THE GUINNESS BOOK OF
TEST CRICKET
CAPTAINS

This book is dedicated to Brian Croudy

THE GUINNESS BOOK OF
TEST CRICKET CAPTAINS

David Lemmon

GUINNESS PUBLISHING

David Lemmon

Published in Great Britain by Guinness Publishing Ltd,
33 London Road, Enfield, Middlesex

Cover design by Stonecastle Graphics Ltd
Text design and layout by Stonecastle Graphics Ltd

Typeset in Palatino by Ace Filmsetting Ltd, Frome, Somerset

Printed and bound in Great Britain by The Bath Press, Bath

'Guinness' is a registered trademark of Guinness Publishing Ltd

A catalogue record for this book is available from the British Library.

ISBN 0-85112-981-1

Contents

The Birth of Test Cricket

International cricket began when Canada played the United States of America in 1844. This was 33 years before what we now accept as the first 'Test' match between England and Australia.

Cricket was immensely popular on the North American continent in the middle of the 19th century. When Canada became a nation in 1867 Prime Minister Sir John A. MacDonald and his cabinet decreed that cricket was the country's national sport, and eight years before this, the first England overseas cricket tour had been to North America.

The England party consisted of 12 professionals under the captaincy of George Parr, the great Nottinghamshire batsman, whose career preceded Test cricket. Organised by W.P. Pickering, an original member of the Surrey County Club and a Cambridge blue who had settled in Montreal, the tour was a great success. The England side was a strong one, and it attracted large crowds. Matches were played against 'odds', 11 of England being pitted against 22 of Lower Canada, or Philadelphia, or Canada and the United States combined. The England XI won every game.

The success of England's tour in North America excited interest in Australia, and the catering firm of Spiers and Pond sent a representative to England to negotiate a tour of the antipodes. Hallam, the Spiers and Pond agent, offered £150 and first-class travelling expenses to the leading professionals of the day if they would make the trip. Parr and his Nottinghamshire colleagues rejected Hallam's offer as inadequate, but the Surrey cricketers, led by H.H. Stephenson, accepted.

Nottinghamshire and Surrey were the foremost counties of the period and were keen rivals. When Stephenson and his men broke ranks over pay, a rift occurred which lasted for a considerable time and caused some animosity.

Stephenson's side was far from representative of the best in English cricket, and they lost two and drew four of their twelve matches. These matches were often referred to as 'tests', tests of strength between Stephenson's XI and 22 of Bendigo, Bathurst, Ballarat or several other communities.

Although the England side was not as strong as the organisers would have liked, the tour was a huge success and financially rewarding for all parties concerned. The tourists were offered more money to extend their trip for another month, but as many had commitments in England, they declined. One of the Surrey men, Charles Lawrence, did remain in Australia. He accepted a post in Sydney and was later to play an important part in fostering cricket between the two nations.

The first tour of Australia had shown that such a venture was not only viable but lucrative, and the Melbourne Club had no difficulty in persuading a side to come to Australia in 1863–64. This time George Parr accepted the terms that were offered and agreed to take with him eleven of the strongest of English cricketers. Of the party that had travelled with Stephenson only William Caffyn remained, although Mortlock had first accepted an invitation before later withdrawing.

Among the most interesting of Parr's selections was a little-known Gloucestershire amateur, Dr E.M. Grace, whose mother had written to Parr suggesting that he should take her son.

The side began and ended their tour in Australia, but they also played five games in New Zealand. They won ten and drew six of their 16 matches and, on and off the field, the trip was even more successful than its predecessor. Once more, however, a Surrey cricketer was lost to English cricket as William Caffyn accepted an engagement in Melbourne.

Both tours had shown a considerable profit, and this prompted Australian businessmen to believe that there was money to be made in sending a team to England. An Aboriginal team of cricketers had drawn large crowds in Melbourne, and W.E.B. Gurnett of Sydney, a man of somewhat dubious character, approached their managers, William Hayman and Tom Wills, with the proposition that it would be financially rewarding if the side was taken to Sydney and then to England.

More players were recruited, but the Australian public was sceptical, fearing, with justification, that the Aboriginals were being exploited. Gurnett's financial backing had less substance than he had indicated, and the trip to Sydney was a disaster. One newspaper commented, 'It is evident that Hayman and his blacks entrusted themselves to hands which were not quite trustworthy.'

The team returned to Melbourne destitute. The players were not paid, and some became ill. Four of the original side died. Nevertheless, the view persisted that the Aboriginal team would prove a worthwhile investment if taken to England. This view was most fervently supported by the ex-Surrey cricketer Charles Lawrence.

Financial backing was obtained from respectable businessmen of Sydney and matches were played in Victoria to raise money for the trip. Following the events surrounding Gurnett's involvement, the Aboriginal Protection Board strongly opposed any plans for further tours. They put forward medical claims that a trip to England would put the lives of the players at risk. The objections were ignored and the Aboriginals left Australia on 8 February 1868. They were captained by Charles Lawrence and were ten years ahead of the first all-white Australian side to tour England.

The original schedule allowed for ten matches but the Aboriginals proved to be so popular that the number was increased to 47. The tour lasted from May until October, with 14 matches being won, 14 lost and the rest drawn.

It was a most arduous tour and it was made more taxing for the Aboriginals in that they were expected to give demonstrations of other sports including spear and boomerang throwing. They played under their nicknames – Bullocky, Red Cap, Dick-a-Dick etc – and, popular as they were, they did not find the English climate to their liking. King Cole died of tuberculosis in June, and Sundown and Jim Crow returned to Australia in August because of ill-health. If it was a successful tour, it was a sad one. Few of the side retained their interest in cricket on their return to Australia, and several died within a few years.

While the Aboriginals were still touring England, Edgar Willsher took a side to North America where he discovered that the standard of cricket had dropped considerably since Parr's

side toured there nine years earlier. The continent had been ravaged by the American Civil War and baseball had now supplanted cricket in the public's affections.

There were still pockets of support for cricket in the United States and R.A. Fitzgerald, secretary of MCC, was approached with a view to selecting a team of amateurs to tour North America in 1872. Although the side was not fully representative in that players of the stature of the Walker brothers of Middlesex were unable to make the trip, it was a huge attraction, no doubt because it was led by W.G. Grace.

Grace was again in charge when an England side went to Australia in 1873–74, but his side was weakened because several of the leading professionals refused the terms that were offered to them. This was unfortunate, as it quickly became apparent that the standard of cricket in Australia was improving as rapidly as it was declining in North America. Grace's side was beaten three times, but in most ways the tour was a success. What emerged, however, was that there was a division between the amateurs and the professionals which caused some

The incomparable W.G. Grace. His presence was a major factor in the success of some of the early tours (Hulton)

lack of harmony in the party. The next time that a team went to Australia, in 1876–77, it was decided to revert to the all-professional format.

Before this tour took place, a party of American baseball players came to England in an attempt to popularise their sport. They gave exhibitions and also played six games of cricket in England and one in Ireland. They were unbeaten, but the opposition that they faced was generally weak. There seemed to be a total lack of vision in England as to the value of tours and the future of international cricket.

Such a vision was really generated by the team that James Lillywhite took to Australia and New Zealand in 1876–77. The tour was organised by Lillywhite himself, and he both managed and captained the side.

Lillywhite's party was a strong one. He was a most respected Sussex bowler, and he had with him one other Sussex man, H.R.J. Charlwood. There were five Yorkshiremen – G. Ulyett, A. Hill, T. Emmett, A. Greenwood and T. Armitage – in the side; two from Nottinghamshire – Alfred Shaw and John Selby; and three from Surrey – H. Jupp, E. Pooley and James Southerton. It can be argued that some of the leading batsmen of the day were missing, but the side was strong in bowling and Pooley was unquestionably the best wicket-keeper in England.

The tour began at Adelaide where Twenty-Two of South Australia were beaten by an innings. This easy win may have lulled the England party into underestimating their opponents, and victory over Fifteen of New South Wales in Sydney was anticipated. There was a shock result. Thirty thousand people watched the game, and New South Wales won by two wickets.

Local sides were beaten with ease, but Fifteen of Victoria followed the example of New South Wales in claiming victory over the Englishmen. The return match with New South Wales proved an even greater disaster with Lillywhite's men being bowled out for 35 and 104 and losing by 13 wickets. The state side immediately challenged the tourists to a match on even terms. This time the Englishmen had the better of a draw, but they were now aware of the strength of cricket in Australia.

Following the draw in Sydney, Lillywhite's side sailed to New Zealand where they played eight matches against 'odds' and won five of them by an innings. Unfortunately, it was in New Zealand that they temporarily lost the services of their one and only wicket-keeper, Ted Pooley.

There was always heavy betting on the matches, and Pooley was never one to keep away from a wager or a drink. He became involved with a local spectator on whom he played a trick involving the naming of the correct score of each batsman before the match. The local man refused to pay his debt and Pooley became involved in a fight. He was arrested and had to await trial while the rest of the party returned to Australia.

The New Zealand part of the tour had been badly arranged and was a financial failure, while the journey back to Melbourne was far from easy. This was certainly poor preparation for what was to be the inaugural Test match, not that any of the 22 cricketers who took part realised that such a title would be given to the game in which they played.

On 15, 16, 17 and 19 March 1877, a Grand Combined Melbourne and Sydney XI played James Lillywhite's Professional Touring XI. This was the first match played on level terms between teams which could be considered representative of England and Australia, and it has subsequently been recognised as the first Test match. It was played at Melbourne Cricket Ground, and Australia won by 45 runs. A fortnight later, a return match was played on the same ground and England, fielding an unchanged eleven, won by four wickets.

Australia's victory over England had aroused considerable comment and, anxious to profit from the interest that had been generated, John Conway decided to arrange a tour of England in the summer of 1878. Conway was a 35-year-old enthusiast who had played for Melbourne and was a fine judge of a cricketer. He asked James Lillywhite to draw up a fixture list while he concentrated on getting together a good representative side.

Scarcely acclimatised, the Australians lost their opening match at Trent Bridge, but a week later they caused a sensation at Lord's by beating MCC inside a day.

MCC batted first and were bowled out for 33. The Australians replied with 41 and then bowled out MCC for 19 before going on to win by nine wickets. Spofforth, 'The Demon', had match figures of 11 for 20. The MCC side was captained by W.G. Grace and included other England captains of the future in A.N. Hornby and Alfred Shaw. Victory over MCC did much to establish the Australians as an outstanding side in the minds of the public, and from that day large crowds flocked to see them, but there were no Test matches.

Melbourne was the home of the third Test match as it had been the home of the first two. The Melbourne Club had invited I.D. Walker, one of the famous Walker brothers from Southgate, to take a side of twelve amateurs to Australia in 1878–79. It was found impossible to gather together an amateur side of sufficient strength, and the side was completed by the Yorkshire professionals G. Ulyett and T. Emmett. I.D. Walker himself was unable to make the trip, and the captaincy passed to Lord Harris.

The side was a weak one, and in no way was it representative of English cricket. The one Test match that was played (originally billed as Gentlemen of England, with Ulyett and Emmett, v The Australian XI) saw England trounced by ten wickets. They never truly recovered from the trauma of being 26 for 7 in their first innings.

It is a measure of the quality of this 'England' side that the wicket-keeper was Leland Hone, who was not a regular 'keeper and had not played for a county. His cricket was mostly for Ireland and he ended his first-class career in 1880 with just eight matches to his credit, five of them on this tour, and an average of 7.08.

It was not a happy tour for the Englishmen, who lost three and won two of their five first-class matches. One of the victories came in the return game against New South Wales although this was the match which caused the greatest upset.

There was a considerable amount of betting on the game and the crowd became passionately involved, no doubt because of the amount of money they had invested. When Murdoch was adjudged run out in New South Wales' second innings angry scenes broke out. It was rumoured that the umpire had wagered heavily on an England victory. The crowd invaded the pitch, and Lord Harris was struck across the body with a whip or stick. The attacker was apprehended, but tempers still raged. Gregory, the New South Wales captain, asked Lord Harris for a change of umpire. His Lordship refused, and Gregory declined to allow his batsmen to continue the innings. Eventually, the impasse was resolved and the game played to a finish.

Harris was critical of the amateur umpiring in Australia and was adamant that the gambling element should be removed from Australian cricket, but he was also aware that the Australians were now close to being the equals of their English counterparts at cricket.

It was possibly the controversy that attended Lord Harris' side in Australia that made the Australians hesitate before sending a party to England in 1880. By the time they reached their decision all the major fixtures for the season had been settled, and they arrived in England to find their programme included only five matches against county sides. There was an attempt to arrange a match against England for the benefit of professional cricketers, but this came to nothing, and when W.G. Grace tried to organise an international match at Lord's he was snubbed. The tourists spent much of their time playing against 'odds' in the North of England. They were highly successful, and the public began to take a great interest in the side.

The Surrey Club, the most vibrant of the era, had been greatly surprised by the size of the crowd that had attended the match between Surrey and the Australians at The Oval in 1878. They had not anticipated such interest, and the Surrey executive had looked on in amazement as spectators circled the playing area and reduced it to half its normal size, so great was their number.

The Surrey secretary, C.W. Alcock, was a man of enterprise and vision, and he was quick to see the potential that was being wasted. He realised the income that a match between England and Australia at The Oval could bring. He knew that Grace, having been snubbed by Lord's, would give his backing to any plan The Oval had to stage a match between England and Australia.

The Surrey Committee saw that the most appropriate date for the game was 6, 7 and 8 September, but those days were scheduled for a match between Sussex and the tourists. The other problem that confronted them was the attitude of Lord Harris, still smarting from the treatment he had received in Australia the previous winter. Alcock was given the task of reconciling both parties to the idea.

He won the support and the trust of both. Sussex readily agreed to postpone their match, while Lord Harris was in fact most eager for the international to take place. He accepted the captaincy and played a prominent part in the selection of the England side. To Alcock and the Surrey executive must go the praise for bringing Test cricket to England. It will ever remain a mystery why Lord's was the venue for the Centenary Test in 1980.

Some 40 000 paid to see the first two days' play in the first Test match between England and Australia at The Oval, and so great was the public's enthusiasm that score-cards gave out towards the finish. Crowds pressed round the printer's box with pieces of paper anxious to have a copy of the official score.

Over the next few years Alcock was to play a major role in arranging schedules for Australian touring sides, and never again was there to be an Australian tour which did not include a Test match.

Privately organised tours by England sides to other countries proliferated, and it was not until 1903–04 that MCC took responsibility for England's tour to Australia and for future major tours until 1976–77.

It was a private tour that brought South Africa into Test cricket. Major R. Gardner Warton served there for five years as a member of the General Staff. He retired at the beginning of 1888 and determined that the following winter he would take to the country which had been his home a party of England cricketers.

This was no easy task as he found it difficult to judge the standard of cricket in South Africa, but his side included eight men who had appeared in first-class cricket regularly in 1888.

The early matches were against 'odds', but at the end of the tour two games were played against a South African XI, and these are now recognised as Test matches.

A much stronger side went to South Africa in 1891–92 and played one Test match, but when a South African side came to England in 1894 it was not even accorded first-class status. First-class status was given to the tours of 1901 and 1904, but it was not until 1907 that South Africa were granted a Test match in England.

Other countries had to be even more patient. An England side first went to India and Ceylon in 1889–90, but the first All-India side did not come to England until 1911 and India did not play Test cricket until 1932.

New Zealand was visited as early as 1864, but no New Zealand side came to England until 1927 and three more years elapsed before the Kiwis played a Test match.

It was not until their fourth tour of England in 1928 that West Indies were granted a Test match, but Pakistan met India in a Test series in 1952–53, only five years after partition.

The number of countries who have engaged in Test cricket was increased to eight in February 1982, when Sri Lanka met England in Colombo. This was the 921st Test match to be played. It had taken 84 years to play the first 500 Test matches; the next 500 were to come in 23 years. We have now passed the 1150 mark.

By the autumn of 1991, 218 men had captained a Test side. They had met with varying fortunes and had received both castigation and accolades. Their appointments and their actions had often led to controversy. The 'evil' that they did has lived after them; the 'good' has often been 'interred with their bones'. They have come from various walks of life, and their selection shows both a changing social pattern and differing attitudes within the game itself.

Key to abbreviations used in tables

W	Wins	I	Innings	RC	Runs conceded
L	Losses	NO	Not Out innings	Wkts	Wickets taken
D	Draws	Runs	Runs scored	Avge	Average (bowling)
+	Tie	HS	Highest score (*)	BB	Best bowling
M	Matches	Avge	Average (batting)	Ct/st	Catches/stumpings
		100s	Hundreds scored		
		*	Not out		

Captains' Test match statistics are correct up to the end of the 1991 English season

ENGLAND

England and Captaincy

In 13 of the first 18 Test matches to be played in Australia, England were led by a professional; but it was to be 72 years before a professional captained England in England.

When Test cricket came to England in 1880 through the energies and enterprise of Charles William Alcock, Lord Harris and the Surrey Committee invited what was considered to be the cream of English cricket to face the Australians. *The Times* described the England side as 'probably the strongest combination that has ever entered a cricket field'. That combination consisted of eight amateurs and three professionals, Shaw, Morley and Barnes.

The dominance of the amateur in Test matches played in England was to continue for several years. In the four home series against Australia between 1895 and 1905, England selected twice as many amateur specialist batsmen as they did professionals. The captaincy was invariably given to the senior of these amateur batsmen.

Contrary to popular belief, the majority of these amateurs were not exceptionally wealthy men able to give all their time to cricket: the demands of business precluded many of them from touring. C.B. Fry went to South Africa shortly after coming down from Oxford in 1895, but he never again represented England abroad. F.S. Jackson's multiplicity of interests and his political activities determined that his 20 Test appearances were all to be made in England.

The fact that many of the leading amateurs could not make themselves available to tour meant that it was easier to win a Test cap in Australia than it was in England. In 1903–04, A.C. MacLaren, C.B. Fry, F.S. Jackson and Gilbert Jessop were among seven amateurs who were forced to decline invitations to tour Australia. In their absence Pelham Warner was appointed as England's captain. He was to lead England in ten Test matches abroad, but he played in only three Tests in England, and never as captain. J.W.H.T. Douglas led England to victory in two Test series abroad before the First World War, but during that period he appeared in only one Test match at home, and that was under the captaincy of C.B. Fry.

Initially, of course, England's tours to Australia and elsewhere were entirely in the hands of professionals. They were the organisers, the managers and the players. James Lillywhite junior organised the tour to Australia and New Zealand in 1876–77, and he combined with Alfred Shaw and Arthur Shrewsbury to take four other sides to Australia between 1881 and 1888. Shaw was captain of the first of these sides, and Shrewsbury of the second and third.

The last tour, in 1887–88, clashed with a rival tour by a party known as G.F. Vernon's team, captained by The Hon. M.B. Hawke. The

Lillywhite, Shaw and Shrewsbury side was officially led by C. Aubrey Smith. The two teams did combine to play one Test match against a weakened Australian side. Neither Hawke nor Smith played in the game, and although Shrewsbury was in the side, the team was captained by the Surrey amateur W.W. Read. In effect, the reign of the professional manager, organiser and captain was at an end.

Changes in leadership and inconsistencies in selection were not restricted to parties touring overseas. A Test selectors' panel did not come into existence until 1899, and before that time the England XI was chosen by the committee of the county club on whose ground the Test was to be played. This caused some anomalies. For The Oval Test in 1888, the Surrey Committee chose five of their own players. England won by an innings, but neither Shuter, the Surrey captain, nor Wood, the wicket-keeper, was asked to play in the next Test at Old Trafford where the Lancashire Committee selected their own wicket-keeper, Pilling.

Six years earlier, in what was the second Test match to be staged in England, the Surrey Committee had chosen the Lancashire captain A.N. Hornby to lead an England side which included five professionals and was a very strong one. Needing only 85 to win, England reached 70 for 5, but lost their last five wickets for seven runs. It was this defeat which caused the mock obituary to appear in the *Sporting Times* in September 1882:

In Affectionate Remembrance
of
ENGLISH CRICKET
which died at The Oval
on
29th August 1882
Deeply lamented by a large circle of
Sorrowing Friends and Acquaintances
R.I.P.
N.B. – The body will be cremated and
the Ashes taken to Australia

Shortly after this notice appeared, an England side was on its way to Australia to regain those 'Ashes'. The tour was made at the instigation of the Melbourne Club, and the England party consisted of eight amateurs and four professionals. The original idea had been that the side should be made up of Cambridge men, but this proved not to be feasible. Nevertheless, it was captained by the Cambridge skipper of

1881, The Hon. Ivo Bligh. Also in the side was A.G. Steel, the light blues' captain in 1880. He was a year senior to Bligh and had played in both of the Test matches that had been staged in England, but Bligh's aristocratic connections gave him precedence when it came to the captaincy of England. It must be emphasised, though, that in 1882–83 the 'Test' matches between England and Australia were being advertised as The Hon. Ivo Bligh's Team versus Mr Murdoch's XI.

Bligh's international career ended with his one and only tour. Hornby and Lord Harris were available in 1884, Steel was a most successful captain in 1886, and W.G. Grace took over in 1888.

That Grace had not captained England before this time is astonishing, but in the social context of the time it is clear to see why he had not been given that honour. He had led a party to Australia, had been with Fitzgerald's side to North America and had been an automatic selection for every England side for which he was available from the very first Test match at The Oval in 1880, by which time he was already 32 years old. He was indisputably the greatest cricketer in the world, and in the century that has passed since his finest days we have seen no greater cricketer. He was the captain of Gloucestershire, whose predominantly amateur eleven he had lifted to great heights by his own prodigious efforts, and he was the best-known man in England, 'the champion'. But he was also the son of a country doctor. He had no aristocratic connections, no public school or university education. Dominant as he was as a cricketer, he was not one of the hierarchy of the Marylebone Club, as is evidenced by the snub he received when he suggested staging England and Australia at Lord's in 1880. W.G. Grace, the colossus of the cricket world, was 40 years old and his best days behind him when he became captain of England, but the social system had decreed that that should be the case.

At the time that Grace ascended to the captaincy of England, cricket in Australia was undergoing something of a trauma. The twin tours by Vernon's team and the professional side of Shaw, Shrewsbury and Lillywhite in 1887–88 had been a disaster, and matters were not helped by the wranglings of the Sydney and Melbourne Clubs. In an effort to revive interest in cricket in Australia, Lord Sheffield agreed to organise a tour in 1891–92, but he did so only on the understanding that Grace would lead the side. This was a measure of the respect and esteem which the champion's prowess had earned him.

By the time that Grace became captain, the principle of the amateur captain was firmly established. This was fine as long as the golden age continued to produce amateurs of the calibre of Jackson, Fry, Stoddart and MacLaren who were worth their place in any side on their ability. The problems began to arise when men of such quality were no longer available. Before these problems arrived, however, there were the more immediate questions of remuneration and selection.

The first Test match of the 1896 season was played at Lord's, and the England team was chosen by the MCC. K.S. Ranjitsinhji was asked to make himself available for this Test.

Ranjitsinhji was then at the beginning of his illustrious career. He had played virtually no organised cricket before going up to Cambridge, but there, and with Sussex, his dazzling footwork and exotic stroke-play marked him as a great player. The idea of an Indian representing England had never arisen before, and Lord Harris, President of MCC and former Governor of Bombay, objected to what he called 'birds of passage'. For this reason, Ranjitsinhji was not chosen for the Lord's Test.

The Lancashire Committee thought that he should have been in the side and stated that he would be chosen for the second Test at Old Trafford. He responded by hitting 62 and 154 not out, scoring a hundred before lunch on the third morning.

Such inconsistencies were to the liking of no one, and the counties were most happy to be relieved of the responsibility of selection when, in 1899, the new MCC Board of Control appointed a panel of selectors.

Before this was brought about, another problem had arisen in the dispute over payments. In spite of Ranjitsinhji's efforts at Old Trafford in 1896, England were beaten, and before the deciding Test at The Oval five of the professionals threatened strike action in a dispute over match fees. Four of the men were Surrey players – Lohmann, Abel, Hayward and Richardson – while the fifth was Gunn of Nottinghamshire.

At the time, a professional who represented England was paid £10. The five wrote to the Surrey executive to the effect that they would not play unless they received £20 each. The Surrey Committee rejected the ultimatum and made provision to find replacements while, at the same time, giving the four Surrey players the opportunity to withdraw the letter they had written. Abel, Richardson and Hayward recanted, but Lohmann was soon to be lost to Surrey and England.

The reason for the action of the five protestors was that they believed that several of the leading amateurs, Grace and Stoddart in particular, were receiving larger amounts in expenses than they, the professionals, were being paid. Both Grace and Stoddart were attacked in the press. Stoddart withdrew from the side and played for Middlesex in a county match; Grace issued a statement relevant to payments made to him and, inevitably, won public sympathy and support. He played in the Test and led England to victory.

It was to be another 60 years before this financial problem was settled, and a further 19 before it was really settled to the satisfaction of all concerned.

As we have seen, the problem of selection had a quicker solution, at least in theory, but the amateurs dominated the corridors of power of selection just as they had dominated the question of captaincy. In 1899, Lord Hawke was appointed chairman of selectors with W.G. Grace and H.W. Bainbridge of Warwickshire to serve with him. They were empowered to co-opt two more *amateur* cricketers if they so desired, and C.B. Fry and A.C. MacLaren were the two who later joined them.

It was not until 1926 when the need to win had become so urgent that the selection committee of P.F. Warner, P.A. Perrin and A.E.R. Gilligan were empowered to co-opt one professional from the North and one from the South. They turned to Wilfred Rhodes and Jack Hobbs.

Not until 1950 was a professional cricketer, Les Ames, named as a member of the selection panel. Within two years of Ames' appointment, a professional was invited to captain England and restore the fortunes of his country. A tradition had been broken and a new age dawned, at least in theory.

James LILLYWHITE junior

Sussex

Born: Westhampnett, Sussex, 23 February 1842
Died: Westerton, Sussex, 25 October 1929

James Lillywhite was not only a good left-arm medium pace bowler, high in delivery and exceptionally accurate, he was also a very useful left-handed batsman and one of cricket's great adventurers. He toured North America with Willsher's team in 1868 and Australia with W.G. Grace's side in 1873–74. In 1876–77, he organised, managed and captained the side that went to Australia and New Zealand and played in what we now regard as the first two Test matches.

He was from a famous cricketing family, and he made an immediate impact with a sensational first-class debut. This was for Sussex against MCC at Lord's in June 1862. He and Stubberfield bowled unchanged throughout both innings, and Lillywhite finished with match figures of 14 for 57. He took 9 for 29 in the second innings, and this, along with his match figures, remains a record for a bowler on his first-class debut in England.

Lillywhite was 35 when he captained England in the inaugural Test match, and when he next organised a tour to Australia, in 1881–82, it was in conjunction with Shaw and Shrewsbury. Lillywhite acted as manager and umpire, so becoming the first former Test cricketer to stand as an umpire in a Test match.

In all, Lillywhite was concerned with the organisation of five tours to Australia, four of them in conjunction with Shaw and Shrewsbury. The last, in 1887–88, was a financial disaster and Lillywhite was unable to meet his obligations. It marked the end of speculative ventures by professionals, but James Lillywhite junior will always have a place in cricket history as a pioneer whose willingness for adventure made Test cricket possible.

Test Record as Captain

			M	I	NO	Runs	HS	Avge	100s	RC	Wkts	Avge	BB	Ct
v Australia	W1	L1	–	2	3	1	16	10	8.00	–	126	8	15.75	4–70	1

Fourth Lord HARRIS
(Hon. Sir George Robert Canning Harris)

Kent

Born: St Anne's, Trinidad, 3 February 1851
Died: Belmont, Faversham, Kent, 24 March 1932

Educated at Eton and Oxford where he gained his blue in 1871, 1872 and 1874 (missing the Varsity match of 1873 because of injury), Lord Harris was, in the words of *Wisden*, 'a great batsman and a brilliant field in his younger days, and all his life a commanding figure in the world of cricket'.

He made his first-class debut for Kent against MCC in 1870 while he was still at school and played his last game for Kent against All India at Catford in 1911. He was then 60 years 151 days old, and he remains the oldest man to have appeared in first-class cricket in England.

In the spring of 1878, I.D. Walker, one of the famous Middlesex brethren, was asked by the Melbourne Cricket Club to take a party of amateurs to tour Australia the following winter. This proved impossible, and two Yorkshire professionals, Ulyett and Emmett, were invited to bolster a team that was far from strong. Walker himself was unable to make the trip and the captaincy passed to Lord Harris, who had become captain of Kent in 1875. He was to hold the position until 1889.

In his first Test match as England's captain, Harris decided to bat on a damp wicket and saw his side reduced to 26 for 7. Australia eventually won by ten wickets. Harris received some rough treatment in the game against New South Wales at Sydney some two months after that Test match, and he was very critical of the gambling that was associated with cricket in Australia at the time.

When C.W. Alcock was attempting to arrange the first Test match in England in 1880 it was essential that he gained the support of Lord Harris, a dominant and influential figure in the game. Harris gave his support and led

England to victory in the first Test match to be played at The Oval.

Business and political commitments prevented him from touring again after the trip to Australia in 1878-79, and he was unable to give much time to playing after 1884 when he led England against Australia in two Tests, including the first to be played at Lord's.

A vigorous upholder of the laws of the game, being particularly severe on suspect bowling actions, breaches of etiquette and rules governing county qualification, Harris was a good friend to the professionals while remaining a stern disciplinarian and never forgetting his rank. He held all the senior positions in the MCC, as well as leading an active political life which restricted his cricket: he was later Governor of Bombay, from 1890-95, during which time he helped to foster cricket in India; Under-Secretary for India; and Under-Secretary for War.

A man born into a ruling class, Lord Harris' influence on cricket extended far beyond the four Test matches in which he played.

Test Record as Captain

				M	I	NO	Runs	HS	Avge	100s	RC	Wkts	Avge	BB	Ct
v Australia	W2	L1	D1	4	6	1	145	52	29.00	–	29	0	–	–	2

Alfred SHAW

Nottinghamshire and Sussex

Born: Burton Joyce, Nottinghamshire, 29 August 1842
Died: Gedling, Nottinghamshire, 16 January 1907

Like James Lillywhite junior, Alfred Shaw was an intrepid traveller and a brave adventurer. He made two tours to North America and was involved in six tours to Australia including one as non-travelling co-organiser. He bowled the first ball in Test cricket and was one of only three professionals deemed worthy of a place in a full-strength England side against Australia at The Oval in 1880. He appeared in seven of the first eight Test matches.

He joined with Lillywhite and Shrewsbury in planning four tours of Australia, leading the side in the first trip, in 1881-82, and acting as manager on later occasions.

Alfred Shaw's first-class career lasted from 1864 until 1895, and for a period he was without question the greatest slow bowler in England. He had begun as a medium-pace bowler but he reduced his speed and started to spin the ball more. He never turned the ball a prodigious amount but was relentlessly accurate and, astonishingly, sent down more overs in his career than he conceded runs. At first a capable bat, he allowed his batting to decline in order to concentrate on his bowling.

Unlike Lord Harris he was not born to the purple, but Shaw was a forceful personality and a natural leader of men. He had no success as captain of England – and there were even accusations, which were refuted, that his side had attempted to 'throw' matches in which they had a wager on their opponents – but he was a highly talented leader of Nottinghamshire. He captained the county from 1883 until 1886, and they were the leading county in all four years of his leadership. They dispensed with his services in 1887 and Shaw moved to Sussex where he was employed as coach by Lord Sheffield. Having qualified by residence, he played ten games for Sussex, the last at the age of 53. He later became an umpire.

The strength of Shaw's personality and his capacity for command can be seen from the fact that he was a strong upholder of the rights of the professional. He refused to go with Grace's side to Australia in 1875 because the professionals were to be allowed only second-class travel facilities, and in 1881 he led a strike of Nottinghamshire professionals.

The strike was brought about by what Shaw and his colleagues saw as the preferential treatment given to the Australians who toured England. Seven in number, the Nottinghamshire faction demanded a formal contract of employment which would guarantee them an automatic benefit on completion of an agreed span of years.

Their action was seen as anarchy and the offenders were dropped by the Nottingham-

shire Committee. Eventually there was reconciliation, but power moved firmly into the hands of the committee. The belief was reinforced that an amateur captain, a man of rank and authority, was essential to control and guide the professionals.

Shaw and Shrewsbury's team of 1894–95 (Hulton)

Shaw's team-mates would later point to the fact that a great county side went rapidly into decline when he was no longer at the helm.

Test Record

			M	I	NO	Runs	HS	Avge	100s	RC	Wkts	Avge	BB	Ct
v Australia			7	12	1	111	40	10.09	–	285	12	23.75	5–38	4

Test Record as Captain

			M	I	NO	Runs	HS	Avge	100s	RC	Wkts	Avge	BB	Ct
v Australia	–	L2 D2	4	7	0	98	40	14.00	–	76	2	38.00	1–12	1

Albert Neilson HORNBY

Lancashire

Born: Blackburn, Lancashire, 10 February 1847
Died: Nantwich, Cheshire, 17 December 1925

'Monkey' Hornby was the England captain who lost the 'Ashes'. He was leading his country for the first time in what was the second Test match to be played in England, at The Oval in August 1882. There has been some surprise as to why he was captain of a side that included Grace, the Hon. Alfred Lyttleton, A.G. Steel and A.P. Lucas, but Hornby was the senior member of the team and had the right pedigree.

Educated at Harrow, he went up to Oxford to play cricket and left the university to return to the family mill in Blackburn as soon as he realised that he was expected to do a certain amount of academic work.

He played for Lancashire from 1867 to 1899, leading the side for much of that time. Small and strong, he was a strict disciplinarian, but his autocracy was spiced with a sense of fun. He was Lord Harris' right-hand man in Australia in 1878–79, and it was Hornby who apprehended the man who attacked his Lordship at Sydney.

A vigorous spirit with what Cardus called a 'passion for taking a risk', Hornby captained England at rugby as well as cricket, and as the aggressive foil to the stone-walling of his opening partner Barlow, he was immortalised in Francis Thompson's poem:

And I look through my tears on a soundless-clapping host
As the run-stealers flicker to and fro,
  To and fro;
O my Hornby and my Barlow long ago!

Between 1870 and 1881 he was the only batsman to hit a century for Lancashire, and in 1881 he was the leading batsman in the country.

His last Test was the first to be played at Old Trafford, in July 1884. It was ruined by rain.

Test Record

		M	I	NO	Runs	HS	Avge	100s	RC	Wkts	Avge	BB	Ct
v Australia		3	6	0	21	9	3.50	–	0	1	0.00	1–0	–

Test Record as Captain

			M	I	NO	Runs	HS	Avge	100s	RC	Wkts	Avge	BB	Ct
v Australia	–	L1 D1	2	4	0	15	9	3.75	–	–	–	–	–	–

Hon. Ivo Francis Walter BLIGH

Kent

Born: Westminster, 13 March 1859
Died: Cobham, Kent, 10 April 1927

To Ivo Bligh has gone the honour of having first regained the 'Ashes', although the accolade thrust upon him is somewhat weak in substance.

The Melbourne Cricket Club had wanted a party of Cambridge University men to tour Australia in 1882–83, for the university had an excellent record against the Australians in England. Such a tour proved to be impracticable, and Bligh instead led a team of eight amateurs and four professionals. A tall, elegant batsman and a good fielder, Bligh had won his blue at Cambridge in all four years in residence, 1878 to 1881, and he was captain in his last year. He was, however, junior to A.G. Steel, who led the light blues in 1880, and who was a far better cricketer than Bligh, but rank determined that Bligh should lead the side to Australia.

The first Test was lost, but the second and third were won, and after the third match some Melbourne ladies burned a bail, sealed the ashes in an urn and presented it to Bligh. In fact, a fourth match was played which Australia won.

Bligh's career was comparatively short, 1877 to 1883, for he did not enjoy good health. When he died his widow presented the 'ashes', the urn and its embroidered velvet bag to MCC.

Test Record as Captain

				M	I	NO	Runs	HS	Avge	100s	RC	Wkts	Avge	BB	Ct
v Australia	W2	L2	–	4	7	1	62	19	10.33	–	–	–	–	–	7

Arthur SHREWSBURY

Nottinghamshire

Born: New Lenton, Nottinghamshire, 11 April 1856
Died: Gedling, Nottinghamshire, 19 May 1903

When asked to name the contemporary batsman he rated above all others, W.G. Grace replied, 'Give me Arthur.' The first-class career of Arthur Shrewsbury lasted from 1875 until 1902, and for much of that time he was unquestionably the finest professional batsman in England.

He joined Lillywhite and Shaw in organising four trips to Australia. He made his Test debut on the first, 1881–82, and he captained the side in 1884–85 and 1886–87. In the fifth Test of the 1884–85 series he hit 105 not out, so becoming the first England captain to score a century in a Test match. He later became the first England batsman to score three Test hundreds and the first batsman to reach 1000 runs in Test cricket.

Shrewsbury was admired and respected by all as both a player and a man, and when Shaw decided to concentrate on management he was the obvious person to lead the all-professional side. He won both the series in which he was captain, but when the tour of 1887–88 clashed with a tour organised by G.F. Vernon and the Melbourne Club he played under the leadership of the amateur W.W. Read. Shrewsbury's last game as captain was at Sydney in 1887; a professional was not to lead England again for another 65 years.

Shrewsbury's Test career lasted until 1893 when he scored his second hundred in a Test at Lord's.

In bearing, attitude, resolve and application, Shrewsbury, like Shaw, did much to raise the status of the professional cricketer. He shot himself within a year of his last first-class match, believing that ill-health and failing sight would prevent him from playing the game he loved and had served so well. He and Shaw were buried within thirty yards of each other.

Test Record

		M	I	NO	Runs	HS	Avge	100s	RC	Wkts	Avge	BB	Ct
v Australia		23	40	4	1277	164	35.47	3	2	0	–	–	29

Test Record as Captain

			M	I	NO	Runs	HS	Avge	100s	RC	Wkts	Avge	BB	Ct
v Australia	W5	L2	–	7	13	3	347	105*	34.70	1	–	–	–	–	9

Allan Gibson STEEL

Lancashire

Born: West Derby, Liverpool, 24 September 1858
Died: Hyde Park, London, 15 June 1914

'It is a strange fact connected with cricket,' wrote A.G. Steel, 'that a good captain is but seldom met with.' He also maintained that few professional cricketers made good captains. Steel himself was an inspiring and intelligent captain, and a very fine cricketer.

He arrived at Cambridge with an impressive record in school cricket for Marlborough where he had been skipper in his last two years. He won his blue in a very strong Cambridge side in all four years of residence, 1878–81, and was captain of the eleven in 1880. He was invited to play in the inaugural Test at The Oval in the same season.

He was also in Hornby's side that lost the 'Ashes' and was a member of Bligh's team that regained them. He hit 135 not out in the fourth match, at Sydney, the first century made by an English amateur in a Test in Australia.

Steel was senior to Bligh and might have led England on that tour but for Bligh's place among the nobility. He played under both Hornby and Lord Harris in 1884 and hit 148 in the first Test match ever staged at Lord's.

In 1886, Hornby withdrew from the side for the first Test because of an injured leg, and the captaincy passed to Steel. That Test was at Old Trafford, and Steel remained as captain for the two other Tests at Lord's and The Oval. All three were won, so Steel became the first captain to claim a one hundred per cent record in a three-match Test series.

He was captain again for the first Test when the Australians next visited in 1888, but that was his last appearance in international cricket although he appeared for Lancashire until 1893.

A batsman with a wide range of strokes and an eagerness to use them, and a bowler with great variations in pace and a viciously spun leg-break, Steel was an all-rounder of exceptional talent whose work as a barrister prevented him from playing more often.

A.G. Steel led England to victory in all three Tests against Australia in 1886. An accomplished man in many fields, he was unable to give much time to cricket (Ken Kelly)

Test Record

	M	I	NO	Runs	HS	Avge	100s	RC	Wkts	Avge	BB	Ct
v Australia	13	20	3	600	148	35.29	2	605	29	20.86	3–27	5

Test Record as Captain

			M	I	NO	Runs	HS	Avge	100s	RC	Wkts	Avge	BB	Ct
v Australia	W3	L1	–	4	6	2	58	19	14.50	–	128	7	18.28	2–34	–

Walter William READ

Surrey

Born: Reigate, Surrey, 23 November 1855
Died: Addiscombe, Surrey, 6 January 1907

An exuberant batsman, Walter Read played for Surrey from 1873 to 1897. His greatest achievement in Test cricket came at The Oval in 1884 when he hit 117 in 113 minutes while batting at number ten. England fielded a strong batting line-up, and Read had dropped down the order because he was feeling unwell. His innings remains a record for a number ten in Test cricket.

Captain of England in both Australia and South Africa, Walter Read of Surrey, one of the most entertaining of batsmen (Ken Kelly)

Never the regular captain of Surrey, he was somewhat fortuitous to lead England on two occasions. He toured Australia with Bligh's side in 1882–83, and was in Vernon's 1887–88 side. The Hon. Martin Hawke was the official captain of this side, but he had to return to England because of the death of his father. G.F. Vernon took over the leadership, but he did not play in the combined team which was fielded in the one Test match. Read was captain of that eleven.

In 1891–92, Read organised a tour of South Africa, and his side played one game which has since been awarded Test status although the South African side was of doubtful quality and a stronger England side, under W.G. Grace, was on tour in Australia.

Read's last Test was at Old Trafford in 1893.

Test Record

	M	I	NO	Runs	HS	Avge	100s	RC	Wkts	Avge	BB	Ct
v Australia	17	26	1	680	117	27.20	1	63	0	–	–	16
v South Africa	1	1	0	40	40	40.00	–	–	–	–	–	–
	18	27	1	720	117	27.69	1	63	0	–	–	16

Test Record as Captain

				M	I	NO	Runs	HS	Avge	100s	RC	Wkts	Avge	BB	Ct
v Australia	W1	–	–	1	2	0	18	10	9.00	–	–	–	–	–	2
v South Africa	W1	–	–	1	1	0	40	40	40.00	–	–	–	–	–	–
	W2	–	–	2	3	0	58	40	19.33	–	–	–	–	–	2

William Gilbert GRACE

Gloucestershire

Born: Downend, Bristol, 18 July 1848
Died: Mottingham, Kent, 23 October 1915

The fourth son of a Gloucestershire doctor, W.G. Grace made his first-class debut in 1865 and played his last match, for the Gentlemen of England, in 1908. During that long career he established or broke virtually every batting record, and for the majority of those who follow the game he remains the most famous and greatest of all cricketers. 'Through Grace,' wrote C.L.R. James, 'cricket, the most complete expression of popular life in pre-industrial England, was incorporated into the life of the nation.'

He toured North America in 1872 and took a side to Australia in 1873–74, yet, in spite of his experience and his stature in the game, he did not captain England until 1888, by which time he was 40 years old.

Grace was the first choice for any Test match for which he was available, and in the inaugural Test in England, at The Oval in 1880, he hit 152, the first century by an England batsman in Test cricket. Two of his brothers, E.M. and G.F., were also in that side.

He played under Lord Harris, Hornby and Steel, two of whom were junior to him, but all three of whom had the kiss of public school and university which Grace did not. By 1888, however, his rivals for the captaincy had disappeared. He led England in his last 13 Test matches.

In his earlier years, Grace was an all-rounder without equal, but he was 32 when he played his first Test match, and he began to bowl less as he grew older. The power of his batting barely diminished, and at The Oval in 1886 he hit 170 out of 216 in 270 minutes, having dominated an opening partnership of 170 with the Nottinghamshire left-hander Scotton who made 34.

He captained Lord Sheffield's team to Australia in 1891–92, and this was the only occasion on which he was able to play Test cricket outside England. The series in Australia was also the only one in which he suffered defeat, but even then he led England to victory by an

Grace with his England side in 1896. On his left is F.S. Jackson, a future Test captain (Hulton)

innings and 230 runs in the final Test, the biggest margin of victory in a Test match at that time.

A member of the selection committee in 1899, he captained England in the first Test at the age of 51 years 320 days. He was the oldest captain in Test history, but it was to be his last Test.

When C.B. Fry arrived at the next selection meeting Grace asked him if he thought that MacLaren should be in the side. Fry said he should. 'That settles it,' said Grace, who had determined before Fry's arrival that he should resign from the England XI as he felt that he no longer fielded nor ran between the wickets as well as was necessary.

Grace had forced his way to the England captaincy because of the strength of his personality and his greatness as a cricketer. He surmounted the obstacles of the Victorian class system just as he did the bowlers of his time. His supremacy was undisputed, for, as Fry wrote, 'he had a formidable eye and a beetling brow; he had a merry heart of the full-blooded English yeoman type, but he knew who he was and who you were, and he possessed, when it came to it, an Olympian dignity.'

Test Record

				M	I	NO	Runs	HS	Avge	100s	RC	Wkts	Avge	BB	Ct
v Australia				22	36	2	1098	170	32.29	2	236	9	26.22	2–12	39

Test Record as Captain

				M	I	NO	Runs	HS	Avge	100s	RC	Wkts	Avge	BB	Ct
v Australia	W8	L3	D2	13	22	1	595	75	28.33	–	108	2	54.00	2–12	18

Sir Charles Aubrey SMITH

Sussex

Born: London, 21 July 1863
Died: Beverly Hills, California, USA,
20 December 1948

An accurate medium-pace bowler who moved the ball in from the off, C. Aubrey Smith was known as 'Round-the-Corner' Smith because of his peculiar approach to the wicket. He won his blue in all four years at Cambridge, 1882–85, and captained Sussex in 1887 and 1888.

He captained Lillywhite, Shaw and Shrewsbury's side to Australia in 1887–88, but he did not play in the one Test match when his side combined with Vernon's side to beat Australia. When Major Warton returned to England from South Africa in 1888 Smith was an obvious man to approach to lead his proposed pioneer tour to South Africa the following winter.

Smith duly captained England in the first Test match, but fever prevented him from playing in the second match so that he remains the only cricketer to have led England in his single Test match.

In conjunction with Monty Bowden he established a firm of stockbrokers in South Africa, and he led Transvaal to victory in the inaugural Currie Cup match.

He returned to England and played his last game for Sussex in 1896 by which time he had begun to pursue his interest in the theatre. His

C. Aubrey Smith had the unique distinction of captaining England in his only Test. He was later to win greater fame in Hollywood (Allsport)

theatrical career culminated in a move to Hollywood where he won fame for his portrayals of the archetypal elderly Englishman in such films as *Lives of a Bengal Lancer*, *The Prisoner of Zenda* and *Rebecca*.

With Boris Karloff, he fostered cricket in California, and he was knighted in 1944 for his contribution to Anglo-American relations.

Test Record as Captain

		M	I	NO	Runs	HS	Avge	100s	RC	Wkts	Avge	BB	Ct
v South Africa	W1	–	–	1	1	0	3	3	3.00	–	61	7	8.71	5–19	–

Montague Parker BOWDEN

Surrey

Born: Stockwell, Surrey, 1 November 1865
Died: Umtali, Mashonaland, 19 February 1892

Monty Bowden first played for Surrey in 1883 shortly after leaving Dulwich College. He toured Australia with Vernon's side in 1887–88, sharing the wicket-keeping with Newton of Somerset. Neither played in the solitary Test.

Bowden enjoyed a fine season in 1888 and, although not a regular 'keeper, he kept for the Gentlemen at both Lord's and The Oval. He went with Warton's side to South Africa in 1888–89, and when C. Aubrey Smith was ill with fever he captained England in the second Test as he was the only other amateur in the side with sufficient first-class experience. He was 23 years 144 days old, and he remains the youngest player to have captained England.

He joined with Smith in establishing a stockbrokers' firm in South Africa and played for

Transvaal in the inaugural Currie Cup match against Kimberley in August 1890. He hit a match-winning 126 not out in the second innings. It proved to be his last innings in first-class cricket.

He trekked north with the Pioneer Column of Cecil Rhodes and led an adventurous life in primitive conditions for more than two years. In February 1892 he fell from a cart and died in Umtali Hospital which was little more than a glorified mud hut. A man with a revolver stood guard over his body to protect it from marauding lions, and Monty Bowden, England's youngest captain, was buried in a coffin made from whisky cases.

Test Record

	M	I	NO	Runs	HS	Avge	100s	RC	Wkts	Avge	BB	Ct
v South Africa	2	2	0	25	25	12.50	–	–	–	–	–	1

Test Record as Captain

			M	I	NO	Runs	HS	Avge	100s	RC	Wkts	Avge	BB	Ct
v South Africa	W1	–	–	1	1	0	25	25	25.00	–	–	–	–	–	–

Andrew Ernest STODDART

Middlesex

Born: Westloe, South Shields, 11 March 1863
Died: St John's Wood, London, 4 April 1915

A gifted sportsman, Stoddart captained England at rugby as well as cricket. He first played for Middlesex in 1885, and the following year, playing for Hampstead against Stoics in a club match, he hit 485 in 370 minutes.

He was a member of Vernon's side in Australia in 1887–88, and played in the Test match when Vernon's team combined with the rival touring party to produce an England XI. He next went to Australia with Lord Sheffield's side in 1891–92. He played in all three Tests under Grace's captaincy and hit 134 in the third match.

When the Australians came to England in 1893 Grace was unfit to play in the first Test. Stoddart deputised as captain and made history by becoming the first captain to declare an innings closed in a Test match.

With Grace unable to lead the side in Australia in 1894–95, Stoddart was invited to captain in his place. It was an eventful and historic tour. In the first Test England followed-on 261 runs in arrears but won by 10 runs. This was the first instance of a Test side winning after being forced to follow-on, and it was to remain the only instance until 1981. In the second Test Stoddart scored 173, the highest score by an England captain in Australia until 1974–75, and in the fourth Test he became the first England captain to ask the opposition to bat first when he won the toss. England lost the match, but won the series three to two, and Stoddart returned home a hero.

In the home series of 1896, Grace was available to lead England, and Stoddart withdrew from The Oval Test because of the threatened strike by professionals over finances.

Stoddart had been so successful and popular a captain in Australia that it was no surprise when the Melbourne and Sydney Clubs invited him to take a side there again in 1897–98. The tour was a disaster for him. He missed the first two Tests because of the death of his mother and stood down from the last Test because of a complete loss of form. He was not to play Test cricket again.

A stylish batsman and a brilliant fielder, he continued to play irregularly and hit 221, the highest score of his career, against Somerset at Lord's in 1900. He did not appear in first-class cricket again.

Worried by ill-health, a worsening financial position and an unhappy marriage, he took his own life in April 1915.

Test Record

	M	I	NO	Runs	HS	Avge	100s	RC	Wkts	Avge	BB	Ct
v Australia	16	30	2	996	173	35.57	2	94	2	47.00	1–10	6

Test Record as Captain

				M	I	NO	Runs	HS	Avge	100s	RC	Wkts	Avge	BB	Ct
v Australia	W3	L4	D1	8	16	1	470	173	31.33	1	63	2	31.50	1–10	3

Sir Timothy Carew O'BRIEN

Middlesex

Born: Dublin, 5 November 1861
Died: Ramsey, Isle of Man, 9 December 1948

A most aggressive batsman and an equally lively character, O'Brien played for Middlesex between 1881 and 1898. He won a blue at Oxford in 1884 and 1885, having gone to the university in order to improve his cricket.

He also played for his native Ireland, and his last first-class match was for L. Robinson's XI against Oxford in 1914 when, at the age of 52, he hit 90 and 111.

He played against Australia at Old Trafford in 1884 and at Lord's in 1888. He went to South Africa with Lord Hawke's team in 1895–96 and led England in the first Test. Hawke played but felt unwell and O'Brien was asked to captain the side.

Test Record

	M	I	NO	Runs	HS	Avge	100s	RC	Wkts	Avge	BB	Ct
v Australia	2	4	0	24	20	6.00	–	–	–	–	–	1
v South Africa	3	4	0	35	17	8.75	–	–	–	–	–	3
	5	8	0	59	20	7.37	–	–	–	–	–	4

Test Record as Captain

		M	I	NO	Runs	HS	Avge	100s	RC	Wkts	Avge	BB	Ct
v South Africa	W1 – –	1	2	0	33	17	16.50	–	–	–	–	–	2

Seventh Lord HAWKE
(Hon. Martin Bladen Hawke)

Yorkshire

Born: Gainsborough, Lincolnshire, 16 August 1860
Died: Edinburgh, 10 October 1938

Educated at Eton and Cambridge, where he gained his blue in three of his four years in residence, Lord Hawke will best be remembered as the man who transformed Yorkshire cricket. He played for the county from 1881 to 1911, captained them from 1883 to 1910 and indeed ruled them for most of his life.

He made Yorkshire the strongest county in the land and did a vast amount to improve the lot of the professionals and, in his various offices with MCC, foster the well-being of the game.

He was captain of Vernon's team in Australia in 1887–88, but he returned home early because of the death of his father. He later took sides to Canada, United States, India, Ceylon and West Indies, but his Test career was limited to the two tours he took to South Africa, 1895–96 and 1898–99. Feeling unwell, he handed over the captaincy to O'Brien for the first Test of the first series, but he still played in the match.

Test Record

	M	I	NO	Runs	HS	Avge	100s	RC	Wkts	Avge	BB	Ct
v South Africa	5	8	1	55	30	7.85	–	–	–	–	–	3

Test Record as Captain

		M	I	NO	Runs	HS	Avge	100s	RC	Wkts	Avge	BB	Ct
v South Africa	W4 – –	4	6	1	25	12	5.00	–	–	–	–	–	3

Archibald Campbell MacLAREN

Lancashire

Born: Whalley Range, Manchester, 1 December 1871
Died: Bracknell, Berkshire, 17 November 1944

As a batsman Archie MacLaren was one of the bright jewels of a golden age; as a captain his credentials are less impressive.

A majestic batsman rich in strokes of classical propensity, he came into the Lancashire side in 1890 straight from Harrow and marked his debut with a century. He hit 424 against Somerset at Taunton in 1895, the highest first-class innings in England, and he hit 200 not out for MCC in New Zealand in his final first-class innings in 1923. He was 52 years old.

He captained Lancashire from 1894–96 and 1899–1907, but a strong side took the championship only once in that period.

He went with Stoddart's side to Australia in 1894–95 and hit 120 in the final Test. Four of his five Test hundreds were to be made in Australia. His success in England was never so great, and he scored only 41 runs in two Tests under Grace in 1896.

In 1897–98, he again went with Stoddart to Australia and led England in the first two Tests when Stoddart withdrew because of the death of his mother. MacLaren also captained the side in the last Test when Stoddart stood down. He hit 109 on the occasion of his debut as captain, and his 124 in the third Test at Adelaide meant that he was the first English batsman to hit two centuries in a rubber.

He played no great innings at the beginning of 1899, but he was brought in for the second Test match at Lord's at the expense of W.G. Grace who had realised that his Test career must end. MacLaren was chosen on the strength of his performances in Australia, and he was appointed captain. C.B. Fry maintained that this was an oversight on the part of Lord Hawke and his selectors who had failed to see that F.S. Jackson was MacLaren's senior and should have led the side.

The MCC agreed to organise the 1901–02 tour of Australia, but they announced in May 1901 that they had found it impossible to muster a representative England side and were withdrawing from the venture. MacLaren was persuaded to gather a party, but without cricketers of the calibre of Ranjitsinhji, Hirst, Rhodes and Fry it could hardly be called a strong one. MacLaren enjoyed a good series and became the first batsman to score four hundreds in Test cricket, but his side was beaten four matches to one.

He retained the captaincy for the 1902 series, but withdrew from the side that went to Australia in 1903–04. He had originally been invited to lead the party, but he refused to go when S.F. Barnes, whom he had introduced to Test cricket, and Lockwood rejected invitations.

In 1905 he played in four Tests under Jackson, but he was back in charge four years later. He was then 37, and his recall was a strange one, for Fry, Warner and Jones, all of whom had captained England, were in the side, and MacLaren himself felt that he was no longer up to the required standard for he was playing irregularly.

He turned out an all-amateur side against the victorious Australians of 1921 and beat them, in a match which has passed into cricket legend; and he ended his career with a highly successful tour of New Zealand in 1922–23.

MacLaren was an authoritative and inflexible leader with a fine knowledge of the game, but he never drew the best from those under him in whom he often seemed to have little confidence. He did not always use his bowlers to good advantage and was insensitive to specialist fielders, and the fact remains that in the five Test series in which he was involved as captain, England were beaten each time.

Test Record

	M	I	NO	Runs	HS	Avge	100s	RC	Wkts	Avge	BB	Ct
v Australia	35	61	4	1931	140	33.87	5	–	–	–	–	29

Test Record as Captain

		M	I	NO	Runs	HS	Avge	100s	RC	Wkts	Avge	BB	Ct
v Australia	W4 L11 D7	22	36	3	1156	116	35.03	2	–	–	–	–	23

Sir Pelham Francis WARNER

Middlesex

Born: Port-of-Spain, Trinidad, 2 October 1873
Died: West Lavington, Sussex, 30 January 1963

'Plum' Warner was not in the top flight of batsmen in the Golden Age, but his record is impressive in that he hit 60 centuries in a first-class career which began in 1894 and ended in 1920. He captained Middlesex from 1908 until that last year, and his career reached a romantic climax with Middlesex beating Surrey in his last game to win the championship. He was later selector, long-serving committee member and ultimately President of MCC, tour manager and journalist. Fry described him as 'a golden treasury of all that ever happened, or was likely to happen, in the game of cricket'. Cricket was his life.

He had a profound knowledge of the game, a sound technique and temperament and a total dedication, but he lacked the flair that would have brought him on a par with MacLaren or Fry. Twelve of his fifteen Test matches were played abroad which is a testimony to the fact that he was not considered in the top flight of batsmen and could not command a place in an England side when the best amateurs were available.

Educated at Rugby and Oxford, he was invited to tour South Africa with Lord Hawke's side in 1898–99, and he carried his bat through the second innings of the first Test for 132.

Archie MacLaren was to have taken a party to Australia in 1903–04, but he withdrew, and MCC organised the tour in his stead. Seven amateurs, including Fry, Jackson, MacLaren and Jessop, refused invitations, and Warner was named as captain with only two other amateurs in the party alongside him. The series was won, but Warner did not play for England again until 1905–06 when he took the side to South Africa, the leading amateurs having once more found it impossible to make the trip. Warner's side was comprehensively beaten.

Ten years after his Test debut, he at last played in a home Test match, against Australia in 1909 when MacLaren was captain.

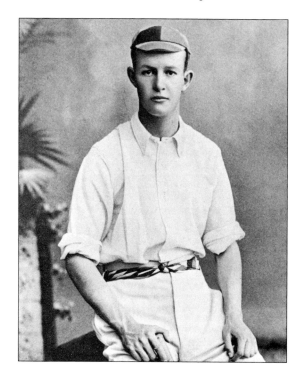

'Plum' Warner – an influential figure for half a century (Ken Kelly)

C.B. Fry was asked to take the England side to Australia in 1911–12, but he could give no answer until August when he declined. Once more MCC fell back on Warner to fill the breach; once more there were only two other amateurs in the party. After one match, in which he scored 151, Warner fell ill, and J.W.H.T.

Douglas took over the captaincy for the rest of the tour, Warner advising from his sickbed. He never enjoyed the best of health, but he lived until he was nearly 90.

He played under Fry in the first two Tests of the triangular series in 1912 and that was the end of his Test career.

Test Record

	M	I	NO	Runs	HS	Avge	100s	RC	Wkts	Avge	BB	Ct
v Australia	7	13	1	287	79	23.91	–	–	–	–	–	2
v South Africa	8	15	1	335	132*	23.92	1	–	–	–	–	1
	15	28	2	622	132*	23.92	1	–	–	–	–	3

Test Record as Captain

				M	I	NO	Runs	HS	Avge	100s	RC	Wkts	Avge	BB	Ct
v Australia	W3	L2	–	5	10	1	249	79	27.66	–	–	–	–	–	2
v South Africa	W1	L4	–	5	10	0	89	51	8.90	–	–	–	–	–	1
	W4	L6	–	10	20	1	338	79	17.78	–	–	–	–	–	3

Sir Francis Stanley JACKSON

Yorkshire

Born: Chapel Allerton, Yorkshire, 21 November 1870
Died: Knightsbridge, London, 9 May 1947

Sir Stanley Jackson's span as captain of England was limited to one series, yet had he been more regularly available, he would surely have led his country more often.

He was educated at Harrow and Cambridge where he won his blue in all four years, 1890–93, and had the rare distinction of leading the side for two seasons. His first-class career extended until 1907, but he was able to play regularly in only one season, 1905, his *annus mirabilis* when he captained England.

Jackson's single tour was to India in 1892–93, and his 20 Test matches were all played in England against Australia.

A stylish middle-order batsman and a fast-medium pace bowler, Jackson was an all-rounder of the very highest quality, the epitome of the Golden Age of English cricket. He made his Test debut at Lord's in 1893 and scored 91 and 5. In the next Test, at The Oval, he made

103, but he was unable to play in the third and final Test.

The problem for Jackson was that cricket was a hobby, not an occupation. He served in the Boer War and was invalided home with enteric fever in June 1900. He was persuaded to play for the Gentlemen at Scarborough although he was still weak, convalescing and had not held a bat for over a year. He hit 134 and 42 against an attack that included Hirst and Rhodes. Then he went back to the Boer War.

As well as his service as a soldier, Jackson was MP for Howdenshire from 1915 to 1926. He was Financial Secretary to the War Office in 1922 and Chairman of the Unionist Party in 1923, and he was later Governor of Bengal where he narrowly escaped assassination.

He was an automatic choice for England when available and played in all the home Tests against Australia from 1896 to 1905. Fry maintained that it was an oversight that Jackson was not asked to be captain in 1899, and it was not until 1905 that he finally gained the leadership. He topped both the batting and the bowling averages in a series which England won two-nil, their first victory in a home rubber since 1896.

A fine captain of England, Jackson, like Hutton half a century later, was not to captain

Yorkshire, and one can only conjecture what he might have achieved had he been able to give himself fully to the game.

Test Record

	M	I	NO	Runs	HS	Avge	100s	RC	Wkts	Avge	BB	Ct
v Australia	20	33	4	1415	144*	48.79	5	799	24	33.29	5–52	10

Test Record as Captain

				M	I	NO	Runs	HS	Avge	100s	RC	Wkts	Avge	BB	Ct
v Australia	W2	–	D3	5	9	2	492	144*	70.28	2	201	13	15.46	5–52	1

Reginald Erskine FOSTER

Worcestershire

Born: Malvern, Worcestershire, 16 April 1878
Died: Kensington, London, 13 May 1914

'Tip' Foster was another Edwardian cricketer of immense talent who was able to give little time to the game because of business commitments. The third of seven sons of a clergyman all of whom played for Malvern and Worcestershire, he was in the Oxford side for four seasons, 1897–1900, leading the eleven in inspiring fashion in his last year. He hit a record 171 in the Varsity match and a fortnight later became the first batsman to hit a century in each innings of a Gentlemen v Players match.

He captained Worcestershire in 1901, the only season in which he was able to play cricket regularly. He accepted an invitation to tour Australia in 1903–04, and hit 287 in the first Test. This remained a record score in Test cricket until 1929–30 and still stands as the highest score by a player in his first Test and the highest score by an English batsman in a Test match in Australia.

He led England in the series against South Africa in 1907, the first time that the South Africans had played Test cricket outside their own country, and he was invited to take the side to Australia the following winter, but he declined.

A soccer international, Foster last played cricket for Worcestershire in 1912. His career was cut short by diabetes, and he died just before the outbreak of the First World War at the age of 36.

Test Record

	M	I	NO	Runs	HS	Avge	100s	RC	Wkts	Avge	BB	Ct
v Australia	5	9	1	486	287	60.75	1	–	–	–	–	8
v South Africa	3	5	0	116	51	23.20	–	–	–	–	–	5
	8	14	1	602	287	46.30	1	–	–	–	–	13

Test Record as Captain

v South Africa	W1	–	D2	*Details as above*

Frederick Luther FANE

Essex

Born: Curragh Camp, Ireland, 27 April 1875
Died: Kelvedon Hatch, Essex, 27 November 1960

A stylish right-handed batsman who played for Essex while still at Oxford, Freddie Fane gained his blue in 1897 and 1898. He went on several tours and led Essex from 1904–06, but captaincy was never really to his liking.

His Test debut came with Warner's side in South Africa in 1905–06, and he enjoyed a highly successful series, hitting 143 in the third Test in Johannesburg.

He was less successful in the series in Australia in 1907–08, although he captained a weak England side in the first three Tests because A.O. Jones was ill. He had a similar experience in South Africa in 1909–10, when Leveson Gower stood down from the last two matches of the series, and Fane captained the side.

The first Essex player to captain England, all five times by default, Fane assisted the county until 1922, and his last first-class match was for Leveson Gower's XI two years later. He was never asked to play for England in a home series.

A reluctant leader – F.L. Fane of Essex (Ken Kelly)

Test Record

	M	I	NO	Runs	HS	Avge	100s	RC	Wkts	Avge	BB	Ct
v South Africa	10	19	1	490	143	27.22	1	–	–	–	–	5
v Australia	4	8	0	192	50	24.00	–	–	–	–	–	1
	14	27	1	682	143	26.23	1	–	–	–	–	6

Test Record as Captain

				M	I	NO	Runs	HS	Avge	100s	RC	Wkts	Avge	BB	Ct
v Australia	W1	L2	–	3	6	0	146	50	24.33	–	–	–	–	–	1
v South Africa	W1	L1	–	2	3	0	57	37	19.00	–	–	–	–	–	2
	W2	L3	–	5	9	0	203	50	22.55	–	–	–	–	–	3

Arthur Owen JONES

Nottinghamshire

Born: Shelton, Nottinghamshire, 16 August 1872
Died: Dunstable, Bedfordshire, 21 December 1914

A highly popular and successful county captain, Jones led Nottinghamshire from 1900 until the outbreak of the First World War, taking his side to the County Championship in 1907. He was a fiercely aggressive batsman – his 296 against Gloucestershire at Trent Bridge in 1903 was a county record at the time – a very useful leg-spin bowler and a fielder who has had few equals in the history of the game. It was said that he invented the position of gully when at Bedford Modern School and that he won his blue at Cambridge in 1893 solely on the strength of his fielding.

He first played for England against Australia at The Oval in 1899, batting at number nine although he invariably opened for his county, and took three wickets in Australia's first innings. These were to be his first and last wickets in Test cricket.

He toured Australia with MacLaren's side in 1901–02 and appeared in all five Test matches, and he played in two Test matches, under Jackson, in 1905. When several of England's leading amateurs announced that they were unavailable for the tour of Australia in 1907–08, the captaincy passed to Jones. He was doubly unfortunate. Illness prevented him from playing in the first three Test matches, and it was reported that he found the burden of leadership and its attendant administrative chores more than he could cope with.

MacLaren was reinstated as England's captain in 1909, and Jones played his last two Test matches in that series. He was dogged by ill-health in the closing years of his career, and he died of tuberculosis in his 43rd year.

Test Record

	M	I	NO	Runs	HS	Avge	100s	RC	Wkts	Avge	BB	Ct
v Australia	12	21	0	291	34	13.85	–	133	3	44.33	3–73	15

Test Record as Captain

			M	I	NO	Runs	HS	Avge	100s	RC	Wkts	Avge	BB	Ct
v Australia	–	L2	–	2	4	0	68	34	17.00	–	–	–	–	–	3

Sir Henry Dudley Gresham LEVESON GOWER

Surrey

Born: Titsey, Surrey, 8 May 1873
Died: Kensington, London, 1 February 1954

Small in stature, hence his nickname 'Shrimp', Leveson Gower was, nevertheless, influential in the cricket world for many years, as captain and president of Surrey for whom he played from 1895 until 1920, Test selector and organiser of the Scarborough Festival.

He was also organiser of several private tours, went to South Africa in 1905–06 but did not play in a Test, and captained the MCC side to the Union in 1909–10. After the mauling that Warner's team had received in 1905–06 MCC attempted to send a stronger side with Leveson Gower, but it was still well below full England strength, and had Fry or any of the other notable amateurs been able to accept invitations, Leveson Gower would not have captained the side.

He was a middle-order batsman and could bowl both slow-medium outswingers and leg-breaks. His most famous achievement was to lead Oxford to victory in the Varsity match of 1896. His side was asked to make 330 to win in the fourth innings and reached the target with three wickets to spare thanks mainly to Leveson Gower's determination to pack his eleven with batsmen, a policy he maintained as a selector, not always to the benefit of England.

In 1953, he was knighted for his services to cricket.

Test Record as Captain

	M	I	NO	Runs	HS	Avge	100s	RC	Wkts	Avge	BB	Ct
v South Africa **W1 L2** –	3	6	2	95	31	23.75	–	–	–	–	–	1

John William Henry Tyler DOUGLAS

Essex

Born: Clapton, Middlesex, 3 September 1882
Died: nr Laeso, Denmark, 19 December 1930

The only man to have captained England before and after the First World War, J.W.H.T. Douglas carried Essex cricket on his shoulders for nearly thirty years. Educated at Felsted School, he first played for his adopted county in 1901, but he did not win a regular place in the side until 1904.

Douglas was not a natural athlete, but, inspired and encouraged by his father, he dedicated his life to sport. He ran, jumped, played hockey, appeared for England against Bohemia in an amateur soccer international and won the gold medal in the middleweight division of boxing in the 1908 Olympics. He bowled fast medium pace, moved the ball appreciably, was unerringly accurate and had immense reserves of stamina and energy. He was a batsman of limited scoring strokes but infinite patience, and in Australia he was nicknamed 'Johnny Won't Hit Today' although his rate of scoring compares favourably with many who have played Test cricket in recent years.

In 1911, Douglas became captain of Essex. It was a surprising appointment, for it had seemed that Percy Perrin was destined for the captaincy. He was six years senior to Douglas and had been playing for the county since 1896. It was generally accepted that Douglas senior was responsible for the appointment of his son as captain and that, holding the mortgage on the Leyton ground, he threatened to foreclose if J.W.H.T. was not given the honour.

Douglas enjoyed a splendid first season as captain, hitting 1279 runs and taking 82 wickets in all matches. He was selected for the Gentlemen against the Players at both The Oval and Lord's, and these matches were looked upon as important trials to help the selectors choose the side to Australia the following winter. At Lord's, Douglas had an outstanding match. He hit 72 in three and a quarter hours on a difficult wicket, made 22 not out in the second innings and finished with match figures of 7 for 91. He played a significant role in the Gentlemen's victory by 130 runs.

Courage and determination, triumph and failure – J.W.H.T. Douglas (Hulton)

A few weeks before this game, MCC had invited eight men to form the nucleus of the side to tour Australia. The eight included the amateurs Fry, Spooner, Warner and F.R. Foster, but both Fry, who was to have led the side, and Spooner later said that they would be unable to make the trip. Jessop was another amateur who stated that he could not accept an invitation, but Douglas, who was selected shortly after his success for the Gentlemen at Lord's, readily agreed to tour. He was in the enviable position of never having to refuse such an invitation, for he had a father eager for his success and wealthy enough in his timber business to allow his son to pursue his sporting activities.

Warner replaced Fry as captain and had only two other amateurs, Douglas and Foster, in his party which was certainly as strong as any that had ever left England. Warner fell ill after the opening match and was to take no further part in the tour. He had been appointed captain and sole selector so it was up to him to name a vice-captain. There were, of course, only two candidates to act as his successor. He wrote:

'Both were county captains of the same standing, both having been appointed to their positions at the beginning of 1911. Foster had a particularly good record, having in his first season led Warwickshire to the top of the tree, but Douglas had done well with Essex, and was senior both in age and in cricketing experience, having played for Essex long before Foster appeared for Warwickshire, and having represented the Gentlemen against the Players at Lord's as far back as 1907. It would have been unfair, then, to have passed over Douglas, and my choice, therefore, fell on him.'

So Douglas found himself captain of England on the occasion of his Test debut. He made a psychological and diplomatic error in opening the bowling with Foster and himself rather than S.F. Barnes, and England lost. He did not make the same mistake again, and England took the series 4–1. The English bowling was outstanding with Barnes taking 34 wickets, Foster 32 and Douglas 15. Douglas was liked and respected by his men, and he returned to England a hero.

In spite of this, he was not in the England side for the first five Test matches in the triangular series of 1912. Fry, Spooner, Jessop and the rest were now available. Douglas appeared in the sixth and last Test, received a tumultuous reception when he went out to bat and was not asked to bowl.

There was no Test series in 1913, but England were to send a side to South Africa in the winter of 1913–14, and having been badly beaten in the two previous tours of the Union, it was important that England fielded a strong side. Lord Harris asked Jessop to captain the team, and when he withdrew he turned to Fane who had relinquished the Essex captaincy in 1906 and was not a noted leader. Fane first agreed and then said 'no'. Tennyson was considered too young so they turned again to Douglas. He hit a century in the first Test, bowled well in the series and England won 4–0 with one match drawn. By the outbreak of war, Douglas' record as a Test captain was eight wins, a loss and a draw in ten matches. Had his Test career ended there, he would be remembered as one of the great Test captains.

Test cricket restarted in 1920–21 with an England tour of Australia. The captaincy was offered to Spooner, but he again declined as did several other amateurs, and the selectors again turned to Douglas. There seemed a marked lack of enthusiasm about the appointment and the tour. The scepticism was well justified. For the first time in Test history, England lost 5–0.

Douglas led England against Australia in the

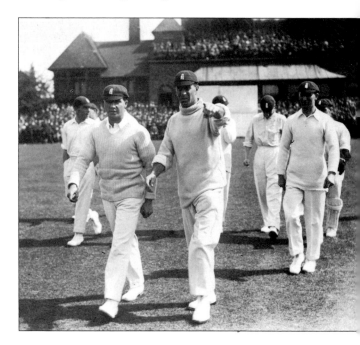

Douglas leads his side out against Australia in 1921. Next to him is Lord Tennyson, who succeeded him as captain (Hulton)

first two Test matches in 1921, one of the grimmest seasons in English cricket history. England were heavily beaten in both Tests, and Douglas was replaced as captain by Tennyson although he retained his place in the side. Ironically, Tennyson was injured during the third Test, and Douglas took over again for a time.

He was surprisingly recalled to the England side against South Africa in 1924 and was asked to be vice-captain to Gilligan in the side that went to Australia in 1924–25. He was now 42, and he was chosen to act as elder statesman and adviser to the younger players, particularly as Gilligan's fitness was in doubt.

Douglas was asked to play in the second Test, but it proved to be a sad end to his international career, Victor Richardson hitting him for a record 21 runs in one eight-ball over.

At the end of the 1928 season, the Essex Committee suggested to Douglas that he should give up the captaincy. He was then 46, but he refused, believing that his successor had not the commitment necessary to lead the county. He was proved right, but his connection with Essex had come to a sorry conclusion.

Two years later, he was drowned when the boat on which he was returning from Finland collided with its sister ship and sank in a matter of minutes. His father drowned with him.

If one has dwelt long on Douglas, it is because he has been unjustifiably maligned and because, in the years of his success, he was never more than second choice as England's captain, a position he attained, it seems, by default.

Test Record

		M	I	NO	Runs	HS	Avge	100s	RC	Wkts	Avge	BB	Ct
v Australia		17	28	2	696	75	26.76	–	1227	35	35.05	5–46	7
v South Africa		6	7	0	266	119	38.00	1	259	10	25.90	4–14	2
		23	35	2	962	119	29.15	1	1486	45	33.02	5–46	9

Test Record as Captain

				M	I	NO	Runs	HS	Avge	100s	RC	Wkts	Avge	BB	Ct
v Australia	W4	L8	–	12	21	1	528	68	26.40	–	885	27	32.77	5–46	3
v South Africa	W4	–	D2	6	7	0	266	119	38.00	1	259	10	25.90	4–14	2
	W8	L8	D2	18	28	1	794	119	29.40	1	1144	37	30.91	5–46	5

Charles Burgess FRY

Sussex and Hampshire

Born: West Croydon, Surrey, 25 April 1872
Died: Hampstead, 7 September 1956

The name of C.B. Fry has occurred so often in this narrative that it is hard to believe that he did not captain England until 1912 and that he was the 23rd cricketer to be so honoured. As we have seen, he was approached to lead England on several occasions, but his other interests never allowed him the time, and the only tour that he was able to make was to South Africa in 1895–96 just after coming down from Oxford. He played in two Test matches on that tour, and

the remaining 24 in which he appeared were all in England.

A first-class honours graduate in Classical Moderations, he won his blue for cricket in all four seasons (1892–95) and also won blues for soccer and athletics. He would also have won a blue for rugby but for injury. He held the world long jump record for 21 years, was capped for England against Ireland at soccer in 1901 and played for Southampton in the FA Cup Final of 1902. An author, an avid talker, a broadcaster, an unsuccessful Liberal candidate in three elections, a representative of India at the League of Nations, captain of Sussex from 1904–08, magazine editor and founder and director of the training ship *Mercury*, Fry was, it will be noted, a man of many talents. After the First World War he was offered and declined the throne of Albania.

A great thinker on the game, a batsman of determination and correct technique, Fry hit six centuries in succession in 1901 and passed 3000 runs in the season. He moved from Sussex to Hampshire after the 1908 season because he had established the training ship *Mercury* and played for his adopted county until 1921. He also played for the Europeans in India in 1922. He said in his charming autobiography, *Life Worth Living* (1939), that he was asked to replace Douglas as captain of England in 1921, but he felt that as he could neither spare the time nor was he in sufficient practice, he suggested that the selectors should ask Tennyson, his Hampshire colleague.

An automatic choice for England when available, Fry captained his country for just one season, 1912. This was the year of the triangular Test tournament between England, Australia and South Africa, the first attempt at a world cup. It was not a success, the weather providing one obstacle, but under Fry, England won four and drew two of their six matches to win the competition. It was said that the selectors met at the beginning of the season, named Fry as captain and then disbanded, leaving the rest of the job to him. He would have enjoyed that.

Supreme all-round athlete and captain of England in 1912, C.B. Fry (Ken Kelly)

Test Record

	M	I	NO	Runs	HS	Avge	100s	RC	Wkts	Avge	BB	Ct
v Australia	18	29	3	825	144	31.73	1	3	0	–	–	14
v South Africa	8	12	0	398	129	33.16	1	–	–	–	–	3
	26	41	3	1223	144	32.18	2	3	0	–	–	17

Test Record as Captain

				M	I	NO	Runs	HS	Avge	100s	RC	Wkts	Avge	BB	Ct
v Australia	W1	–	D2	3	4	0	145	79	36.25	–	–	–	–	–	2
v South Africa	W3	–	–	3	4	0	55	29	13.75	–	–	–	–	–	
	W4	–	D2	6	8	0	200	79	25.00	–	–	–	–	–	2

Third Lord TENNYSON
(Hon. Lionel Hallam Tennyson)

Hampshire

Born: Westminster, 7 November 1889
Died: Bexhill-on-Sea, Sussex, 6 June 1951

A grandson of Alfred Lord Tennyson, the great Victorian poet, Lionel Tennyson was one of cricket's memorable eccentrics. Educated at Eton, he was a fierce, attacking batsman who began his first-class career in 1913 with a century. He led Hampshire from 1919 until 1933 and played his last first-class match, for MCC, in 1937. Like his batting, his captaincy was unpredictable. He changed batting orders as the mood took him, and many felt that Hampshire

had the talent to have fared better than they did during his period of captaincy.

He went on numerous tours, some organised by himself, and played his first five Test matches in South Africa under Douglas' leadership in 1913–14. He was chosen for the second Test against Australia at Lord's in 1921, with Douglas again as captain, and took over from the Essex man for the last three Tests.

In his first Test as captain, at Headingley, he split a finger fielding and batted one-handed against the furious pace of Gregory and McDonald. That series marked the end of the Test career of one who was too impatient and too dedicated to the joy of good living ever to be at home in post-war international cricket.

Walter Livesey, the Hampshire wicket-keeper, was his butler.

Test Record

	M	I	NO	Runs	HS	Avge	100s	RC	Wkts	Avge	BB	Ct
v Australia	4	5	1	229	74*	57.25	–	–	–	–	–	2
v South Africa	5	7	0	116	52	16.57	–	1	0	–	–	4
	9	12	1	345	74*	31.36	–	1	0	–	–	6

Test Record as Captain

		M	I	NO	Runs	HS	Avge	100s	RC	Wkts	Avge	BB	Ct
v Australia	– L1 D2	3	3	0	150	63	50.00	–	–	–	–	–	2

Francis Thomas MANN

Middlesex

Born: Winchmore Hill, Middlesex, 3 March 1888
Died: Milton Lilbourne, Wiltshire, 6 October 1964

Frank Mann was a middle-order batsman who hit with tremendous power. He won his blue at Cambridge in all three years, 1909–11, and first played for Middlesex in 1909. Although wounded three times in the First World War, he succeeded Warner as captain of Middlesex in 1921, a position he held until the end of the 1928 season.

Extremely popular with his men, he led

A popular cricketer and an unassuming captain of Middlesex and England – Frank Mann (Allsport)

Middlesex to a notable Championship triumph in his first season as captain in 1921, and led the England side to South Africa in 1922–23. The only defeat his side suffered was in the first Test, but they came back to win the series.

His final first-class match was in 1933, for H.D.G. Leveson Gower's XI. His son, George Mann, was also to lead England in South Africa.

Test Record as Captain

				M	I	NO	Runs	HS	Avge	100s	RC	Wkts	Avge	BB	Ct
v South Africa	W2	L1	D2	5	9	1	281	84	35.12	–	–	–	–	–	4

Arthur Edward Robert GILLIGAN

Surrey and Sussex

Born: Denmark Hill, Surrey, 23 December 1894
Died: Mare Hill, Pulborough, Sussex, 5 September 1976

In the years immediately following the First World War, the problem as to who should captain the England side began to loom large. The great amateurs of the Edwardian age, Fry, MacLaren, Foster etc, had passed from the scene or reached the veteran stage. Warwick Armstrong and his Australians had wrenched Test cricket onto a more professional and competitive plain. By the mid-twenties, England were still shell-shocked from the batterings that they had received in 1920 and 1921. Tennyson and Mann were stop-gap captains, and the dearth of amateur talent was becoming apparent. It was in 1925 that Lord Hawke, replying to a vote of thanks at the AGM of Yorkshire County Cricket Club, made his famous utterance –

'Pray God, no professional shall ever captain England. I love and admire them all but we have always had an amateur skipper and when the day comes when we shall have no more amateurs captaining England it will be a thousand pities.'

The England captain at the time was Arthur Gilligan who, for a short period at least, was genuinely worth his place in the England side as a fast bowler, excellent fielder and aggressive late middle-order batsman. He played three matches for Surrey in 1919, the first of his two years at Cambridge. He won his blue both years and then moved to Sussex for whom he played until 1932 and whom he captained with zest and intelligence from 1922 until 1929.

He went to South Africa with Mann's team in 1922–23 and played in the first and fifth Test matches. The fifth Test decided the series. Gilligan took six wickets and in the second innings, batting number eleven, he shared a stand of 92 with Russell of Essex. This remains a last-wicket record stand for England against South Africa. England went on to win by 109 runs and gained their first successful rubber for nine years.

Gilligan was now at his best, and in 1923 he hit 1183 runs and took 163 wickets. This was the inspiration that England had been needing, and he was named as captain for the series against South Africa in 1924. In the first Test, at Edgbaston, he opened the bowling with his county new-ball partner Maurice Tate. They bowled the South Africans out for 30 in 48 minutes. Gilligan took 6 for 7 in 6.3 overs; Tate had 4 for 12 in six. Gilligan took five wickets in the second innings, and England won by an innings, their first home Test victory for 12 years.

He led England to an equally emphatic victory in the second Test at Lord's, and by the end of June he had 74 first-class wickets to his credit. He went straight from Lord's to captain the Gentlemen against the Players at The Oval. His side was beaten, but he played an astonishing innings of 112 in just over an hour and a half. It was, however, an unwise innings. He had received a severe blow over the heart from a ball by fast bowler Howell, but insisted on playing on. The accident took its toll of him. He captured only another 29 wickets during the season, had to stand down from the fourth Test and, in the opinion of many, he was never the same cricketer again.

He led England to Australia in 1924–25, and to victory in the fourth Test of the series, England's first over Australia since 1912, but his international career was at an end, for his own performances with bat and ball were most disappointing.

Gilligan served Sussex cricket well all his life, and he became a noted writer and broadcaster.

Test Record

	M	I	NO	Runs	HS	Avge	100s	RC	Wkts	Avge	BB	Ct
v Australia	5	9	2	64	31	9.14	–	519	10	51.90	3–114	1
v South Africa	6	7	1	145	39*	24.16	–	527	26	20.26	6–7	2
	11	16	3	209	39*	16.07	–	1046	36	29.05	6–7	3

Test Record as Captain

				M	I	NO	Runs	HS	Avge	100s	RC	Wkts	Avge	BB	Ct
v Australia	W1	L4		5	9	2	64	31	9.14	–	519	10	51.90	3–114	1
v South Africa	W3	–	D1	4	3	0	77	36	25.66	–	322	17	18.94	6–7	1
	W4	L4	D1	9	12	2	141	36	14.10	–	841	27	31.14	6–7	2

Arthur William CARR

Nottinghamshire

Born: Mickleham, Surrey, 21 May 1893
Died: West Wilton, Yorkshire, 7 February 1963

Arthur Carr was a vigorous, aggressive batsman who hit more than 21 000 runs in his career, but he was just a little short of Test class. He made his first-class debut in 1910 when still at school and led Nottinghamshire from 1919 until 1934, taking them to the Championship in 1929. A forthright and uncompromising captain who did not suffer fools gladly, he was immensely popular with his players and looked upon with some distrust by the Establishment.

He was with Mann's team in South Africa in 1922–23, having earned selection following a good season in England, and he played in all five Tests. He did not appear in a Test match again until 1926 when he was named as captain against Australia. With the choice of captain restricted to amateurs, there was not a wide field, and, ultimately, the selectors had to decide between Carr and Fender, neither of whom was docile by nature.

The first Test match, at Trent Bridge, saw only 50 minutes' play. In the second, at Lord's, Australia made 383 and 194 for 5, while England, with Hobbs and Hendren making centuries and three other batsmen reaching fifty, scored 475 for 3 declared. The third Test

Arthur Carr – strong and uncompromising (Lemmon)

was to be a bad one for Carr. He won the toss and asked Australia to bat first. Bardsley was caught at slip off the first ball of the match, and three balls later, Macartney was dropped at slip, by Carr. Macartney went on to hit a century before lunch. Woodfull and A.J. Richardson also scored hundreds, and England were forced to follow-on. Hobbs and Sutcliffe put on 156 for the first wicket, and the match was saved. The fourth Test, at Old Trafford, was restricted by bad weather and was also drawn. Carr went down with tonsilitis, and Jack Hobbs took over the captaincy for the second and third days although there was an amateur, G.T.S. Stevens, in the side.

It is interesting to note that Carr believed that Hobbs, for whom he had the greatest admiration as a batsman, was a 'rotten captain'. It is also interesting to recall that Percy Chapman had to be called from bed where he was sleeping late after a night of jollity in order to field as substitute for Carr.

The final Test against Australia in 1926 began some three weeks after the game at Old Trafford. Carr travelled to London to help pick the side. What happened is best told in his own words.

'I very soon sensed that something was not quite right where I was concerned, and it was not very long before I found out what it was. I was to be sacked.

'As Chairman of Selectors, P.F. Warner put it to me, after the preliminaries of the meeting, that I was not fit or in any real form and that "for the sake of England" I should stand down.

'To put it mildly, I was very much taken aback; I was perfectly fit and said so at once. Then, seeing that matters were rather strained and to save as much embarrassment as I could, I withdrew from the meeting.'

Carr was replaced by Percy Chapman, but he was to lead England again, in the last two Tests against South Africa in 1929. Carr's batting was in keeping with his personality. He had a powerful straight drive, and he hit hard and often. In his autobiography, *Cricket With the Lid Off*, he revealed a strong dislike of Australians, and it was he who helped Jardine to evolve the theory of body-line bowling. It was his unflinching support for this type of bowling, and for Larwood and Voce, that was to bring an end to his reign at Nottinghamshire.

He was aggressive, but he was generous, and he was well liked by those who served him. The strength of his influence on cricket has, perhaps, never been quite fully realised.

Test Record

			M	I	NO	Runs	HS	Avge	100s	RC	Wkts	Avge	BB	Ct
v Australia			4	1	0	13	13	13.00	–	–	–	–	–	1
v South Africa			7	12	1	224	63	20.36	–	–	–	–	–	2
			11	13	1	237	63	19.75	–	–	–	–	–	3

Test Record as Captain

				M	I	NO	Runs	HS	Avge	100s	RC	Wkts	Avge	BB	Ct
v Australia	–	–	D4	4	1	0	13	13	13.00	–	–	–	–	–	1
v South Africa	W1	–	D1	2	2	0	25	15	12.50	–	–	–	–	–	1
	W1	–	D5	6	3	0	38	15	12.66	–	–	–	–	–	2

Arthur Percy Frank CHAPMAN

Kent

Born: Reading, Berkshire, 3 September 1900
Died: Alton, Hampshire, 16 September 1961

The gods of cricket gave all the gifts to Percy Chapman, and then they took them away again and left him a tragic figure. His prodigious efforts for Uppingham were noted by *Wisden* which, in 1919, named him as one of the Five Public School Cricketers of the Year. He was a physical symbol of all that seemed good and desirable. His large frame was surmounted by golden curls. He was courteous and abundant in friendship. It was as if Apollo had come to play cricket. He made a century on the occasion of his first-class debut for Cambridge University, and history has decreed that he will be the only batsman ever to score a hundred in the Varsity match, for the Gentlemen against the Players and for England against Australia at Lord's.

Tall and left-handed, he was a ferocious hitter with a touch of majesty, and in the field he was brilliant. He transmitted joy when he played cricket. He first played for England in 1924, appearing in the first two Tests against South Africa when he was, in fact, still a Berkshire player qualifying for Kent by residence. He played in four of the five Tests in Australia in 1924–25, and was in the England side for the first three Tests of the 1926 series, being relegated to twelfth man for the fourth match. When it was decided that Carr should be dropped for the deciding, 'timeless' Test, Percy Chapman was named as captain in his place. He was a month short of his 26th birthday. He was the youngest man to lead England in England, and he had virtually no experience of captaincy. He had appeared in only 15 matches for Kent over a period of three years.

Twenty-two runs behind on the first innings, England won a memorable match by 289 runs. It marked England's first series victory over Australia for 14 years. It was the end of a drought, and Chapman was an instant national hero.

These had been troubled times, with the General Strike and the aftermath of the Great War causing much distress, and people reacted to England's win at The Oval in a way which we find hard to understand today. They crowded the streets and sang and cheered.

Chapman was not able to lead the side that went to South Africa, but he captained England to three wins in three Tests against West Indies in 1928, and the following winter he led the party to Australia where the first four Tests were won. He stood down from the fifth Test to give others in the party a chance, and England lost.

Visits to New Zealand and Canada and a string of social engagements kept him out of the series against South Africa in 1929, and there was even press speculation that he should not lead the side against Australia in 1930, but public opinion demanded that he should. At Trent

A joyful captain and a national hero who sank into a sad decline, Percy Chapman (centre) takes the field at Leeds in 1926 (Hulton)

Bridge, he scored 52 and 29, and England won by 93 runs. It was his ninth game as England's captain, and the ninth victory, a record.

At Lord's, England made 425 and Australia responded with 729 for 6 declared. At 147 for 5, England faced an innings defeat, but Chapman hit 121 in 155 minutes. His innings included four sixes and 12 fours, and the crowd rose to him. Australia needed 72 to win, but they lost three wickets in getting the runs, one to an astonishing catch in the gully by Chapman which accounted for Bradman.

The third Test match was drawn. England had had to follow-on, but appeals against the light by Leyland and Sutcliffe were upheld, wrongly it was thought, and the match was saved. Very little play was possible after the first two days in the fourth Test match, but there was an undercurrent of murmuring which suggested that the selectors were about to drop Chapman. Warner, in *The Cricketer*, waged a subtle campaign which hinted that Chapman was not the captain he had been and was not in form – he was averaging 43.16 in the series. The press, outraged as they realised what was about to happen, countered with a 'Don't Drop Chapman' campaign. The selectors announced a party of 14 for the final Test. It included two wicket-keepers, but it did not include Percy Chapman. No explanation was given; nor, at the time, was a captain named. Wyatt was later told he was to lead the side.

Chapman had already agreed to take the England side to South Africa the following winter, but there the side was beaten in the first Test and the rest were drawn. Having won his first nine Test matches, he did not taste success in his remaining eight as leader. He put on weight, and he drank heavily. Once people had gathered round him in the street and cheered him; now they avoided him.

He was neither a great thinker nor a great tactician. His success was founded on his genial personality, and the charm he exuded created the best of atmospheres for a side in which all wanted to do well for him. For five years, he was a national hero. His tragedy was that he believed that the good times would last for ever, and he ended a shell of the man he once was. Few, however, have been blessed as was Chapman in being allowed to climb so high.

Chapman as seen by the Australian leg-spinner, cartoonist and journalist Arthur Mailey (Allsport)

"AFTER A HOT DAY IN THE FIELD."

To Percy Chapman. With apologies: Arthur Mailey

Test Record

	M	I	NO	Runs	HS	Avge	100s	RC	Wkts	Avge	BB		Ct
v Australia	16	25	3	784	121	35.64	1	20	0	–	–		18
v South Africa	7	8	0	83	28	10.37	–	–	–	–	–		8
v West Indies	3	3	1	58	50	29.00	–	–	–	–	–		6
	26	36	4	925	121	28.90	1	20	0	–	–	–	32

Test Record as Captain

				M	I	NO	Runs	HS	Avge	100s	RC	Wkts	Avge	BB	Ct
v Australia	W6	L1	D2	9	15	0	492	121	32.80	1	–	–	–	–	15
v South Africa	–	L1	D4	5	7	0	75	28	10.71	–	–	–	–	–	7
v West Indies	W3	–	–	3	3	1	58	50	29.00	–	–	–	–	–	6
	W9	L2	D6	17	25	1	625	121	26.04	1	–	–	–	–	28

Ronald Thomas STANYFORTH

Yorkshire

Born: Chelsea, 30 May 1892
Died: Kirk Hammerton, Yorkshire, 20 February 1964

Stanyforth became a regular army officer after his time at Oxford, where he did not get a blue, and rose to the rank of Lieutenant-Colonel. Nearly all of his cricket was for the Army and for MCC. A competent wicket-keeper, he toured South Africa in 1927–28 and was asked to lead the side when G.R. Jackson of Derbyshire withdrew because of illness. As both Stevens and Wyatt were in the side, which was a strong one, the choice of Stanyforth as captain was surprising, for he had never appeared in county cricket. Indeed, his only three county matches, for Yorkshire, where he was not born, were in 1928. His leadership of the side also meant that Elliott, the highly respected Derbyshire keeper, was relegated to second string. A lively personality and a man with strong ties with MCC, Stanyforth received a severe blow under the eye in the fourth Test in Johannesburg and did not play in the final Test.

Test Record as Captain

				M	I	NO	Runs	HS	Avge	100s	RC	Wkts	Avge	BB	Ct/st
v South Africa	W2	L1	D1	4	6	1	13	6*	2.60	–	–	–	–	–	7/2

Greville Thomas Scott STEVENS

Middlesex

Born: Hampstead, 7 January 1901
Died: Islington, 19 September 1970

Greville Stevens was one of the greatest hopes for English cricket in the 1920s. He was an exciting batsman and a leg-break and googly bowler who had had legendary success as a schoolboy at University College School, and he was in the side at Oxford in all four years, 1920 to 1923. He played an important part in two Championship title successes by Middlesex, and he was chosen to tour South Africa in 1922–23 when still at Oxford. He played in one Test on that tour and in the last two Tests against Australia in 1926. In South Africa in 1927–28 he took over the captaincy of the side for the last Test when Stanyforth was absent through injury. A brilliant fielder, a highly talented cricketer and a likeable and popular man, Stevens never reached the heights for which he had seemed destined, for he had to devote most of his time to business.

He played in the first two matches in the series against West Indies in 1929–30, taking 5 for 105 and 5 for 90 in the first game. He played no Test cricket after that tour.

Test Record

	M	I	NO	Runs	HS	Avge	100s	RC	Wkts	Avge	BB	Ct
v Australia	2	3	0	63	24	21.00	–	184	5	36.80	3–86	3
v South Africa	6	10	0	149	69	14.90	–	223	4	55.75	3–58	5
v West Indies	2	4	0	51	29	12.75	–	241	11	21.90	5–90	1
	10	17	0	263	69	15.47	–	648	20	32.40	5–90	9

Test Record as Captain

				M	I	NO	Runs	HS	Avge	100s	RC	Wkts	Avge	BB	Ct
v South Africa	–	L1	–	1	2	0	31	18	15.50	–	11	0	–	–	–

John Cornish WHITE

Somerset

Born: Holford, Somerset, 19 February 1891
Died: Combe Florey, Somerset, 2 May 1961

An accurate slow left-arm bowler, 'Farmer' White did not spin the ball greatly, nor was he in the top flight of bowlers, but he was very successful on the hard wickets in Australia in 1928–29, when he was vice-captain to Percy Chapman. He led the side in the fifth Test when Chapman was unavailable, and he was captain in the first three Tests against South Africa the following summer before being replaced by Carr. He served as a Test selector in 1929–30, being one of the men responsible for the dropping of Chapman.

He was vice-captain to Chapman in 1928–29 as he was one of only three amateurs on the tour, and the only one who was a county captain. He was not, however, a good or popular captain. In his history of Somerset CCC, Peter Roebuck says of him that he was '. . . distant from his players and his severe manner had a dampening effect upon their enthusiasm'.

White first played for England in 1921, one of 30 players to appear for the home country against Australia in a series in which they were overwhelmed, and his last appearance was in the fifth Test against South Africa in 1931.

'Farmer' White – his most successful series was as vice-captain to Chapman in Australia (Lemmon)

Test Record

	M	I	NO	Runs	HS	Avge	100s	RC	Wkts	Avge	BB	Ct
v Australia	7	12	6	110	29	18.33	–	1033	31	33.32	8–126	1
v South Africa	7	9	2	108	23	15.42	–	495	15	33.00	3–21	4
v West Indies	1	1	1	21	21*	–	–	53	3	17.66	3–41	1
	15	22	9	239	29	18.38	–	1581	49	32.26	8–126	6

Test Record as Captain

				M	I	NO	Runs	HS	Avge	100s	RC	Wkts	Avge	BB	Ct
v Australia	–	L1	–	1	2	1	13	9*	13.00	–	164	2	82.00	2–136	–
v South Africa	W1	–	D2	3	4	2	51	20*	25.50	–	187	5	37.40	3–40	2
	W1	L1	D2	4	6	3	64	20*	21.33	–	351	7	50.14	3–40	2

Alfred Herbert Harold GILLIGAN

Sussex

Born: Denmark Hill, Surrey, 29 June 1896
Died: Shamley Green, Surrey, 5 May 1978

In 1929–30, England played Test series in New Zealand and West Indies concurrently. Neither England party could be said to be fully representative as several of the leading players had declined to go on either tour. The side to New Zealand was to have been led by Arthur Gilligan, but he was forced to withdraw through ill health, and his younger brother Harold took over.

Harold had led Sussex when Arthur was absent and became captain in his own right in 1930. An impetuous batsman and an occasional leg-spinner, he had flown in the First World War and played his cricket in a cavalier fashion. He lived life fully, and did all in what we have come to accept as the amateur spirit.

He was honorary treasurer and vice-president of Surrey, and his daughter married P.B.H. May.

Test Record as Captain

				M	I	NO	Runs	HS	Avge	100s	RC	Wkts	Avge	BB	Ct
v New Zealand	W1	–	D3	4	4	0	71	32	17.75	–	–	–	–	–	–

Hon. Frederick Somerset Gough CALTHORPE

Warwickshire and Sussex

Born: Kensington, 27 May 1892
Died: Worplesden, Surrey, 19 November 1935

Freddie Calthorpe played for Sussex before the First World War in which, like Harold Gilligan, he was a flier. His career at Cambridge was interrupted by the First World War, and he led Warwickshire from 1920 to 1929. He led England in the inaugural series in the Caribbean while Harold Gilligan, whose cavalier methods he mirrored, was captaining the side in New Zealand. He was a capable all-rounder, a golfer of high quality and a man who enjoyed cricket and life to the full. He completed the 'double' of 1000 runs and 100 wickets in the 1920 season.

Test Record as Captain

				M	I	NO	Runs	HS	Avge	100s	RC	Wkts	Avge	BB	Ct
v West Indies	W1	L1	D2	4	7	0	129	49	18.42	–	91	1	91.00	1–38	3

Robert Elliott Storey WYATT

Warwickshire and Worcestershire

Born: Milford, Surrey, 2 May 1901

'Never fortunate as England's captain' was the information on the back of a cigarette card in the 1930s, nor was Wyatt ever a popular choice. He was a consistent and tenacious batsman and a useful medium pace bowler who made his Test debut against South Africa with Stanyforth's side in 1927–28. He hit the first of his two Test centuries against South Africa at Old Trafford in 1929, and the following year he led England for the first time.

His appointment was controversial, for he replaced the popular Percy Chapman for the final Test against Australia at The Oval. It was Wyatt's first appearance against Australia, and there were two other amateurs in the side, Duleepsinhji and Peebles, but Duleepsinhji was Indian and Peebles was junior to Wyatt.

Wyatt served under Chapman in South Africa in 1930–31, and was vice-captain to Jardine in Australia and New Zealand in 1932–33. He led England in one Test against West Indies in 1933, when Jardine was unavailable, and when England entered the 1934 series against Australia without Jardine, Wyatt was named as captain. A broken thumb prevented him from playing in the first Test, which England lost. England won at Lord's, but surrendered the Ashes at The Oval where they were heavily beaten.

Wyatt captained England in West Indies in 1934–35, but the tour was something of a disaster. West Indies won a series for the first time, Wyatt twice made bizarre alterations in the second innings batting order, and his jaw was broken by a ball from Martindale in the first innings of the fourth and final Test.

He was reappointed captain for the series against South Africa in 1935 and hit 149 in the first Test at Trent Bridge where he opened with Sutcliffe. At Lord's, South Africa won by 157 runs, their first win in a Test match in England,

and they took the series. That marked the end of Wyatt's rather unfortunate career as England captain. He played under Allen against India in 1936 and in Australia in 1936–37 although he only received a late invitation for this tour when Errol Holmes of Surrey was unable to make the trip.

When Australia came to England in 1938 they played an MCC side at Lord's. There were eight amateurs in the MCC side, which was led by Robins, and Wyatt made 84 not out. He was asked if he was available for the first Test, and he said that he was contracted to write for the

'Never fortunate as England's captain' – Bob Wyatt (Ken Kelly)

Daily Mail, but that he was hopeful that they would release him to play. He was not contacted again; his Test career was over.

He played for Warwickshire from 1923 to 1939, captaining them from 1930 to 1937 when he resigned over a disagreement with the com-mittee. He was never at ease with authority. He played for Worcestershire from 1946 to 1951, leading them in his last two seasons, and he later became a selector. He was 56 when he played his last first-class game, and in 1991 he was the oldest living Test cricketer.

Test Record

	M	I	NO	Runs	HS	Avge	100s	RC	Wkts	Avge	BB	Ct
v Australia	12	21	2	633	78	33.31	–	98	1	98.00	1–58	6
v South Africa	17	27	2	873	149	34.92	2	291	8	36.37	3–4	6
v West Indies	8	13	2	253	71	23.00	–	238	9	26.44	3–33	2
v New Zealand	2	2	0	80	60	40.00	–	–	–	–	–	1
v India	1	1	0	0	0	0.00	–	15	0	–	–	1
	40	64	6	1839	149	31.70	2	642	18	35.66	3–4	16

Test Record as Captain

				M	I	NO	Runs	HS	Avge	100s	RC	Wkts	Avge	BB	Ct
v Australia	W1	L2	D2	5	8	0	206	64	25.75	–	86	1	86.00	1–58	3
v South Africa	–	L1	D4	5	8	1	317	149	45.28	1	64	1	64.00	1–1	2
v West Indies	W2	L2	D1	5	8	2	139	71	23.16	–	88	4	22.00	3–33	2
v New Zealand	–	–	D1	1	1	0	60	60	60.00	–	–	–	–	–	–
	W3	L5	D8	16	25	3	722	149	32.81	1	238	6	39.66	3–33	7

Douglas Robert JARDINE

Surrey

Born: Malabar Hill, Bombay, India, 23 October 1900
Died: Montreux, Switzerland, 18 June 1958

Few captains have excited as much passion and controversy as Douglas Jardine; none has been more successful.

Jardine was born in India where his father, who had scored a century in the Varsity match of 1892, had a most successful career in the legal profession. Jardine returned to Britain at the age of nine and went to Winchester in 1914. He was at Oxford from 1920 to 1923, and he was known as a rather cold intellectual and a batsman of outstanding ability, with great courage and powers of concentration. He was also a fearless fielder, and in his refusal to bow to pain, he anticipated Brian Close.

He began to play for Surrey while still at university, and he won his first Test cap in 1928, playing against West Indies both at Lord's and Old Trafford where he was run out for 83. He was an automatic choice for Chapman's side in Australia in 1928–29, and he averaged 46.62 in the five Tests.

Cold and aloof, batting in the brightly col-oured Harlequin cap, Jardine was barracked by the Australians who saw him as symbolic of the Imperial order, the British establishment. He remained the patrician.

Had he been able to give his time to cricket, it is likely that he would have won the captaincy of England in 1930, but he was able to play only eight innings at the start of the season and took no part in the series. Jardine was an amateur without independent means, and, passionate as he was about the game of cricket, he had to spend much of his time earning a living.

Jardine became England captain in 1931, leading the side in the three Tests against New

Zealand. The following season, he was England's captain in India's inaugural Test match, and he was top scorer with innings of 79 and 85 not out. That winter, he took England to Australia and New Zealand. There are those who conjecture that he was not the first choice, that his air of arrogance worried the hierarchy of the game, and that Hubert Ashton was approached.

Jardine himself says nothing of this. Indeed, he later wrote –

'As a race, we run ourselves down and write ourselves off at any mention of efficiency and rationalisation. "We muddle through" has become almost a boast, but anything less like muddling than the manner in which the Marylebone Cricket Club set about recovering the Ashes would be hard to imagine.'

This appealed to Jardine who was meticulously thorough and *professional* in his approach to the game. He was unequivocal in his opinion that, other things being equal, he would unhesitatingly select a Northerner before a Southerner because the Northerners' attitude and determination were akin to his own.

He prepared thoroughly for the 1932–33 tour, and, in consultation with men like Arthur Carr, he evolved the theory of fast bowling to a leg-side field which the Australians dubbed 'body-line'. He had, in Larwood, the bowler capable of carrying out the theory. The Nottinghamshire bowler was very fast and very accurate, and he had an able, if lesser partner in Voce.

England won the first Test, lost at Melbourne – Jardine's only defeat as captain – and won the last three. Jardine should have returned home a hero, but the vacillations of Warner, one of the tour managers, and the collapse of the English cricketing authorities in face of Australian criticism of Jardine's tactics caused a split in the game.

Those who played under Jardine, with the possible exception of Allen, remained steadfastly loyal to him. He was a man much respected and admired by those who knew him best.

He led England in two Tests against West Indies in 1933, and when Martindale and Constantine attacked him with his own leg theory, he countered with a fine century. He took the England side to India the following winter.

Leg theory had been evolved to counter the run-gorging feats of Don Bradman, and when the Australians arrived in England in 1934 there

The architect of 'body-line', Douglas Jardine, one of the finest of England's captains (Allsport)

was a belief that Jardine, the people's hero, would adopt the tactics again. Warner was opposed to him being made captain, and Jardine himself refused to compromise. If he was to be captain, *he* would dictate the tactics and no one else. In India, he had had Tarrant removed as umpire after two Tests because he believed the Australian was biased in favour of the Indians.

On 31 March 1934, Jardine announced through the pages of the *Evening Standard*, 'I have neither the intention nor the desire to play cricket against Australia this summer.' He covered the series from the press box in an attempt to augment his meagre salary from banking, and he played for neither England nor Surrey again.

Jardine was only 33 years old when he retired from cricket, and he was arguably the best number five batsman in the world at the time. It is doubtful if England has had a better captain, and he was one of the few amateurs of his period who won a place in the side on the merit of his batting.

Jardine (centre) leads England out at Melbourne in 1933. The Test was won by Australia but was England's only defeat of the series (Hulton)

Test Record

	M	I	NO	Runs	HS	Avge	100s	RC	Wkts	Avge	BB	Ct
v Australia	10	18	1	540	98	31.76	–	10	0	–	–	13
v West Indies	4	4	0	253	127	63.25	1	–	–	–	–	3
v New Zealand	4	5	3	118	45	59.00	–	–	–	–	–	2
v India	4	6	2	385	85*	96.25	–	–	–	–	–	8
	22	33	6	1296	127	48.00	1	10	0	–	–	26

Test Record as Captain

				M	I	NO	Runs	HS	Avge	100s	RC	Wkts	Avge	BB	Ct
v Australia	W4	L1	–	5	9	0	199	56	22.11	–	–	–	–	–	9
v West Indies	W1	–	D1	2	2	0	148	127	74.00	1	–	–	–	–	–
v New Zealand	W1	–	D3	4	5	3	118	45	59.00	–	–	–	–	–	2
v India	W3	–	D1	4	6	2	385	85*	96.25	–	–	–	–	–	8
	W9	L1	D5	15	22	5	850	127	50.00	1	–	–	–	–	19

Cyril Frederick WALTERS

Glamorgan and Worcestershire

Born: Bedinog, Glamorgan, 1905

An elegant opening batsman, Cyril Walters left Glamorgan in 1928 to become secretary of Worcestershire whom he captained from 1931 to 1935. He played three Tests against West Indies in 1933 and went to India with Jardine's side the following winter. Selected for the first Test against Australia in 1934, he suddenly found himself captain when Wyatt withdrew with a broken thumb. The only other amateurs in the side were Farnes, who was just down from Cambridge, and the Nawab of Pataudi, who was Indian. Professionals of ability and experience such as Hendren, Sutcliffe, Verity, Hammond and Ames were playing, but such were the ethics of the time that they could not be considered for the captaincy. Walters retired in 1935 to the surprise and regret of many.

Cyril Walters – captain only once, against Australia in 1934 (Lemmon)

Test Record

	M	I	NO	Runs	HS	Avge	100s	RC	Wkts	Avge	BB	Ct
v Australia	5	9	1	401	82	50.12	–	–	–	–	–	5
v West Indies	3	3	0	99	51	33.00	–	–	–	–	–	–
v India	3	6	2	284	102	71.00	1	–	–	–	–	1
	11	18	3	784	102	52.26	1	–	–	–	–	6

Test Record as Captain

			M	I	NO	Runs	HS	Avge	100s	RC	Wkts	Avge	BB	Ct
v Australia	–	L1	–	1	2	0	63	46	31.50	–	–	–	–	–	–

Sir George Oswald Browning ALLEN

Middlesex

Born: Bellevue Hill, Sydney, 31 July 1902
Died: St John's Wood, 29 November 1989

'Gubby' Allen's first-class career lasted from 1921, the year before he went to Cambridge University, to 1950, yet rarely was he able to appear in more than a handful of games for Middlesex in any season. He was probably the fastest bowler to play for the county, and he had one of the most perfect actions imaginable. By 1930, he had developed into a correct, stylish and hard-hitting batsman.

In 1929, he became the only man to take all ten wickets in an innings of a county match at Lord's, Lancashire being the opponents, and the following year he made his debut for England, against Australia. His selection was strongly criticised in some sections of the press, for he had been born in Australia whom his uncle had represented in 1886–87.

The following season, he played in all three Tests against New Zealand and, in the first, he hit 122 and shared a record eighth-wicket partnership of 246 with Les Ames. He went with Jardine's team to Australia in 1932–33 and had a successful series, taking 21 wickets, although he refused to bowl leg theory. There are two schools of thought on his refusal to adopt Jardine's tactics: the first says that Allen believed they destroyed the beauty of the game; the second, voiced by men like the Yorkshire pace bowler Bill Bowes, maintains that Allen was not accurate enough to bowl leg theory.

Allen played one Test in 1933 and two in 1934, and, in 1936, led England against India although he was not, nor had he ever been, a regular captain of Middlesex. His appointment as captain against India was in anticipation of his leading the side to Australia in 1936–37. The tour was the first by a full England side since the 'body-line' series, and Allen's family connections with Australia were seen as an aid to restoring normal relations.

England won the first two Tests and lost the next three when Bradman ran into form, but there are those who believe that Allen's selection was at fault. Neither Paynter, nor Bowes, Northern stalwarts at the height of their powers, was included in the tour party and they were replaced by lesser performers.

Allen played no more Test cricket before the Second World War, but, astonishingly, he was recalled to captain England in West Indies in 1947–48. He had played in only one match for Middlesex in 1947, had failed to take a wicket and was 45 years old. Tom Pearce, the Essex captain, had been approached by Warner and invited to lead the side to the Caribbean. Pearce had agreed and made arrangements to be released from his work as a wine merchant so that he could go on the tour, only to read in an evening paper that Allen had been named as captain.

Leading players like Compton, Edrich, Bedser and, initially, Hutton were unable to make the trip, and the strength of the West Indians was grossly underestimated. Allen pulled a calf muscle while skipping on the ship deck on the way out, missed the first of the four Test matches and was never fully fit. For the first time in cricket history MCC went through an overseas tour without a single victory.

Allen was very close to Warner and succeeded him as the most influential administrator in the game, although the breadth of his influence was resented by many who thought that his reputation was out of proportion to his performance. E.M. Wellings wrote of him, 'Allen was a very fine cricketer, better at playing than at administration.'

He was knighted for services to cricket in 1986.

'Gubby' Allen captained England in 1936 and in 1947–48, but his influence was felt right up until his death in 1989 (Hulton)

Test Record

	M	I	NO	Runs	HS	Avge	100s	RC	Wkts	Avge	BB	Ct
v Australia	13	21	1	479	68	23.95	–	1603	43	37.27	5–36	15
v West Indies	4	7	1	110	36	18.33	–	251	8	31.37	2–13	3
v New Zealand	5	2	0	134	122	67.00	1	195	10	19.50	5–14	1
v India	3	3	0	27	13	9.00	–	330	20	16.50	7–80	1
	25	33	2	750	122	24.19	1	2379	81	29.37	7–80	20

Test Record as Captain

				M	I	NO	Runs	HS	Avge	100s	RC	Wkts	Avge	BB	Ct
v Australia	W2	L3	–	5	9	1	150	68	18.75	–	526	17	30.94	5–36	6
v India	W2	–	D1	3	3	0	27	13	9.00	–	330	20	16.50	7–80	1
v West Indies	–	L2	D1	3	6	1	94	36	18.80	–	205	5	41.00	2–82	3
	W4	L5	D2	11	18	2	271	68	16.93	–	1061	42	25.26	7–80	10

Robert Walter Vivian ROBINS

Middlesex

Born: Stafford, 3 June 1906
Died: Marylebone, London, 12 December 1968

'I would have died for that man on the cricket field,' says Mike Murray, Chairman of Middlesex, of Walter Robins, one of the finest captains in the history of county cricket.

An aggressive, impetuous batsman, a legbreak bowler who spun the ball prodigiously, and a brilliant fielder, Robins played for Middlesex while still at Highgate School in 1925, and scored a century and took eight wickets in the last of his three Varsity matches for Cambridge in 1928. He made his Test debut the following year and played in at least one Test match every season, with the exception of 1934, until 1937 when he led England against New Zealand.

His blunt manner and dynamic approach to the game did not always endear him to the authorities although he himself was later to become a selector and manager of England sides.

One of the finest of county captains, Walter Robins led England for only one series, against New Zealand in 1937 (Lemmon)

Test Record

	M	I	NO	Runs	HS	Avge	100s	RC	Wkts	Avge	BB	Ct
v Australia	6	10	2	183	61	22.88	–	558	14	39.85	4–51	2
v South Africa	4	5	1	136	108	34.00	1	343	14	24.50	3–32	2
v West Indies	2	2	0	63	55	31.50	–	220	11	20.00	6–32	1
v New Zealand	4	6	1	103	38*	20.60	–	337	13	25.92	4–40	2
v India	3	4	0	127	76	31.75	–	300	12	25.00	3–50	5
	19	27	4	612	108	22.60	1	1758	64	27.46	6–32	12

Test Record as Captain

	M	I	NO	Runs	HS	Avge	100s	RC	Wkts	Avge	BB	Ct
v New Zealand W1 – D2	3	5	1	91	38*	22.75	–	173	8	21.65	4–40	2

Walter Reginald HAMMOND

Gloucestershire

Born: Buckland, Dover, Kent, 19 June 1903
Died: Durban, South Africa, 1 July 1965

Wally Hammond first played for Gloucester-shire in 1920, as an amateur, but Kent's attempts to claim him by reason of birth delayed the start of his professional career until 1923. He became the greatest English batsman of the inter-war years, and one of the very greatest in the history of the game, tall, majestic, powerful and athletic. He was also a very good medium pace bowler and a slip fielder who has had few equals. He was the dominant force in English cricket in the 1930s.

His 905 runs in the 1928–29 series has been beaten only by Don Bradman, and his 336 not out in 318 minutes in 1932–33 was a record score for Test cricket until 1938. His ten sixes in the innings remains a Test record.

In the autumn of 1937, Hammond announced that he would in future play as an amateur. Obviously, he had an eye to the England captaincy. He had been an automatic choice for the England side and missed only two Tests, one in 1929 and one in 1936, both through injury, between his debut in South Africa in 1927–28 and his retirement from international cricket after the 1946–47 tour of Australia and New Zealand.

England had had four captains since Jardine's day. Allen had played little in 1937 and there were doubts about his fitness while Warner, in his accounts of the time, does not mention that either Wyatt or Robins was con-sidered. Warner and his fellow selectors chose Hammond and Allen as captains for the Test trial of June 1938, which was to be played ten days before the first Test against Australia.

Batsman supreme, but a distant and enigmatic skipper – Wally Hammond (Hulton)

Allen withdrew the afternoon before the match, and Hammond became captain of England.

Supreme cricketer as he was, Hammond was not among the best of captains. He was aloof, distant and had little understanding or compassion for those less gifted than himself.

He hit 240 in the Lord's Test of 1938, which remains the highest score against Australia at that famous ground, and he had the luxury of being able to declare at 903 for 7 in the Oval Test. England drew the series and claimed the solitary victory in the series in South Africa the following winter. There was also victory over West Indies in 1939.

Hammond was 43 when cricket resumed after the Second World War. He led England against India and then on the ill-fated and unwise tour of Australia and New Zealand in 1946–47. He, like many of his team, was not fit enough, and he was a shadow of the great player he had once been. He enjoyed the hospitality of the Australians, but had insufficient regard for the needs of his side. He did not play in the fifth Test in Australia, and his last appearance was in Christchurch when he hit 79.

He is best remembered as one of the finest of sights with a bat in his hand, and the memory of his off-drive still creates a thrill.

Hammond (right) and a pin-striped Bradman toss at the Oval in 1938. Between them is the groundsman Roger Martin (Hulton)

Test Record

	M	I	NO	Runs	HS	Avge	100s	RC	Wkts	Avge	BB	Ct
v Australia	33	58	3	2852	251	51.85	9	1612	36	44.77	5–57	43
v South Africa	24	42	7	2188	181	62.51	6	1041	34	30.61	5–36	30
v West Indies	13	20	2	639	138	35.50	1	176	3	58.66	1–20	22
v New Zealand	9	11	2	1015	336*	112.77	4	188	6	31.33	2–19	9
v India	6	9	2	555	217	79.28	2	121	4	30.25	3–9	6
	85	140	16	7249	336*	58.45	22	3138	83	37.80	5–36	110

Test Record as Captain

				M	I	NO	Runs	HS	Avge	100s	RC	Wkts	Avge	BB	Ct
v Australia	W1	L3	D4	8	14	0	571	240	40.78	1	67	0	–	–	14
v South Africa	W1	–	D4	5	8	1	609	181	87.00	3	161	3	53.66	1–11	6
v West Indies	W1	–	D2	3	6	1	279	138	55.80	1	–	–	–	–	5
v India	W1	–	D2	3	4	1	119	69	39.66	–	3	0	–	–	2
v New Zealand	–	–	D1	1	1	0	79	79	79.00	–	–	–	–	–	1
	W4	L3	D13	20	33	3	1657	240	55.23	5	231	3	77.00	1–11	28

Norman Walter Dransfield YARDLEY

Yorkshire

Born: Gawber, Barnsley, 19 March 1915
Died: Sheffield, 4 October 1989

Highly successful in his four years at Cambridge, 1935 to 1938, and captain in his last term, Norman Yardley first played for Yorkshire in 1936 and was close to selection for England against Australia in 1938. He won his first Test cap on the tour of South Africa in 1938–39, but, like others, he was robbed of important years of cricket development by the Second World War, and, in truth, as a player, he never quite reached Test standard.

He was a late and surprising nomination as vice-captain to Hammond for the 1946–47 tour of Australia but he acquitted himself well, averaging 31.50 with the bat and topping the bowling averages with his medium pace in the five Tests. He led England for the first time in the last Test.

He succeeded Hammond as England's captain and won the series against South Africa, playing a match-saving innings of 99 in the first Test at Trent Bridge. In 1948, he was confronted by the strongest Australian side ever to visit this country, and England were trounced. Business commitments prevented him from playing Test cricket in 1949 and from touring again, but, with competent amateurs becoming harder to find,

Norman Yardley – faced strong opposition as captain in home series against Australia and West Indies (Lemmon)

he returned to lead England in the first three Tests against West Indies in 1950, only to see his side confused at Lord's and Trent Bridge by the spin wizardry of Ramadhin and Valentine.

Yardley was a stylish batsman, a useful, but under-used bowler, and a sympathetic and intelligent captain. He was a well-liked leader of men and an astute reader of the game who had the misfortune to captain England when bowling resources were at their lowest and the opposition of the strongest.

Test Record

	M	I	NO	Runs	HS	Avge	100s	RC	Wkts	Avge	BB	Ct
v Australia	10	19	2	402	61	23.65	–	576	19	30.32	3–67	4
v South Africa	6	8	0	280	99	35.00	–	25	0	–	–	7
v West Indies	3	6	0	108	41	18.00	–	94	1	94.00	1–82	3
v New Zealand	1	1	0	22	22	22.00	–	12	1	12.00	1–12	–
	20	34	2	812	99	25.37	–	707	21	33.66	3–67	14

Test Record as Captain

				M	I	NO	Runs	HS	Avge	100s	RC	Wkts	Avge	BB	Ct
v Australia	–	L5	D1	6	11	0	163	44	14.81	–	219	9	24.33	2–32	2
v South Africa	W3	–	D2	5	7	0	273	99	39.00	–	25	0	–	–	7
v West Indies	W1	L2	–	3	6	0	108	41	18.00	–	94	1	94.00	1–82	3
	W4	L7	D3	14	24	0	544	99	22.66	–	338	10	33.80	2–32	12

Kenneth CRANSTON

Lancashire

Born: Aigburth, Liverpool, 20 October 1917

A dentist by profession who came to the fore in wartime cricket and played only two seasons of regular first-class cricket, captaining Lancashire in 1947 and 1948. An aggressive middle-order batsman and a fast-medium pace bowler, he played in three Tests against South Africa in 1947, and went as vice-captain under Allen to the Caribbean the following winter. Allen's injury, sustained on the boat, meant that Cranston led England in the first Test. He played one Test against Australia in 1948.

Test Record

	M	I	NO	Runs	HS	Avge	100s	RC	Wkts	Avge	BB	Ct
v Australia	1	2	0	10	10	5.00	–	79	1	79.00	1–28	2
v South Africa	3	4	0	71	45	17.75	–	186	11	16.90	4–12	1
v West Indies	4	8	0	128	36	16.00	–	196	6	32.66	4–78	–
	8	14	0	209	45	14.92	–	461	18	25.61	4–12	3

Test Record as Captain

				M	I	NO	Runs	HS	Avge	100s	RC	Wkts	Avge	BB	Ct
v West Indies	–	–	D1	1	2	0	10	8	5.00	–	60	1	60.00	1–31	–

Francis George MANN

Middlesex

Born: Byfleet, Surrey, 6 September 1917

George Mann emulated his father, F.T., in that he captained England in every Test in which he played.

After the Second World War fewer amateurs of quality were able to give their time to cricket, and when Yardley announced that he would not be able to tour South Africa in 1948–49 George Mann was chosen as his successor although he had been captain of Middlesex for only one season. There were strong criticisms that he was not a good enough batsman, but he hit a brilliant century in the final Test which turned possible defeat into victory by three wickets. He led England in the first two Tests against New Zealand in 1949, but then stated that he would not be able to play regularly in future because of the demands of the family brewery business.

He was a hard-hitting batsman and a most popular and capable captain. If not an outstanding tactician, he had a gift of leadership which brought the best out of others and men were happy to play under him.

Test Record as Captain

				M	I	NO	Runs	HS	Avge	100s	RC	Wkts	Avge	BB	Ct
v South Africa	W2	–	D3	5	8	1	254	136*	36.28	1	–	–	–	–	3
v New Zealand	–	–	D2	2	4	1	122	49*	40.66	–	–	–	–	–	–
	W2	–	D5	7	12	2	376	136*	37.60	1	–	–	–	–	3

Frederick Richard BROWN

Surrey and Northamptonshire

Born: Lima, Peru, 16 December 1910
Died: 24 July 1991

Freddie Brown was a belligerent middle-order batsman and a leg-break and googly bowler who later added medium pace off-cutters to his repertoire. His career falls into two distinct parts.

He won his blue at Cambridge in 1930 and 1931, played for Surrey and did the 'double' and made his Test debut against New Zealand in 1931. He went with Jardine's team to Australia in 1932–33, but played only in the two Tests in New Zealand after the end of that tour. He played again against New Zealand in 1937, but by that time his appearances in first-class cricket had become spasmodic.

He took up a business appointment in Northampton immediately after the Second World War and in 1949 became captain of Northamptonshire whom he led until 1953. With both Yardley and Mann unavailable and with the majority of counties struggling to find efficient and willing captains, England turned to Brown to lead the side against New Zealand in the last two Tests in 1949, and they turned to him again in 1950 when Yardley said he would be unable to take the party to Australia.

In Australia, Brown displayed enthusiasm and tremendous spirit, and, having lost the first four Tests, his side won the fifth, the first defeat suffered by Australia since 1938. Brown continued as captain against South Africa in 1951.

Brown was neither a great tactician, nor a good manager of men. His biggest asset was his whole-heartedness. He was of a breed that was passing from the game.

He became a Test selector, and, in 1953, when chairman of selectors, he was persuaded to play in the Lord's Test where he scored 22 and 28 and took 4 for 82 in the second Australian innings.

Test Record

	M	I	NO	Runs	HS	Avge	100s	RC	Wkts	Avge	BB	Ct
v Australia	6	10	0	260	79	26.00	–	524	22	23.81	5–49	5
v New Zealand	9	9	1	307	74	38.37	–	440	12	36.66	3–81	11
v India	1	2	0	30	29	15.00	–	102	3	34.00	2–54	–
v West Indies	1	2	0	15	15	7.50	–	74	1	74.00	1–74	–
v South Africa	5	7	0	122	42	17.42	–	258	7	36.85	3–107	6
	22	30	1	734	79	25.31	–	1398	45	31.06	5–49	22

Test Record as Captain

				M	I	NO	Runs	HS	Avge	100s	RC	Wkts	Avge	BB	Ct
v Australia	W1	L4	–	5	8	0	210	79	26.25	–	389	18	21.61	5–49	4
v New Zealand	W1	–	D3	4	5	1	162	62	40.50	–	202	4	50.50	2–71	8
v West Indies	–	L1	–	1	2	0	15	15	7.50	–	74	1	74.00	1–74	–
v South Africa	W3	L1	D1	5	7	0	122	42	17.42	–	258	7	36.85	3–107	6
	W5	L6	D4	15	22	1	509	79	24.33	–	923	30	30.76	5–49	18

Nigel David HOWARD

Lancashire

Born: Gee Cross, Hyde, Cheshire, 18 May 1925
Died: Douglas, Isle of Man, 31 May 1979

Regarded as one of the most promising and stylish of batsmen when he first played for Lancashire in 1946, Nigel Howard never fulfilled that promise, and once he was appointed captain of the county in 1949, Lancashire's youngest ever captain, his form began to decline. He retired in 1953.

With the leading amateurs and professionals declaring themselves unavailable, Howard was asked to lead the party to India in 1951–52. The party was rather cruelly dubbed 'England's second string', although two of the side, Graveney and Statham, went on to perform great things. Howard was ill and unable to play in the final Test.

Test Record as Captain

				M	I	NO	Runs	HS	Avge	100s	RC	Wkts	Avge	BB	Ct
v India	W1	–	D3	4	6	1	86	23	17.20	–	–	–	–	–	4

Donald Bryce CARR

Derbyshire

Born: Wiesbaden, Germany, 28 December 1926

Heralded as a future star when, as an unknown schoolboy, he played in a Victory Test at Lord's in 1945, Donald Carr was a good batsman, a capable left-arm bowler and a brilliant fielder. He was a very fine captain of Derbyshire (1955–62) and later became an intelligent and sympathetic administrator. He was vice-captain to Howard on the tour of India in 1951–52, and led England in the final Test when India won a Test match for the first time.

Test Record

				M	I	NO	Runs	HS	Avge	100s	RC	Wkts	Avge	BB	Ct
v India				2	4	0	135	76	33.75	–	140	2	70.00	2–84	–

Test Record as Captain

				M	I	NO	Runs	HS	Avge	100s	RC	Wkts	Avge	BB	Ct
v India	–	L1	–	1	2	0	45	40	22.50	–	84	2	42.00	2–84	–

Sir Leonard HUTTON

Yorkshire

Born: Fulneck, Pudsey, 23 June 1916
Died: Kingston upon Thames, Surrey, 6 September 1990

The quality of the side that had gone to India in 1951–52, and India's victory in the final Test, had served to emphasise something of a crisis in English cricket, and it was apparent that much of the problem revolved around the question of captaincy. The advance made by West Indies and India had drawn attention to the fact that it was now necessary to field the strongest eleven in every Test match. There was no longer any room for a passenger, nor was there an abundance of amateur cricketers who could hold their own at international level.

By 1952, Sussex and Warwickshire were captained by professionals, and Compton shared the captaincy of Middlesex with Edrich, a professional who had turned amateur. Within the next two years, Gloucestershire, Lancashire and Northamptonshire were to appoint professional captains.

Of the county captains in 1952, Wooller and

Brown were at the veteran stage, and Yardley could no longer give his time to play Test cricket although, along with Brown, Wyatt and Ames, he was a selector. The only county captains of Test cricket standard were Insole and Simpson, but the first was, as yet, untried and the second unsure of a place.

There had been a significant move in 1950 when Les Ames was the first professional to be appointed an England selector. In 1952, Len Hutton became the first professional cricketer to be chosen as captain of England since Arthur Shrewsbury had led Shaw's all-professional side in Australia in 1887.

Hutton's appointment caused an uproar, for it was a violent break with tradition, and many saw it as a threat to the very structure of the game. Under the professional captaincy of Dollery, Warwickshire had won the County Championship in 1951, but Dollery pointed out later that, as a professional, he could never show his displeasure at opponents' tactics by any gesture of contempt as amateurs like Simpson and Wooller had done. From the moment of his appointment, Hutton was under close scrutiny, and his every move was open to criticism.

The Cricketer viewed the appointment with some scepticism, but suggested that encouragement should be the keynote. They saw the appointment as a short-term measure when it might have been better to have chosen a less experienced leader with a view to training him for the coming contests with the Australians in 1953 and 1954–55.

Hutton had made his Test debut in the 1937 series with New Zealand. He made 0 and 1 on his debut at Lord's, but was retained for the next Test when he hit 100 and 14 at The Oval. The following year, he hit a century on the occasion of his debut against Australia, and in the final Test of the series, at The Oval, which was to remain a ground particularly dear to him, he made 364 which was a record score for Test cricket. He was 23 years old.

An injury sustained in an accident early in the war caused him to be invalided out of the army in 1942, and his left arm was now two inches shorter than his right. If he was never again quite the batsman he had been in 1939 when he and Hammond put on 264 in three hours against West Indies, he remained until the end of his career the finest opening batsman in the world and among the greatest that the game has known.

Troubled by the pace of Lindwall and Miller, he was dropped from the England side for the Old Trafford Test of 1948, but he was brought back for the last two Tests of the series. This was the only time in his career that he was not an automatic choice for the England side.

Against the spinners Ramadhin and Valentine, he carried his bat for an innings of 202 out of 344 at The Oval in 1950, but England were still beaten by an innings. In Australia in 1950–51, he remained supreme in spite of Brown's perversity of dropping him down the order.

He was 36 when he became captain of England, and he was his country's leading batsman. His first Test as captain was on his own ground at Headingley. Freddie Trueman was making his international debut, and India were 0 for 4 in their second innings. England won by seven wickets, and they won the next two Tests with Hutton scoring a century in each of them. S.C. Griffith wrote of him that he 'handled the team with admirable skill both on and off the field, and there is no doubt that his tactical appreciation is exceptionally sound'.

Len Hutton (left) opening the England innings with David Sheppard in the match against India at Old Trafford in 1952. Hutton was the first professional to captain England; Sheppard captained when Hutton was unavailable (Hulton)

The following season, after four drawn Tests, England beat Australia at The Oval and regained the Ashes which Australia had held for a record period of just under 19 years. Hutton became the first captain to win a rubber after losing the toss in all five matches, and he was a national hero.

His bad luck with the toss and his heroics continued in the West Indies. He lost the toss four times out of five, but England came back from two down to level the series. In the final match, at Sabina Park, Hutton hit 205, the first double century by an England captain in an overseas Test.

In spite of these triumphs, Hutton could not escape criticism. There were suggestions of ill discipline and rude behaviour, and the argument was raised again that only an amateur was a suitable person to lead an England side at a time when diplomacy was becoming as important as cricketing ability. For the series against Pakistan, Hutton was appointed captain only on a match to match basis. He fell ill after the first Test, and David Sheppard replaced him as captain.

To the traditionalists, Sheppard appeared to have all the attributes necessary for leadership, in education and upbringing, and there was a powerful lobby that he should take the side to Australia. Public opinion and the press were strongly in favour of Hutton, and once he was fit again, it was hard to fault his record. Hutton took the side to Australia and, with the power of Tyson and Statham at his disposal, he triumphed by winning the series three to one, the defeat coming in the first Test.

He played his last two Test matches in New Zealand at the end of that tour. Batting at number five, he was England's top scorer with 53 in his final Test innings, and he orchestrated the dismissal of New Zealand for 26, the lowest score in Test history.

Partly through back trouble, but mainly, one feels, through weariness, he retired shortly after that grand finale. He had led English cricket out of the wilderness, but he had received more than his share of criticism for what was seen as too professional an approach and the slowing down of over-rates.

He retired to Surrey and a successful business career, and he was knighted for his services to the game. He must rank with Jardine as among the very best of England captains.

Test Record

	M	I	NO	Runs	HS	Avge	100s	RC	Wkts	Avge	BB	Ct
v Australia	27	49	6	2428	364	56.46	5	60	1	60.00	1–2	22
v South Africa	19	34	4	1564	158	52.13	4	39	0	–	–	18
v West Indies	13	24	3	1661	205	79.09	5	88	1	88.00	1–45	9
v New Zealand	11	17	0	777	206	45.70	3	45	1	45.00	1–4	5
v India	7	11	2	522	150	58.00	2	–	–	–	–	3
v Pakistan	2	3	0	19	14	6.33	–	–	–	–	–	–
	79	138	15	6971	364	56.67	19	232	3	86.66	1–2	57

Test Record as Captain

				M	I	NO	Runs	HS	Avge	100s	RC	Wkts	Avge	BB	Ct
v Australia	W4	L1	D5	10	18	1	663	145	39.00	1	2	1	2.00	1–2	6
v West Indies	W2	L2	D1	5	8	1	677	205	96.71	2	43	0	–	–	1
v New Zealand	W2	–	–	2	3	0	67	53	22.33	–	–	–	–	–	1
v India	W3	–	D1	4	6	1	399	150	79.80	2	–	–	–	–	3
v Pakistan	–	L1	D1	2	3	0	19	14	6.33	–	–	–	–	–	–
	W11	L4	D8	23	38	3	1825	205	52.14	5	45	1	45.00	1–2	11

Rt Rev. David Stuart SHEPPARD

Sussex

Born: Reigate, Surrey, 6 March 1929

A stylish opening batsman who played for Sussex when still at school and for England while still at Cambridge (1950–52), his first Test appearance was against West Indies at The Oval in 1950. He led England against Pakistan at Trent Bridge and Old Trafford when Hutton was unavailable in 1954.

He was seen as the Establishment's choice for the captaincy, but, ironically, he was a far from Establishment figure with his outspoken pronouncements on social and political issues. He was a fine but short-lived captain of Sussex, for he was ordained in 1955, and thereafter could give little time to cricket. He made dramatic returns to Test cricket from time to time, making 113 against Australia in 1956 and the same score in Melbourne in 1962–63, when he had taken a sabbatical winter to take part in that tour. His Test career ended with the three matches in New Zealand at the end of the tour.

He became Bishop of Liverpool in 1975.

Test Record

	M	I	NO	Runs	HS	Avge	100s	RC	Wkts	Avge	BB	Ct
v Australia	9	16	0	580	113	36.25	2	–	–	–	–	2
v West Indies	3	4	0	148	68	37.00	–	–	–	–	–	2
v New Zealand	4	6	1	92	42	15.33	–	–	–	–	–	3
v India	2	2	0	153	119	71.50	1	–	–	–	–	1
v Pakistan	4	5	1	199	83	49.75	–	–	–	–	–	4
	22	33	2	1172	119	37.80	3	–	–	–	–	12

Test Record as Captain

				M	I	NO	Runs	HS	Avge	100s	RC	Wkts	Avge	BB	Ct
v Pakistan	W1	–	D1	2	2	0	50	37	25.00	–	–	–	–	–	4

Peter Barker Howard MAY

Surrey

Born: Reading, Berkshire, 31 December 1929

The outstanding English batsman of the post-war era, Peter May first appeared for Surrey in 1950, his first year at Cambridge, and for England a year later. He marked his Test debut with an innings of 138 against South Africa at Headingley. He had a successful series against India in 1952, but was dropped after the first Test against Australia the following year. Recalled for the final, victorious Test at The Oval, he was an automatic choice for England from that point onwards.

A tall, elegant batsman with the full range of classical stroke-play, he was immediately recognised as the natural successor to Hutton.

He was brought up under the two outstanding captains of the time, Hutton at Test level, and Surridge, the ebullient and audacious Surrey captain. In style of leadership, May resembled Hutton more than Surridge, for there was a hard vein of professionalism and ruthless determination in a man who was, by nature, a little shy and reticent. It was this aspect of his character that did not allow him the best of relationships with the press although he was admired and respected by his players and has always enjoyed the companionship of cricketers.

Hutton was named as captain for all five Tests against South Africa in 1955, but he withdrew because of back trouble, and May took over and won an exciting series by three matches to two. In all, he was to captain England a record 41 times. He led his country to victory on 20 occasions, which is also a record.

It was not until South Africa in 1956–57 that

he suffered a bad run with the bat, and the home country fought back to level the series, but the following summer he ended the West Indian supremacy over England. In the first Test, at Edgbaston, Ramadhin had once more held sway over England with his masterly spin bowling in the first innings, but in the second, May hit 285 not out, the highest score by an England captain, and shared a record fourth-wicket stand of 411 with Colin Cowdrey. The stand virtually ended Ramadhin's Test career.

The greatest disappointment came in Australia in 1958–59, when a side which looked strong on paper seemed to disintegrate and lost by four Tests to nil. May and Cowdrey were the only batsmen to perform to their full ability.

In West Indies, a year later, England were one up after three Tests when May was forced to return home for treatment for an illness, and he missed the whole of the following summer recovering from an operation. He returned in 1961 and was chosen for the second Test against Australia, but Cowdrey led the side. May cap-

One of the greatest batsmen of the post-war period, Peter May led England more times than any other player (Lemmon)

tained in the last three Tests and then announced his retirement from Test cricket. He was still short of his 32nd birthday, and the retirement, brought about by his illness, by pressures and, like Hutton, by a general weariness, was a very sad one.

He was later to hold every high office in the game, but his period as chairman of selectors was not a happy one. The players with whom he dealt spoke a language that was different from his, and values had changed.

Test Record

	M	I	NO	Runs	HS	Avge	100s	RC	Wkts	Avge	BB	Ct
v Australia	21	37	3	1566	113	46.05	3	–	–	–	–	10
v South Africa	12	22	1	906	138	43.14	3	–	–	–	–	10
v West Indies	13	21	2	986	285*	51.89	3	–	–	–	–	5
v New Zealand	9	11	2	603	124*	67.00	3	–	–	–	–	6
v India	7	10	1	356	106	39.55	1	–	–	–	–	8
v Pakistan	4	5	0	120	53	24.00	–	–	–	–	–	3
	66	106	9	4537	285*	46.77	13	–	–	–	–	42

Test Record as Captain

				M	I	NO	Runs	HS	Avge	100s	RC	Wkts	Avge	BB	Ct
v Australia	W3	L6	D4	13	23	3	1091	113	54.55	2	–	–	–	–	4
v South Africa	W5	L4	D1	10	19	1	735	117	40.83	2	–	–	–	–	9
v West Indies	W4	–	D4	8	11	1	572	285*	57.20	2	–	–	–	–	5
v New Zealand	W5	–	D2	7	8	2	532	124*	88.66	3	–	–	–	–	5
v India	W3	–	–	3	4	1	150	106	50.00	1	–	–	–	–	5
	W20	L10	D11	41	65	8	3080	285*	54.03	10	–	–	–	–	28

Sir Michael Colin COWDREY

Kent

Born: Putumala, Ootacamund, India, 24 December 1932

One of the very finest of post-war batsmen, Colin Cowdrey was a prolific scorer and a stylist who resembled Wally Hammond without ever having Hammond's confident arrogance.

He was Peter May's lieutenant for several series, and it seemed that he would be his successor, but he had to give way first to Ted Dexter and then to Mike Smith. It was, perhaps, his periods of introspection in which he questioned his own technique and his seemingly too benign approach to the game which made selectors lose confidence in him.

He made his Test debut on Hutton's 1954–55 tour of Australia, and first led England, as deputy for May, against India in 1959. In 1962, Cowdrey and Dexter were put on trial in the series against Pakistan. Cowdrey led the side in the third Test and won an innings victory with some intelligent manipulation of his bowlers, but Dexter took the party to Australia.

In 1966, against West Indies, he took over from Smith and then lost the captaincy to Close. Following Close's misdemeanour, Cowdrey was reinstated for the 1967–68 tour of West Indies and, against all expectation, won a series in which he himself scored two centuries.

The England captaincy now appeared to be his. He achieved a famous victory over Australia at The Oval in 1968, and led England through a troubled and aborted tour in Pakistan the following winter. He was named as captain for the series against West Indies and New Zealand in 1969, but he tore his left Achilles tendon in a Sunday league match at the end of May, and Illingworth took over. Illingworth made a success of the job, and it was he who took the side to Australia in 1970–71. After some delay, Cowdrey accepted the vice-captaincy, but his disappointment was apparent, and it was not a happy tour for him.

He played his last Tests when, in 1974–75, at the age of 42, he was called to Australia in an emergency to help combat the pace bowlers, his sixth tour of a country where he was very popular. A surprisingly revolutionary president of MCC and a most active chairman of the ICC, he was knighted for services to cricket in 1991.

Test Record

	M	I	NO	Runs	HS	Avge	100s	RC	Wkts	Avge	BB	Ct
v Australia	43	75	4	2433	113	34.26	5	45	0	–	–	40
v South Africa	14	27	1	1021	155	39.26	3	4	0	–	–	23
v West Indies	21	36	2	1751	154	51.50	6	20	0	–	–	21
v New Zealand	18	24	5	1133	128*	59.63	2	–	–	–	–	15
v India	8	11	2	653	160	72.55	3	34	0	–	–	11
v Pakistan	10	15	1	633	182	45.21	3	1	0	–	–	10
	114	188	15	7624	182	44.06	22	104	0	–	–	120

Test Record as Captain

				M	I	NO	Runs	HS	Avge	100s	RC	Wkts	Avge	BB	Ct
v Australia	W1	L2	D3	6	10	0	265	104	26.50	1	–	–	–	–	5
v South Africa	W3	–	D2	5	9	0	312	155	34.66	1	4	0	–	–	7
v West Indies	W1	L2	D7	10	18	0	916	148	50.88	3	16	0	–	–	6
v India	W2	–	–	2	3	0	82	67	27.33	–	–	–	–	–	3
v Pakistan	W1	–	D3	4	5	0	140	100	28.00	1	–	–	–	–	1
	W8	L4	D15	27	45	0	1715	155	38.11	6	20	0	–	–	22

Edward Ralph DEXTER

Sussex

Born: Milan, Italy, 15 May 1935

Making his Test debut against New Zealand at Old Trafford in 1958, Ted Dexter was sent out to Australia the following winter to boost a flagging England side. A batsman of regal splendour, authority and immense power, capable of dealing with the quickest of bowling in an imperious manner, he also bowled erratic but effective fast medium.

He captained England in Pakistan and India in 1961–62, and led the side from then until the end of 1964, with the exception of the Headingley Test against Pakistan in 1962, when Cowdrey had his 'trial'.

For such an entertaining cricketer, he was a surprisingly dull and unenterprising captain.

Dexter in the nineties – supremo of English cricket (Allsport)

His judgment and handling of men, as in the case of John Murray, the leading wicket-keeper in the world at the time, was often poor, and there were few who enjoyed playing under him. His problem was that he was a multi-talented man who easily became bored and lost interest.

His period of captaincy bridged the years in which the distinction between amateur and professional was abolished, and he was the last man to captain the Gentlemen against the Players, at Lord's in 1962. In style and attitude, leadership was to remain in the hands of those with amateur backgrounds for some years.

He missed the 1963–64 tour to India but led the side against Australia in 1964. He then stood as a Conservative candidate against the future Labour Prime Minister, James Callaghan, at the General Election in October that year, but, as he was unsuccessful, he went to South Africa under Mike Smith. In 1965, he broke a leg and retired, but he made infrequent appearances for Sussex and played his last two Tests for England in 1968.

A great theorist, he has shown a vigorous, if sometimes haphazard, approach to his post as cricket 'supremo'.

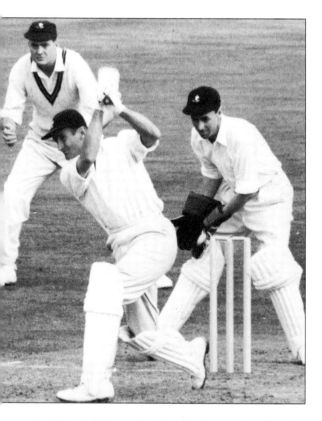

Ted Dexter hits out in the fifth Test against South Africa at The Oval in 1960. A brilliantly exciting batsman, Dexter was a surprisingly dry and unadventurous captain (Hulton)

Test Record

	M	I	NO	Runs	HS	Avge	100s	RC	Wkts	Avge	BB	Ct
v Australia	19	35	0	1358	180	38.80	2	742	23	32.26	3–16	10
v South Africa	10	16	1	585	172	39.00	1	310	7	44.28	3–79	4
v West Indies	10	19	1	866	136*	48.11	2	397	12	33.08	4–38	2
v New Zealand	8	10	2	477	141	59.62	1	142	4	35.50	3–23	4
v India	7	12	2	467	126*	46.70	1	311	7	44.42	2–24	2
v Pakistan	8	10	2	749	205	93.62	2	404	13	31.07	4–10	7
	62	102	8	4502	205	47.89	9	2306	66	34.93	4–10	29

Test Record as Captain

				M	I	NO	Runs	HS	Avge	100s	RC	Wkts	Avge	BB	Ct
v Australia	W1	L2	D7	10	18	0	865	174	48.06	1	491	14	35.07	3–65	6
v West Indies	W1	L3	D1	5	10	0	340	73	34.00	–	227	7	32.42	4–38	1
v New Zealand	W3	–	–	3	3	0	84	46	28.00	–	48	0	–	–	3
v India	–	L2	D3	5	9	2	409	126*	58.42	1	240	4	60.00	2–84	2
v Pakistan	W4	–	D3	7	9	2	729	205	104.14	2	370	8	46.25	3–86	6
	W9	L7	D14	30	49	4	2427	205	53.93	4	1376	33	41.69	4–38	18

Michael John Knight SMITH

Leicestershire and Warwickshire

Born: Westcotes, Leicestershire, 30 June 1933

A prolific scorer in county cricket, M.J.K. Smith made his debut for Leicestershire before going up to Oxford (1954–56). He moved on to Warwickshire in 1956 and captained them from 1957 to 1967. Immensely popular with his players who considered him fair and kind, he was less popular with the public who saw his period of stewardship of the England side as being concurrent with one of the dullest periods in Test history. Although an admirable ambassador on an overseas tour, he seemed to lack the drive necessary to win a game.

He first led England in India in 1963–64, when Dexter was unavailable, and in South Africa in 1964–65, when Dexter's position was uncertain due to his contesting a seat at the General Election. He was deposed after losing the first Test to West Indies in 1966, but was

Test Record

	M	I	NO	Runs	HS	Avge	100s	RC	Wkts	Avge	BB	Ct
v Australia	9	15	2	248	41	19.07	–	8	0	–	–	8
v South Africa	12	18	1	561	121	33.00	1	43	0	–	–	16
v West Indies	6	11	0	319	108	29.00	1	15	0	–	–	5
v New Zealand	9	12	1	312	87	28.36	–	–	–	–	–	14
v India	11	18	2	639	100	39.93	1	52	0	–	–	6
v Pakistan	3	4	0	199	99	49.75	–	10	1	10.00	1–10	4
	50	78	6	2278	121	31.63	–	128	1	128.0	1–10	53

recalled to the England side as a player for three Tests against Australia in 1972.

A brilliant short-leg, Mike Smith also represented England at rugby in 1956, two years before his Test cricket debut.

Test Record as Captain

				M	I	NO	Runs	HS	Avge	100s	RC	Wkts	Avge	BB	Ct
v Australia	W1	L1	D3	5	7	1	107	41	17.83	–	8	0	–	–	4
v South Africa	W1	L1	D6	8	12	1	369	121	33.54	1	43	0	–	–	12
v West Indies	–	L1	–	1	2	0	11	6	5.50	–	–	–	–	–	2
v New Zealand	W3	–	D3	6	8	1	255	87	36.42	–	–	–	–	–	11
v India	–	–	D5	5	8	2	306	75*	51.00	–	52	0	–	–	4
	W5	L3	D17	25	37	5	1048	121	32.75	1	103	0	–	–	33

Dennis Brian CLOSE

Yorkshire and Somerset

Born: Rawdon, Leeds, 24 February 1931

In his first season, 1949, Brian Close did the 'double', becoming the youngest Yorkshire player to be capped – he was 18 – and playing for England against New Zealand. He never quite lived up to that promise as a player, and his 22 appearances for England were spread over a period of 27 years.

A hard-hitting left-handed batsman, an off-break or seam right-arm bowler and one of the most courageous close to the wicket fielders in the history of the game, Brian Close captained Yorkshire from 1963 to 1970 and led them to four Championships. He left the county after a disagreement regarding his attitude to one-day cricket, and he took over at Somerset whose status he helped raise, particularly in one-day cricket.

Something of a cricket eccentric, honest and caring to his players, he was a popular choice to lead England after they had been overwhelmed by West Indies for much of the series in 1966. Under Close, England won the last Test at The Oval by an innings. He seemed to symbolise all that the people desired. He was an honest, no-nonsense professional, outstandingly brave and an astute tactician. He was unquestionably a national hero, but his reign was to be short-lived.

In 1967, he led England to triumph over India and Pakistan, and he was invited to

Brian Close – outstandingly brave, an astute tactician, but never far from controversy (Lemmon)

captain the side to the Caribbean. Late in the season, he used delaying tactics in a vital Championship match against Warwickshire, slowing down the over-rate at the end of the match to prevent Warwickshire from winning. He had a brush with a spectator, and MCC withdrew their invitation to lead the side in the West Indies.

At Tony Greig's insistence, he was recalled to the England side for three Tests against West Indies in 1976 when he was 45 years old. He batted and fielded as bravely as ever.

He retired from county cricket at the end of the following season, but he appeared in the Scarborough Festival until he was 55. He has been an England selector and manager and chairman of Yorkshire, and he has never been far from controversy.

Test Record

	M	I	NO	Runs	HS	Avge	100s	RC	Wkts	Avge	BB	Ct
v Australia	2	4	0	42	33	10.50	–	61	1	61.00	1–20	3
v South Africa	1	2	0	47	32	23.50	–	–	–	–	–	–
v West Indies	11	20	1	574	70	30.21	–	124	1	124.00	1–21	9
v New Zealand	1	1	0	0	0	0.00	–	85	1	85.00	1–39	–
v India	4	5	1	129	47	32.25	–	197	13	15.15	4–35	6
v Pakistan	3	5	0	95	41	19.00	–	65	2	32.50	1–4	6
	22	37	2	887	70	25.34	–	532	18	29.55	4–35	24

Test Record as Captain

				M	I	NO	Runs	HS	Avge	100s	RC	Wkts	Avge	BB	Ct
v West Indies	W1	–	–	1	1	0	4	4	4.00	–	28	1	28.00	1–21	1
v India	W3	–	–	3	4	1	102	47	34.00	–	144	8	18.00	4–68	2
v Pakistan	W2	–	D1	3	5	0	95	41	19.00	–	65	2	32.50	1–4	6
	W6	–	D1	7	10	1	201	47	22.33	–	237	11	21.54	4–68	9

Thomas William GRAVENEY

Gloucestershire and Worcestershire

Born: Riding Mill, Northumberland, 16 June 1927

Tom Graveney, one of the most elegantly artistic batsmen, played for Gloucestershire from 1948 to 1960 before moving to Worcestershire because he had been deprived of the captaincy. He later captained Worcestershire. He first played for England in 1951, against South Africa, and, although he did not appear between 1963 and 1966, he was recalled that year on his 39th birthday to face West Indies. His last Test was against the same opponents three years later.

He captained England once, at Headingley in 1968, when Cowdrey was injured.

Test Record

	M	I	NO	Runs	HS	Avge	100s	RC	Wkts	Avge	BB	Ct
v Australia	22	38	4	1075	111	31.61	1	74	1	74.00	1–34	24
v South Africa	6	10	0	234	60	23.40	–	–	–	–	–	9
v West Indies	19	31	5	1532	258	58.92	5	73	0	–	–	26
v New Zealand	8	10	1	293	46	32.55	–	–	–	–	–	6
v India	11	18	3	805	175	53.66	2	9	0	–	–	4
v Pakistan	13	16	0	943	153	58.93	3	11	0	–	–	11
	79	123	13	4882	258	44.38	11	167	1	167.00	1–34	80

Test Record as Captain

				M	I	NO	Runs	HS	Avge	100s	RC	Wkts	Avge	BB	Ct
v Australia	–	–	D1	1	2	0	78	41	39.00	–	–	–	–	–	2

Raymond ILLINGWORTH

Yorkshire and Leicestershire

Born: Pudsey, Yorkshire, 8 June 1932

An accomplished middle-order batsman and a tantalisingly accurate off-break bowler, Ray Illingworth played for Yorkshire from 1951 to 1969 and won 30 Test caps during that period. He left Yorkshire over a contractual disagreement in 1969 and became captain of Leicestershire. He had led the side in only eight first-class matches when he was called upon to captain England, the chosen captain, Colin Cowdrey, having been injured.

So successful was Illingworth – immediate victory over West Indies and a century in his second Test as captain – that he was invited to lead the side to Australia in 1970–71, although England had lost to a Rest of the World side in 1970 in a series which was hastily arranged to compensate for the cancellation of the South African tour.

Illingworth regained the Ashes and successfully defended them in 1972. He did not suffer defeat in a Test match until his 20th appearance as England's captain when India won an historic victory at The Oval in 1971. Heavy defeats at the hands of a strong West Indies side in 1973 ended his reign of captaincy and his Test career, but his record places him alongside Hutton, whom he admired greatly, Brearley and Close among post-war England captains.

Illingworth was a shrewd tactician who got the best out of his men as he proved at

Test Record

	M	I	NO	Runs	HS	Avge	100s	RC	Wkts	Avge	BB	Ct
v Australia	18	28	3	663	57	25.52	–	1094	34	32.17	6–87	16
v South Africa	4	6	2	81	37	20.25	–	146	6	24.33	3–15	1
v West Indies	13	21	2	369	113	19.42	1	1077	19	56.68	3–50	7
v New Zealand	13	16	1	320	65	21.33	–	597	22	27.13	4–34	10
v India	8	12	2	321	107	32.10	1	592	31	19.09	6–29	11
v Pakistan	5	7	1	82	45	13.66	–	301	10	30.10	3–58	–
	61	90	11	1836	113	23.24	2	3807	122	31.20	6–29	45

Leicestershire where the county enjoyed a golden period under his leadership. If he had a fault, it was that, as captain, he was a reluctant bowler in times of adversity, but he was a great fighter, and they were halcyon days when he led England.

He later returned to Yorkshire as manager and captain, but the move was not a success. He was offered the management of the England side, but he wanted more power than the TCCB could grant him, and he followed his career as a respected commentator.

Test Record as Captain

				M	I	NO	Runs	HS	Avge	100s	RC	Wkts	Avge	BB	Ct
v Australia	W4	L2	D5	11	18	3	527	57	35.13	–	546	17	32.11	3–39	10
v West Indies	W2	L2	D2	6	10	1	270	113	30.00	1	529	11	48.09	3–50	4
v New Zealand	W5	–	D3	8	12	0	249	65	20.75	–	395	10	39.50	4–37	6
v India	–	L1	D2	3	5	0	175	107	35.00	1	202	7	28.85	5–70	4
v Pakistan	W1	–	D2	3	4	0	67	45	16.75	–	162	6	27.00	3–58	–
	W12	L5	D14	31	49	4	1288	113	28.62	2	1834	51	35.96	5–70	24

Anthony Robert LEWIS

Glamorgan

Born: Uplands, Swansea, 6 July 1938

An elegant and popular batsman, Tony Lewis played for Glamorgan before going up to Cambridge where he won his blue in all three seasons (1960–62). He was a most able captain of Glamorgan, and when Illingworth was unable to take the side to India and Pakistan in 1972–73, he was asked to lead England. He proved an admirable and tactful captain, and his popularity has remained high on the Indian sub-continent ever since. In effect, he was worthy of a place in the England side, but the team was strong in batting, and the call for Lewis came too late. He played one Test under Illingworth in 1973, but was forced out of the game with a leg injury.

He became a highly successful journalist and broadcaster.

Tony Lewis – a most popular leader in India and Pakistan and later a most successful journalist and broadcaster (Adrian Murrell/Allsport)

Test Record

	M	I	NO	Runs	HS	Avge	100s	RC	Wkts	Avge	BB	Ct
v India	5	9	2	234	125	33.42	1	–	–	–	–	–
v Pakistan	3	5	0	219	88	43.80	–	–	–	–	–	–
v New Zealand	1	2	0	4	2	2.00	–	–	–	–	–	–
	9	16	2	457	125	32.64	1	–	–	–	–	–

Test Record as Captain

				M	I	NO	Runs	HS	Avge	100s	RC	Wkts	Avge	BB	Ct
v India	W1	L2	D2	5	9	2	234	125	33.42	1	–	–	–	–	–
v Pakistan	–	–	D3	3	5	0	219	88	43.80	–	–	–	–	–	–
	W1	L2	D5	8	14	2	453	125	37.75	1	–	–	–	–	–

Michael Henry DENNESS

Kent and Essex

Born: Bellshill, Lanarkshire, Scotland,
1 December 1940

Mike Denness had played only once for England, against New Zealand at The Oval in 1969, before being appointed vice-captain to Tony Lewis for the tour of India in 1972–73, a Scotsman vice-captain to a Welshman. It was then apparent that he was the most likely candidate to succeed Illingworth, for he was a successful and unselfish captain of Kent from 1972 to 1976.

A fine stroke-maker either as opener or in the middle order, Denness was a particularly good player of spin. He did not play against West Indies or New Zealand in 1973, but he led the side to the Caribbean the following winter, and England drew the series.

England won all three Tests against India in 1974, and Denness hit two centuries. It was in Australia in 1974–75 that his downfall came. England were in disarray against the pace and fire of Lillee and Thomson, and Denness dropped himself from the fourth Test match. He returned for the next match, and, in the sixth, with Thomson absent, he hit 188. He followed this with an innings of 181 in New Zealand, and he led England to the semi-final of the World

Mike Denness captained England at a most difficult time when the pace of Lillee and Thomson was too much for his side (Sporting Pictures)

Test Record

	M	I	NO	Runs	HS	Avge	100s	RC	Wkts	Avge	BB	Ct
v Australia	6	11	0	329	188	29.90	1	–	–	–	–	7
v West Indies	5	9	0	231	67	25.66	–	–	–	–	–	5
v New Zealand	3	4	2	297	181	148.50	1	–	–	–	–	3
v India	8	12	1	546	118	49.63	2	–	–	–	–	5
v Pakistan	6	9	0	264	68	29.33	–	–	–	–	–	8
	28	45	3	1667	188	39.69	4	–	–	–	–	28

Cup. But, confronted again by the pace of Lillee and Thomson, England lost by an innings in the first Test of the series against Australia which followed the 1975 World Cup. Denness was dropped from the next match and did not appear again in Test cricket.

Relieved of the Kent captaincy as politics raged within the county, he moved to Essex and played for them from 1977 to 1980, playing a significant part in that county's capturing of their first major honours.

Test Record as Captain

				M	I	NO	Runs	HS	Avge	100s	RC	Wkts	Avge	BB	Ct
v Australia	W1	L4	D1	6	11	0	329	188	29.90	1	–	–	–	–	7
v West Indies	W1	L1	D3	5	9	0	231	67	25.66	–	–	–	–	–	5
v New Zealand	W1	–	D1	2	2	1	240	181	240.00	1	–	–	–	–	–
v India	W3	–	–	3	4	1	289	118	96.33	2	–	–	–	–	2
v Pakistan	–	–	D3	3	4	0	91	44	22.75	–	–	–	–	–	4
	W6	L5	D8	19	30	2	1180	188	42.14	4	–	–	–	–	18

John Hugh EDRICH

Surrey

Born: Blofield, Norfolk, 21 June 1937

A member of a great cricketing family, John Edrich was a solid and dependable left-handed opening batsman who played for England from 1963 to 1976 and hit 39 790 runs in his first-class career which lasted from 1958 to 1978. He was vice-captain to Denness in Australia in 1974–75 and led the side at Sydney when Denness dropped himself. He had his ribs broken by the first ball he received from Lillee in the second innings, but, typically, he returned to bat for two and a half hours for 33 not out.

His highest innings was one of 310 not out against New Zealand at Headingley in 1965. He led Surrey from 1973 to 1977, but his period of captaincy was not the happiest time for himself or for the club.

Test Record

	M	I	NO	Runs	HS	Avge	100s	RC	Wkts	Avge	BB	Ct
v Australia	32	57	3	2644	175	48.96	7	–	–	–	–	16
v South Africa	1	2	1	7	7*	7.00	–	–	–	–	–	1
v West Indies	14	25	2	792	146	34.43	1	–	–	–	–	11
v New Zealand	11	15	1	840	310*	60.00	3	6	0	–	–	6
v India	10	14	1	494	100*	38.00	1	17	0	–	–	5
v Pakistan	9	14	1	361	70	27.76	–	–	–	–	–	4
	77	127	9	5138	310*	43.54	12	23	0	–	–	43

Test Record as Captain

				M	I	NO	Runs	HS	Avge	100s	RC	Wkts	Avge	BB	Ct
v Australia	–	L1	–	1	2	1	83	50	83.00	–	–	–	–	–	–

Anthony William GREIG

Sussex

Born: Queenstown, South Africa, 6 October 1946

Tony Greig excites the same conflicting passions in followers of cricket as did Jardine, but for very different reasons. At six feet seven and a half inches, he was the tallest cricketer to represent England, and his blond hair and good looks, allied to his height, made him a dominant and attractive personality.

Born in South Africa of a Scottish squadron leader who had won high honours in Bomber Command and of a South African mother, he was coached by Mike Buss who recommended him to his own county, Sussex. A hard-hitting batsman and a medium pace bowler who could also produce some devastating spells of off-breaks, Greig made a sensational debut for Sussex, hitting 156 against Lancashire in his first Championship match in 1967.

He captivated all who saw him, and he played for England against Rest of the World in 1970. Two years later, he made his Test debut, hitting 57 and 62 and taking 1 for 21 and 4 for 53 against Australia at Old Trafford. It was the first in an unbroken sequence of 58 Test matches.

The first of his eight Test centuries came against India at Bombay in 1972–73. He hit 148, and he was to make the same score against West Indies at Bridgetown the following winter when

Saint or sinner? Tony Greig, one of England's most controversial captains. He revitalised England's Test side after a period of despondency (Allsport)

he was vice-captain to Mike Denness. He hit two centuries in this series and had figures of 8 for 86 and 5 for 70 in the fifth Test with his off-breaks. These figures remain the best both for innings and match for England against West Indies.

The series was not without controversy, however, for, at the end of the second day of the first Test, Greig had run out Kallicharran when the batsman began to leave his crease and walk towards the pavilion. The appeal was later withdrawn, but Greig suffered much criticism in some quarters and was deprived of the vice-captaincy for the tour to Australia in 1974–75. Nothing could detract from his courage and combative spirit, and he scored a fine century in difficult conditions against Lillee and Thomson in the first Test.

He led Sussex from 1973 to 1977, and when Denness was sacked it was apparent that he would be the man to take over. He was immensely popular, and he instilled self-belief and fighting spirit into a flagging England side. England drew the three Tests under his captaincy against Australia in 1975.

The next summer, West Indies were the opponents, and he claimed before the start of the series that his side would try to make the West Indians 'grovel'. They did not, but Greig's words, fine in the context in which they were used, were turned against him, and his critics were ever ready to remind people that he was South African born.

In 1976–77, he took the side to India where he inspired them to a memorable series victory. He had elevated English cricket to a level where it was again respected and joyful. No man stood higher in cricket esteem than Tony Greig, and he had earned his position.

He led England in the Centenary Test in Melbourne, but it was then revealed that he was negotiating to recruit players for Kerry Packer's World Series Cricket. He became the recipient of much abuse as he was regarded by some as a traitor to England and to cricket. He was relieved of the England captaincy, but Brearley insisted that Greig and the other players contracted to Packer should play in the series against Australia in 1977. After that, Greig faded from cricket and settled in Australia.

On the tour of India in 1976–77, he had become the first man to score 3000 runs and take 100 wickets for England in Test cricket, just as he had been the first to score a hundred and

take five wickets in an innings for England at Bridgetown in 1973–74. His record in Test cricket will stand comparison with anyone's.

He is the only England captain not to be honoured by MCC, and there are still those who are angered by what he did in 1977. Cricketers are not among them; before Greig and Packer, there was little or no sponsorship in international cricket, and wages were poor. Greig helped revolutionise all that, just as he introduced the raised-bat stance, another thing for which many will not forgive him. He was a great enthusiast who inspired his team-mates and was loved by them. His passion for the game and his commitment were infectious. It was later revealed that he suffered from a mild form of epilepsy.

His place in the history of the game and among the most influential of England captains is secure.

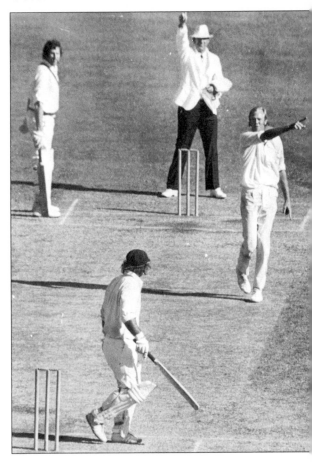

Greig points Rodney Marsh towards the pavilion on England's 1974–75 tour of Australia (Hulton)

Test Record

	M	I	NO	Runs	HS	Avge	100s	RC	Wkts	Avge	BB	Ct
v Australia	21	37	1	1303	110	36.19	1	1663	44	37.79	4–53	37
v West Indies	13	23	1	795	148	36.13	3	1281	36	35.58	8–86	18
v New Zealand	5	6	0	267	139	44.50	1	361	20	18.05	5–51	2
v India	13	18	2	883	148	55.18	3	759	27	28.11	5–24	16
v Pakistan	6	9	0	351	72	39.00	–	477	14	34.07	4–86	14
	58	93	4	3599	148	40.43	8	4541	141	32.20	8–86	87

Test Record as Captain

				M	I	NO	Runs	HS	Avge	100s	RC	Wkts	Avge	BB	Ct
v Australia	–	L1	D3	4	8	0	328	96	41.00	–	345	9	38.33	3–107	8
v West Indies	–	L3	D2	5	9	1	243	116	30.37	1	336	5	67.20	2–42	6
v India	W3	L1	D1	5	8	0	342	103	42.75	1	336	10	33.60	3–64	5
	W3	L5	D6	14	25	1	913	116	38.04	2	1017	24	42.37	3–64	19

John Michael BREARLEY

Middlesex

Born: Harrow, Middlesex, 28 April 1942

A cultured man, academically brilliant, with a warmth and charm as a communicator, Mike Brearley has a record unsurpassed by any other England captain.

In four years at Cambridge, he hit more runs than anyone had hit before, and he went with the England side to South Africa in 1964–65 without playing in a Test match. Although his appearances were limited because of his academic pursuits, he led the MCC Under-25 side to Pakistan in 1966–67, and hit 312 not out on the first day against North Zone at Peshawar.

In the mid-sixties, he was torn between cricket and an academic life, and in 1968 he took a job teaching philosophy in Newcastle, appearing for Middlesex in the summer vacation. On his own admission, he was lured back to cricket by the offer of the Middlesex captaincy: 'I like to be bossy. I hate to get bored. I want to be doing something all the time, and the tactics of the game fascinated me. I liked the idea of interrelation with people, and, above all, I like trying to get the best out of people.'

Brearley led Middlesex from 1971 to 1982, and he transformed the county's fortunes. They won three Championships and shared one under his leadership and twice won the Gillette Cup.

The distinction between amateur and professional had been abolished in 1963, but, in background and attitude, Brearley was in every way an *amateur*. This amateur aspect of his character came to be one of his greatest strengths. As John Arlott said of him, 'You're the only England captain who knows it doesn't *really* matter.' This was a fact, but it did not stop Brearley from having an efficient and, at times, ruthless approach to captaincy, and few captains have been lucky enough to have been able to ally an intelligent and professional approach to a sense of detachment which allowed them to accept that there were things in the world more important than cricket.

Brearley's early promise as a batsman was never to be fulfilled, and, unquestionably, he was short of Test standard, but it must be remembered that he was first selected for England under Tony Greig as a batsman for the first two Tests against West Indies in 1976, and that he went with Greig's side to India in 1976–77 and made 91 in the final Test at Bombay. He was vice-captain to Greig, and when Greig's contacts with Kerry Packer were revealed Brearley became captain of England in 1977.

He insisted that Greig and the other Packer players should retain their places in the England side, and, like Greig, he wanted his men to be well paid for their labours.

Under Brearley, England regained the Ashes against a rather demoralised and below-strength Australian side in 1977. That winter he led England in Pakistan, but he broke his arm after the second Test match and could not go on the New Zealand part of the tour.

There were overwhelming victories against Pakistan and New Zealand in 1978, and, in Australia in 1978–79, England won five of the six Test matches and lost one. Brearley was the first man to lead England to five victories in a rubber, but the Australian side, like the Pakistan side, had been ravaged by World Series Cricket and was well below strength.

India were beaten in a dull series in 1979, and at the end of that year, Brearley took an England side to Australia for a hastily-arranged three-match series to help consolidate the end to the warring between the Australian Board and the Packer organisation. Confronted by a full-strength Australian side for the first time, Brearley's side was beaten in all three Tests.

After the Golden Jubilee Test against India in February 1980, Brearley announced his retirement from Test cricket, but the following year, under Botham's captaincy, England performed miserably against Australia at Trent Bridge and

Lord's. Botham resigned, and Brearley was persuaded to lead England in the last four Tests. Three of them were won, two in astonishing fashion, and, under Brearley, Botham performed heroic deeds.

Brearley did not play Test cricket again, and he left behind him an amazing record, yet it must be pointed out that on the one occasion he was faced by a full-strength Australian side he lost all three games, and he never led England against West Indies, the strongest side in the world at that period. The debate about his true worth continues, not least because it symbolises a North-South and amateur-professional divide. This is somewhat ironic, for, as we have indicated, he was totally professional in his approach, even mercenary in some matters, and was a frequent scourge of the Establishment.

A wicket-keeper who became a very fine slip fielder, he gave delight in his handling of the England side. One was ever conscious that here was a sharp mind at work, and the intelligent application was always spiced with good humour.

Mike Brearley's side for the Edgbaston Test against Australia in 1981 includes no less than eight England captains. Back row, left to right: Bob Taylor, Graham Gooch, John Emburey, Peter Willey, David Gower, Mike Gatting. Front: Ian Botham, Bob Willis, Mike Brearley, Geoff Boycott, Chris Old (Patrick Eagar)

Test Record

	M	I	NO	Runs	HS	Avge	100s	RC	Wkts	Avge	BB	Ct
v Australia	19	37	2	798	81	22.80	–	–	–	–	–	20
v West Indies	2	4	0	70	40	17.50	–	–	–	–	–	1
v New Zealand	3	5	1	104	50	26.00	–	–	–	–	–	5
v India	10	14	0	316	91	22.57	–	–	–	–	–	17
v Pakistan	5	6	0	154	74	25.66	–	–	–	–	–	9
	39	66	3	1442	91	22.88	–	–	–	–	–	52

Test Record as Captain

				M	I	NO	Runs	HS	Avge	100s	RC	Wkts	Avge	BB	Ct
v Australia	W11	L4	D3	18	35	2	743	81	22.51	–	–	–	–	–	19
v New Zealand	W3	–	–	3	5	1	104	50	26.00	–	–	–	–	–	5
v India	W2	–	D3	5	6	0	101	34	16.83	–	–	–	–	–	8
v Pakistan	W2	–	D3	5	6	0	154	74	25.66	–	–	–	–	–	9
	W18	L4	D9	31	52	3	1102	81	22.48	–	–	–	–	–	41

Geoffrey BOYCOTT

Yorkshire

Born: Fitzwilliam, Yorkshire, 21 October 1940

Unequalled powers of concentration, application and single-minded dedication to the art of batting made Geoffrey Boycott the most prolific scorer in post-war cricket, but his career was ever tinged with controversy.

He opened the innings for Yorkshire from 1962 to 1986, having been sacked, then reinstated in 1983 when his supporters overthrew the committee. His England career lasted from 1964 until 1982, although he exiled himself from international cricket from midway through 1974 until 1977. It was generally believed that it was his unwillingness to play under Mike Denness that caused him to withdraw from Test cricket for a period.

He was never a successful captain of Yorkshire (1971–78), and he became the centre of a schism within the county which has never truly healed. His approach to the game was seen by many as selfish, and although his knowledge of the game was profound, his dogmatic attitude did not make communication easy, and he failed to get players behind him.

It was an ambition ultimately realised for Geoff Boycott when he captained England against Pakistan and New Zealand in 1977–78 (Adrian Murrell/Allsport)

He nursed great ambitions of becoming captain of England, and he led them once against Pakistan and three times against New Zealand in 1977–78, after Brearley had broken his arm. His second match as captain saw New Zealand gain their first victory over England.

Test Record

		M	I	NO	Runs	HS	Avge	100s	RC	Wkts	Avge	BB	Ct
v Australia		38	71	9	2945	191	47.50	7	107	2	53.50	2–32	12
v South Africa		7	12	2	373	117	37.30	1	217	5	43.40	3–47	2
v West Indies		29	53	5	2205	128	45.93	5	16	0	–	–	7
v New Zealand		15	25	1	916	131	38.16	2	30	0	–	–	5
v India		13	22	3	1084	246*	57.05	4	8	0	–	–	7
v Pakistan		6	10	3	591	121*	84.42	3	4	0	–	–	–
		108	193	23	8114	246*	47.72	22	382	7	54.57	3–47	33

Test Record as Captain

				M	I	NO	Runs	HS	Avge	100s	RC	Wkts	Avge	BB	Ct
v New Zealand	W1	L1	D1	3	5	0	166	77	33.20	–	–	–	–	–	2
v Pakistan	–	–	D1	1	2	0	87	56	43.50	–	–	–	–	–	–
	W1	L1	D2	4	7	0	253	77	36.14	–	–	–	–	–	2

Ian Terence BOTHAM

Somerset, Worcestershire and Durham

Born: Heswall, Cheshire, 24 November 1955

The greatest all-round cricketer to represent England this century, Ian Botham was named by Mike Brearley as the man who should succeed him as England captain, a view which was supported by several critics who later chose to forget their recommendation. A glorious entertainer as a mighty, belligerent batsman, fast-medium pace bowler always probing for wickets with his late swing and superb slip-fielder, Botham first played for England against Australia at Trent Bridge in 1977 when he took 5 for 74 on his debut. His Test career has been littered with records ever since.

Only Richard Hadlee has taken more wickets in Test cricket; Botham shares with Alan Knott the record of having played 65 consecutive Test matches for England; he hit 50 off 32 balls

Ian Botham – such men are our joys, not our leaders (David Munden)

against New Zealand at The Oval in 1986. The list is almost endless.

At several points his Test career has seemed to be at an end, but he has defied logic, as in 1991 when, after injury, he was recalled for the final Test against West Indies and for the Test against Sri Lanka.

The worst patch of his Test career came when, in 1980 and 1981, he led England in nine Tests against West Indies and three against Australia. His own form suffered. There was disaffection with his behaviour, and, having

demanded more of his team in the Lord's Test against Australia, he was out for 0 and 0 and resigned the captaincy before he could be relieved of it. Under Brearley, his form blossomed again, and he virtually won the series for England with some heroic deeds.

He stated publicly that he wanted to be captain of England again, but that was not to be. He was born to be a man of instant pleasure and future memory. Such men are our joys, not our leaders.

Test Record

		M	I	NO	Runs	HS	Avge	100s	RC	Wkts	Avge	BB	Ct
v Australia		36	59	2	1673	149*	29.35	4	4093	148	27.65	6–78	57
v West Indies		20	38	1	792	81	21.40	–	2146	61	35.18	8–103	19
v New Zealand		14	21	2	830	138	43.68	3	1424	61	23.34	6–34	13
v India		14	17	0	1201	208	70.64	5	1558	59	26.40	7–48	14
v Pakistan		12	19	1	639	108	35.50	2	1210	40	30.25	8–34	12
v Sri Lanka		3	3	0	41	22	13.66	–	310	11	28.28	6–90	2
		99	157	6	5176	208	34.27	14	10741	380	28.26	8–34	117

Test Record as Captain

				M	I	NO	Runs	HS	Avge	100s	RC	Wkts	Avge	BB	Ct
v Australia	–	L1	D2	3	5	0	34	33	6.80	–	281	7	40.14	2–34	2
v West Indies	–	L3	D6	9	16	0	242	57	15.12	–	877	28	31.32	4–77	7
	–	L4	D8	12	21	0	276	57	13.14	–	1158	35	33.08	4–77	9

Keith William Robert FLETCHER

Essex

Born: Worcester, 20 May 1944

Brearley returned to lead the England side in 1981, but he made it clear that he would not be available thereafter. The selectors appointed Keith Fletcher to take the side to India and Sri Lanka in 1981–82. He had not played in a Test since the Centenary Test in Melbourne, 1977.

Fletcher had played for Essex since 1962 and he captained them from 1974 to 1985 and again in 1988. Under his leadership, Essex won the first honours in their history and dominated county cricket in the early eighties.

Keith Fletcher had a splendid Test record as a middle-order batsman with a wide range of strokes. His knowledge of the game was profound, and his tactical acumen was sharper than anyone else's on the county circuit, but he had suffered badly at the hands of the press and of the Yorkshire crowd when he first played Test cricket at Headingley against Australia in 1968. He was scarred by his early experiences, and he tended to remain introspective and taciturn, known only to those who played under him. He was highly respected by all who played with and against him, and he was a fierce adversary, but the captaincy of England came to him too late. He lacked the flamboyant personality that made Tony Greig so successful and popular in India, and the 1981–82 series, with Gavaskar captain of India and Fletcher captain of England, was exceedingly tedious as the rival leaders failed to establish any rapport between them.

Fletcher's cause was not helped by the fact that his leading players were engaged in arranging a clandestine tour of South Africa. He lost the series in India, but, after a fright, won the inaugural Test in Sri Lanka. He was unceremoniously sacked from the captaincy by Peter May at the beginning of the 1982 season, but he has since given good service to England as the manager of 'A' teams on tour.

Keith Fletcher takes a spectacular catch at short-leg to dismiss Sandeep Patil in the fourth Test against India in 1981–82. Bob Taylor is the wicket-keeper (Adrian Murrell/Allsport)

Test Record

	M	I	NO	Runs	HS	Avge	100s	RC	Wkts	Avge	BB	Ct
v Australia	15	27	1	661	146	25.42	1	101	1	101.00	1–48	10
v West Indies	7	13	3	528	129*	52.80	1	5	0	–	–	6
v New Zealand	8	11	0	578	216	52.54	2	14	0	–	–	12
v India	19	29	7	874	123*	39.72	2	20	1	20.00	1–6	17
v Pakistan	9	14	2	586	122	48.83	1	53	0	–	–	6
v Sri Lanka	1	2	1	45	45	45.00	–	–	–	–	–	3
	59	96	14	3272	216	39.90	7	193	2	96.50	1–6	54

Test Record as Captain

				M	I	NO	Runs	HS	Avge	100s	RC	Wkts	Avge	BB	Ct
v India	–	L1	D5	6	9	2	252	69	36.00	–	20	1	20.00	1–6	5
v Sri Lanka	W1	–	–	1	2	1	45	45	45.00	–	–	–	–	–	3
	W1	L1	D5	7	11	3	297	69	37.12	–	20	1	20.00	1–6	8

Robert George Dylan WILLIS

Surrey and Warwickshire

Born: Sunderland, 30 May 1949

One of the greatest fast bowlers to have represented England, Bob Willis began his Test career in 1970–71 when he was flown out to Australia as a replacement for the injured Alan Ward. Thirteen years later, at Headingley in 1984, he became England's leading wicket-taker in Test cricket when he overtook Freddie Trueman's record of 307 wickets.

Never as successful in county cricket – either as an uncapped player with Surrey or as captain of Warwickshire – as in Test cricket, he was a bowler of heart and passion and his 8 for 43 at Headingley in 1981, which gave England victory over Australia by 18 runs, was one of the most inspiring bowling performances ever seen on a cricket field.

He was rather a surprising appointment as captain of England in 1982, for he was always seen as more of a sergeant-major than a commissioned officer, but he led his country until 1984 when he was replaced by David Gower. He played under Gower in the first three Tests against West Indies that season.

Bob Willis – a lion-hearted leader (Adrian Murrell/ Allsport)

Test Record

	M	I	NO	Runs	HS	Avge	100s	RC	Wkts	Avge	BB	Ct
v Australia	35	58	21	383	26	10.35	–	3346	128	26.14	8–43	16
v West Indies	13	22	13	139	24*	15.44	–	1381	38	36.34	5–42	7
v New Zealand	14	20	9	117	25*	10.63	–	1132	60	18.86	5–32	4
v India	17	17	7	118	28	11.80	–	1441	62	23.24	6–53	4
v Pakistan	10	10	5	83	28*	16.60	–	820	34	24.11	5–47	6
v Sri Lanka	1	1	0	0	0	0.00	–	70	3	23.33	2–46	2
	90	128	55	840	28*	11.50	–	8190	325	25.20	8–43	39

Test Record as Captain

				M	I	NO	Runs	HS	Avge	100s	RC	Wkts	Avge	BB	Ct
v Australia	W1	L2	D2	5	9	3	63	26	10.50	–	486	18	27.00	5–66	4
v New Zealand	W3	L2	D2	7	11	3	81	25*	10.12	–	579	32	18.09	5–35	4
v India	W1	–	D2	3	3	1	35	28	17.50	–	330	15	22.00	6–101	–
v Pakistan	W2	L1	–	3	5	3	37	28*	18.50	–	268	12	22.33	3–55	4
	W7	L5	D6	18	28	10	216	28*	12.00	–	1663	77	21.59	6–101	12

David Ivon GOWER

Leicestershire and Hampshire

Born: Tunbridge Wells, Kent, 1 April 1957

David Gower made his Test debut against Pakistan at Edgbaston in 1978. He hit the first ball he received in Test cricket for four and so began a career which has brought him 8081 runs. Only Boycott stands ahead of him among England Test cricketers.

Tall, blond, left-handed, David Gower has a languid eloquence with the bat which has marked him as one of the most beautiful sights that the cricket field has known. So delicate is his timing, so felicitous his touch, that there is always a suggestion of human frailty and vulnerability about his batting which only adds to the attraction, but the very characteristics which help give delight to the batting have proved to be his Achilles heel as a captain.

The background, the style, the carefree 'amateur' attitude were seen by many as providing the substance of which captains are made, and there were journalists who wrote of him as having been born for the job. As deputy for Bob Willis, he first led England against Pakistan at Lord's in 1982 and it was the first occasion that Pakistan won a Test match at Lord's. He was again deputy to Willis in Pakistan in 1983–4. He captained in two Tests and hit centuries in both, but failed to save the series.

He replaced Willis as captain for the series against West Indies the following summer when, for the first time in England, England lost a series by five matches to nil. He retained the captaincy for the tour of India in 1984–85 and led with tact and shrewdness through a most difficult time, which saw the assassination of the Indian Prime Minister Mrs Gandhi and of Mr Percy Norris, the British Deputy High Commissioner. England lost the first Test but won the series, not least because of Gower's calm and control.

In 1985 Gower regained the Ashes from an Australian side weakened by defections to a rebel tour of South Africa, but he hit 732 runs in the series and his standing was high. It slumped again, however, when England lost by five matches to nil in the Caribbean, and Gower

David Gower at Old Trafford, 1989. England lost this Test and with it the Ashes (Allsport/Murrell)

took much of the blame for his apparently diffident approach and for a lack of team discipline. When England lost to India at Lord's in the first Test match of 1986, Gower's languid attitude was again criticised and Gatting replaced him as captain.

With the fall of Gatting and the retirement of Peter May, Ted Dexter, the new chairman of selectors, restored Gower to the England captaincy for the series against Australia in 1989. Australia won four of the six Tests, two were drawn and Gower was not only deprived of the captaincy for the tour of the West Indies but was not even selected for the trip.

In 1990 he won back a place in the England side for the three Tests against India and hit a century at The Oval to win a place in Gooch's

side to go to Australia. He made two centuries in that series, but was guilty of a breach of discipline with an ill-judged flying escapade and played an irresponsible shot just before lunch in the fourth Test at Adelaide. His apparently lackadaisical approach caused his relations with skipper Gooch, who had pressed for his selection, to become strained, and he was not chosen for the home series against West Indies.

For Hampshire, he achieved little. In truth, he has never seemed to have a great appetite for the county game. Perhaps he was born out of his time. He should have been an Edwardian amateur, playing as the mood took him and expenses allowed. He would have graced the golden age, as indeed he would have graced any age in which he batted.

Test Record

	M	I	NO	Runs	HS	Avge	100s	RC	Wkts	Avge	BB	Ct
v Australia	42	77	4	3269	215	44.78	9	–	–	–	–	26
v West Indies	19	38	3	1149	154*	32.82	1	–	–	–	–	11
v New Zealand	13	22	1	1051	131	50.04	4	5	0	–	–	11
v India	24	37	6	1391	200*	44.87	2	15	1	15.00	1–1	13
v Pakistan	14	22	1	1035	173*	49.28	2	–	–	–	–	7
v Sri Lanka	2	3	1	186	89	93.00	–	–	–	–	–	5
	114	199	16	8081	215	44.15	18	20	1	20.00	1–1	73

Test Record as Captain

				M	I	NO	Runs	HS	Avge	100s	RC	Wkts	Avge	BB	Ct
v Australia	W3	L5	D4	12	20	0	1115	215	55.75	4	–	–	–	–	10
v West Indies	–	L10	–	10	20	1	541	90	28.47	–	–	–	–	–	6
v India	W2	L2	D2	6	9	1	193	78	24.12	–	13	0	–	–	6
v Pakistan	–	L1	D2	3	5	1	363	173*	90.75	2	–	–	–	–	3
v Sri Lanka	–	–	D1	1	1	0	55	55	55.00	–	–	–	–	–	1
	W5	L18	D9	32	55	3	2267	215	43.59	6	13	0	–	–	26

Michael William GATTING

Middlesex

Born: Kingsbury, Middlesex, 6 June 1957

A stocky, belligerent batsman, capable of shredding most attacks, Mike Gatting made his

Test debut in Pakistan in 1977–78, but he did not score his first Test hundred until his 54th Test innings at Bombay in 1984–85. He hit a double century later the same series and runs flowed from his bat thereafter.

He succeeded Mike Brearley as captain of Middlesex in 1983, and although Gatting had lost his place in the England side against West

Indies in the preceding series, he was named as vice-captain to Gower for the 1984–85 tour of India. When Gower fell out of favour after defeat in the first Test by India in 1986, Gatting was made captain. He lost the series against India and the one against New Zealand which followed, but in Australia he led a harmonious side to a surprise Ashes victory.

This success could not be maintained, and Pakistan were victors in England in 1987 when Gatting's tactical limitations were apparent and his powers of diplomacy viewed with anxiety.

A dreadful reverse sweep cost him his wicket in the World Cup Final of 1987 and England went on to lose a match that they seemed to be winning. From that point, Gatting's fortunes declined swiftly. In Pakistan, he and umpire Shakoor Rana had a confrontation which, due to the absurdity of both parties, cost a day's Test cricket and soured a series.

Gatting led England in the first Test against West Indies in 1988, but he was the subject of an article in a tabloid newspaper which made allegations regarding his social activities during the Test match. He was deprived of the captaincy, stood down after the third Test and played only once more, against Australia the following season, after which it was revealed that, disenchanted, he had contracted to lead a rebel tour to South Africa. A ban on his playing Test cricket was automatically imposed.

Like Willis, Gatting was seen as a sergeant-major who barked orders more than as a commissioned officer, but if he lacked distinction in the finer points of his game, he had a rugged honesty which was respected.

Honesty and endeavour – Mike Gatting (Adrian Murrell/Allsport)

Test Record

	M	I	NO	Runs	HS	Avge	100s	RC	Wkts	Avge	BB	Ct
v Australia	20	35	4	1388	160	44.77	3	68	0	–	–	14
v West Indies	9	17	0	258	56	15.17	–	–	–	–	–	7
v New Zealand	11	17	2	435	121	29.00	1	103	3	34.33	1–14	9
v India	13	21	6	936	207	62.40	3	50	0	–	–	7
v Pakistan	15	27	2	853	150*	34.12	2	96	1	96.00	1–17	14
	68	117	14	3870	207	37.57	9	317	4	79.25	1–14	51

Test Record as Captain

				M	I	NO	Runs	HS	Avge	100s	RC	Wkts	Avge	BB	Ct
v Australia	W2	L1	D3	6	10	0	406	100	40.60	1	39	0	–	–	5
v West Indies	–	–	D1	1	2	0	34	29	17.00	–	–	–	–	–	1
v New Zealand	–	L1	D5	6	9	1	276	121	34.50	1	61	2	30.50	1–21	2
v India	–	L1	D1	2	4	2	253	183*	126.50	1	10	0	–	–	2
v Pakistan	–	L2	D6	8	14	1	573	150*	44.07	2	40	0	–	–	3
	W2	L5	D16	23	39	4	1542	183*	44.05	5	150	2	75.00	1–21	13

John Ernest EMBUREY

Middlesex

Born: Peckham, London, 20 August 1952

Throughout the 1980s John Emburey was England's leading off-spinner, and for most of the time their only spinner. Joining a rebel tour to South Africa in 1981–82 caused him to be banned from Test cricket for three years, and he was banned again when he returned to South Africa in 1989–90.

An accurate bowler, brilliant fielder and effective if unorthodox batsman, he first played for Middlesex in 1973 and for England, against New Zealand, five years later. Vice-captain to Gatting at Middlesex, he led England against West Indies at Lord's and Old Trafford in 1988 after Gatting's dismissal, but he himself was dropped after the Manchester Test.

An astute thinker on the game, he led England intelligently in both his Tests as captain, but his side was well beaten and his own form seemed to be in decline.

A brief reign for a thoughtful captain – John Emburey (Adrian Murrell/Allsport)

Test Record

	M	I	NO	Runs	HS	Avge	100s	RC	Wkts	Avge	BB	Ct
v Australia	24	34	8	667	69	25.65	–	2548	75	33.97	7–78	15
v West Indies	14	24	5	218	35*	11.47	–	1178	30	39.26	5–78	7
v New Zealand	6	7	1	200	75	33.33	–	417	9	46.33	2–87	2
v India	7	11	1	86	38	8.60	–	363	10	36.30	2–35	5
v Pakistan	7	11	3	369	74*	46.12	–	473	7	67.57	3–49	3
v Sri Lanka	2	2	0	0	0	0.00	–	126	7	18.00	6–33	1
	60	89	18	1540	75	21.69	–	5105	138	36.99	7–78	33

Test Record as Captain

			M	I	NO	Runs	HS	Avge	100s	RC	Wkts	Avge	BB	Ct
v West Indies	–	L2	–	2	4	0	46	30	11.50	–	133	1	133.00	1–17	3

Christopher Stuart COWDREY

Kent

Born: Farnborough, Kent, 20 October 1957

Although he was selected for the tour of India in 1984–85, few considered Chris Cowdrey to be of Test class. An aggressive batsman, medium-pace bowler and excellent fielder, he was a most enthusiastic all-rounder best suited to the one-day game.

Eldest son of a famous England captain, he first played for Kent in 1977 and was appointed captain in 1985. He proved to be an inspiring leader of a moderate team, and in 1988 he was made captain of England following the sacking of Gatting and heavy defeats under Emburey. It was also indicated to him that he would lead the side for the rest of the summer and would be captain on the winter tour of India. But a foot injury forced him out of the final Test against West Indies, and he was never called upon again.

His appointment as captain was an attempt to restore a former order in which a captain was thought to be good enough to lead a side even if he were not up to standard as a player. Nothing was learned about Cowdrey in his one Test as captain that had not been previously known. He was shabbily treated and, embittered, he joined the rebel tour of South Africa in 1989–90. He resigned as Kent captain at the end of the 1990 season and was not re-engaged after 1991. It was a sad end for a cricketer who never played the game without zest and enjoyment.

Chris Cowdrey – a man sadly used (Adrian Murrell/Allsport)

Test Record

	M	I	NO	Runs	HS	Avge	100s	RC	Wkts	Avge	BB	Ct
v West Indies	1	2	0	5	5	2.50	–	21	0	–	–	–
v India	5	6	1	96	38	19.20	–	288	4	72.00	2–65	5
	6	8	1	101	38	14.42	–	309	4	77.25	2–65	5

Test Record as Captain

				M	I	NO	Runs	HS	Avge	100s	RC	Wkts	Avge	BB	Ct
v West Indies	–	L1	–	1	2	0	5	5	2.50	–	21	0	–	–	–

Graham Alan GOOCH

Essex

Born: Leytonstone, Essex, 23 July 1953

When Graham Gooch was appointed captain of England against West Indies at The Oval in August 1988, he became England's fourth captain of the summer. By that time he had become his country's leading batsman, although his start in Test cricket had been inauspicious.

He made his debut for Essex in 1973 and was soon seen as a very powerful and aggressive batsman. He was called into the Test side a little prematurely, making his debut against the pace of Lillee and Thomson at Edgbaston in 1975. He made 0 and 0. He was retained for the second Test at Lord's but then disappeared from Test cricket until 1978, when he returned against Pakistan as Boycott's opening partner.

His first Test century came at Lord's against West Indies in 1980, and during that period it was his mighty batting that played a prominent

The keeper of the flame – Graham Gooch (David Munden)

part in Essex's success in all competitions. Following the tour of India and Sri Lanka in 1981–82, he captained a rebel England tour of South Africa and was banned from Test cricket for three years.

He returned to the England side in 1985 and hit 196 at The Oval as England won the series against Australia. He became captain of Essex in 1986 but relinquished the post after two seasons because he felt his form was affected adversely. He was reappointed in 1989, by which time he had led England against West Indies and Sri Lanka. He had been named as captain of England for the tour of India in 1988–89, but the tour was cancelled because of the South African connections of Gooch and other members of the party.

Gooch became a national hero when he led England to victory over West Indies at Kingston in 1989–90, and he came close to leading them to victory at Port-of-Spain, where he himself was forced to retire hurt with a broken finger.

The year of 1990 was to belong to him. He hit 154 as England beat New Zealand at Edgbaston and followed this with innings of 333 and 123 in the victory over India at Lord's. His triple century was the highest innings ever played by an England captain.

Injury again kept him out of a Test match in Australia in 1990–91, where he was England's sole success in a disappointing series defeat. In the first Test against West Indies at Headingley in 1991 he hit a brilliant century in difficult conditions and England drew the series. He notched another century against Sri Lanka in the final Test of the summer.

A useful, if under-used, seam bowler and a fine slip fielder, Gooch has changed his batting style over the years, adding a watchful defence to his strength and belligerence. He is capable of the destruction of any attack. With his drooping moustache, the man presents an air of brooding melancholy and he has a streak of obstinacy that does not suffer fools gladly; yet he has lifted the spirits of English cricket by his own supreme example after a few years of unhappiness and controversy.

He is a captain who insists on full fitness and whose own form has thrived on responsibility. His career has been littered with scars, most of them self-inflicted, but his rehabilitation is now as complete as it is remarkable.

Test Record

	M	I	NO	Runs	HS	Avge	100s	RC	Wkts	Avge	BB	Ct
v Australia	31	57	0	1714	196	30.07	2	338	7	48.28	2–16	27
v West Indies	26	51	2	2197	154*	44.83	5	136	4	34.00	2–18	28
v New Zealand	9	15	2	764	183	58.76	2	92	1	92.00	1–23	10
v India	17	29	2	1678	333	62.14	5	230	5	46.00	2–12	20
v Pakistan	5	8	0	299	93	37.37	–	4	0	–	–	5
v Sri Lanka	3	6	0	376	174	62.66	1	–	–	–	–	4
	91	166	6	7028	333	43.92	15	800	17	47.05	2–12	94

Test Record as Captain

				M	I	NO	Runs	HS	Avge	100s	RC	Wkts	Avge	BB	Ct
v Australia	–	L2	D2	4	8	0	426	117	53.25	1	69	2	34.50	1–23	6
v West Indies	W3	L3	D2	8	15	2	701	154*	53.92	1	14	0	–	–	10
v New Zealand	W1	–	D2	3	5	0	306	154	61.20	1	25	0	–	–	3
v India	W1	–	D2	3	6	0	752	333	125.33	3	70	1	70.00	1–26	4
v Sri Lanka	W2	–	–	2	4	0	323	174	80.75	1	–	–	–	–	3
	W7	L5	D8	20	38	2	2508	333	69.66	7	178	3	59.33	1–23	26

Allan Joseph LAMB

Northamptonshire

Born: Langebaanweg, South Africa, 20 June 1954

Allan Lamb learned his cricket in South Africa where he played for Western Province before coming to England to assist Northamptonshire. His English parentage and residence allowed him to qualify for England in 1982, and he was immediately selected to play against India, hitting a century in his third match.

A hard-hitting batsman, he took three centuries off the West Indian attack in the 1984 series. He became captain of Northamptonshire in 1989, but although he is a joyful cricketer and a man who enjoys life fully, there has been considerable criticism of his captaincy and general man-management.

He was vice-captain to Gooch in both West Indies in 1989–90 and Australia in 1990–91, and he led England when Gooch was injured. It became apparent at the beginning of the 1991 season, however, that he would not be cast in the role of vice-captain again.

Test Record

	M	I	NO	Runs	HS	Avge	100s	RC	Wkts	Avge	BB	Ct
v Australia	20	35	2	1138	125	34.48	1	10	0	–	–	20
v West Indies	22	42	3	1342	132	34.41	6	1	0	–	–	20
v New Zealand	11	18	3	603	137*	40.20	2	–	–	–	–	13
v India	13	22	2	877	139	43.85	3	6	1	6.00	1–6	13
v Pakistan	6	11	0	126	33	11.45	–	–	–	–	–	5
v Sri Lanka	2	3	0	178	107	59.33	1	6	0	–	–	2
	74	131	10	4264	139	35.23	13	23	1	23.00	1–6	73

Test Record as Captain

				M	I	NO	Runs	HS	Avge	100s	RC	Wkts	Avge	BB	Ct
v Australia	–	L1	–	1	2	0	46	32	23.00	–	–	–	–	–	–
v West Indies	–	L2	–	2	4	0	201	119	50.25	1	–	–	–	–	2
	–	L3	–	3	6	0	247	119	41.16	1	–	–	–	–	2

AUSTRALIA

Australia and Test Captaincy

According to Jack Pollard, the noted historian of Australian cricket, the 'Captaincy of the Australian Test cricket team remains the most prestigious job in Australian sport.' Pollard gives as his reason for this that the men who have captained Australia 'have had a unique blend of toughness and skill, and in building up Australia's exceptional record they helped give a young country an identity all could appreciate.'

If Pollard's assertion that all of the men who have been captain of Australia 'have had a special aura' seems rather naive, the captaincy of Australia has generally excited less debate and controversy than the captaincy of England, and Australian leaders tend to have a longer tenure of office than their English counterparts. Since Allan Border became captain of Australia in 1985, England has had six different leaders.

Whereas English selectors have wrestled over the problem of picking an effective leader of men and have constantly been influenced by questions of class structure and school background, the Australians have adopted the policy of choosing the best 11 men and then nominating the captain as the most respected player amongst the eleven. There has rarely, if ever, been a case of an Australian captain being chosen for what the English would see as qualities of leadership. In Australia, it has first been necessary to make the team on merit as a player. It would have been inconceivable for a Stanyforth, Harold Gilligan or Howard to have captained Australia.

The Australians, of course, were not burdened by the distinction between amateur and professional. It was not possible to earn a full-time living as a cricketer in Australia, and their players were classified as amateurs. The former Glamorgan captain and stalwart J.C. Clay gave a clear indication of the truth when he wrote, 'The only sane view of the amateur or professional question is the Australian one – "Call us what you something well like but we want half the gate."'

The first captain of Australia was David Gregory, and he was elected by his fellow players. This was the method generally adopted by the Australians in the early days of what later became known as Test cricket, and in essence it established a tradition to which selectors have generally adhered. The naming of an Australian captain has rarely been greeted with surprise.

Giffen, Harry Trott and Darling were among the earlier Australian captains to be elected to the post by their team-mates, and all were men with a certain streak of toughness in them. This toughness is a quality which the Australians admire and an area in which they believe they are superior to their English opponents. They also believe that they learned how to be tough from W.G. Grace.

The first England tour of Australia was in 1861–62 and a second party toured two years later. Grace took a side in 1873–74 and prided himself on the influence he had had in raising standards in Australia. He advised on the improvement of wickets and umpiring and commented on the lack of important matches.

Grace was quick to note that 'the best cricketers we met were, as a rule, English University and Public School men, who had settled in the Colony, but some of the native born showed considerable aptitude, especially in bowling.' By the time of the first Test match in March 1877, five of the Australian side were 'native born'. Indeed, Australia have had only two captains who were born overseas: Horan, in Ireland, and McDonnell, in London. England's list of captains abounds with men born in foreign lands.

However undeveloped Grace may have found Australian cricket to have been in 1873, it was the national sport four years later. Of the first nine Test matches played between England and Australia, five were won by Australia and two were drawn. The Australians learned very quickly.

David William GREGORY

New South Wales

Born: Fairy Meadow, New South Wales, 15 April 1845
Died: Turramurra, New South Wales, 4 August 1919

A member of a famous family which gave half a dozen cricketers to Australia and New South Wales, David Gregory was not, in fact, captain of New South Wales when he was elected to lead the 'Grand Combined Melbourne and Sydney XI' against James Lillywhite's professional touring team in March 1877. A big man with a full black beard, he had a commanding presence, and he was tactically aware and able to readjust to conditions and circumstances. 'Like many Australian batsmen in those early days, he had no grace or style to recommend him, but his defence was stubborn, and he lacked neither pluck nor patience.'

He led the Australians in England in 1878 and it was the victory over MCC in one day at Lord's that made all realise that Australia were now on level terms with England.

Test Record as Captain

				M	I	NO	Runs	HS	Avge	100s	RC	Wkts	Avge	BB	Ct
v England	W2	L1	–	3	5	2	60	43	20.00	–	9	0	–	–	–

William Lloyd MURDOCH

New South Wales and Sussex

Born: Sandhurst, Victoria, 18 October 1854
Died: Melbourne, 18 February 1911

For the second Test match in 1877, Gregory dropped his brother Ned, Horan and the ex-Rugby batsman Cooper to bring in Spofforth, Kelly and Murdoch. Although Murdoch was in the side, Blackham continued to keep wicket. This was the first of 16 consecutive Test matches in which Murdoch played, and he led Australia in 14 of them.

Murdoch was Australia's first truly great batsman and in world cricket only W.G. Grace stood ahead of him in his era. He first toured England in 1878 and was a member of the side that beat MCC in one day. He stumped two off the fearsome fast bowling of Spofforth, 'The Demon'. When Australia returned to England in 1880 Murdoch was captain. It was the first of four tours on which he led Australia.

In his first Test as captain, at The Oval in 1880, he hit 153 not out, so becoming the first Test captain to score a hundred. It was his first century in first-class cricket.

At The Oval in 1884, he scored 211, the first double century in Test cricket, and shared a third wicket stand of 207 with Dr Henry Scott.

A man of great personal charm, he overcame Lord Harris' opposition to matches between the two countries after his lordship's treatment at Sydney in 1879, and he furthered the cause of Australian cricket in his negotiations for fixtures. A member of the legal profession, he allied a fine knowledge of the game to a sense of fun. Men were happy to play under Murdoch, and if he had a fault as a captain, it was that he was prepared to listen to too many opinions.

He kept wicket less as he grew older, and in any case Blackham was the regular Australian 'keeper. Murdoch led Australia against England in the first Test of the 1884–85 series after which

he, together with the other 10 members of his side, stepped down following a dispute with officials over terms. He retired to his legal practice and did not play again until 1890 when he was persuaded to lead Australia in England. He was then 36 years old and after the tour the selectors dropped him on account of his age. Murdoch responded by emigrating to England and captaining Sussex from 1893 to 1899.

In 1891–92 he toured South Africa with W.W. Read's side and appeared in the Test match. It was while watching Australia play South Africa at Melbourne that Murdoch died of a heart attack.

Test Record

	M	I	NO	Runs	HS	Avge	100s	RC	Wkts	Avge	BB	Ct/st
v England	18	33	5	896	211	32.00	2	–	–	–	–	13/1
For England v South Africa	1	1	0	12	12	12.00	–	–	–	–	–	–/1
	19	34	5	908	211	31.31	2	–	–	–	–	13/2

Test Record as Captain

				M	I	NO	Runs	HS	Avge	100s	RC	Wkts	Avge	BB	Ct/st
v England	W5	L7	D4	16	29	4	877	211	35.08	2	–	–	–	–	12/1

Thomas Patrick HORAN

Victoria

Born: Midleton, County Cork, Ireland,
8 March 1854
Died: Malvern, Victoria, 16 April 1916

'Felix' Horan was brought to Australia as a child and first played for Victoria in 1874–75. He batted number three in the inaugural Test match and hit 12 and 20, which was top score in the second innings. A powerful batsman and a round-arm medium pace bowler, he sported mutton chop whiskers and wore black pads and no batting gloves.

He was a strong personality, but his two matches as captain of Australia were in most

The black-padded Irishman Tom Horan whose two Test matches as captain of Australia proved disastrous because he led a side weakened by dispute (Ken Kelly)

unfortunate circumstances and Australia were crushed in both games. When Murdoch stood down from the second Test in 1884–85, Horan captained a side which included nine men new to Test cricket and five of them were never to play for Australia again. Massie captained in the third Test, and Blackham in the fourth. Horan was captain again for the fifth Test and this proved to be his last appearance for Australia.

His two sons played for Victoria while he won renown as a journalist under the name of 'Felix'.

Test Record

	M	I	NO	Runs	HS	Avge	100s	RC	Wkts	Avge	BB	Ct
v England	15	27	2	471	124	18.84	1	143	11	13.00	6–40	6

Test Record as Captain

				M	I	NO	Runs	HS	Avge	100s	RC	Wkts	Avge	BB	Ct
v England	–	L2	–	2	4	0	99	63	24.75	–	5	0	–	–	2

Hugh Hamon MASSIE

New South Wales

Born: nr Belfast (now Port Fairy), Victoria, 11 April 1854
Died: Point Piper, New South Wales, 12 October 1938

A batsman of admirable physique, Massie was invited to tour England in 1880 but was forced to decline for business reasons. His Test debut came in the first match of the 1881–82 series when Horan hit a century and shared Australia's first three-figured partnership with Giffen. Massie himself recorded his single Test fifty at The Oval in 1882.

He captained Australia in the third Test match of 1884–85, succeeding Murdoch and Horan. Needing 214 to win, England were 194 for 6 but Australia gained a sensational victory by six runs. Blackham was made captain for the next match and Massie did not play Test cricket again. His career in banking prevented him from playing as often as he would have wished.

Test Record

	M	I	NO	Runs	HS	Avge	100s	RC	Wkts	Avge	BB	Ct
v England	9	16	0	249	55	15.56	–	–	–	–	–	5

Test Record as Captain

				M	I	NO	Runs	HS	Avge	100s	RC	Wkts	Avge	BB	Ct
v England	W1	–	–	1	2	0	23	21	11.50	–	–	–	–	–	1

John McCarthy BLACKHAM

Victoria

Born: North Fitzroy, Victoria, 11 May 1854
Died: Melbourne, 28 December 1932

Spofforth declined to play in the inaugural Test match because Billy Murdoch was not chosen as wicket-keeper. That honour went to Jack Blackham who kept wicket for Australia in each of the first 17 Test matches and went on every one of the first eight tours to England.

He was described as 'the prince of wicket-keepers' and his team-mate Giffen recalled, 'One could not help admiring him as he stood behind the stumps at critical periods of a game. With dark eyes as keen as a hawk, and regardless of knocks, he would take the fastest bowling with marvellous dexterity, and woe betide the batsman who even so much as lifted the heel of his back foot as he played forward and missed the ball.' Occasionally, for a rest, Blackham would field as Murdoch kept wicket.

His ability in standing close to the stumps for even the quickest of bowlers was a contributory factor in the disappearance of long-stop as a fielding position. Blackham was also a useful defensive batsman, but it was felt that, reliable as he was in all other fields, he tended to be too nervous as a captain. He first led Australia in the fourth Test of the 1884–85 series. His side won to level the rubber but he was replaced by Felix Horan for the final Test and did not

captain Australia again until 1891–92.

He led the Australian side in England in 1893 and in the first Test against England in 1894–95. England followed-on 261 runs in arrears but hit 437 in their second innings. Needing 177 to win, Australia fell 11 short of their target to give England a sensational victory. Blackham's gloom and nervousness did not encourage a side who were caught on a damp wicket drying under a hot sun. He damaged a thumb in the second England innings and the injury brought an end to a great career.

Test Record

	M	I	NO	Runs	HS	Avge	100s	RC	Wkts	Avge	BB	Ct/st
v England	35	62	11	800	74	15.68	–	–	–	–	–	37/24

Test Record as Captain

				M	I	NO	Runs	HS	Avge	100s	RC	Wkts	Avge	BB	Ct/st
v England	W3	L3	D2	8	14	7	154	74	22.00	–	–	–	–	–	11/4

Dr Henry James Herbert SCOTT

Victoria

Born: Toorak, Victoria, 26 December 1858
Died: Scone, New South Wales, 23 September 1910

To take the fifth Australian side to England in 1886, the Melbourne Cricket Club, who were organising the tour, chose H.J.H. Scott, then completing a degree in medicine.

A defensive right-handed batsman, Scott had toured England in 1884, played in all three Tests and hit 102 in the third when he and Murdoch created a Test record by adding 207 for the third wicket. He had also played in two of the

matches in the 1884–85 series, which had seen the selectors change the captaincy for each Test, and he had the most difficult of tasks in 1886.

Injuries to Spofforth and Bonnor dispirited the side. The fielding was slovenly and there were internal divisions which Scott, inexperienced as a captain, was unable to handle. All three Tests were lost and Scott played no more Test cricket.

He became a pioneer doctor in the bush, became mayor of Scone and died of typhoid contracted on one of his ventures to a remote outpost. A hospital was named after him, and the Australian poet Banjo Paterson, a close friend, was among the chief mourners at his funeral.

Test Record

	M	I	NO	Runs	HS	Avge	100s	RC	Wkts	Avge	BB	Ct
v England	8	14	1	359	102	27.61	1	26	0	–	–	8

Test Record as Captain

				M	I	NO	Runs	HS	Avge	100s	RC	Wkts	Avge	BB	Ct
v England	–	L3	–	3	6	0	110	47	18.33	–	–	–	–	–	2

Percy Stanislaus McDONNELL

Victoria, New South Wales and Queensland

Born: Kensington, London, 13 November 1858
Died: Brisbane, 24 September 1896

A joyful man whose passionate study of Greek prevented him from playing cricket on several occasions and kept him out of the 1886 tour of England, 'Greatheart' McDonnell was a right-handed batsman with a sound defence and plenty of attacking shots. He was noted for his tenacious batting on rain-affected wickets.

His debut for Australia was in the Oval Test of 1880, the first Test match to be played in England. In the fourth match in which he played, at Sydney in 1882, he made 147. He became the first batsman to score centuries in successive Test innings when he hit 103 at The Oval in 1884 and 124 at Adelaide four months later, and came close to making three centuries in succession, run out for 83 in the second innings at Adelaide.

He had the reputation of being a splendid team man and he succeeded Scott as captain of Australia after the 1886 tour of England. His period of stewardship came at a most unfortunate time. Australia were at their weakest and England at their strongest. McDonnell was lacking in experience and even his jollity could not lift the side.

McDonnell was forced out of cricket through ill health and died of consumption before his 38th birthday.

'Greatheart' McDonnell led Australia at a time when England were at their strongest. His main interest was the study of Greek (Allsport)

Test Record

	M	I	NO	Runs	HS	Avge	100s	RC	Wkts	Avge	BB	Ct
v England	19	34	1	950	147	28.78	3	53	0	–	–	6

Test Record as Captain

				I	NO	Runs	HS	Avge	100s	RC	Wkts	Avge	BB	Ct
v England	W1	L5	–	6	12	0	138	35	11.50	–	–	–	–	–	1

George GIFFEN

South Australia

Born: Adelaide, 27 March 1859
Died: Adelaide, 29 November 1927

Regarded as the W.G. Grace of Australia, George Giffen was a right-handed batsman who liked to attack and a slow-medium pace bowler. In his 30th and penultimate Test match at Old Trafford in 1896, he became the first man to complete 1000 runs and take 100 wickets in Test cricket.

His Test debut was at Melbourne in 1881–82 but it was not until the series a year later that he was used fully as a bowler. He toured England five times and completed the 'double' on the last three occasions, 1886, 1893 and 1896.

At Sydney in December 1894, he hit 161 and

41, and took 4 for 75 and 4 for 164, so becoming the only player to score 200 runs and take eight wickets in a Test match between England and Australia. Ironically, he finished on the losing side as England won after being forced to follow-on.

Blackham was injured in that match and Giffen took over as captain for the remainder of the rubber. He was elected captain by the rest of the players, but he was too involved with his own all-round contribution to be a good captain He over-bowled himself, and the jibe was that he changed the bowling simply by putting himself on at the other end.

He did not captain Australia again after the 1894–95 series and his Test career ended in England in 1896. His book *With Bat and Ball* remains one of the treasures of cricket literature, with its comments on the cricketers of Giffen's period.

Test Record

	M	I	NO	Runs	HS	Avge	100s	RC	Wkts	Avge	BB	Ct
v England	31	53	0	1238	161	23.35	1	2791	103	27.09	7–117	24

Test Record as Captain

	W2	L2	–	4	7	0	273	58	39.00	–	581	26	22.34	6–155	4
v England															

George Henry Stevens TROTT

Victoria

Born: Collingwood, 5 August 1866
Died: Albert Park, Victoria, 10 November 1917

'No Australian Captain was more popular in England, and good judges thought him as great as any Australian Captain. By his pleasant character he won the regard of cricketers wherever he played.' So wrote Pelham Warner of Harry Trott, a high-class right-handed batsman adaptable to all conditions and situations, and a medium pace leg-break bowler. He was the elder brother of Albert Trott, of Australia and Middlesex, and Fred Trott.

He toured England four times, in 1888, 1890, 1893 and 1896, and it was on the first of those trips that he made his Test debut. He captained Australia for the first time on the 1896 tour as his side was beaten by two Tests to one. In Australia in 1897–98, Australia lost the first Test but won the last four to regain the Ashes. 'Blessed with a humour that nothing could ruffle, Harry Trott was always master both of himself and of his team.'

His one Test century came at Lord's in 1896 when he made a valiant attempt to ward off defeat after his side had been bowled out for 53 in their first innings.

Harry Trott's health broke down after the 1897–98 series, and for a time he received treat-

A fine captain and a top class all-rounder, Harry Trott (Ken Kelly)

ment in a psychiatric institution. Happily, with help from friends and public, he recovered and played occasionally for Victoria from 1903–04 until 1907–08.

Test Record

	M	I	NO	Runs	HS	Avge	100s	RC	Wkts	Avge	BB	Ct
v England	24	42	0	921	143	21.92	1	1019	29	35.13	4–71	21

Test Record as Captain

				M	I	NO	Runs	HS	Avge	100s	RC	Wkts	Avge	BB	Ct
v England	W5	L3	–	8	12	0	350	143	29.16	–	396	11	36.00	2–13	11

Joseph DARLING

South Australia

Born: Glen Osmond, Adelaide, 21 November 1870
Died: Hobart, Tasmania, 2 January 1946

Son of a member of the Legislative Council of South Australia who was responsible for introducing the bill granting a lease on parklands that became known as the Adelaide Oval, Joe Darling excelled in cricket for Prince Alfred College. He worked for a time in a bank after leaving school, but he was appointed manager of one of the family's wheat farms and seemed lost to sport.

In 1893–94 he returned to Adelaide to open a sports store. He immediately re-established himself as a left-handed batsman capable of sound defence and bold hitting. Thickset with a face browned by the sun, he made his Test debut in 1894–95, playing in all five matches of the rubber in which Australia were beaten 3–2.

He moved up to open the innings on the first of his four tours of England in 1896 and captained the side on his next three visits, in 1899, 1902 and 1905. His supremacy was asserted against MacLaren's team in 1897–98, when he became the first batsman to hit three centuries in a Test rubber and the first to aggregate 500 runs in a series. His 160 in the final Test came in

only 175 minutes and contained a record 20 fours. In the third Test at Adelaide he had made 178, reaching his century with the first six ever hit in Test cricket. (At this time, a batsman had to hit the ball out of the ground in order to be awarded six.)

Darling's captaincy began with a winning series in England in 1899 and continued in the same vein in 1901–02, when he missed the last two matches, and 1902. He then led the first Australian team to South Africa in 1902–03. He did not play against England the following season but returned to lead the side to England in 1905, when his tactics seemed over-cautious and he lost the series to Jackson's men. This proved to be the end of Darling's Test career. He led Australia in 18 Tests against England, a number bettered only by Bradman and Border.

Darling was a man of the utmost integrity, as strong in mind as he was in body. He had been elected to the captaincy by his fellow players who revered him. He worked tirelessly to improve their conditions and terms, and he led them with discipline that was uncompromising.

He retired in 1905 in order to help his wife raise their ten sons and five daughters. In 1908 he sold the sports shop in Adelaide and settled in Tasmania, where he reared merino sheep and served in the parliament from 1921 until 1946. In politics, as in cricket, he was forceful, popular and incorruptible.

Test Record

	M	I	NO	Runs	HS	Avge	100s	RC	Wkts	Avge	BB	Ct
v England	31	55	2	1632	178	30.79	3	–	–	–	–	23
v South Africa	3	5	0	25	14	5.00	–	–	–	–	–	4
	34	60	2	1657	178	28.56	3	–	–	–	–	27

Test Record as Captain

				M	I	NO	Runs	HS	Avge	100s	RC	Wkts	Avge	BB	Ct
v England	W5	L4	D9	18	32	2	725	73	25.89	–	–	–	–	–	11
v South Africa	W2	–	D1	3	5	0	25	14	5.00	–	–	–	–	–	4
	W7	L4	D10	21	37	2	750	73	21.42	–	–	–	–	–	15

Hugh TRUMBLE

Victoria

Born: Abbotsford, Victoria, 12 May 1867
Died: Hawthorn, Victoria, 14 August 1938

Hugh Trumble toured England five times and, after the first tour in 1890, was immensely successful as a right-arm fast-medium pace bowler of infinite variety and as a capable middle-order batsman. Pelham Warner described him as a great camel, and his prominent ears and large nose were usually surmounted by a large stetson specially imported from America.

Grace called him the 'best bowler Australia has sent us', and Fry considered him not only one of the best bowlers of all time but also a most acute judge and observer of the game, 'a perfect master of the whole art of placing fieldsmen and changing bowlers'.

He played for Australia from 1890 until 1903–04. In 1901–02 he performed the hat-trick against England at Melbourne; and two years later, on the same ground, he again performed the hat-trick, taking 7 for 28 in what proved to be his last first-class match.

At The Oval in 1902 he took 8 for 65 and 4 for 108, and scored 64 not out and 7 not out to become the first Australian to take 10 wickets and score 50 in a Test match. In the absence of Darling, he led Australia twice in 1901–02 and proved to be a most intelligent and able captain.

One of the most intelligent of cricketers and one of the greatest of bowlers, Hugh Trumble. That he captained Australia only twice was a surprise to all (Allsport)

Test Record

	M	I	NO	Runs	HS	Avge	100s	RC	Wkts	Avge	BB	Ct
v England	31	55	13	838	70	19.95	–	2945	141	20.88	8–65	45
v South Africa	1	2	1	13	13	13.00	–	127	0	–	–	–
	32	57	14	851	70	19.79	–	3072	141	21.78	8–65	45

Test Record as Captain

		M	I	NO	Runs	HS	Avge	100s	RC	Wkts	Avge	BB	Ct
v England	W2	2	3	0	31	22	10.33	–	191	11	17.36	5–62	4

Montague Alfred NOBLE

New South Wales

Born: Sydney, 28 January 1873
Died: Randwick, New South Wales, 22 June 1940

Banker, dentist, manufacturer's agent, writer, broadcaster, right-handed batsman with a sound defence and the ability to hit hard when necessary, off-break bowler at medium pace and brilliant fielder, Monty Noble stood over six feet tall and was a master of the game.

On the occasion of his Test debut, against England at Melbourne in January 1898, he took 6 for 49, and he followed this with eight wickets in his next Test. He first captained Australia in the 1903–04 series against England and hit his only Test century in his first match as captain, at Sydney. He was also captain in 1907–08 and 1909.

He was a most experienced cricketer by the time that he came to lead Australia and he proved to be even a stronger disciplinarian than Darling. He rebuked his players for talking to spectators and urged abstinence during a Test match. Throughout his life he was dedicated to the ethics of the game. He was solid, alert and competent, deeply respected by his opponents.

Test Record

	M	I	NO	Runs	HS	Avge	100s	RC	Wkts	Avge	BB	Ct
v England	39	68	6	1905	133	30.72	1	2860	115	24.86	7–17	26
v South Africa	3	5	1	92	53*	23.00	–	165	6	27.50	3–75	–
	42	73	7	1997	133	30.25	1	3025	121	25.00	7–17	26

Test Record as Captain

				M	I	NO	Runs	HS	Avge	100s	RC	Wkts	Avge	BB	Ct
v England	W8	L5	D2	15	29	3	992	133	38.15	1	745	31	24.03	7–100	12

Clement HILL

South Australia

Born: Adelaide, 18 March 1877
Died: Melbourne, 5 September 1945

A short, powerful left-handed batsman with a crouched stance, Clem Hill delighted observers with both his defence and his explosive attack. He was particularly fine on hard wickets and in placing the ball on the leg side, but he also had the best of temperaments and rarely failed on big occasions. He was an outstanding fielder in the deep, where he took some memorable catches. His catch to dismiss Lilley at Old Trafford in 1902 has become of Test match legend.

A prolific scorer as a schoolboy cricketer, he topped the South Australian batting averages at the age of 18. He was not in the side that was originally chosen to tour England in 1896, but a double century against New South Wales caused a public outcry at his omission and a late invitation.

He played in all three Tests on that tour, but with no success. His potential was obvious, however, and 96 in the first Test of 1897–98 was followed by innings of 58, 81 and 188. This last innings, at Melbourne, remains the highest score made by a batsman under 21 in Test matches between England and Australia.

In three successive Test innings in 1901–02, he was dismissed for 99, 98 and 97, the first batsman to suffer such a fate, and in 1902 he scored 119 in the only Test match ever to be played at Bramall Lane, Sheffield.

He declined to tour England in 1909 because he said that he distrusted the Australian Board of Control's terms, and he refused to tour again in 1912 because, in company with five others, he protested against the players not being allowed to choose their own manager. By that time he had become captain of Australia.

Hill succeeded Noble as captain for the 1910–11 series against South Africa and hit 191 in his first Test in charge. Australia won the series 4–1 but the scores were reversed the following season when England, under Johnny Douglas, were the visitors.

To lose at home to England does not put an Australian captain in the top bracket, and Hill's period of office was shot with controversy. In 1911, he had a widely-reported fist fight with fellow selector Peter McAlister over the composition of the Test side. The fight is said to have lasted twenty minutes.

Hill was a man of principle, and he was popular with his team-mates. Although his Test career ended in 1911–12, he played for South Australia until 1922–23, and at the time of his retirement he was the leading run-scorer in Sheffield Shield cricket.

It was said that Hill's severest critic was his wife, who scored at each match and confronted him about errors at the end of the day.

Test Record

	M	I	NO	Runs	HS	Avge	100s	RC	Wkts	Avge	BB	Ct
v England	41	76	1	2660	188	35.46	4	–	–	–	–	30
v South Africa	8	13	1	752	191	62.66	3	–	–	–	–	3
	49	89	2	3412	191	39.21	7	–	–	–	–	33

Test Record as Captain

				M	I	NO	Runs	HS	Avge	100s	RC	Wkts	Avge	BB	Ct
v England	W1	L4	–	5	10	0	274	98	27.40	–	–	–	–	–	8
v South Africa	W4	L1	–	5	8	0	425	191	53.12	2	–	–	–	–	3
	W5	L5	–	10	18	0	699	191	38.83	2	–	–	–	–	11

Sydney Edward GREGORY

New South Wales

Born: Randwick, New South Wales, 14 April 1870
Died: Randwick, New South Wales, 1 August 1929

Known as 'Little Tich' because he was only 5ft 4in tall, Syd Gregory was a quick-scoring, technically sound batsman whose consistency and brilliant fielding at cover kept him in the Australian side for 22 years. He made the first of his eight tours to England in 1890 and played in two of the three Tests. His first Test century came at Sydney in December 1894 when he hit 201 in 244 minutes. This was the first double century to be scored in a Test match in Australia. He also made hundreds at Lord's in 1896, The Oval in 1899 and Adelaide in 1903–04.

Syd Gregory played for Australia for 22 years but was left to lead a poor side in the Triangular tournament of 1912 (Ken Kelly)

When Clem Hill and five other leading players refused to play in the Triangular Tournament in England in 1912 because of their disagreement with the Australian Board, Syd Gregory was recalled after being out of Test cricket for three years to captain the side. It was a woefully weak and ill-disciplined party, and Gregory was then 42 and past his best.

He was the nephew of Australia's first captain, and the cousin of pace bowler Jack Gregory.

Test Record

	M	I	NO	Runs	HS	Avge	100s	RC	Wkts	Avge	BB	Ct
v England	52	92	7	2193	201	25.80	4	33	0	–	–	24
v South Africa	6	8	0	89	37	11.12	–	–	–	–	–	1
	58	100	7	2282	201	24.53	4	33	0	–	–	25

Test Record as Captain

				M	I	NO	Runs	HS	Avge	100s	RC	Wkts	Avge	BB	Ct
v England	–	L1	D2	3	3	0	12	10	4.00	–	–	–	–	–	–
v South Africa	W2	–	D1	3	3	0	60	37	20.00	–	–	–	–	–	–
	W2	L1	D3	6	6	0	72	37	12.00	–	–	–	–	–	–

Warwick Windridge ARMSTRONG

Victoria

Born: Kyneton, Victoria, 22 May 1879
Died: Darling Point, New South Wales,
13 July 1947

If the name of Jardine can still excite anger in the breasts of Australians, the name of Warwick Armstrong can have the same effect on Englishmen. The two leaders had something in common: they were both totally professional in their approach to the game and they were both winners. Those whom they beat accused them of arrogance and contemptuousness.

Everything about Warwick Armstrong was on the grand scale. He was over six feet tall and by the time he retired in 1921–22 he weighed 22 stone. His cricket began in the golden age, but he became the bridge to the modern game with captaincy that was forthright, relentless, shrewd, calculating, persistent and even ruthless. He was the forerunner of much that was to come later.

He made his debut for Victoria in 1898–99, and for Australia in 1901–02. He first toured England in 1902, and this was to be the only occasion in four visits to England when he did not perform the 'double'. Armstrong was a great all-rounder. He was a relentlessly accurate leg-break bowler, having originally bowled fast-medium pace, and he was a fine stroke-player who relished a fight when his colleagues were failing.

He became the only Australian to carry his bat through an innings against South Africa in 1902–03, and he became a mighty force in the Australian side of the Edwardian period although his relationships with the Board were always strained. He was one of the six players who refused to appear in the Triangular Tournament of 1912, and he was a constant champion of his fellow cricketers.

Armstrong moved into the captaincy of his country when cricket resumed after the First World War. He hit 158 against England in his first match as captain and scored two more centuries in the series which Australia won by five matches to nil, an unprecedented achievement. In spite of this, he was not a unanimous choice to lead Australia in England in 1921, for there were many in administration who resented his power and authority, but Armstrong's players never wavered in their loyalty to him.

The first three Tests in England were won and the last two drawn. He retired from Test cricket after that series with a record that has remained the envy of all ever since.

It was perhaps unfortunate that his career as a journalist should be punctuated with some bitter attacks on others, but nothing can detract from the achievements of 'The Big Ship'.

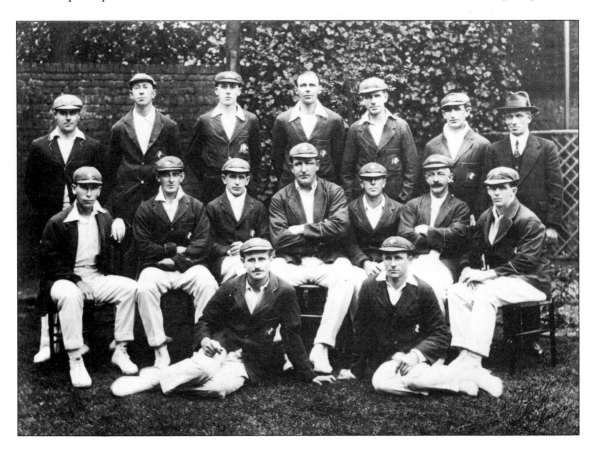

The all-conquering Australian side of 1921 led by Warwick Armstrong. Back row, left to right: W. Bardsley, J. Ryder, H.S.T.L. Hendry, J.M. Gregory, E.R. Mayne, T.J.E. Andrews, S. Smith (manager). Front: A.A. Mailey, E.A. McDonald, H.L. Collins, W.W. Armstrong, C.G. Macartney, H. Carter, J.M. Taylor. On ground: C.E. Pellew and W.A.S. Oldfield. Collins and Bardsley were both to captain Australia after Armstrong (Lemmon)

Test Record

	M	I	NO	Runs	HS	Avge	100s	RC	Wkts	Avge	BB	Ct
v England	42	71	9	2172	158	35.03	4	2288	74	30.91	6–35	37
v South Africa	8	13	1	691	159*	57.58	2	635	13	48.84	4–103	7
	50	84	10	2863	159*	38.68	6	2923	87	33.59	6–35	44

Test Record as Captain

		M	I	NO	Runs	HS	Avge	100s	RC	Wkts	Avge	BB	Ct
v England	W8 – D2	10	13	2	616	158	56.00	3	416	17	24.47	4–26	8

Herbert Leslie COLLINS

New South Wales

Born: Darlinghurst, New South Wales,
21 January 1889
Died: Sydney, 28 May 1959

Herbie Collins made his debut for New South Wales in 1909–10 and went with Australian sides to New Zealand and North America before the First World War. He first came to prominence as captain of the Australian Imperial Forces team which played in England in 1919. He performed the 'double' in that season with his slow left-arm bowling supporting his sound right-handed opening batting.

He played in eight Tests under Armstrong, and took over the captaincy in South Africa on the way back to Australia in 1921–22, when Armstrong declared himself unfit. Collins continued to lead Australia, against England in 1924–25 and 1926, when he missed two Tests through illness.

He was a thoughtful captain who attempted to analyse a day's play and to draw up campaigns in advance, but he was also rather lax with his players and could not maintain the same ruthless efficiency that Armstrong had shown with a great side which, in fairness, began to show signs of decline when Collins took over.

Test Record

	M	I	NO	Runs	HS	Avge	100s	RC	Wkts	Avge	BB	Ct
v England	16	26	0	1012	162	38.92	3	236	3	78.66	2–47	11
v South Africa	3	5	1	340	203	85.00	1	16	1	16.00	1–9	2
	19	31	1	1352	203	45.06	4	252	4	63.00	2–47	13

Test Record as Captain

				M	I	NO	Runs	HS	Avge	100s	RC	Wkts	Avge	BB	Ct
v England	W4	L2	D2	8	14	0	384	114	27.42	1	113	1	113.00	1–36	4
v South Africa	W1	–	D2	3	5	1	340	203	85.00	1	16	1	16.00	1–9	2
	W5	L2	D4	11	19	1	724	203	40.22	2	129	2	64.50	1–9	6

Warren BARDSLEY

New South Wales

Born: Nevertire, Warren, New South Wales,
7 December 1882
Died: Collaroy, New South Wales, 20 January 1954

A stylish left-handed opening batsman of impeccable technique, Warren Bardsley made his Test debut on the tour of England in 1909 and, at The Oval, became the first batsman to score a century in each innings of a Test match. He hit 193 not out in the Lord's Test of 1926, the highest score in a Lord's Test at that time, and captained Australia in that series when Collins was in hospital.

Test Record

	M	I	NO	Runs	HS	Avge	100s	RC	Wkts	Avge	BB	Ct
v England	30	49	4	1487	193*	33.04	3	–	–	–	–	6
v South Africa	11	17	1	982	164	61.37	3	–	–	–	–	6
	41	66	5	2469	193*	40.47	6	–	–	–	–	12

Test Record as Captain

				M	I	NO	Runs	HS	Avge	100s	RC	Wkts	Avge	BB	Ct
v England	–	–	D2	2	2	0	15	15	7.50	–	–	–	–	–	1

John RYDER

Victoria

Born: Collingwood, Victoria, 8 August 1889
Died: Fitzroy, Victoria, 3 April 1977

Jack Ryder made his Test debut in the 1920–21 series against England and toured England in 1921 without appearing in a Test match. An aggressive middle-order batsman and medium pace bowler, he hit his maiden Test century against South Africa in 1921–22 and made a double century against England at Adelaide in 1924–25. He could not find his form in England in 1926 and was dropped for the final Test, but

he was appointed captain for the series against England in 1928–29 and hit a century at Melbourne.

Not helped by some strange selections, Australia were trounced in that series by Chapman's powerful England side. Ryder was not selected for the tour of England in 1930, although he was one of the selectors – it was felt that he was too old at 41. There were public protests at his omission but he did not play Test cricket again, although he was a selector for many years. He was a shrewd and diplomatic captain who had the misfortune to lead Australia at the end of a good era against a strong England side.

Test Record

	M	I	NO	Runs	HS	Avge	100s	RC	Wkts	Avge	BB	Ct
v England	17	28	4	1060	201*	44.16	2	630	13	48.46	2–20	15
v South Africa	3	4	1	334	142	111.33	1	113	4	28.25	2–25	2
	20	**32**	**5**	**1394**	**201***	**51.62**	**3**	**743**	**17**	**43.70**	**2–20**	**17**

Test Record as Captain

				M	I	NO	Runs	HS	Avge	100s	RC	Wkts	Avge	BB	Ct
v England	W1	L4	–	5	10	1	492	112	54.66	1	180	5	36.00	2–29	8

William Maldon WOODFULL

Victoria

Born: Maldon, Victoria, 22 August 1897
Died: nr Tweed Heads, New South Wales, 11 August 1965

Bill Woodfull was a right-handed opening batsman with so stout a defence that he was termed 'unbowlable'. His career began in 1921–22 and ended after the tour of England in 1934. His Test career began in 1926, and in his third match he hit 141 and shared a record second wicket partnership of 235 with Macartney.

He was a surprising and somewhat controversial choice to lead Australia to England in 1930, but with Bradman in devastating form, he won the series. Woodfull himself hit 155 at Lord's.

Under Woodfull, Australia ravaged both West Indies and South Africa, but against Jardine, Larwood and 'bodyline' in 1932–33, the outcome was much different. A schoolmaster, the son of a clergyman and a man of calm and dignity, Woodfull accused England of not playing the game, and his and the general Australian response to Jardine and Larwood virtually ensured that those two would not oppose Australia in 1934 when, with Bradman again in dominant form and the England attack toothless and ill-led, they regained the Ashes.

A true assessment of Woodfull as a captain is difficult, for the deeds of Bradman intrude. Australia had been given little hope in England in 1930 but they won in spite of having a very limited attack. Woodfull was a traditionalist in a changing world. A man of calm and common sense, he was highly respected by his players. His record as a captain is an impressive one.

The 'unbowlable' schoolmaster – Bill Woodfull (Allsport)

Test Record

	M	I	NO	Runs	HS	Avge	100s	RC	Wkts	Avge	BB	Ct
v England	25	41	3	1675	155	44.07	6	–	–	–	–	5
v South Africa	5	7	1	421	161	70.16	1	–	–	–	–	1
v West Indies	5	6	0	204	83	34.00	–	–	–	–	–	1
	35	54	4	2300	161	46.00	7	–	–	–	–	7

Test Record as Captain

				M	I	NO	Runs	HS	Avge	100s	RC	Wkts	Avge	BB	Ct
v England	W5	L6	D4	15	25	2	878	155	38.17	1	–	–	–	–	–
v South Africa	W5	–	–	5	7	1	421	161	70.16	1	–	–	–	–	1
v West Indies	W4	L1	–	5	6	0	204	83	34.00	–	–	–	–	–	1
	W14	L7	D4	25	38	3	1503	161	42.94	2	–	–	–	–	2

Victor York RICHARDSON

South Australia

Born: Unley, Adelaide, 7 September 1894
Died: Fullarton Park, Adelaide, 29 October 1969

Victor Richardson, the grandfather of the Chappell brothers, made his Test debut in the 1924–25 series against England and hit his only Test century in the second match of the rubber. A forceful, right-handed middle-order batsman, he could not hold a regular place in the Australian side and missed the 1926 tour of England. He played in only two Tests in the 1928–29 series and had no success, but was named as vice-captain for the tour of England in 1930. Again his form was poor, and he did not play in the final Test.

He batted bravely against Larwood and Voce in 1932–33 but, as a veteran, he was not chosen for the 1934 tour of England. Following Woodfull's retirement, Richardson led Australia in South Africa in 1935–36. Bradman was not on the tour, but Australia were highly successful and Richardson proved a good motivator and a wise and considerate leader. He was an outstanding all-round sportsman.

Test Record

	M	I	NO	Runs	HS	Avge	100s	RC	Wkts	Avge	BB	Ct
v England	14	25	0	622	136	24.88	1	–	–	–	–	15
v South Africa	5	5	0	84	45	16.80	–	–	–	–	–	9
	19	30	0	706	136	23.53	1	–	–	–	–	24

Test Record as Captain

				M	I	NO	Runs	HS	Avge	100s	RC	Wkts	Avge	BB	Ct
v South Africa	W4	–	D1	5	5	0	84	45	16.80	–	–	–	–	–	9

Sir Donald George BRADMAN

New South Wales and South Australia

Born: Cootamundra, New South Wales, 27 August 1908

There has been no greater batsman in world cricket than Don Bradman, nor has there been a more successful captain in Test cricket.

His achievements as a batsman are unparalleled. His lowest average on four tours of England, on which he never failed to score 2000 runs, was 84.16 in 1934. In his last Test match, at The Oval in 1948, most probably overcome by the emotion of the reception he received, he was bowled second ball by Eric Hollies. Had he scored four, his average in Test cricket from 80 innings would have been 100. No other batsman has remotely challenged such scoring in Test cricket, nor, indeed, in first-class cricket where he scored over 28 000 runs and averaged 95.14.

Bradman first played for New South Wales in 1927–28, making 118 at number seven against South Australia. There was a second century, against Victoria, and he made his Test debut in the first game of the rubber the following season. He made 18 and 1 against Chapman's England side and was dropped for the second Test. He returned for the third Test, scored 79 and 112, and never again was he omitted from an Australian side.

In 1928–29 he hit 452 not out in 415 minutes against Queensland at Sydney, a world record which stood for nearly 30 years, yet still there were those who had doubts as to whether he would succeed in England. The critics were soon silenced in 1930 when he hit 8 and 131 at Trent Bridge, 254 and 1 at Lord's, 334 at Headingley, 14 at Old Trafford, and 232 at The Oval. His 974 runs, average 139.14, remains a world record for any Test rubber, as does his 309 on the first day of the Headingley Test.

He was to hit another triple century at Headingley in 1934 and at The Oval he scored 244, sharing a record stand of 451 in 316 minutes with Ponsford for the second wicket. By

The great Don Bradman (Hulton)

then he had plundered the bowling of West Indies and South Africa and had suffered only the indignity of the 'bodyline' series in which, incidentally, he hit fifty in all four Tests in which he played, including a century in the second match of the series.

Throughout this period, indeed throughout his life, Bradman was a world figure, the focus of attention for the press. He was on a par with film stars and politicians of his time and such attention tended to draw him apart from his colleagues, some of whom may have become envious of the adulation he received. By instinct, he was a loner, and there were some who did not relish the inevitability of his becoming captain. Ponsford is reputed to have retired early to avoid playing under Bradman, and both Fingleton and O'Reilly, whom Bradman rated as the finest bowler he ever faced, later wrote disparagingly of him.

Bradman was unwell throughout most of the 1934 tour of England and only an emergency operation at the end of the tour prevented peritonitis and saved his life. He played no cricket in 1934–35 and did not go to South Africa in 1935–36. Had he been available it is likely that he would have been captain, for the recall of Richardson was seen as only a temporary measure.

In 1936–37, G.O.B. Allen brought over the first England side to play a Test series in Australia since the bodyline tour and Bradman was named as captain of the Australian side. His career as a captain had an inauspicious begin-

Worcester, 1948, the start of the last, triumphant tour. Alongside Bradman (left) as he leads his side onto the field are his vice-captain and successor Lindsay Hassett and the tall Ernie Toshack. Colin McCool is just behind them (Hulton)

ning. Caught on sticky wickets, Australia were beaten in the first two Tests by an England side that had been poorly selected and was not of the strongest. In the last three Tests, Bradman played innings of 270, 212 and 169, and for the first time in the history of Test cricket, a country won a rubber after losing the first two matches. Bradman's aggregate of 810 runs was the highest recorded by a captain in any Test rubber.

Bradman was to lose only one more Test in the four other series in which he led Australia, and that was at The Oval in 1938 when Australia, facing England's 903 for 7 declared, batted without Bradman and Fingleton, both of whom were injured. England's victory enabled them to draw the series, and this was the only occasion on which Bradman did not win the rubber.

A weakened, ill-fed and under-prepared England side were trounced in 1946–47, and in 1948 Bradman brought to England the finest international side which one has ever seen. They went through the tour unbeaten, and Bradman's Test career, like all else in his life, ended in triumph.

Bradman was not a supreme stylist but there was magic in the air when he batted. On the field, he was unmistakable. Like a great actor or dancer, he had an aura about him so that one never had to ask, 'Which one is Bradman?'

If there were those who found him initially too distant and did not relish the idea of playing under him, none, by the end of his career, could deny that he was a great captain as well as a great batsman. He was a tough negotiator with the deepest possible knowledge of the game. He had a total tactical awareness and a vision with which few are blessed. He smiled and laughed, but he knew only the art of winning. Test cricket has known no better captain, nor greater player.

Test Record

	M	I	NO	Runs	HS	Avge	100s	RC	Wkts	Avge	BB	Ct
v England	37	63	7	5028	334	89.78	19	51	1	51.00	1–23	20
v South Africa	5	5	1	806	299*	201.50	4	2	0	–	–	2
v West Indies	5	6	0	447	223	74.50	2	15	1	15.00	1–8	4
v India	5	6	2	715	201	178.75	4	4	0	–	–	6
	52	80	10	6996	334	99.94	29	72	2	36.00	1–8	32

Test Record as Captain

				M	I	NO	Runs	HS	Avge	100s	RC	Wkts	Avge	BB	Ct
v England	W11	L3	D5	19	32	5	2432	270	90.07	10	6	0	–	–	12
v India	W4	–	D1	5	6	2	715	201	178.75	4	4	0	–	–	6
	W15	L3	D6	24	38	7	3147	270	101.51	14	10	0	–	–	18

William Alfred BROWN

New South Wales and Queensland

Born: Toowoomba, Queensland, 31 July 1912

A fine right-handed opening batsman and a brilliant fielder, Bill Brown toured England in 1934, 1938 and 1948. He hit 105 at Lord's in 1934 in what was his second Test, and 206 not out on the same ground in 1938. He played in two Tests in 1948, having dropped down the order to accommodate Barnes and Morris, and that marked the end of a Test career which had seen this handsome player give Australia fine service.

In 1945–46, Australia sent a side to New Zealand to play a match which was only later accorded Test status. As the senior batsman in the side, Brown was appointed captain. Among the debutants for Australia were Miller, Lindwall, Tallon and Toshack, while O'Reilly was playing his last Test. New Zealand were bowled out for 42 and 54, and Brown top scored with 67 as his side won by an innings.

Bill Brown (right), who led Australia against New Zealand after the Second World War, goes out with Bradman at Trent Bridge in 1938 (Hulton)

Test Record

	M	I	NO	Runs	HS	Avge	100s	RC	Wkts	Avge	BB	Ct
v England	13	24	1	980	206*	42.60	3	–	–	–	–	9
v South Africa	5	7	0	417	121	59.57	1	–	–	–	–	1
v New Zealand	1	1	0	67	67	67.00	–	–	–	–	–	–
v India	3	3	0	128	99	42.66	–	–	–	–	–	4
	22	35	1	1592	206*	46.82	4	–	–	–	–	14

Test Record as Captain

		M	I	NO	Runs	HS	Avge	100s	RC	Wkts	Avge	BB	Ct
v New Zealand	**W1**	–	–	1	1	0	67	67	67.00	–	–	–	–	–

Arthur Lindsay HASSETT

Victoria

Born: Geelong, Victoria, 28 August 1913

A diminutive right-handed batsman of considerable power, Lindsay Hassett faced no easy task in succeeding Bradman as captain of Australia, and although he had a good record, he failed to gain the full confidence of the selectors or, indeed, the general public.

He was passed over in favour of Bill Brown when Bradman was unavailable for the match in New Zealand in 1945–46, and when Bradman retired in 1948, Hassett only narrowly won election to lead Australia in South Africa in 1949–50. He hit 112 in his first Test as captain. Australia won the series handsomely, as they did when England were the opponents in 1950–51

and when West Indies were the visitors in 1951–52.

There was some criticism of Hassett when an unfancied South African side drew the series in 1952–53, and that criticism increased when England regained the Ashes in 1953, for Australia had held them for nearly 19 years.

These criticisms were, perhaps, unfair. Bradman's great side was in decline by 1953 and Hassett himself, a cunning and tactically inventive leader with impish wit and charm, was no Bradman. He was well-liked by his side but his easy-going manner was what worried the administrators.

He was a fine batsman who made his Test debut at Trent Bridge in 1938, but he had to wait until the first Test of 1946–47 for his maiden Test century. His highest Test innings was his 198 not out against India at Adelaide in 1947–48.

Test Record

	M	I	NO	Runs	HS	Avge	100s	RC	Wkts	Avge	BB	Ct
v England	24	42	1	1572	137	38.34	4	60	0	–	–	16
v South Africa	10	14	0	748	167	53.42	3	18	0	–	–	7
v New Zealand	1	1	0	19	19	19.00	–	–	–	–	–	1
v West Indies	4	8	1	402	132	57.42	2	–	–	–	–	2
v India	4	4	1	332	198*	110.66	1	–	–	–	–	4
	43	69	3	3073	198*	46.56	10	78	0	–	–	30

Test Record as Captain

				M	I	NO	Runs	HS	Avge	100s	RC	Wkts	Avge	BB	Ct
v England	W4	L2	D4	10	19	0	731	115	38.47	2	8	0	–	–	4
v South Africa	W6	L2	D2	10	14	0	748	167	53.42	3	18	0	–	–	7
v West Indies	W4	–	–	4	8	1	402	132	57.42	2	–	–	–	–	2
	W14	L4	D6	24	41	1	1881	167	47.02	7	26	0	–	–	13

Arthur Robert MORRIS

New South Wales

Born: Dungog, New South Wales, 19 January 1922

A century in each innings on the occasion of his first-class debut for New South Wales against

Queensland in 1940–41 heralded the career of one of the most accomplished of left-handed opening batsmen to have graced the Test arena. The style was the man. He exuded charm and good humour.

He made his Test debut in 1946–47 and hit 155 in his third match. He was highly successful in England in 1948, hitting centuries at Lord's, Headingley and The Oval. He scored 206 against Brown's team at Adelaide in 1950–51, when he was vice-captain to Hassett. He was also subsequently vice-captain to Ian Johnson, although he had been expected to succeed to the captaincy.

He deputised once for Hassett, against West Indies in 1951–52, and once for Johnson, against England in 1954–55, but was beaten on both occasions.

Test Record

	M	I	NO	Runs	HS	Avge	100s	RC	Wkts	Avge	BB	Ct
v England	24	43	2	2080	206	50.73	8	39	1	39.00	1–5	9
v South Africa	10	17	0	792	157	46.58	2	11	1	11.00	1–11	2
v West Indies	8	14	0	452	111	32.28	1	–	–	–	–	1
v India	4	5	1	209	110*	52.25	1	–	–	–	–	3
	46	79	3	3533	206	46.48	12	50	2	25.00	1–5	15

Test Record as Captain

				M	I	NO	Runs	HS	Avge	100s	RC	Wkts	Avge	BB	Ct
v England	–	L1	–	1	2	0	22	12	11.00	–	–	–	–	–	–
v West Indies	–	L1	–	1	2	0	46	45	23.00	–	–	–	–	–	–
	–	L2	–	2	4	0	68	45	17.00	–	–	–	–	–	–

Ian William JOHNSON

Victoria

Born: North Melbourne, 8 December 1918

In the history of Australian Test cricket, the appointment of Ian Johnson to succeed Lindsay Hassett as captain of Australia remains among the most astonishing. In the first place, Morris, Hassett's vice-captain, Miller, Harvey and Lindwall were still active in Test cricket; and in the second place, Johnson was not sure of a place in the Australian side. A capable batsman and an off-break bowler who relied more on flight than spin and was essentially defensive in character, he had first played for Victoria in 1935–36 but had not won a Test cap until 1945–46. He did reasonably well against England in 1946–47, taking 6 for 42 in the second Test, but he had featured little in England in 1948 and had not been selected for the side to tour England in 1953.

His reign as captain began brightly with an

Test Record

	M	I	NO	Runs	HS	Avge	100s	RC	Wkts	Avge	BB	Ct
v England	22	35	6	485	77	16.72	–	1590	42	37.85	6–42	14
v South Africa	6	7	1	117	66	19.50	–	519	22	23.59	5–34	4
v New Zealand	1	1	1	7	7*	–	–	–	–	–	–	–
v West Indies	9	13	3	254	66	25.40	–	668	22	30.36	7–44	8
v India	6	8	0	124	73	15.50	–	339	19	17.84	4–35	3
v Pakistan	1	2	1	13	13*	13.00	–	66	4	16.50	4–50	1
	45	66	12	1000	77	18.51	–	3182	109	29.19	7–44	30

innings victory over England and five wickets for himself at Brisbane in 1954–55, but for the remainder of the series Australia were savaged by Hutton's side and the pace of Tyson and Statham. Against expectation, Australia then won in the Caribbean against a West Indian side that was in need of reshaping and riven by debate over the captaincy. Ian Johnson played a major part in Australia's win in the third Test, taking 7 for 44 in the second innings.

Such form was not to continue in England in 1956 when Australia fell foul of Laker at Old Trafford on a pitch which, however helpful to spin, saw Johnson take 4 for 151 in 47 overs, figures which disappointed him bitterly. It was apparent that he could not get the best out of players like Miller and Harvey, and his own contribution was so minimal as to lead Australian commentators to refer to him as the 'non-playing captain'.

He retained the captaincy for the tour to India where, thanks mainly to Benaud, Australia won. In his last Test match, Johnson completed the 'double'. He later became secretary of Melbourne Cricket Club.

Test Record as Captain

				M	I	NO	Runs	HS	Avge	100s	RC	Wkts	Avge	BB	Ct
v England	W2	L4	D3	9	15	5	177	41	17.70	–	546	18	30.33	4–151	3
v West Indies	W3	–	D2	5	6	2	191	66	47.75	–	406	14	29.00	7–44	4
v India	W2	–	–	2	3	0	79	73	26.33	–	78	3	26.00	1–15	1
v Pakistan	–	L1	–	1	2	1	13	13*	13.00	–	66	4	16.50	4–50	1
	W7	L5	D5	17	26	8	460	73	25.55	–	1096	39	28.10	7–44	9

Raymond Russell LINDWALL

New South Wales and Queensland

Born: Mascot, New South Wales, 3 October 1921

The outstanding fast bowler of the immediate post-war period, Ray Lindwall formed a lethal partnership with Keith Miller which made Australia supreme in world cricket for the best part of a decade. He made his Test debut in New Zealand in 1945–46 and his last Test match was against India at Calcutta in January 1960.

Although he captained Queensland for five seasons, he was never seriously in contention for the Australian captaincy as there has ever been a prejudice against the main strike bowler leading a side. He captained Australia once, at Bombay in 1956–57 when Johnson was unavailable. Lindwall was also a most capable, hard-hitting batsman.

Test Record

	M	I	NO	Runs	HS	Avge	100s	RC	Wkts	Avge	BB	Ct
v England	29	43	7	795	100	22.08	1	2559	114	22.44	7–63	17
v South Africa	8	10	2	107	41	13.37	–	631	31	20.35	5–32	3
v New Zealand	1	1	0	0	0	0.00	–	29	2	14.50	1–13	–
v West Indies	10	15	2	398	118	30.61	1	1121	41	27.34	6–95	2
v India	10	11	2	173	48*	19.22	–	725	36	20.23	7–38	3
v Pakistan	3	4	0	29	23	7.25	–	186	4	46.50	2–72	1
	61	84	13	1502	118	21.15	2	5251	228	23.03	7–38	26

Test Record as Captain

				M	I	NO	Runs	HS	Avge	100s	RC	Wkts	Avge	BB	Ct
v India	–	–	D1	1	1	1	48	48*	–	–	100	2	50.00	1–40	1

Ian David CRAIG

New South Wales

Born: Yass, New South Wales, 12 June 1935

When Ian Craig played for Australia against South Africa in Melbourne in February 1953, he was 17 years 239 days old, the youngest Australian ever to appear in a Test match. A middle-order batsman, he scored 53 and 47. He was never to do so well in a Test match again.

He toured England in 1953 but did not play in a Test match, and he did not appear in an Australian side again until the 1956 tour of England when he played in two Tests. Craig had found it hard to adapt to English conditions and never fully recovered from the pressure that surrounded him after he had hit 213 not out for New South Wales against the South Africans in 1952–53. He had been hailed as the new Bradman – and clearly he was nothing of the sort.

To the astonishment of the cricket world, Craig was appointed captain of the side to tour South Africa in 1957–58. He had already led a party to New Zealand – no Tests were played – but at 22 years 194 days he was, at the time, the youngest man ever to captain a Test side; and in six Tests he had had a poor record as a batsman.

The prestige of Australian cricket was sagging badly towards the end of the 1950s, but Craig's side lifted spirits by going through the tour unbeaten and convincingly winning the Test series. Craig's contribution was again minimal but he had an air of authority – as befitted a Congregational lay preacher – and he led the side intelligently. Above all, he created an excellent team spirit. His successors were to pay credit to him, but to the cricket world at large he remains a strange interlude in the game in Australia.

Craig was expected to lead Australia against England in 1958–59, but an attack of hepatitis effectively ended his international career although he played occasionally for New South Wales until 1961–62.

Test Record

	M	I	NO	Runs	HS	Avge	100s	RC	Wkts	Avge	BB	Ct
v England	2	4	0	55	38	13.75	–	–	–	–	–	–
v South Africa	6	9	0	203	53	22.55	–	–	–	–	–	1
v India	2	3	0	82	40	27.33	–	–	–	–	–	1
v Pakistan	1	2	0	18	18	9.00	–	–	–	–	–	–
	11	18	0	358	53	19.88	–	–	–	–	–	2

Test Record as Captain

				M	I	NO	Runs	HS	Avge	100s	RC	Wkts	Avge	BB	Ct
v South Africa	W3	–	D2	5	7	0	103	52	14.71	–	–	–	–	–	1

Richard BENAUD

New South Wales

Born: Penrith, New South Wales, 6 October 1930

Richie Benaud has always argued that he would not have won a place in the Australian side had he not learned to bat. Certainly, he was a fine right-handed middle-order batsman who loved to attack, but he will be best remembered as one of the great leg-break and googly bowlers, and as a captain of Australia who must rank alongside Bradman and Armstrong. He, more than any other man, lifted Australian cricket from a period of gloom and tedium to a position of joyful supremacy.

Benaud first played for New South Wales in 1948–49 and made his Test debut in the fifth match of the 1951–52 series against West Indies. He played in four of the five Test matches

The most daring and knowledgeable of captains, Richie Benaud (Hulton)

against South Africa the following season and made the first of his three tours of England in 1953. He did little in the three Tests in which he appeared, but, as in all he did, Benaud was ever learning.

He played in all five matches in 1954–55 when Tyson and Statham shattered Australia, but a few weeks later he had a highly successful series in the Caribbean. His all-round cricket did much to win the third Test, and in the fifth he scored 121, his hundred coming in 78 minutes.

In England in 1956 he played a significant part in Australia's victory at Lord's where he hit 97, but it was in India that he had his greatest success, taking 7 for 72 at Madras and bowling Australia to victory. In Calcutta, he took 6 for 52 and 5 for 53, and his match analysis of 11 for 105 remains a record for a Test match at Eden Gardens.

Benaud, Harvey or Burke might have expected to succeed Ian Johnson as captain of Australia but the job was given to Ian Craig. In South Africa, under Craig, in 1957–58, Benaud had an outstanding series. He hit centuries in the first and fourth Tests and took 30 wickets in the rubber, wreaking havoc among the South African batsmen. He was also recognised as the outstanding *personality* of the tour. When Craig fell ill, Benaud was appointed captain of Australia ahead of Neil Harvey.

Benaud's first opponents were Peter May's England side, on paper an immensely strong combination. Australia took the series four to nil, and Benaud's own contribution, as an all-round cricketer and as a captain, was immense. Impressive victories in Pakistan and India followed, with Benaud the bowler and captain supreme.

Australian cricket was now buoyant and the 1960–61 series against West Indies was described as the most exciting and entertaining in living memory. The first match was tied and Australia went on to take the rubber. Both captains, Benaud and Worrell, were lauded. No sportsman stood higher in esteem in Australia than Richie Benaud.

He now faced the supreme test, the tour of England in 1961. He was troubled by a shoulder injury and missed the Lord's Test. The sides went to the fourth Test at Old Trafford level at one Test each. On the last afternoon, England needed 256 runs in 230 minutes to win the match. Ted Dexter blasted 76 in 84 minutes, and

England were in sight of victory. Benaud elected to bowl round the wicket into the bowlers' rough. He had Dexter caught behind and bowled May round his legs. In 25 balls, he took 5 for 12 and won the match.

He had a tactical genius which was always brilliantly inventive. His vision, his joy and his ability to carry his side with him in enthusiasm and confidence made him an outstanding captain in every possible way, but the tour of England took its toll of him. The next rubber with England in 1962–63 was drawn, and it did not sparkle as others had done.

Benaud led Australia against South Africa in 1963–64 and hit 43 and took 5 for 68 in the first Test, so becoming the first Australian to score 2000 runs and take 200 wickets in Test cricket. Troubled by his injury, he gave up the captaincy after that Test, although he did play three times more in the series.

He departed Test cricket with a record which left no doubt as to his ability as both a player and a captain. Of the six Test series in which he led Australia, five were won and the other drawn.

He became a journalist and he worked to establish Kerry Packer's World Series Cricket. His wit, his charm, his lucidity and his deep knowledge of the game have made him an outstanding commentator.

Test Record

	M	I	NO	Runs	HS	Avge	100s	RC	Wkts	Avge	BB	Ct
v England	27	41	2	767	97	19.66	–	2641	83	31.81	6–70	32
v South Africa	13	21	2	684	122	36.00	2	1413	52	27.17	5–49	15
v West Indies	11	17	0	462	121	27.17	1	1278	42	30.42	5–96	11
v India	8	12	2	144	25	14.40	–	956	52	18.38	7–72	5
v Pakistan	4	6	1	144	56	20.80	–	416	19	21.89	5–93	2
	63	97	7	2201	122	24.45	3	6704	248	27.03	7–72	65

Test Record as Captain

				M	I	NO	Runs	HS	Avge	100s	RC	Wkts	Avge	BB	Ct
v England	W6	L2	D6	14	18	1	404	64	23.76	–	1760	63	27.93	6–70	21
v South Africa	–	–	D1	1	1	0	43	43	43.00	–	72	5	14.40	5–68	1
v West Indies	W2	L1	D1+1	5	9	0	194	77	21.55	–	779	23	33.86	5–96	3
v India	W2	L1	D2	5	8	2	91	25	15.16	–	568	29	19.58	5–43	5
v Pakistan	W2	–	D1	3	4	1	84	29	28.00	–	380	18	21.11	5–93	2
	W12	L4	D11+1	28	40	4	816	77	22.66	–	3559	138	25.78	6–70	32

Robert Neil HARVEY

Victoria and New South Wales

Born: Fitzroy, Victoria, 8 October 1928

A brilliant left-handed batsman who made his Test debut against India in 1947–48, Neil Harvey was the first left-hander to score a hundred in his first Test against England, at Headingley in 1948. He was an automatic choice for Australia for 15 years. A modest man, he was consistently passed over for the captaincy of Australia, but he was successful on the one occasion he led his country, at Lord's in 1961 when Benaud was injured.

Test Record

	M	I	NO	Runs	HS	Avge	100s	RC	Wkts	Avge	BB	Ct
v England	37	68	5	2416	167	38.34	6	15	0	–	–	25
v South Africa	14	23	3	1625	205	81.25	8	20	1	20.00	1–9	6
v West Indies	14	25	1	1054	204	43.91	3	18	0	–	–	10
v India	10	13	0	775	153	59.61	4	59	2	29.50	1–8	17
v Pakistan	4	8	1	279	96	39.85	–	8	0	–	–	6
	79	137	10	6149	205	48.41	21	120	3	40.00	1–8	64

Test Record as Captain

		M	I	NO	Runs	HS	Avge	100s	RC	Wkts	Avge	BB	Ct
v England	W1	–	–	1	2	0	31	27	15.50	–	–	–	1

Robert Baddeley SIMPSON

New South Wales and Western Australia

Born: Marrickville, New South Wales, 3 February 1936

The Test career of Bobby Simpson is divided into two distinct parts. He made his Test debut against South Africa in 1957–58, and succeeded Benaud as captain after the first Test against South Africa in 1963–64. When he took over the captaincy he had not hit a Test century although he was a reliably attractive right-handed opening batsman. He was also a very useful leg-break bowler and a slip fielder who has had no superior in Test cricket.

His maiden Test hundred came in his 52nd innings. It was at Old Trafford in July 1964 and he hit 311, sharing an opening stand of 201 with Bill Lawry. Australia won the only Test that was decided in a rather mundane series, and it was a

mark of Simpson's captaincy that he tended to be ultra-cautious. Caution was also a characteristic of his batting.

At the beginning of the 1967–68 season, Simpson announced that he was retiring from first-class cricket at the end of the year. He led Australia against India in the first two Tests, scored centuries in both, and then stood down and handed over to Bill Lawry. For reasons of sentiment, Simpson was recalled to the side for the fourth Test at Sydney and returned match figures of 8 for 97; and that, it was believed, was the end of his international career.

But in 1977–78, with Australia decimated by the Packer revolution which saw their leading players defect to World Series Cricket, Simpson came out of retirement to captain Australia against India and West Indies. It was a testament to the man's fitness and dedication that he hit two centuries against India and won the series by three matches to two. Against the strong West Indies side he was less successful, but he

Test Record

	M	I	NO	Runs	HS	Avge	100s	RC	Wkts	Avge	BB	Ct
v England	19	31	3	1405	311	50.17	2	838	16	52.37	5–57	30
v South Africa	15	27	2	980	153	39.20	1	533	13	41.00	2–10	27
v West Indies	15	28	2	1043	201	40.11	1	846	18	47.00	4–83	29
v India	11	21	0	1125	176	53.57	4	647	23	28.13	5–49	21
v Pakistan	2	4	0	316	153	79.00	2	137	1	137.00	1–47	3
	62	111	7	4869	311	46.81	10	3001	71	42.26	5–57	110

gave Australia firm, traditional values in attitude, dress, behaviour and application at a time when the Test team was in danger of falling apart. He was not always backed by a Board vacillating over its relationships with broadcasting companies, and he retired for a second time.

He was not among the best of Australian captains but he was a good teacher of the young,

and he gave his best work as coach to Allan Border's side in the late 1980s. He also became manager of Leicestershire, but here he was much less successful.

Bobby Simpson in action against West Indies at Brisbane in the tied Test match of 1960. The other batsman is Neil Harvey (Hulton)

Test Record as Captain

				M	I	NO	Runs	HS	Avge	100s	RC	Wkts	Avge	BB	Ct
v England	W2	–	D6	8	12	2	813	311	81.30	2	240	1	240.00	1–14	14
v South Africa	W2	L4	D3	9	18	1	798	153	46.94	1	481	12	40.08	2–10	13
v West Indies	W2	L5	D3	10	18	1	598	201	35.17	1	629	12	52.41	4–83	16
v India	W6	L3	D1	10	19	0	1098	176	57.78	4	550	15	36.66	4–45	16
v Pakistan	–	–	D2	2	4	0	316	153	79.00	2	137	1	137.00	1–47	3
	W12	L12	D15	39	71	4	3623	311	54.07	10	2037	41	49.68	4–45	62

Brian Charles BOOTH

New South Wales

Born: Perthville, Bathurst, New South Wales, 19 October 1933

A slim, lean batsman, graceful in every stroke he played, Brian Booth first played for Australia in the last two Tests of the 1961 series in England. He batted admirably in both matches, and in his third Test, the first of the home series against England at Brisbane in 1962–63, he hit

112; he followed this with 103 in the second Test at Melbourne.

A quietly effective member of the Australian side for the first half of the sixties, his courtesy and traditional attitude to sportsmanship was, perhaps, becoming less fashionable at that time. He led Australia at Brisbane and Sydney in 1965–66 and was beaten in the second encounter. He was promptly discarded as Australia sought to rebuild, although he continued to prosper in Sheffield Shield cricket for another three seasons.

Test Record

	M	I	NO	Runs	HS	Avge	100s	RC	Wkts	Avge	BB	Ct
v England	15	26	5	824	112	39.23	2	4	0	–	–	8
v South Africa	4	7	1	531	169	88.50	2	3	0	–	–	1
v West Indies	5	8	0	234	117	29.25	1	48	0	–	–	5
v India	3	5	0	112	74	22.40	–	58	2	29.00	2–33	2
v Pakistan	2	2	0	72	57	36.00	–	33	1	33.00	1–18	1
	29	48	6	1773	169	42.21	5	146	3	48.66	2–33	17

Test Record as Captain

				M	I	NO	Runs	HS	Avge	100s	RC	Wkts	Avge	BB	Ct
v England	–	L1	D1	2	3	0	51	27	17.00	–	–	–	–	–	1

William Morris LAWRY

Victoria

Born: Thornbury, Victoria, 11 February 1937

A left-handed opening batsman who automatically succeeded Simpson as captain of Australia in 1967–68 by reason of seniority, Bill Lawry was a stubborn, pugnacious player. Tall, with relentless concentration, he did not take easily to captaincy. He brushed with umpires and spectators, appeared fidgety and frustrated in the way he used his bowlers, and above all, he roused the anger of the press against him.

He was outstanding on his first visit to England in 1961 and hit two centuries in his maiden series, but at a time when cricket was fighting

for its existence, his dourness began to wear down spectators. The media focused upon his unwillingness to walk when it was obvious that he had touched a ball to the wicket-keeper. He was cited as being a prime reason for the decline in the standard of manners in the game. This was hardly fair on him, but he had left himself vulnerable.

He had fought many brave battles for Australia, but in 1970–71, things began to go wrong against Illingworth's England side. With the English press, in particular, hounding him, Lawry was dropped from the final Test and the captaincy given to Ian Chappell. Thus, Bill Lawry had the unenviable record of being the first Australian captain to be sacked in the middle of a series.

Test Record

	M	I	NO	Runs	HS	Avge	100s	RC	Wkts	Avge	BB	Ct
v England	29	51	5	2233	166	48.54	7	0	0	–	–	16
v South Africa	14	28	1	985	157	36.48	1	–	–	–	–	9
v West Indies	10	17	2	1035	205	69.00	4	–	–	–	–	1
v India	12	23	4	892	100	46.94	1	6	0	–	–	4
v Pakistan	2	4	0	89	47	22.25	–	–	–	–	–	–
	67	123	12	5234	205	47.15	13	6	0	–	–	30

Test Record as Captain

				M	I	NO	Runs	HS	Avge	100s	RC	Wkts	Avge	BB	Ct
v England	W1	L2	D6	9	17	3	594	135	42.42	1	–	–	–	–	7
v South Africa	–	L4	–	4	8	0	193	83	24.12	–	–	–	–	–	6
v West Indies	W3	L1	D1	5	8	0	667	205	83.37	3	–	–	–	–	1
v India	W5	L1	D1	7	14	3	466	64	42.36	–	6	0	–	–	3
	W9	L8	D8	25	47	6	1920	205	46.82	4	6	0	–	–	17

Barrington Noel JARMAN

South Australia

Born: Hindmarsh, Adelaide, 17 February 1936

A capable wicket-keeper who began his career in the shadow of the great Wally Grout and ended it under the challenge of Taber, Jarman toured England three times, in 1961, 1964 and 1968, On his third tour, he was vice-captain to Lawry and, like Booth and Harvey before him, he led Australia when the captain was injured.

By a bizarre coincidence, when Jarman led Australia at Headingley Tom Graveney was captaining England for the only time in his career because Cowdrey was injured.

Test Record

	M	I	NO	Runs	HS	Avge	100s	RC	Wkts	Avge	BB	Ct/st
v England	7	11	3	111	41	13.87	–	–	–	–	–	18/–
v West Indies	4	6	0	40	17	6.66	–	–	–	–	–	12/1
v India	7	12	0	216	78	18.00	–	–	–	–	–	17/2
v Pakistan	1	1	0	33	33	33.00	–	–	–	–	–	3/1
	19	30	3	400	78	14.81	–	–	–	–	–	50/4

Test Record as Captain

				M	I	NO	Runs	HS	Avge	100s	RC	Wkts	Avge	BB	Ct/st
v England	–	–	D1	1	2	0	14	10	7.00	–	–	–	–	–	3/–

Ian Michael CHAPPELL

South Australia

Born: Unley, South Australia, 26 September 1943

Ian Chappell first played for Australia against Pakistan in December 1964, but he failed to win a regular place in the side until the tour of South Africa in 1966–67. The series was not a happy one for him but he was now established in the Test side.

A determined and gritty, rather than stylish, right-handed batsman, an occasional leg-spin bowler and a brilliant slip fielder, he hit his first Test hundred in 1967–68 against India at Melbourne. He toured England in 1968, finishing second to Lawry in the Test batting averages, and scored heavily against West Indies and India. Like other Australians, he had a poor series in South Africa in 1969–70, and when Illingworth's side began to gain the upper hand in the 1970–71 Ashes series, Australian morale became low. Lawry was dropped from the sixth and final Test and Ian Chappell took over the captaincy.

Like McDonnell, Giffen and Simpson before him, Chappell invited the opposition to bat first when he won the toss in his first Test as captain. It seemed a master-stroke when England were bowled out for 184 and Australia took a first innings lead of 80, but England went on to win by 62 runs. It proved to be the last serious setback that Ian Chappell encountered in his reign as captain of Australia.

Leading a not particularly strong side in England in 1972, he drew the rubber by winning the last Test at The Oval where both he and his brother Greg hit centuries. This was followed by victory over Pakistan in all three Tests, and a new, confident Australian side had begun to emerge. West Indies were beaten in the Caribbean in spite of the loss of Lillee through injury, and by 1974–75, with Thomson joining the fit-again Lillee and Walker in attack, Australia were one of the most formidable post-war Test sides the game had seen

Following victory over England in 1975, Ian Chappell stood down as captain and handed over to brother Greg. He played in one more series, against West Indies, and then announced his retirement. When World Series Cricket came into being, Chappell re-emerged as one of the brains behind the Packer organisation, and the bulk of the fine Australian side followed him into the rebel world series.

Once peace reigned again in 1979–80 he was recalled to the Test side and played once against West Indies and twice against England who, confronted by a full-strength Australian side, were totally outplayed. Chappell later became a commentator for Packer's Australian television channel.

Shrewd captain, hard negotiator and tough commentator who led Australia out of the wilderness – Ian Chappell, seen here interviewing Allan Border (Allsport/Adrian Murrell)

His achievements as a captain are undeniable. He took a side which was low in morale and performance and led them to the top of world cricket, yet he was never far away from controversy. Verbal abuse of opponents on the field, casual dress at official functions off it, and attacks on officials became permanently associated with Chappell's sides. Even in public, his language was colourful, and he suffered suspension and fines for what he said and did to officials. His relations with the Board were always strained, but his team were devoted to him and he ran them as a self-contained unit answerable only to himself.

In the Packer era, Simpson was brought out of retirement to lead Australia and to re-establish some decorum in the wake of Chappell's regime. Traditionalists were glad to see the back of Chappell, but his record as a captain is a magnificent one. He inspired loyalty and had strength of purpose. His tactical sense and deployment of his forces would have been exceptional in any age.

Test Record

			M	I	NO	Runs	HS	Avge	100s	RC	Wkts	Avge	BB	Ct
v England			30	56	4	2138	192	41.11	4	429	6	71.50	1–10	31
v South Africa			9	18	1	288	49	16.94	–	296	5	59.20	2–91	11
v New Zealand			6	10	0	486	145	48.60	2	21	2	10.50	1–4	16
v West Indies			17	31	4	1545	165	57.22	5	254	6	42.33	2–21	24
v India			9	15	1	536	151	38.28	2	199	1	199.00	1–55	17
v Pakistan			4	6	0	352	196	58.66	1	117	0	–	–	6
			75	136	10	5345	196	42.42	14	1316	20	65.80	2–21	105

Test Record as Captain

				M	I	NO	Runs	HS	Avge	100s	RC	Wkts	Avge	BB	Ct
v England	W7	L4	D5	16	30	1	1181	192	40.72	2	192	3	64.00	1–10	22
v New Zealand	W3	L1	D2	6	10	0	486	145	48.60	2	21	2	10.50	1–4	16
v West Indies	W2	–	D3	5	9	2	542	109	77.42	2	48	1	48.00	1–17	6
v Pakistan	W3	–	–	3	5	0	341	196	68.20	1	37	0	–	–	2
	W15	L5	D10	30	54	3	2550	196	50.00	7	298	6	49.66	1–4	46

Gregory Stephen CHAPPELL

South Australia, Queensland and Somerset

Born: Unley, South Australia, 7 August 1948

Very different from his elder brother in style and appearance, Greg Chappell was a tall, lean, elegant batsman who sharpened his technique by playing county cricket for Somerset in 1968 and 1969. He hit the first century in the Sunday League, and 18 months later, in December 1970, scored a century on his Test debut against England at Perth.

From that point onwards, he was a regular member of the Australian side, an integral part of his brother's plan to revive the country's cricket. He hit centuries at Lord's and The Oval in the 1972 Ashes series, and in The Oval match, he and Ian provided the first instance of brothers scoring hundreds in the same innings of a Test.

Under his brother's tutelage, he was groomed for the captaincy of Australia and he took over for the series against West Indies in 1975–76. At Brisbane, he became the first player to score a century in each innings in his first Test match as captain. Australia won the series by five matches to one.

All went well for Australia and Greg Chappell until the 1977 tour of England when they were heavily beaten, but by then they were playing under the cloud of Packer's World Series Cricket, news of which had just been released. Greg Chappell and the bulk of the Australian side defected to Packer, and they did not return to Test cricket until the television rights problem had been resolved in 1979–80. Greg Chappell was immediately reinstated as captain; he lost to West Indies but trounced England.

Whenever he made himself available Greg Chappell captained Australia, but he elected not to go to Pakistan nor to tour England in 1981. He led Australia for the last time against

Sri Lanka in Kandy in April 1983, although he did play one more series, against Pakistan under Kim Hughes in 1983–84.

There were many who resented the cavalier way in which he chose when he would captain Australia and when not, but the Board seemingly condoned his attitude. Indeed, in the post-Packer era, the Australian Board did seem frightened to criticise or hinder their leading players in any way.

A much less flamboyant leader than his elder brother, Greg Chappell did not always wear the

Greg Chappell during his innings of 115 for Australia against England at Adelaide in December 1982. A batsman incapable of an ineloquent gesture, and a thoughtful and firm captain (Allsport/Adrian Murrell)

mantle of captain easily. He often looked under strain although his batting never suffered. He had a dignified air which concealed an urgent desire to win, and his detachment did not always make him the most pleasant of opponents.

In February 1981, in a one-day international against New Zealand at Melbourne, he ordered his brother Trevor to bowl the last ball of the match under-arm to prevent New Zealand from hitting the six that they needed to win the game. The incident caused anger and resentment, and few forgave Greg Chappell for what he had done. Perhaps the captaincy of Australia and the responsibility that accompanied the position drained him more than he cared to admit, but one will always take delight from the memory of that tall, upright, elegant batting.

Originally a bowler of leg-spin, he turned to medium pace with good effect.

Test Record

				M	I	NO	Runs	HS	Avge	100s	RC	Wkts	Avge	BB	Ct
v England				35	65	8	2619	144	45.94	9	679	13	52.23	2–36	61
v New Zealand				14	22	3	1076	247*	56.63	3	464	13	36.69	3–54	18
v West Indies				17	31	6	1400	182*	56.00	5	323	8	40.37	2–10	16
v India				3	5	0	368	204	73.60	1	27	1	27.00	1–4	5
v Pakistan				17	27	2	1581	235	63.24	6	418	12	34.83	5–61	22
v Sri Lanka				1	1	0	66	66	66.00	–	2	0	–	–	–
				87	151	19	7110	247*	53.86	24	1913	47	40.70	5–61	122

Test Record as Captain

				M	I	NO	Runs	HS	Avge	100s	RC	Wkts	Avge	BB	Ct
v England	W6	L4	D5	15	29	4	1225	117	49.00	4	244	6	40.66	2–36	27
v New Zealand	W4	L1	D3	8	12	1	517	176	47.00	1	171	5	34.20	2–7	9
v West Indies	W6	L4	D2	12	23	5	1058	182*	58.77	4	97	4	24.25	2–10	10
v India	W1	L1	D1	3	5	0	368	204	73.60	1	27	1	27.00	1–4	5
v Pakistan	W3	L3	D3	9	16	0	975	235	60.93	3	142	7	20.28	3–49	8
v Sri Lanka	W1	–	–	1	1	0	66	66	66.00	–	2	0	–	–	–
	W21	L13	D14	48	86	10	4209	235	55.38	13	683	23	29.69	3–49	59

Graham Neil YALLOP

Victoria

Born: Balwyn, Victoria, 7 October 1952

Graham Yallop, a left-handed middle-order batsman, first played for Australia in three Test matches against West Indies in 1975–76. He was not called upon again until the last Test against India in 1977–78 when the leading Australian batsmen had defected to World Series Cricket. He hit 121 and was picked to tour West Indies.

When Simpson resigned after that tour, Yallop was appointed captain against Brearley's England side. He hit centuries in the first and sixth Tests, but a weak Australian side, not helped by his dull and unimaginative captaincy and lack of motivation, was trounced.

He also led Australia in the first of two Tests against Pakistan who, inspired by Sarfraz Nawaz, snatched a most improbable victory on the last afternoon. Yallop was injured and unable to play in the second Test; Hughes stood in for him and won. Yallop never captained

Australia again, playing another 24 Tests under Hughes and Greg Chappell.

Against Pakistan in 1983–84 he hit two centuries, including 268 at Melbourne, but 2 and 1 against West Indies in the first Test the following season marked the end of his international cricket.

An unhappy period as captain of Australia for Graham Yallop. A placard reminds him and Rodney Hogg (left) of the series outcome after the final Test against England in 1978–79 (Allsport/ Adrian Murrell)

Test Record

	M	I	NO	Runs	HS	Avge	100s	RC	Wkts	Avge	BB	Ct
v England	13	25	0	709	121	28.36	3	17	0	–	–	10
v West Indies	8	15	2	499	81	38.38	–	8	0	–	–	6
v India	7	14	1	568	167	43.69	2	62	1	62.00	1–21	–
v Pakistan	10	15	0	882	268	58.80	3	29	0	–	–	6
v Sri Lanka	1	1	0	98	98	98.00	–	–	–	–	–	1
	39	70	3	2756	268	41.13	8	116	1	116.00	1–21	23

Test Record as Captain

				M	I	NO	Runs	HS	Avge	100s	RC	Wkts	Avge	BB	Ct
v England	W1	L5	–	6	12	0	391	121	32.58	2	–	–	–	–	3
v Pakistan	–	L1	–	1	2	0	33	28	16.50	–	–	–	–	–	–
	W1	L6	–	7	14	0	424	121	30.28	2	–	–	–	–	3

Kimberley John HUGHES

Western Australia

Born: Maragert River, Western Australia, 26 January 1954

An attractive right-handed batsman, Kim Hughes toured England in 1977. One of the few players on the trip who was not engaged by World Series Cricket, he was something of a lost figure and appeared in only the final Test, when he scored 1. With the mass defections to Kerry Packer's cricket, Hughes must have expected a regular place in the Australian side, but he played only twice against India in 1977–78, and although picked in the party to tour West Indies under Simpson, he did not appear in a Test match.

The resignation of Simpson and the failure in the Caribbean saw Hughes drafted in for all six Tests against England in 1978–79. He hit a patient century in the first Test but otherwise struggled like his compatriots. An innings of 84 in the bad-tempered Test with Pakistan in Melbourne gave him some prestige, and when Yallop stood down from the second match with injury, Hughes was appointed captain. Australia won, and an air of optimism prevailed. He took the side to India and hit a century in the first Test, but again a raw and inexperienced side was well beaten.

Hughes had arrived as a Test captain without any previous experience of captaincy at first-class level. His naivety was most apparent, but he also had a sense of discipline and honesty in what he did. When he was ultimately made captain of Western Australia, he went through a season without appearing for the state of which he was captain, so great had become the international commitments.

With peace resolved between Packer and the Australian Board, Greg Chappell returned to take over as captain of Australia once more and Hughes was named as his vice-captain. He held his place in the side with some exciting if erratic stroke-play. When Greg Chappell declined to tour England in 1981, Hughes became captain again. The Test series was a disaster for Australia. They won the first Test and should have won more, but the Botham–Brearley–Willis combination conjured the impossible. Australia lost by three Tests to one, and Hughes' standing as a captain was low.

Greg Chappell returned as captain. Hughes reverted to being a player until Chappell declined to go to Pakistan in 1982–83 when he became captain again. His side lost 3–0, and Chappell was captain in the Ashes series later the same year.

After that, Chappell retired, and Hughes was captain against Pakistan, with Chappell in the side, and won. In the Caribbean, however, he and his side were totally out of their depth. West Indies visited Australia the following season, 1984–85, and won the first two Tests most convincingly. There had been a constant barrage of criticism against Hughes, and it was quite obvious that he did not have the full support of the Australian Board, the very people who had chosen him to lead Australia. At another time, Hughes might have been able to lead a national side, but in the turbulent years in Australia during and after the Packer revolution and after the break-up of Ian Chappell's great side, he was certainly not the man to captain Australia.

In the second Test match at Brisbane in November 1984, there were verbal exchanges on the field between players, Hughes dropped a vital and simple catch which allowed

Kim Hughes' dejection is plain to see after England's extraordinary recovery to win the 1981 series (Allsport/Adrian Murrell)

Richardson to go on to reach a century, and West Indies won inside four days. At the end of the match, Hughes called a press conference at which he read a prepared statement in which he said, 'The constant criticism, speculation and innuendo by former players and a section of the media over the past four or five years have finally taken their toll.' He was unable to fight back the tears. He had resigned as captain of Australia, and he left no doubt that he felt that he had been betrayed.

He played in the next two Test matches under Allan Border and scored 0, 2, 0 and 0. He did not play Test cricket again. Embittered, he took a team to South Africa and later played for Natal, whom he captained. Even there, things went badly for him, and he resigned in the middle of the 1990–91 South African season.

His 213 at Sydney in January 1981 remains a record for Australia against India, while his century in the Centenary Test at Lord's in 1980 was probably the most attractive of his Test innings.

Test Record

		M	I	NO	Runs	HS	Avge	100s	RC	Wkts	Avge	BB	Ct
v England		22	40	1	1499	137	38.43	3	–	–	–	–	12
v West Indies		15	30	2	774	130*	27.64	2	0	0	–	–	9
v New Zealand		6	8	1	138	51	19.71	–	0	0	–	–	–
v India		11	21	2	988	213	52.00	2	1	0	–	–	10
v Pakistan		16	25	0	1016	106	40.64	2	27	0	–	–	10
		70	124	6	4415	213	37.41	9	28	0	–	–	50

Test Record as Captain

				M	I	NO	Runs	HS	Avge	100s	RC	Wkts	Avge	BB	Ct
v England	W1	L3	D2	6	12	0	300	89	25.00	–	–	–	–	–	3
v West Indies	–	L5	D2	7	14	0	294	37	21.00	–	–	–	–	–	3
v India	–	L2	D4	6	12	2	594	100	59.40	1	–	–	–	–	5
v Pakistan	W3	L3	D3	9	13	0	538	106	41.38	1	6	0	–	–	7
	W4	L13	D11	28	51	2	1726	106	35.22	2	6	0	–	–	18

Allan Robert BORDER

New South Wales, Queensland and Essex

Born: Cremorne, New South Wales, 27 July 1955

It is indicative of the times that Kim Hughes played in more Test matches than Don Bradman and captained Australia on more occasions than the 'Don', yet throughout his period of office there were those who thought that Allan Border should be leading the side.

Border came to notice during the Packer revolution of 1978–79. He made his Test debut against England in the third game of the rubber, at Melbourne, and was the only batsman of the

newcomers to excite the interest of World Series Cricket, who were anxious to sign him. His quality was confirmed by innings of 20, 105, 85 and 66 not out in the two matches against Pakistan which followed the Ashes series, and he continued to score heavily in India.

He survived the return of Greg Chappell and the rest of the Packer players in 1979–80 and hit his first century against England that season. Later the same year, he became the first batsman to score 150 in both innings of a Test match, hitting 150 not out and 153 against Pakistan at Lahore.

In England in 1981, he shone bravely as Australia struggled. At Old Trafford, he batted for 377 minutes with a broken finger to reach the slowest century recorded by an Australian in a

Test match, but this was most unusual for the chunky left-hander who is quick to attack the bowling whenever the opportunity presents itself. At The Oval, he recorded another unbeaten century and scored 84 in the second innings.

Against West Indies in 1983–84, only Border's batting saved Australia from greater humiliation. At Port-of-Spain, he played memorable innings of 98 not out and 100 not out to stave off defeat, and when, at the beginning of the series against West Indies the following year, Kim Hughes stood down, there was no doubt as to who would succeed him as captain of Australia. Throughout the chopping and changing of leadership and the political machinations of the early eighties, Border alone had offered consistency and stability, and this is what he now brought to the captaincy of Australia after a time of trial.

The first Test match in which Border was captain was lost, but the fifth Test of the series was won. Yet it was apparent that Australia were some way from being a challenging or formidable side. Defeats by England, two series losses

Stability, passion and success – Allan Border (Allsport/Pascal Rondeau)

to New Zealand and a drawn rubber at home to India did nothing to increase confidence, and Border reacted angrily at the attitude – and ineptitude – of some of his colleagues. The loss of another Ashes series in 1986–87 was softened by victory in the final Test, and against all expectation, Australia went on to win the World Cup in India and Pakistan.

Border's task had not been made easier in his early days as captain by a rebel tour to South Africa which robbed him of key players in 1985, but now a new, young, keen and stable side was beginning to take shape, and he led them with sympathy, strength and intelligence. Honesty, endeavour and a passion for the game sparkled from his ever-smiling blue eyes. He had never been a willing captain of Australia, nor had he sought the job, but he was determined to do it properly.

Two seasons with Essex revealed him as a man of total commitment, always willing to submerge himself in the needs of the side and to treat supporters with warmth and friendship. It was those qualities which were helping to mould a good Australian side.

When Australia entertained West Indies in 1988–89 the visitors took the rubber, but Australia won at Sydney with Border taking 7 for 46 and 4 for 50, a record match analysis by an Australian captain. In the same match, he recorded the slowest fifty by an Australian in a Test. He has, perhaps, never quite trusted his slow left-arm bowling sufficiently, for he was to claim another five-wicket haul against West Indies at Bourda in 1990–91.

In 1989, Border and his men routed England in England, and they retained the Ashes in 1990–91 with another overwhelming victory in the series in Australia. There were disappointments in New Zealand and in an unpleasant series in the Caribbean in 1990–91, where verbal abuse of the opposition seemed to have come into vogue; but that Australia, under Border, had become a power in world cricket again was undeniable.

Border has played in more Test matches than any other Australian and led Australia more times, and in consecutive Tests. There have been occasions when his captaincy has seemed too defensive, too conservative, but the early years were hard and bred such an attitude. He has never failed to lead by example, nor to encourage a young side which has come to maturity with the help of his wise counsel.

Test Record

	M	I	NO	Runs	HS	Avge	100s	RC	Wkts	Avge	BB	Ct
v England	41	73	18	3115	196	56.63	7	339	3	113.00	1–25	49
v West Indies	26	50	7	1754	126	40.79	2	414	19	21.78	7–46	19
v New Zealand	17	25	3	1130	205	51.36	4	103	5	20.60	3–20	25
v India	15	26	1	1292	163	51.68	4	179	4	44.75	2–60	9
v Pakistan	22	36	8	1666	153	59.50	6	208	5	41.60	2–35	22
v Sri Lanka	4	5	1	300	88	75.00	–	49	1	49.00	1–11	6
	125	215	38	9257	205	52.29	23	1292	37	34.91	7–46	130

Test Record as Captain

				M	I	NO	Runs	HS	Avge	100s	RC	Wkts	Avge	BB	Ct
v England	W9	L5	D9	23	39	8	1843	196	59.45	4	195	2	97.50	1–25	25
v West Indies	W3	L6	D4	13	24	3	717	75	34.14	–	333	18	18.50	7–46	11
v New Zealand	W2	L4	D5	11	18	3	986	205	65.73	4	58	1	58.00	1–12	17
v India	–	–	D5+1	6	9	1	543	163	67.87	2	41	0	–	–	2
v Pakistan	W1	L1	D4	6	10	3	364	113*	52.00	1	63	1	63.00	1–10	5
v Sri Lanka	W2	–	D1	3	4	0	253	88	63.25	–	38	0	–	–	3
	W17	L16	D28+1	62	104	18	4706	205	54.72	11	728	22	33.09	7–46	63

SOUTH AFRICA

Test Cricket in South Africa

It was the British Army who brought cricket to South Africa, just as they did to many other parts of a far-flung Empire. Garrison troops first occupied the Cape in the early years of the Napoleonic Wars, and there is evidence that the military men were playing cricket in Cape Town by the time the British had reoccupied the Cape in 1806.

By the middle of the 19th century, the game was well established in various parts of the country, with cricket being played in schools and clubs having been founded. In 1862, a match between the Mother Country and the Colonial Born was played in Cape Town. It was the first of a long series of such games which were the highlight of the season.

In 1888, South Africa's two most famous cricket grounds, Newlands in Cape Town and Wanderers in Johannesburg, were opened. This was the year that Major R.G. Warton returned to England.

Warton had been attached to the Army General Staff in Cape Town since 1883, was a member of the Western Province Club which had been formed in 1864, and played a prominent part in cricket in the Cape. On his return to England, he negotiated for a tour of South Africa by a team of first-class cricketers. Warton himself managed the side, which was captained by the Sussex bowler C. Aubrey Smith, later to gain greater fame as a film actor.

The side was not a strong one but it proved more than adequate for the South African opposition. Most matches were played against 'odds', but there were two that were contested on equal terms. These matches were played in Port Elizabeth and Cape Town in March 1889 and were subsequently recognised as first-class and as Test matches, a decision which has displeased many connoisseurs.

To put the matches into perspective, it must be pointed out that J.E.P. McMaster, who batted number nine for England in the second Test and made 0, was playing in his one and only first-class match, and that South Africa were dismissed for 47 and 43 in the second Test. Briggs took 8 for 11, all eight wickets being bowled.

The most significant outcome of the tour was the inauguration of the Currie Cup competition. Sir Donald Currie, the head of the Castle Mail Packets Company, whose ship had brought the Englishmen to South Africa, presented a cup to commemorate the tour. The tourists were to award it to the team which had excelled most against them, and thereafter it was to be competed for by the provinces.

A second England side, under the captaincy of W.W. Read of Surrey, toured South Africa in 1891–92. Again the standard can be measured in that another England side was engaged in playing a Test match in Australia at the same time that Read's side was playing its one Test match in Cape Town. Ferris and Murdoch, who had played for Australia, appeared for England; and Frank Hearne, who had played for England, was in the South African side. His brothers, Alec and George, were his opponents in the England side. Again South Africa were overwhelmed, with Harry Wood, the Surrey wicketkeeper, hitting the only century of his career.

In 1894, the South African Cricket Association (SACA) was formed and a South African team toured England for the first time. No Test match was played and the tour was a financial disaster in a very wet summer.

Lord Hawke brought a side to South Africa in 1895–96, but the home side fared no better than they had done against previous English sides. In two of the three Test matches they were beaten by an innings, and in the second innings of the first match they were bowled out for 30 in 94 balls, Lohmann taking 8 for 7.

There were similar disasters against Hawke's side in 1898–99, although in the first match at Johannesburg Sinclair hit 86 – the first South African to reach fifty in a Test – and in the second in Cape Town he hit 106, only for South Africa to be bowled out for 35 in their second innings.

A visit to England in 1901, with no Test matches played, was again a financial failure, but the enthusiasm of the South Africans was unabated and in 1902 the Australians were persuaded to break their journey home after their tour of England and play six matches in South Africa. In the first Test match, Australia were forced to follow-on, but the visitors avoided defeat and won the other two Tests.

In 1904 South Africa toured England and again no Tests were played, but this was the last tour without an international fixture. It was on this tour that Schwarz was to develop his prowess as a leg-break and googly bowler, and it was this type of bowling which was to revolutionise the country's cricket. When Pelham Warner led MCC to South Africa in 1905–06, the home selectors named the same XI for each of the five Tests. Four of the side were capable googly bowlers and South Africa won the series by four matches to one, their first victories in Test cricket.

South Africa were now established as worthy of a place in world cricket. They beat England again in 1909–10, toured Australia in 1910–11 and played in the ill-conceived and ill-fated triangular tournament of 1912.

Matches in South Africa before the First World War were all played on matting wickets. On the coast the matting was set in grass outfields, while in the interior they were on hard soil ground. Shrewd judges had for several years agitated for a change to grass pitches, and in 1926–27 in Durban there took place the first Currie Cup match to be played on a grass pitch. When Chapman led England in South Africa in 1930–31, the Tests at Cape Town and Durban were played on grass, and when the Australians toured five years later all the Tests were played on turf. By that time, South Africa had won their first rubber in England.

In the period immediately after the Second World War, South Africa displayed considerable graceful ability, but won very few Tests. By the beginning of the 1950s South African cricket appeared to be heading towards a trough. In 1952–53, Jack Cheetham led a young and inexperienced side to Australia for what seemed to be a hopeless cause. But one of the most brilliant fielding sides in Test history drew the rubber and a golden age in South African cricket began.

It lasted until the beginning of the sixties when a lean and rather dull period took over. Then in 1965, van der Merwe's side won the series in England, and this was followed by victory in Australia for the first time; but warning clouds were already gathering.

England were due to tour South Africa in 1968–69. When Tom Cartwright withdrew from the party through injury, Basil D'Oliveira, the Cape Coloured cricketer who had qualified for England, was called in to replace him. B.J. Vorster, the South African Prime Minister, accused England of mixing sport and politics and told MCC that D'Oliveira was unacceptable as a member of the touring party. The series was cancelled.

In 1969–70, South Africa beat Australia in all four Tests that were played in the Republic. It was unquestionably the greatest of all South African sides, but the tour of England due in 1970 was cancelled under pressure from the British Government who feared, rightly, the strength of demonstrations that would ensue if the tour went ahead. So began South Africa's isolation from international cricket.

The captain of the last, great South African side was Ali Bacher, and since 1970 he has worked tirelessly to bring his country back into the fold and to bring about multi-racial cricket in his country. Political developments in South Africa helped his cause and in 1991 South Africa were readmitted to the cricketing brotherhood; it was decided that they should be allowed to participate in the World Cup in 1992.

In the years of isolation, teams from Sri Lanka, England, Australia and West Indies have played in the Republic, and the players who have been engaged in the tours have faced lengthy exclusions from Test cricket. The significance of these tours should not be underestimated, however, for the presence of Rowe and his West Indian side in South Africa, playing a 'Test' series, brought about something which

would have seemed impossible in the 1950s – a cricket match between a team of black men and a team of white men in South Africa. It was a far cry from the 1929 series in England when Duleepsinhji was withdrawn from the England side after the first Test so as not to offend the South African visitors.

The saddest aspect of South Africa's isolation from Test cricket is that it has deprived liberally-minded men like Clive Rice, an outstanding captain, Ken McEwan, Jimmy Cook, Mandy Yachad and Ray Jennings of the international recognition that they have deserved.

Owen Robert DUNELL

Eastern Province

Born: Port Elizabeth, 15 July 1856
Died: Lyon, France, 21 October 1929

Educated at Eton and Oxford but unable to gain

a first team place at either, Owen Dunell was a right-handed batsman who led South Africa in their first ever Test because it was played at his home ground, St George's Park, Port Elizabeth. He also appeared in the second Test, when the captaincy passed to the skipper of Western Province.

Test Record

	M	I	NO	Runs	HS	Avge	100s	RC	Wkts	Avge	BB	Ct
v England	2	4	1	42	26*	14.00	–	–	–	–	–	1

Test Record as Captain

				M	I	NO	Runs	HS	Avge	100s	RC	Wkts	Avge	BB	Ct
v England	–	L1	–	1	2	1	37	26*	37.00	–	–	–	–	–	1

Sir William Henry MILTON

Western Province

Born: Little Marlow, Buckinghamshire,
3 December 1854
Died: Cannes, France, 6 March 1930

A fine all-round sportsman who won two rugby caps for England, Milton was educated at Marl-

borough where his prowess as a hitter was noted. He captained Western Province from 1885–96 and it was for this reason that he led South Africa at Newlands against Warton's side in 1889 and against Read's side in 1892. He had played an important role in bringing Warton's side to South Africa, and was a prominent figure in South African cricket for many years. He later became an administrator in Southern Rhodesia.

Test Record

	M	I	NO	Runs	HS	Avge	100s	RC	Wkts	Avge	BB	Ct
v England	3	6	0	68	21	11.33	–	48	2	24.00	1–5	1

Test Record as Captain

				M	I	NO	Runs	HS	Avge	100s	RC	Wkts	Avge	BB	Ct
v England	–	L2	–	2	4	0	48	21	12.00	–	43	1	43.00	1–27	–

Ernest Austin HALLIWELL

Transvaal and Middlesex

Born: Ealing, Middlesex, 7 September 1864
Died: Johannesburg, 2 October 1919

Son of Richard Halliwell, who kept wicket for Middlesex in the late 1860s, Ernest Halliwell was himself one of the finest wicket-keepers of his day, standing up to the fastest of bowling when such a style had gone out of fashion. Eventually, he came to the conclusion that on English wickets it was better to stand back to the fast men.

Born in Ealing, he emigrated to the Gold Coast at the age of 18 and then moved to India before settling in South Africa in 1891. The fol-

lowing year, he hit 139 not out and shared an opening stand of 289 for Mother Country against Colonial Born. He had made his Test match debut a few months earlier, keeping wicket against Read's side.

In 1895–96, he captained South Africa in the first two Tests against Lord Hawke's side, the leadership passing to the local man, Richards, for the third Test at Newlands. He also captained South Africa in the final Test against Australia in 1902–03.

He created a tremendous impression as a wicket-keeper in England in 1901 and 1904, and kept in one game for Middlesex on his first tour, when he also appeared for the Gentlemen against the Players at Hastings. He died in 1919 following an operation for gangrene of the leg.

Test Record

	M	I	NO	Runs	HS	Avge	100s	RC	Wkts	Avge	BB	Ct/st
v England	5	10	0	113	41	11.30	–	–	–	–	–	5/–
v Australia	3	5	0	75	57	15.00	–	–	–	–	–	4/2
	8	15	0	188	57	12.53	–	–	–	–	–	9/2

Test Record as Captain

				M	I	NO	Runs	HS	Avge	100s	RC	Wkts	Avge	BB	Ct
v England	–	L2	–	2	4	0	70	41	17.50	–	–	–	–	–	3
v Australia	–	L1	–	1	2	0	14	13	7.00	–	–	–	–	–	–
	–	L3	–	3	6	0	84	41	14.00	–	–	–	–	–	3

Alfred Renfrew RICHARDS

Western Province

Born: Grahamstown, 1868

Died: Salisbury, Rhodesia, 9 January 1904

A right-handed batsman who, as senior local player, led South Africa in his solitary Test match, against England at Newlands in 1895–96.

Test Record as Captain

				M	I	NO	Runs	HS	Avge	100s	RC	Wkts	Avge	BB	Ct
v England	–	L1	–	1	2	0	6	6	3.00	–	–	–	–	–	–

Sir Murray BISSET

Western Province

Born: Port Elizabeth, 14 April 1876
Died: Salisbury, Rhodesia, 24 October 1931

An extremely popular man and a capable and skilful captain, Murray Bisset led South Africa in the two Tests against Lord Hawke's side in 1898–99, keeping wicket in the first. He was a forcing batsman and a good wicket-keeper who was unfortunate to be contemporary with Halliwell. He captained the South African side in England in 1901 and batted impressively. The tour was criticised in many quarters by those who thought the players should have stayed at home to fight the Boers.

He kept wicket in the final Test against England in 1909–10, and later became Chief Justice of Rhodesia. He was acting Governor-General at the time of his death.

Test Record

	M	I	NO	Runs	HS	Avge	100s	RC	Wkts	Avge	BB	Ct/st
v England	3	6	2	103	35	25.75	–	–	–	–	–	2/1

Test Record as Captain

			M	I	NO	Runs	HS	Avge	100s	RC	Wkts	Avge	BB	Ct/st
v England	–	L2	–	2	4	1	72	35	24.00	–	–	–	–	–	1/1

Henry Melville TABERER

Natal, Rhodesia, Transvaal and Essex

Born: Keiskama Hoek, Cape Province,
7 October 1870
Died: Colesburg, 5 June 1932

Educated at St Andrew's School, Grahamstown, Taberer went up to Oxford in 1889, but although he played for the university as a pace bowler and right-handed batsman, he failed to get his blue. He did win a blue for rugby and represented Oxford in the long jump. He played for Essex before the county attained first-class status, and his games for Rhodesia and Transvaal were also in non-first-class matches.

His last first-class game was his one Test match, when he led South Africa against Australia in 1902–03, made the opposition follow-on and bowled the great Victor Trumper.

At the time of his death, he was vice-chairman of the South African Cricket Association.

Test Record as Captain

			M	I	NO	Runs	HS	Avge	100s	RC	Wkts	Avge	BB	Ct
v Australia	–	–	D1	1	1	0	2	2	2.00	–	48	1	48.00	1–25	–

John Henry ANDERSON

Western Province

Born: South Africa, 26 April 1874
Died: Bredasdorp, Cape Province, 11 March 1926

A hard-hitting right-handed batsman, he captained South Africa against Australia in Johannesburg in 1902–03, for reasons which remain obscure. It was his only Test match.

Test Record as Captain

					M	I	NO	Runs	HS	Avge	100s	RC	Wkts	Avge	BB	Ct
v Australia	–	L1	–	1	2	0	43	32	21.50	–	–	–	–	–	1

Percy William SHERWELL

Transvaal and Cornwall

Born: Isipingo, Natal, 17 August 1880
Died: Bulawayo, Southern Rhodesia, 17 April 1948

Brought to England at an early age and educated at Bedford County School and the Royal School of Mines, Camborne, he played for Cornwall before going to the Transvaal, where he held a senior post in the mining industry.

He was a wicket-keeper of the highest quality and a captain cheerful in disposition, but stern in command and tactically adept. He kept wicket to South Africa's battery of googly bowlers and showed variety and intelligence in the way he used them.

He first led South Africa against England in 1905–06. Transvaal had defeated MCC on the eve of the first Test, and eight of the victorious side were selected in the XI that represented South Africa in all five Tests. This is only the second occasion on which a side has been unchanged throughout a five-match series. Sherwell's Test career saw him as captain in all of his 13 matches in three series.

He had the most romantic of beginnings. His side trailed by 93 on the first innings and eventually needed 284 to win. When Sherwell, batting at number 11, joined 'Dave' Nourse, 45 runs were still needed for victory. With dedication and concentration, they scored the runs to give South Africa their first win in Test cricket. Sherwell's side were victorious three more times in the series to take the rubber in convincing fashion.

Sherwell led the side to England in 1907, and although he had not batted higher than nine in the previous series, he opened in the first Test at Lord's. This was the first Test South Africa had played outside their own country, and they were forced to follow-on. Sherwell hit a maiden first-class century to save the match.

He took the South African side to Australia in 1910–11, and although his side lost the series, he claimed honour again with the first Test victory on foreign soil, in Adelaide.

His work in the mining industry had kept him out of the series against England in 1909–10, and it prevented him from playing international cricket after the tour of Australia, but he was a Test selector until 1924. He was also Lawn Tennis Singles Champion of South Africa in 1904. His place in the history of South African cricket is a permanent one.

Test Record as Captain

				M	I	NO	Runs	HS	Avge	100s	RC	Wkts	Avge	BB	Ct/st
v England	W4	L2	D2	8	12	3	247	115	27.44	1	–	–	–	–	12/7
v Australia	W1	L4	–	5	10	1	180	60	20.00	–	–	–	–	–	8/9
	W5	L6	D2	13	22	4	427	115	23.72	1	–	–	–	–	20/16

Sibley John SNOOKE

Border, Western Province and Transvaal

Born: St Mark's, Tembuland, 1 February 1881
Died: Port Elizabeth, 14 August 1966

A genuine all-rounder, 'Tip' Snooke first played in the Currie Cup at the age of 16, and his Test debut came in the triumphant series against England in 1905–06. His stylish batting and fast-medium pace bowling played a significant part in winning the series. In the third Test, at Johannesburg, he took 4 for 57 and 8 for 70 to become the first South African bowler to take 12 wickets in a Test and eight in a Test innings. He took 24 wickets in the series, but bowled less after that.

His one Test century came in Australia in 1910–11, and he captained South Africa successfully against England in 1909–10 when Sherwell was unavailable.

He was recalled to the South African side for the last three Tests against England in 1922–23, and at the age of 42, he opened the bowling and finished his Test career with figures of 3 for 17 and 2 for 41.

Test Record

	M	I	NO	Runs	HS	Avge	100s	RC	Wkts	Avge	BB	Ct
v England	19	33	1	713	63	22.28	–	626	35	17.88	8–70	16
v Australia	7	13	0	295	103	22.69	1	76	0	–	–	8
	26	46	1	1008	103	22.40	1	702	35	20.05	8–70	24

Test Record as Captain

				M	I	NO	Runs	HS	Avge	100s	RC	Wkts	Avge	BB	Ct
v England	W3	L2	–	5	10	0	259	53	25.90	–	141	4	35.25	2–23	6

Frank MITCHELL

Transvaal and Yorkshire

Born: Market Weighton, Yorkshire, 13 August 1872
Died: Blackheath, Kent, 11 October 1935

One of those men who seem to be gifted in all walks of life, Frank Mitchell was educated at St Peter's, York, and at Cambridge University, where he gained his blue for cricket in all four years (1894–97). He also gained blues for rugby and putting the weight. He later won six England caps for rugby and kept goal for Sussex.

As captain of Cambridge University in 1896, he adopted tactics which led to a change in the laws concerning the follow-on, and Lord Hawke eyed Mitchell as his likely successor as captain of Yorkshire. He had highly successful seasons for the county in 1899 and 1901, serving in the Boer War in the intervening year. He had gone to South Africa with Hawke's side in 1898–99 and played in both Tests as an opening batsman.

He was entranced by South Africa and a business opportunity persuaded him to emigrate there. He returned to England as captain of the South African side in 1904 and in 1912 led the side in the Triangular tournament. His form was poor and he stood down from three of the Tests, handing over the captaincy to Tancred. *Wisden*

Frank Mitchell who played for England against South Africa and captained South Africa against England (Allsport)

suggested that both he and his deputy were *passé* for international cricket, and that tour virtually marked the end of Mitchell's first-class career.

He served with distinction in the First World War, and he became an author of repute. His son, T.F., played for Kent.

Test Record

	M	I	NO	Runs	HS	Avge	100s	RC	Wkts	Avge	BB	Ct
For England v South Africa	2	4	0	88	41	22.00	–	–	–	–	–	2
v England	3	6	0	28	12	4.66	–	–	–	–	–	–
	5	10	0	116	41	11.60	–	–	–	–	–	2

Test Record as Captain

				M	I	NO	Runs	HS	Avge	100s	RC	Wkts	Avge	BB	Ct
v England	–	L3	–	3	6	0	28	12	4.66	–	–	–	–	–	–

Louis Joseph TANCRED

Transvaal

Born: Port Elizabeth, 7 October 1876
Died: Johannesburg, 28 July 1934

One of three brothers who played for South Africa, Louis Tancred was an opening batsman with a crouched style and the utmost patience. He made four tours of England and captained South Africa in the Triangular Tests when Mitchell stood down. He hit his highest score on his Test debut against Australia in 1902–03, and his last Test was against Douglas' England side in 1913–14.

Test Record

	M	I	NO	Runs	HS	Avge	100s	RC	Wkts	Avge	BB	Ct
v England	9	17	0	279	73	16.41	–	–	–	–	–	1
v Australia	5	9	0	251	97	27.88	–	–	–	–	–	2
	14	26	0	530	97	20.38	–	–	–	–	–	3

Test Record as Captain

				M	I	NO	Runs	HS	Avge	100s	RC	Wkts	Avge	BB	Ct
v England	–	L2	–	2	4	0	54	39	13.50	–	–	–	–	–	–
v Australia	–	–	D1	1	1	0	30	30	30.00	–	–	–	–	–	–
	–	L2	D1	3	5	0	84	39	16.80	–	–	–	–	–	–

Herbert Wilfred TAYLOR

Natal, Transvaal and Western Province

Born: Durban, 5 May 1889
Died: Cape Town, 8 February, 1973

'Herbie' Taylor was one of the first giants of South African cricket. A right-handed batsman of impeccable technique, he was the one success of the South African side that played in the Triangular Tournament in 1912. Taylor appeared in all six Tests, hit 97 against Australia and won praise all round.

When England toured South Africa in 1913–14, Taylor captained the South African side and in the first Test at Durban hit 109 out of 182. Johnny Douglas also hit a century so that this was the first instance of both captains scoring hundreds in a Test match. Taylor was alone among the South Africans in being able to deal with the bowling of S.F. Barnes and scored 508 runs in the series.

He captained South Africa in three series after the First World War, and his 176 against England in Johannesburg in 1922–23 remains the highest score by a South African in a home Test against England. He hit two more centuries in that series and scored 582 runs, which also remains a record for a home rubber against England.

He was a shrewd, knowledgeable and respected captain, but he had little success leading South Africa and after his one lean series, against England in 1924, he stood down as captain. He continued to play Test cricket, moving down the order and still scoring heavily. His final Test was his country's first against New Zealand, in February 1932. Of the pre-First World War Test players, only Woolley remained in international cricket longer.

He captained South Africa in 18 consecutive Tests, which is a record in the country.

Test Record

	M	I	NO	Runs	HS	Avge	100s	RC	Wkts	Avge	BB	Ct
v England	30	54	3	2287	176	44.84	7	113	5	22.60	3–15	15
v Australia	11	21	1	640	93	32.00	–	43	0	–	–	3
v New Zealand	1	1	0	9	9	9.00	–	–	–	–	–	1
	42	76	4	2936	176	40.77	7	156	5	31.20	3–15	19

Test Record as Captain

				M	I	NO	Runs	HS	Avge	100s	RC	Wkts	Avge	BB	Ct
v England	W1	L9	D5	15	27	2	1287	176	51.48	4	92	4	23.00	3–15	9
v Australia	–	L1	D2	3	6	0	200	80	33.33	–	12	0	–	–	2
	W1	L10	D7	18	33	2	1487	176	47.96	4	104	4	26.00	3–15	11

Hubert Gouvaine DEANE

Natal and Transvaal

Born: Eshowe, Zululand, 21 July 1895
Died: Johannesburg, 21 October 1939

Nicknamed 'Nummy' because of a numbness he suffered in the hand following the loss of a finger joint in a boyhood accident, Deane toured England in 1924 and played in all five Tests, but enjoyed only limited success.

He moved from Natal to Transvaal in 1923–24 and proved a most successful captain of the strongest side in the Union. A free-scoring batsman, he was appointed captain of South Africa for the 1927–28 series against England and proved to be a master tactician as he brought his side from two Tests down to level the series. He was victorious on the two occasions on which he put England in to bat.

This ploy did not work when he used it at The Oval in 1929, but he shared a fourth wicket stand of 214 with Taylor and South Africa led by 234 on the first innings. His leadership on the tour was exemplary and his young side did far

Test Record

	M	I	NO	Runs	HS	Avge	100s	RC	Wkts	Avge	BB	Ct
v England	17	27	2	628	93	25.12	–	–	–	–	–	7

better than had been expected.

He was unavailable for the first Test in 1930–31, and a reluctant skipper in the second and third Tests, after which he resigned, feeling that

his international days were behind him.

A selector and administrator, he brought a touch of self-belief to South Africa's cricket and did much to raise the standard of the fielding.

Test Record as Captain

				M	I	NO	Runs	HS	Avge	100s	RC	Wkts	Avge	BB	Ct
v England	W2	L4	D6	12	20	1	485	93	25.52	–	–	–	–	–	7

Eiulf Peter NUPEN

Transvaal

Born: Johannesburg, 1 January 1902
Died: Johannesburg, 29 January 1977

Born of Norwegian parents and blinded in one eye at the age of four, 'Buster' Nupen captained South Africa with great success in one Test match, but played in only two matches thereafter and never again as captain. A bowler of brisk, medium pace leg-cutters and off-cutters, he was lethal on matting, less effective on turf.

He made his Test debut against Australia in 1921–22, played well against England the following season, but had a disappointing tour of England in 1924. He played in four Tests against England in 1927–28 and had a major part in levelling the series. With Deane unavailable, Nupen led South Africa against England in the first Test match at Johannesburg in 1930–31. He took 5 for 63 and 6 for 87, and South Africa won by 28 runs. He played only twice more in the series, when Deane and Cameron captained.

Nupen was recalled for one Test against Australia in 1935–36.

Test Record

	M	I	NO	Runs	HS	Avge	100s	RC	Wkts	Avge	BB	Ct
v England	14	25	5	300	69	15.00	–	1545	47	32.87	6–46	8
v Australia	3	6	2	48	22	12.00	–	243	3	81.00	1–42	1
	17	31	7	348	69	14.50	–	1788	50	35.76	6–46	9

Test Record as Captain

		M	I	NO	Runs	HS	Avge	100s	RC	Wkts	Avge	BB	Ct
v England	W1 – –	1	2	0	1	1	0.50	–	150	11	13.63	6–87	1

Horace Brakenridge CAMERON

Transvaal, Eastern Province and Western Province

Born: Port Elizabeth, 5 July 1905
Died: Johannesburg, 2 November 1935

One of the very finest wicket-keepers that South Africa has produced, 'Jock' Cameron was also a belligerent middle-order batsman, a cricketer who exuded charm in all he did. 'He was,' wrote *Wisden*, 'a very fine personality, one

who enriched the game, and his manliness and popularity extended far beyond the cricket field.'

He made his Test debut against England in 1927–28, and captained the side in two Tests in 1930–31 when Deane resigned. He was captain in Australia and New Zealand and maintained his own form in difficult circumstances. He was a sympathetic leader, but he did not relish the job and was happy to hand over to Wade for the 1935 tour of England. He hit 90 in the Lord's Test and played a significant part in his side's victory in this match, a victory which gave them the series.

Some weeks after his return from the tour of England, he died of enteric fever.

Test Record

	M	I	NO	Runs	HS	Avge	100s	RC	Wkts	Avge	BB	Ct/st
v England	19	32	3	971	90	33.48	–	–	–	–	–	28/8
v Australia	5	10	0	155	52	15.50	–	–	–	–	–	9/–
v New Zealand	2	3	1	113	47	56.50	–	–	–	–	–	2/4
	26	45	4	1239	90	30.21	–	–	–	–	–	39/12

Test Record as Captain

				M	I	NO	Runs	HS	Avge	100s	RC	Wkts	Avge	BB	Ct/st
v England	–	–	D2	2	4	2	116	69*	58.00	–	–	–	–	–	3/1
v Australia	–	L5	–	5	10	0	155	52	15.50	–	–	–	–	–	9/–
v New Zealand	W2	–	–	2	3	1	113	47	56.50	–	–	–	–	–	2/4
	W2	L5	D2	9	17	3	384	69*	27.42	–	–	–	–	–	14/5

Herbert Fredrick WADE

Natal

Born: Durban, 14 September 1905
Died: Johannesburg, 22 November 1980

Herbert Wade first played for Natal in 1924–25. He was a dashing right-handed batsman who scored well in the Currie Cup, and he also played league cricket in Yorkshire, whom he represented at rugby. Short of Test class as a batsman, he was chosen to lead South Africa in England in 1935 purely because of his qualities as a captain. Wade was respected by his team, and his leadership was quietly effective. His knowledge of English conditions was a vital asset. Under his captaincy, South Africa won the Test match at Lord's, their first victory in a Test in England, and took the series. Against an Australian side – even without Bradman – Wade and his men fared less happily.

Test Record as Captain

				M	I	NO	Runs	HS	Avge	100s	RC	Wkts	Avge	BB	Ct
v England	W1	–	D4	5	8	2	132	40*	22.00	–	–	–	–	–	2
v Australia	–	L4	D1	5	10	0	195	39	19.50	–	–	–	–	–	2
	W1	L4	D5	10	18	2	327	40*	20.43	–	–	–	–	–	4

Alan MELVILLE

Natal, Transvaal and Sussex

Born: Carnarvon, Cape Province, 19 May 1910
Died: Kruger National Park, Transvaal, 18 April 1983

Tall and elegant, Alan Melville was among the most stylish and graceful batsmen of his era. He first played for Natal at the age of 17 and was picked for the side to tour England in 1929, but the invitation was declined as Melville was preparing to go to Oxford. He won his blue in all four years at university (1930–33) and was captain in 1931 and 1932, in which year he first appeared for Sussex. He captained Sussex in 1934 and 1935. He was an inspiring captain, a man of dignity and charm, tactically persuasive and a fine leader of men.

He returned to South Africa in 1936 to take up an appointment in Johannesburg and became captain of Transvaal. When England toured South Africa in 1938–39 he was the obvious choice to captain the home side. He was not fully fit during the series, but he hit 78 and 103 in the final Test, the famous 'Timeless Test', when he had moved up to open the innings.

He had injured his back in a car accident in his youth and the injury recurred while he was serving in the Second World War. It was believed that he would not play cricket again, but he recovered sufficiently to lead South Africa in England in 1947. He scored a century in each innings of the first Test, which England saved only by a great rearguard action. Then another century in the first innings of the Lord's Test meant that he became the first batsman to score four consecutive centuries against England in Tests. Thereafter, the series belonged to Compton and Edrich.

Melville was immensely popular and his side played entertaining cricket, but he was exhausted at the end of the tour and announced his retirement. He was persuaded to reappear against England in 1948–49 and played in the Test at Cape Town under Nourse's captaincy. He later served as a Test selector.

Melville's record as a captain gives no indication as to how effective and respected he was.

Test Record

	M	I	NO	Runs	HS	Avge	100s	RC	Wkts	Avge	BB	Ct
v England	11	19	2	894	189	52.58	4	–	–	–	–	8

Test Record as Captain

			M	I	NO	Runs	HS	Avge	100s	RC	Wkts	Avge	BB	Ct
v England	–	L4 D6	10	17	2	855	189	57.00	4	–	–	–	–	7

Arthur Dudley NOURSE

Natal

Born: Durban, 12 November 1910
Died: Durban, 14 August 1981

The son of 'Dave' Nourse, Dudley Nourse was among the most gifted and successful of South African batsmen. In the years either side of the Second World War, he would have claimed a place in a World XI. He made his Test debut against England in 1935, playing in four matches in the series.

It was in the rubber against Australia in 1935–36 that he first showed his international class. He hit 231 in 289 minutes at Johannesburg in the second Test, and from that time, he straddled the South African batting like a Colossus for the next 15 years.

He was vice-captain to Melville for the 1947 tour of England and took over as captain when MCC visited South Africa in 1948–49. He led against Australia and against England in 1951, but by then he was 41, and he failed to top the Test averages for the first time since 1935. He hit 208 in the first Test at Trent Bridge, even though he was batting with a broken thumb. This was his seventh century against England, and so he equalled the record set by H.W. Taylor and B. Mitchell.

Nourse possessed a thorough knowledge of

Test Record

	M	I	NO	Runs	HS	Avge	100s	RC	Wkts	Avge	BB	Ct
v England	24	43	6	2037	208	55.05	7	9	0	–	–	10
v Australia	10	19	1	923	231	51.27	2	0	0	–	–	2
	34	62	7	2960	231	53.81	9	9	0	–	–	12

the game, but he ascended to the captaincy on seniority rather than on qualities of leadership and is best remembered as one of South Africa's greatest batsmen.

Test Record as Captain

				M	I	NO	Runs	HS	Avge	100s	RC	Wkts	Avge	BB	Ct
v England	W1	L5	D4	10	18	3	837	208	55.80	3	9	0	–	–	3
v Australia	–	L4	D1	5	9	0	405	114	45.00	1	0	0	–	–	2
	W1	L9	D5	15	27	3	1242	208	51.75	4	9	0	–	–	5

John Erskine CHEETHAM

Western Province

Born: Cape Town, 26 May 1920
Died: Johannesburg, 21 August 1980

There are cricketers who have an indefinable quality which makes them outstanding leaders of men. They are cricketers to whom others respond and, by some mystery, they persuade ordinary players to perform above the ability which one thought they possessed. Such a man was Jack Cheetham.

He first played for Western Province shortly before the outbreak of the Second World War, and he was picked to play for South Africa in the first Test match against George Mann's side in 1948–49. He was a dour middle-order batsman, and his record would suggest that he was short of Test class.

In three Tests against Australia in 1949–50 he failed to establish himself, but the following season he hit 271 not out for Western Province against Orange Free State, set up a new Currie Cup record for the province and won a place in the side for England in 1951. He played in all five Tests but failed to distinguish himself although he scored heavily in matches against the counties.

The retirement of Nourse meant that South Africa were in search of a leader, and Cheetham was the surprise choice to take a young and inexperienced side to Australia in 1952–53. In the post-Bradman era, Australia were still a very strong side, and the South Africans were greeted as a team inadequate for a Test series. What followed was one of the most remarkable achievements in Test history as South Africa levelled the series at two Tests each. They won the final Test by six wickets to draw the series even though Australia had scored 520 in their first innings.

Endean was the only South African batsman to hit a century in the series, and although Tayfield bowled splendidly, this was essentially a team victory. In conjunction with manager Viljoen, Cheetham had emphasised fitness and fielding. In his dedication to these aspects of the game, Cheetham was the first of the modern captains. He set a pattern which others have followed. His team had no stars. He was strict and demanding, and South Africa enjoyed a golden period. There were victories in New Zealand and at home to New Zealand, when Cheetham hit his highest Test score of 89.

The end of his Test career was an anti-climax, as he suffered a chipped elbow in the second Test of the 1955 rubber in England and missed

Test Record

	M	I	NO	Runs	HS	Avge	100s	RC	Wkts	Avge	BB	Ct
v England	9	17	2	335	54	22.33	–	–	–	–	–	4
v Australia	8	15	1	240	66	17.14	–	–	–	–	–	7
v New Zealand	7	11	3	308	89	38.50	–	2	0	–	–	2
	24	43	6	883	89	23.86	–	2	0	–	–	13

the next two encounters. He led in the three matches which were lost.

A strong churchman, he worked hard as an administrator in South African cricket where his concern for non-white cricketers was paramount.

Test Record as Captain

				M	I	NO	Runs	HS	Avge	100s	RC	Wkts	Avge	BB	Ct
v England	–	L3	–	3	6	2	96	54	24.00	–	–	–	–	–	–
v Australia	W2	L2	D1	5	9	1	160	66	24.87	–	–	–	–	–	3
v New Zealand	W5	–	D2	7	11	3	308	89	38.50	–	2	0	–	–	2
	W7	L5	D3	15	26	6	564	89	28.20	–	2	0	–	–	5

Derrick John McGLEW

Natal

Born: Pietermaritzburg, 11 March 1929

An obdurate opening batsman with infinite patience and a fine cover fielder, Jackie McGlew took longer to win the captaincy of South Africa in his own right than had been expected, for he was a highly respected and competent captain of Natal for several seasons.

He played in two Tests on the 1951 tour of England and in four against Australia under Cheetham in 1952–53. He had accomplished little until he hit 255 not out against New Zealand at Wellington in March 1953. He became only the second player to be on the field throughout a Test match, and his innings was at that time the highest ever played by a South African in Test cricket.

He was appointed vice-captain to Cheetham for the 1955 tour of England and led South Africa to victory in the third and fourth Tests when Cheetham was injured. He hit centuries in both these Tests in which he was captain.

McGlew had proved himself as the ideal replacement for Cheetham and was appointed as captain for the series against England in 1956–57. A shoulder injury forced him to withdraw from the first Test. He played in the second, but aggravated the injury and did not appear again in the series as he required surgery. Clive van Ryneveld led the side successfully and was asked to continue as captain for the rubber against Australia in 1957–58. Van Ryneveld was unable to play in the first Test, and McGlew deputised and hit a hundred, but van Ryneveld returned for the rest of the series before retiring.

The way was now clear for McGlew to lead the side to England in 1960 and against New Zealand in 1961–62, but a dull series in England was lost and New Zealand surprisingly drew the rubber in South Africa. McGlew's last match ended in defeat, and he finished with a thumb in splints and a shoulder in plaster.

Test Record

	M	I	NO	Runs	HS	Avge	100s	RC	Wkts	Avge	BB	Ct
v England	13	26	2	736	133	30.66	2	–	–	–	–	3
v Australia	9	17	0	604	108	35.52	2	23	0	–	–	6
v New Zealand	12	21	4	1100	255*	64.70	3	–	–	–	–	9
	34	64	6	2440	255*	42.06	7	23	0	–	–	18

Test Record as Captain

				M	I	NO	Runs	HS	Avge	100s	RC	Wkts	Avge	BB	Ct
v England	W2	L4	D2	8	16	2	518	133	37.00	2	–	–	–	–	2
v Australia	–	–	D1	1	2	0	114	108	57.00	1	7	0	–	–	–
v New Zealand	W2	L2	D1	5	9	2	426	127*	60.85	2	–	–	–	–	3
	W4	L6	D4	14	27	4	1058	133	46.00	5	7	0	–	–	5

Clive Berrange VAN RYNEVELD

Western Province

Born: Cape Town, 19 March 1928

Clive van Ryneveld was one of those gifted men, capable of whatever he turned his hand to. He spent four years at Oxford, where he won his blue for rugby and cricket, and represented England four times at rugby before returning home to play for South Africa. He was a stand-off half with considerable flair, and he brought that flair to his batting and to his erratic but effective leg-break bowling.

He qualified as a barrister and toured England in 1951, claiming Hutton as his first Test wicket. Studies restricted his Test appearances, but he played against New Zealand in 1953–54 and took over the captaincy of South Africa against England in 1956–57 when McGlew withdrew through injury. His side won the last two Tests to draw the series and van Ryneveld was retained as captain for the Australians' visit the following year. This time South Africa were well beaten, and van Ryneveld retired to enter politics.

In some ways he was an anachronism, an amateur of the old style in contrast to the professional application of men like Cheetham and McGlew. He was an enthusiast who kept his side jolly, but he lacked the total commitment that was becoming increasingly necessary by the 1960s.

Test Record

	M	I	NO	Runs	HS	Avge	100s	RC	Wkts	Avge	BB	Ct
v England	10	19	2	383	83	22.52	–	249	5	49.80	2–38	10
v Australia	4	7	2	107	43	21.40	–	117	2	58.50	2–37	–
v New Zealand	5	7	2	234	68*	46.80	–	305	10	30.50	4–67	4
	19	33	6	724	83	26.81	–	671	17	39.47	4–67	14

Test Record as Captain

				M	I	NO	Runs	HS	Avge	100s	RC	Wkts	Avge	BB	Ct
v England	W2	L1	D1	4	8	1	141	36	20.14	–	150	4	37.50	2–38	3
v Australia	–	L3	D1	4	7	2	107	43	21.40	–	117	2	58.50	2–37	–
	W2	L4	D2	8	15	3	248	43	20.66	–	267	6	44.50	2–37	3

Trevor Leslie GODDARD

Natal and North Eastern Transvaal

Born: Durban, 1 August 1931

The only South African to score 2000 runs and take 100 wickets in Test cricket, Trevor Goddard was a solidly dependable left-handed opening batsman, a medium-pace left-arm bowler and a brilliant close to the wicket fielder. He first made his mark on the tour of England in 1955, when he took 25 wickets in the five-Test series and hit 235 runs. He was an automatic choice for South Africa for the next ten years. Although he scored consistently, he failed to reach a century, being caught at slip for 99 in the Oval Test of 1960.

He missed the 1961–62 series against New Zealand because he was temporarily living in England, but he was asked to lead South Africa in Australia in 1963–64, and the series was drawn. Both McLean and van Ryneveld had been offered the post before Goddard who, great all-rounder though he was, never enjoyed the full confidence of the selectors in the matter of captaincy. He was criticised for his negative approach in the final Test in Sydney. The match was drawn, but the feeling was that South Africa would have won had they ventured more.

In spite of this criticism, Goddard was invited to lead South Africa against England in 1964–65. The first Test was lost and the last four were drawn. During the third Test, the selectors asked him to stand down as captain and to issue a statement that he had asked to be relieved of the leadership. He refused, and announced that he would retire from Test cricket at the end of the series. In the fourth Test, he hit his one and only Test century.

When the side to tour England in 1965 was chosen, Goddard was asked to revoke his decision and to lead the side. He refused to alter his decision, but was persuaded to return for the series against Australia in 1966–67. He had a triumph, with 26 wickets and 294 runs in the rubber, which South Africa won.

The political storm clouds were now gathering fast, but Goddard played in the first three Test matches against Australia in 1969–70. He announced that he would not be available for the forthcoming tour of England, so he was dropped from the fourth and final Test, which was to prove to be South Africa's last for 22 years. His last ball in Test cricket accounted for Connolly.

Goddard was a great all-rounder, but as a captain, he believed that his side were adults who needed no goading for they knew what to do and when to do it. He could not bring himself to hurt men's feelings. That was his weakness. It was no surprise that he became a minister of the church.

Test Record

	M	I	NO	Runs	HS	Avge	100s	RC	Wkts	Avge	BB	Ct
v England	20	40	1	1193	112	30.58	1	1622	63	25.74	5–31	26
v Australia	18	33	4	1090	93	35.17	–	1462	53	27.58	6–53	21
v New Zealand	3	5	0	233	73	46.60	–	142	7	20.28	4–18	1
	41	78	5	2516	112	34.46	–	3226	123	26.22	6–53	48

Test Record as Captain

				M	I	NO	Runs	HS	Avge	100s	RC	Wkts	Avge	BB	Ct
v England	–	L1	D4	5	10	0	405	112	40.50	1	310	6	51.66	2–34	3
v Australia	W1	L1	D3	5	10	3	454	93	64.85	–	420	11	38.18	5–60	7
v New Zealand	–	–	D3	3	5	0	233	73	46.60	–	142	7	20.28	4–18	1
	W1	L2	D10	13	25	3	1092	112	46.93	1	872	24	36.33	5–60	11

Peter Lawrence VAN DER MERWE

Western Province and Eastern Province

Born: Paarl, nr Cape Town, 14 March 1937

Making his first-class debut for South African Universities in 1956–57, Peter van der Merwe was a steady middle-order batsman and slow left-arm bowler who was not of Test quality as a performer, but highly successful as a captain. A chartered accountant, he was a most intelligent captain who inspired a passionate team spirit.

He was fortunate to have cricketers of the calibre of Barlow, Bacher and the Pollocks in his sides, but none could have bettered his results.

Bespectacled, quietly efficient, totally unfussy, he made his Test debut against Australia in 1963–64 but could never hold a regular place in the South African side. He was a surprise choice to succeed Goddard as captain of the side to tour England in 1965, and South Africa won the rubber. In 1966–67 he led South Africa to their first win in a rubber against Australia, after which he retired.

Test Record

	M	I	NO	Runs	HS	Avge	100s	RC	Wkts	Avge	BB	Ct
v England	5	8	1	181	66	25.85	–	–	–	–	–	5
v Australia	8	12	1	300	76	27.27	–	4	0	–	–	4
v New Zealand	2	3	0	52	44	17.33	–	18	1	18.00	1–6	2
	15	23	2	533	76	25.38	–	22	1	22.00	1–6	11

Test Record as Captain

				M	I	NO	Runs	HS	Avge	100s	RC	Wkts	Avge	BB	Ct
v England	W1	–	D2	3	6	0	110	38	18.33	–	–	–	–	–	2
v Australia	W3	L1	D1	5	7	0	225	76	32.14	–	–	–	–	–	2
	W4	L1	D3	8	13	0	335	76	25.76	–	–	–	–	–	4

Dr Aron BACHER

Transvaal

Born: Roodepoort, 24 May 1942

Ali Bacher was a right-handed middle-order batsman and brilliant fielder who made his Test debut in 1965, playing in all three matches of the series in England. He was part of van der Merwe's side which trounced the Australians in 1966–67, and he led South Africa in the final series against Australia in 1969–70, before the Republic was ostracised from Test cricket. One of the most brilliant of combinations, with Procter and Richards now alongside the Pollocks, Barlow, Lindsay and Goddard,

Ali Bacher was South Africa's last Test captain and fought for over 20 years to bring his country back to Test cricket (Adrian Murrell/Allsport)

triumphed in all four Tests. They were men of diverse and positive personalities, and Bacher led them with intelligence, sympathy, tact and firmness.

When South Africa became isolated he fought tirelessly for multi-racial cricket and for his country's return to the Test arena.

Test Record

	M	I	NO	Runs	HS	Avge	100s	RC	Wkts	Avge	BB	Ct
v England	3	6	0	218	70	36.33	–	–	–	–	–	2
v Australia	9	16	1	461	73	30.73	–	–	–	–	–	8
	12	22	1	679	73	32.33	–	–	–	–	–	10

Test Record as Captain

				M	I	NO	Runs	HS	Avge	100s	RC	Wkts	Avge	BB	Ct
v England	W4	–	–	4	7	0	217	73	31.00	–	–	–	–	–	2

NEW ZEALAND

Cricket and New Zealand

The first report of a cricket match in New Zealand we owe to Charles Darwin. In *The Voyage of the Beagle*, he tells how, in 1835, he saw the son of a missionary and some freed Maori slaves engaged in a game at Waimate North.

In the next five years, the population of New Zealand increased dramatically, and the official stamp of colonisation was placed on the islands in 1840. The population continued to grow as farm labourers and factory hands from England were attracted to New Zealand by the subsidised emigration schemes.

In 1842, the *Wellington Spectator* noted that the Wellington Club had enjoyed a game between themselves before enjoying a hearty Christmas dinner, while in 1844 the *Nelson Examiner* recorded with pleasure the revival of the 'truly English game of cricket' in the area. Over the next few years, there were reports of cricket matches in Auckland, Dunedin, Otago and elsewhere.

In 1857, a group of citizens of Wellington, frustrated by plans by builders to develop their cricket ground, petitioned that the proposed site for the Canal and Basin at Te Aro should be set aside as a public park and cricket ground. The petition was granted and prison labour was used to drain what had become a swamp. By 1868 it was ready for cricket, and in January 1930 Basin Reserve saw the first century by a New Zealander in Test cricket as Mills (117)

and Dempster (136) put on 276 for the first wicket in the second Test match against England.

Wellington was not, however, the scene of the first first-class game in New Zealand. That honour belongs to the Dunedin Oval. Inspired by the presence of George Parr's team in Australia, Shadrach Jones, a Dunedin hotelier and theatrical entrepreneur, decided to stage a cricket tournament in the town involving teams from Canterbury, Otago, Southland and Parr's All England XI, whose expenses he agreed to pay if they would interrupt their tour to Australia. On 27, 28 and 29 January 1864, Otago beat Canterbury by 76 runs, and first-class cricket had begun in New Zealand.

Parr's team, with cricketers like E.M. Grace, Tinley, Jackson, Caffyn and Hayward, were too strong for the New Zealanders and were able to beat Twenty-Two of Otago and Twenty-Two of Canterbury, but much interest was aroused and Shadrach Jones made a profit.

For the next ten years, the annual encounters between Otago and Canterbury were the only first-class matches in New Zealand, and it was not until 1873–74 that Wellington, Auckland and Nelson began to compete at first-class level.

In 1876–77, Lillywhite's team played eight matches in New Zealand before returning to Australia to play in what we now regard as the first Test match. It was in Christchurch that

Pooley, the great Surrey wicket-keeper, got involved in a betting argument, was arrested and so missed his one chance of playing in a Test match. In 1878, the Australians played a series of matches in New Zealand as preparation for their scheduled tour of England, and Murdoch's team also visited New Zealand in 1880. Four years later, Tasmania became the first Australian colony to send a side to New Zealand.

In spite of these visits, first-class cricket in New Zealand was slow to develop. There was an abortive attempt to raise a national side in 1886, and by the time that the Plunket Shield was instigated in 1906–07, teams from India, South Africa, Canada, West Indies and the United States had all toured England.

New South Wales and Queensland both visited New Zealand and in 1898–99 a New Zealand side did tour Australia. In the Edwardian period, Lord Hawke's side, MCC and Australia were visitors, but the most significant and exciting tour of New Zealand came after the First World War when A.C. MacLaren led an MCC side which included Percy Chapman, 'Tich' Freeman and Freddie Calthorpe. In two of the three 'Tests', New Zealand were beaten by an innings, and the third was drawn; but the home side were not without honour. They could console themselves, too, with the fact that the leading run scorer on the MCC side in the series was a New Zealander, Tom Lowry.

The New Zealanders had now got the taste of international cricket and they were eager for better things. In 1927 they engaged in a full-scale tour of England, although they were not granted a Test match. In the words of the secretary of MCC, 'The New Zealand team is bent on something of a sporting and educational trip, and makes no pretence of throwing down a gauge for testing its merits against the full strength of England.' This may well have been the case, but the New Zealand Cricket Council instructed the selectors to choose players who had at least ten years of cricket ahead of them. The thoughts and plans were of the future and of Test cricket.

The side had seven wins and five losses in 26 first-class matches. Lowry led the side, and four of the men in the party, Dempster, James, Dacre and Merritt, later qualified for English counties. Indeed, Dacre remained in England in order to begin his two-year period of qualification for Gloucestershire, and so he was lost to New Zealand and Test cricket.

In 1929–30, England played a four-Test series in New Zealand under the captaincy of Harold Gilligan. Concurrently, an England side was engaged in a Test series in the Caribbean. Pace bowler Maurice Allom took four wickets in five balls as England beat New Zealand in the first Test, and the remaining three were drawn. New Zealand also lost one Test on the first major tour of England in 1931.

By the outbreak of the Second World War, New Zealand had played only 14 Test matches, 12 of them against England. They did not meet Australia until a hastily arranged match in 1945–46, nor did they meet them again until 1973–74. They were as badly treated in their formative years as Sri Lanka were to be in theirs, but by the 1980s they were a formidable side, a match for anyone in the world.

The appointment of a New Zealand captain has rarely been a subject of controversy, more a case of natural progression. As the authors of *Men in White* were to write in 1986:

'For much of its history, New Zealand cricket has been free of the grimmer aspects of the professional game. Perhaps at some cost to its win–lose ratio in international matches, the sport has until recently enjoyed an aura of amateur innocence. This came about more from necessity than choice – this country's small population inhibited the growth of professional cricket – but it did result in New Zealand touring teams receiving praise for their sportsmanship and a sunny, adventurous disposition.'

Thomas Coleman LOWRY

Auckland, Wellington and Somerset

Born: Fernhill, 17 February 1898
Died: Hastings, 20 July 1976

There was never any doubt as to who would captain New Zealand in their inaugural Test match, for Tom Lowry had been educated in England and won a blue in his last year at Cambridge. He had also provided some spice to the Somerset side during his years at university, 1921–24. He was a hard-hitting right-handed batsman, a medium pace off-break bowler and more than an occasional wicket-keeper.

A born leader and a man of immense strength, he was a member of the Hellfire Club at Cambridge and lived life to the full. He once went off to Newmarket with a £5 note in his pocket and returned driving a small car. Tom

Pearce, the former Essex captain, tells how once at Southend after a bout of drinking, Lowry carried a cigarette machine from the ground floor to the first floor of the hotel in which he was staying. Next morning, it took four porters to carry the machine back to its rightful place. Lowry was a brave man who did not suffer fools gladly, admired courage above all else, and constantly commented on the game in colourful language.

He returned to New Zealand in 1924, and led his country on the tour of England in 1927 and in their first seven Test matches, all of them against England. He also managed the 1937 side to England. One of his sisters married Percy Chapman, the England captain, and another married the Australian R.H. Bettington, who captained Oxford.

Lowry did much to help raise the standard of cricket in New Zealand and to bring Test cricket to the country.

Test Record as Captain

				M	I	NO	Runs	HS	Avge	100s	RC	Wkts	Avge	BB	Ct
v England	–	L2	D5	7	8	0	223	80	27.87	–	5	0	–	–	8

Milford Laurenson PAGE

Canterbury

Born: Lyttleton, 8 May 1902
Died: Christchurch, 13 February 1987

A right-handed middle-order batsman and a slow-medium pace bowler, 'Curly' Page was a fine all-round sportsman who was an All Black scrum-half in 1928. He toured England in 1927 and was vice-captain to Lowry on the 1931 tour. In the first Test at Lord's, he played a major part

in New Zealand's fightback with an innings of 104.

Following the retirement of Lowry, he led New Zealand against South Africa in 1931–32 and would have captained them against Australia in 1933–34 had the tour not been cancelled. The New Zealand cricket authorities objected to the weakness of the party that the Australians intended to send and withdrew the invitation for the tour.

A modest, gentle and kindly man, Page subsequently led the New Zealand side to England, after which he retired.

Test Record

	M	I	NO	Runs	HS	Avge	100s	RC	Wkts	Avge	BB	Ct
v England	12	16	0	440	104	27.50	1	160	4	40.00	2–31	3
v South Africa	2	4	0	52	23	13.00	–	71	1	71.00	1–30	3
	14	20	0	492	104	24.60	1	231	5	46.20	2–31	6

Test Record as Captain

			M	I	NO	Runs	HS	Avge	100s	RC	Wkts	Avge	BB	Ct
v England	–	L1	D4	5	7	0	152	53	21.85	–	79	2	39.50	2–21	1
v South Africa	–	L2	–	2	4	0	52	23	13.00	–	71	1	71.00	1–30	3
	–	L3	D4	7	11	0	204	53	18.54	–	150	3	50.00	2–21	4

Walter Arnold HADLEE

Canterbury

Born: Lincoln, 4 June 1915

A bespectacled batsman who often opened the innings, Walter Hadlee came to England in 1937 and played in all three Tests, hitting 93 at Old Trafford. He became captain of New Zealand after the war, leading them first against Australia, in 1945–46, in a match which was not recognised as a Test until much later. He made his one Test century against England in 1946–47, and led the side to England in 1949 and at home against England in 1950–51, in a series which marked the end of his career.

He was an able, quiet, but stern captain, and his side drew all four Tests in England in 1949. New Zealand were a strong combination and only three days had been allocated to each Test. The series convinced MCC that opposition was now stronger than it had been in the thirties, and five days were scheduled for Test matches thereafter.

Hadlee is the father of five sons, two of whom, Richard and Dayle, have played Test cricket for New Zealand, while Barry appeared in the 1975 World Cup. Walter Hadlee has also made his mark as an administrator in New Zealand cricket.

Test Record

	M	I	NO	Runs	HS	Avge	100s	RC	Wkts	Avge	BB	Ct
v England	10	17	1	534	116	33.37	1	–	–	–	–	4
v Australia	1	2	0	9	6	4.50	–	–	–	–	–	2
	11	19	1	543	116	30.16	1	–	–	–	–	6

Test Record as Captain

			M	I	NO	Runs	HS	Avge	100s	RC	Wkts	Avge	BB	Ct
v England	–	L1	D6	7	11	1	383	116	38.30	1	–	–	–	–	3
v Australia	–	L1	–	1	2	0	9	6	4.50	–	–	–	–	–	2
	–	L2	D6	8	13	1	392	116	32.66	1	–	–	–	–	5

Bert SUTCLIFFE

Auckland, Otago and Northern District

Born: Auckland, 17 November 1923

A left-handed opening batsman and a useful slow left-arm bowler, Bert Sutcliffe must rank with the great left-handers in world cricket. He captained New Zealand against West Indies in 1951–52, and again in South Africa in 1953–54 when Rabone was injured, but captaincy was not a job he relished. In India in 1955–56 he hit two centuries in the Test series and his 230 not out in Delhi was the highest score made for New Zealand in Test cricket at that time.

His Test career seemed to be over in 1958–59 when he played twice against England, but he was recalled in 1965 for the tours of India, Pakistan and England. He made 151 not out against India in Calcutta, but he played in only the Edgbaston Test in England where he was struck on the ear by a ball from Fred Trueman.

Test Record

	M	I	NO	Runs	HS	Avge	100s	RC	Wkts	Avge	BB	Ct
v England	16	28	2	1049	116	40.34	2	106	1	106.00	1–17	5
v South Africa	7	13	1	455	80*	37.91	–	50	0	–	–	9
v West Indies	4	8	1	196	48	28.00	–	17	0	–	–	2
v India	9	16	3	885	230*	68.07	3	129	0	–	–	1
v Pakistan	6	11	1	142	25*	14.20	–	42	3	14.00	2–38	3
	42	76	8	2727	230*	40.10	5	344	4	86.00	2–38	20

Test Record as Captain

				M	I	NO	Runs	HS	Avge	100s	RC	Wkts	Avge	BB	Ct
v South Africa	–	L2	–	2	4	0	113	52	28.25	–	–	–	–	–	4
v West Indies	–	L1	D1	2	4	1	103	45	34.33	–	1	0	–	–	2
	–	L3	D1	4	8	1	216	52	30.85	–	1	0	–	–	6

Walter Mervyn WALLACE

Auckland

Born: Auckland, 19 December 1916

Wallace topped the tour averages in 1937, and 12 years later, in England for the second time, he scored 910 runs before the end of May; but he could not reproduce that form in the Tests nor for the rest of the tour. He was vice-captain to Hadlee on that tour and led New Zealand against South Africa in 1952–53, but that marked the end of his Test career.

Test Record

	M	I	NO	Runs	HS	Avge	100s	RC	Wkts	Avge	BB	Ct
v England	10	16	0	386	66	24.12	–	5	0	–	–	5
v Australia	1	2	0	24	14	12.00	–	–	–	–	–	–
v South Africa	2	3	0	29	23	9.66	–	–	–	–	–	–
	13	21	0	439	66	20.90	–	5	0	–	–	5

Test Record as Captain

				M	I	NO	Runs	HS	Avge	100s	RC	Wkts	Avge	BB	Ct
v South Africa	–	L1	D1	2	3	0	29	23	9.66	–	–	–	–	–	–

Geoffrey Osbourne RABONE

Wellington and Auckland

Born: Gore, 6 November 1921

A capable all-rounder who could and did bowl medium pace, off-breaks or leg-breaks as the occasion demanded, Rabone made his Test debut in England in 1949, playing in all four games. There was surprise when he was named as captain for the tour of South Africa in 1953–54, for he had originally stated that he was unavailable. Wallace, one of the selectors, was not among the touring party although most had believed that he would be captain. It transpired that Wallace had only accepted the captaincy after Hadlee's retirement in order to lend a young side some experience, and that he had pleaded the case for Rabone to be made captain.

Rabone opened the innings in the first Test at Durban and hit 107. A broken bone in the foot, sustained on the eve of the fourth Test, caused him to miss the end of the tour.

A highly respected captain, Rabone led his country against England in 1954–55 when in the second match, New Zealand were bowled out for 26, the lowest score in Test history. Rabone was not available for the tour of India and Pakistan later the same year and did not appear in Test cricket again

Test Record

	M	I	NO	Runs	HS	Avge	100s	RC	Wkts	Avge	BB	Ct
v England	6	10	1	209	39*	23.22	–	331	4	82.75	3–116	4
v South Africa	4	7	1	289	107	48.16	1	239	12	19.91	6–68	1
v West Indies	2	3	0	64	37	21.33	–	65	0	–	–	–
	12	20	2	562	107	31.22	1	635	16	39.68	6–68	5

Test Record as Captain

				M	I	NO	Runs	HS	Avge	100s	RC	Wkts	Avge	BB	Ct
v England	–	L2	–	2	4	0	61	29	15.25	–	4	0	–	–	1
v South Africa	–	L2	D1	3	5	0	254	107	50.80	1	131	8	16.37	6–68	–
	–	L4	D1	5	9	0	315	107	35.00	1	135	8	16.87	6–68	1

Henry Butler CAVE

Wellington and Central Districts

Born: Wanganui, 10 October 1922
Died: Wanganui, 15 September 1989

Harry Cave made his Test debut in England in 1949. A medium pace bowler noted for his accuracy and a late-order batsman good enough to score two first-class centuries, he missed the tour to South Africa under Rabone, whom he then succeeded as captain of New Zealand for the tour of India and Pakistan in 1955–56.

Test Record

	M	I	NO	Runs	HS	Avge	100s	RC	Wkts	Avge	BB	Ct
v England	8	13	2	74	14*	6.72	–	658	9	73.11	3–103	4
v West Indies	3	6	1	16	11	3.20	–	186	12	15.50	4–21	–
v India	5	7	2	87	22*	17.40	–	412	7	58.85	3–77	2
v Pakistan	3	5	0	52	21	10.40	–	211	6	35.16	3–45	2
	19	31	5	229	22*	8.80	–	1467	34	43.14	4–21	8

Respected for the tactful way in which he negotiated his country's first tour of the Indian subcontinent, he also captained New Zealand in the first Test against West Indies in 1955–56, but after a humiliating innings defeat in that Test he was dropped for the second and Reid was appointed captain. He was recalled for the third Test and played under Reid, as he did in the fourth. This was New Zealand's 45th Test match and they claimed their first victory in Test cricket by 190 runs. In taking 4 for 22 and 4 for 21, Cave played a major part in the historic victory. It was a fine way to end a Test career.

Test Record as Captain

				M	I	NO	Runs	HS	Avge	100s	RC	Wkts	Avge	BB	Ct
v West Indies	–	L1	–	1	2	0	0	0	0.00	–	47	2	23.50	2–47	–
v India	–	L2	D3	5	7	2	87	22*	17.40	–	412	7	58.85	3–77	2
v Pakistan	–	L2	D1	3	5	0	52	21	10.40	–	211	6	35.16	3–45	2
	–	L5	D4	9	14	2	139	22*	11.58	–	670	15	44.66	3–45	4

John Richard REID

Wellington and Otago

Born: Auckland, 3 June 1928

No man has captained New Zealand more often nor in more difficult times than John Reid, nor has New Zealand produced a more complete all-round cricketer. He was a hard-hitting middle-order batsman, a brisk bowler of off-cutters and a wicket-keeper of no mean ability. He scored 50 and 25 in his debut Test at Old Trafford in 1949 and hit 93 and kept wicket in his second Test.

He did not really blossom until the 1953–54 series in South Africa when he hit his maiden Test century in the third match in Cape Town. A year later, he and Sutcliffe were the only New Zealanders to gain praise after the defeat by Hutton's side, and it was felt that New Zealand cricket was at a low ebb.

The despair became deeper in 1955–56 when New Zealand lost the first Test of a four-match series with West Indies by an innings and 71 runs. Reid was appointed captain for the rest of the series and New Zealand won an historic victory in the final encounter, with Reid top scorer on 84.

Defeats by England followed, but in South Africa in 1961–62 Reid led New Zealand in a series that was drawn, each side winning two of the five Tests. Never before had New Zealand won two Tests in a series, and Reid topped both the batting and bowling averages.

There were to be no more team successes for Reid after that tour, and by the mid-sixties, New Zealand had earned a reputation for dullness in their efforts to avoid defeat. Nine Tests in succession were drawn. In 1965, New Zealand played exhausting successive series against India, Pakistan and England. The tour of England was a sad failure for Reid, New Zealand

Test Record

	M	I	NO	Runs	HS	Avge	100s	RC	Wkts	Avge	BB	Ct/st
v England	19	36	2	953	100	28.09	1	584	16	36.50	4–36	13/1
v South Africa	15	28	1	914	142	33.85	2	991	37	26.78	6–60	13/–
v West Indies	6	11	0	212	84	19.27	–	316	7	45.14	3–68	6/–
v India	9	16	2	691	120	49.35	2	446	9	49.55	3–19	4/–
v Pakistan	9	17	0	658	128	38.70	1	498	16	31.12	4–38	7/–
	58	108	5	3428	142	33.28	6	2835	85	33.35	6–60	43/1

losing all three Tests and acquitting themselves poorly. He retired at the end of the tour.

Reid was bitterly disappointed. He felt that New Zealand had made no material progress since the wins in South Africa, and his ambition of leading New Zealand to a victory over England was never realised. He led his country in 34 consecutive Test matches, a record bettered only by Border and Sobers. He was highly respected for his knowledge of the game and for his unstinting efforts to raise the standard of New Zealand cricket.

Test Record as Captain

				M	I	NO	Runs	HS	Avge	100s	RC	Wkts	Avge	BB	Ct/st
v England	–	L11	D2	13	25	2	602	100	26.17	1	465	12	38.75	3–47	7/1
v South Africa	W2	L2	D4	8	16	1	634	142	42.66	1	495	23	21.52	6–60	5/–
v West Indies	W1	L2	–	3	6	0	170	84	28.33	–	215	7	30.71	3–68	2/–
v India	–	L1	D3	4	7	0	198	82	28.29	–	175	3	58.33	1–3	3/–
v Pakistan	–	L2	D4	6	11	0	525	128	47.72	1	277	9	30.77	3–80	5/–
	W3	L18	D13	34	65	3	2129	142	34.33	3	1627	54	30.12	6–60	22/1

Murray Ernest CHAPPLE

Canterbury and Central Districts

Born: Christchurch, 25 July 1930
Died: Hamilton, 30 July 1985

Murray Chapple began his Test career as Sutcliffe's opening partner against South Africa at Auckland in 1952–53. He later dropped down the order, and he could never command a regular place in the side. He was not selected for a tour to England, but surprisingly, he appeared in two of New Zealand's winning Test teams of the period.

He was a very strange choice as successor to Reid. His abilities as a leader and tactician were never in doubt, but his own form in domestic cricket was poor. He took his one Test wicket as his side drew with England, but he was injured and replaced by Sinclair for the rest of the series.

Test Record

	M	I	NO	Runs	HS	Avge	100s	RC	Wkts	Avge	BB	Ct
v England	2	4	0	35	15	8.75	–	24	1	24.00	1–24	1
v South Africa	11	21	1	458	76	22.90	–	60	0	–	–	8
v West Indies	1	2	0	4	3	2.00	–	–	–	–	–	1
	14	27	1	497	76	19.11	–	84	1	84.00	1–24	10

Test Record as Captain

				M	I	NO	Runs	HS	Avge	100s	RC	Wkts	Avge	BB	Ct
v England	–	–	D1	1	2	0	15	15	7.50	–	24	1	24.00	1–24	1

Barry Whitley SINCLAIR

Wellington

Born: Wellington, 23 October 1936

When he was asked to captain New Zealand in the second Test against England in 1965–66, Barry Sinclair became New Zealand's third captain in as many Tests, and his experience of captaining in first-class cricket was limited to one match. He was, however, an admirable choice. A diminutive, defiant batsman, he exuded grit and determination and had already hit two Test centuries.

His reign was brief. After two Tests against England, he led in the first Test against India in 1967–68 but missed the next two through illness. He returned to play in the fourth and final Test under Dowling, and that ended his Test career.

Test Record

	M	I	NO	Runs	HS	Avge	100s	RC	Wkts	Avge	BB	Ct
v England	9	18	0	459	114	25.50	1	–	–	–	–	1
v South Africa	3	6	0	264	138	44.00	1	–	–	–	–	4
v India	4	7	0	79	30	11.28	–	–	–	–	–	1
v Pakistan	5	9	1	346	130	43.12	1	32	2	16.00	2–32	2
	21	40	1	1148	138	29.43	3	32	2	16.00	2–32	8

Test Record as Captain

				M	I	NO	Runs	HS	Avge	100s	RC	Wkts	Avge	BB	Ct
v England	–	–	D2	2	4	0	195	114	48.75	1	–	–	–	–	1
v India	–	L1	–	1	2	0	8	8	4.00	–	–	–	–	–	1
	–	L1	D2	3	6	0	203	114	33.83	1	–	–	–	–	2

Graham Thorne DOWLING

Canterbury

Born: Canterbury, 4 March 1937

A thoughtful cricketer, Graham Dowling established himself in the New Zealand side as an eminently reliable opening batsman, an outstanding close to the wicket fielder and a dependable reserve wicket-keeper. His career was tinged with success. He made his Test debut against South Africa at Johannesburg in 1961–62 and played in the two Tests which New Zealand won to square the series.

His first Test century came against India in

Test Record

	M	I	NO	Runs	HS	Avge	100s	RC	Wkts	Avge	BB	Ct
v England	11	22	1	517	66	24.61	–	–	–	–	–	1
v South Africa	5	10	0	271	78	27.10	–	–	–	–	–	6
v West Indies	5	10	0	277	76	27.70	–	–	–	–	–	2
v India	11	22	2	964	239	48.20	3	19	1	19.00	1–19	7
v Pakistan	7	13	0	277	83	21.30	–	–	–	–	–	7
	39	77	3	2306	239	31.16	3	19	1	19.00	1–19	23

1965, and it was against India that he first captained New Zealand in 1967–68. When Sinclair was ill, Dowling, who had scored 143 in the first Test of the series, was appointed captain. He made 239, then a New Zealand record, and his innings included five sixes. New Zealand won by six wickets to record their first victory over India.

This was the first of four wins which Dowling was to achieve as captain, and under him, New Zealand beat West Indies and Pakistan as well

as India so that two series were drawn, and one, against Pakistan in 1969–70, was won. This was New Zealand's first victory in a rubber, after 40 years of Test cricket. It was a magnificent achievement for which Dowling took great credit.

He still plays a prominent part in the administration of cricket in New Zealand. Sadly, his Test career ended when, after two drawn Tests in West Indies, he was forced to return home with a back injury.

Test Record as Captain

				M	I	NO	Runs	HS	Avge	100s	RC	Wkts	Avge	BB	Ct
v England	–	L3	D2	5	10	1	227	53	25.22	–	–	–	–	–	1
v West Indies	W1	L1	D3	5	10	0	277	76	27.70	–	–	–	–	–	2
v India	W2	L3	D1	6	12	1	575	239	52.27	1	–	–	–	–	5
v Pakistan	W1	–	D2	3	6	0	79	40	13.16	–	–	–	–	–	4
	W4	L7	D8	19	38	2	1158	239	32.16	1	–	–	–	–	12

Bevan Ernest CONGDON

Central Districts, Wellington, Otago
and Canterbury

Born: Motueka, 11 February 1938

Bev Congdon took over the captaincy of New Zealand when Graham Dowling broke down with a back injury in the Caribbean in 1971–72. Congdon had hit 166 not out in the second Test in Trinidad, and he scored 126 in the next match in Barbados, his first as captain.

Originally an opening batsman when he first played Test cricket against Pakistan and India in 1964–65, he settled at number three, and his

medium pace bowling and fine fielding made him one of the very best of New Zealand's all-rounders. He had unlimited powers of concentration and determination, and he could display a wide range of shots. His first Test century came against England in 1965–66.

A thoughtful, kind and eminently sound captain who was rarely prepared to be too adventurous, Congdon led from the front. His record as captain, just one win in 17 games, does scant justice to his achievement. His side lost two of the three Tests in England in 1973, yet they came close to winning the series. At Trent Bridge, having been bowled out for 97 in their first innings, they were left to score 479 to win the match. Congdon and Pollard put on 177 for

Test Record

	M	I	NO	Runs	HS	Avge	100s	RC	Wkts	Avge	BB	Ct
v England	22	41	1	1143	176	28.57	3	569	8	71.12	2–14	12
v Australia	8	15	2	456	132	35.07	2	441	16	27.56	4–46	5
v West Indies	8	14	2	764	166*	63.66	2	446	13	34.30	3–56	3
v India	13	24	1	713	78	31.00	–	354	14	25.28	5–65	15
v Pakistan	10	20	1	372	67	19.57	–	344	8	43.00	2–15	9
	61	114	7	3448	176	32.22	7	2154	59	36.50	5–65	44

the fifth wicket and New Zealand reached 440 to lose by 38 runs. Congdon's 176 was the first century by a New Zealander in a Test in England since 1949. In the next Test, at Lord's, he hit 175; had Fletcher not played a mighty innings and had New Zealand held their catches, England would have been beaten.

He did lead New Zealand to their first victory over Australia, at Christchurch in 1973–74, and the series was drawn.

Following the home series with England in 1974–75, Congdon said that he would not be available for the 1975 World Cup and Turner took over the captaincy for the second one-day international. Congdon remained in the side and hit 101. He was to continue to play Test cricket under the leadership of Turner and Burgess until 1978, and he was in the New Zealand side that gained the first ever victory over England.

Bev Congdon took over the New Zealand captaincy at a difficult time, but he led his side to their first victory over Australia in 1973–74 (Hulton)

Test Record as Captain

				M	I	NO	Runs	HS	Avge	100s	RC	Wkts	Avge	BB	Ct
v England	–	L3	D2	5	8	0	420	176	52.50	2	265	5	53.00	2–54	3
v Australia	W1	L3	D2	6	11	1	300	132	30.00	1	405	16	25.31	4–46	4
v West Indies	–	–	D3	3	4	1	256	126	85.33	1	290	7	41.42	2–26	1
v Pakistan	–	L1	D2	3	6	1	91	35	18.20	–	220	5	44.00	2–44	3
	W1	L7	D9	17	29	3	1067	176	41.03	4	1180	33	35.75	4–46	11

Glenn Maitland TURNER

Otago, Northern Districts and Worcestershire

Born: Dunedin, 26 May 1947

Glenn Turner adopted a thorough and professional approach to cricket from an early age. He worked tirelessly to earn the fare to England, where he played for Worcestershire from 1967 until 1982. An opening batsman, he developed from the 'strokeless wonder' of his early days to a man who was capable of some fierce innings, as he displayed when hitting 311 not out against Warwickshire in 1982.

He began his Test career with a 'duck' against West Indies in 1968–69, but in the second Test he hit 74 and New Zealand won. His first Test century came in Pakistan in November 1969, when he batted for over seven hours for 110.

It was in the 1971–72 series against West Indies in the Caribbean that Turner established himself as one of the most accomplished batsmen in world cricket and as the most successful batsman that New Zealand had produced. He averaged 96 in the series and his 672 runs included two double centuries.

On the 1973 tour of England, he reached 1000 runs before the end of May, the first New Zealander ever to achieve this feat, but he had a disappointing Test series. He took over as captain of New Zealand when Bev Congdon declared that he was unavailable for the 1975 World Cup, and Turner then led the side to a draw in the series against India in 1975–76, each side winning one Test.

In 1978, he decided to give his efforts to his benefit and to Worcestershire, and the first rift occurred between Turner and the New Zealand cricketing authorities. He did return to Test cricket in 1982–83 for the inaugural series against Sri Lanka in New Zealand, and he played for New Zealand in the World Cup of 1983. His relationship with the New Zealand Board was never an easy one, but he subsequently managed touring sides and planned campaigns.

Turner brought to New Zealand cricket a steel and professionalism which was not easily, nor readily, absorbed, but it was a dimension that was to be important when success was consistently achieved in the 1980s.

A young Glenn Turner playing for the New Zealanders against Middlesex in 1969 comes close to being caught by keeper John Murray (Lemmon)

Test Record

	M	I	NO	Runs	HS	Avge	100s	RC	Wkts	Avge	BB	Ct
v England	9	16	2	510	98	36.42	–	–	–	–	–	8
v Australia	7	12	1	541	110*	49.18	2	–	–	–	–	4
v West Indies	8	14	1	855	259	65.76	2	5	0	–	–	9
v India	9	16	1	583	117	38.85	2	–	–	–	–	11
v Pakistan	6	12	1	431	110	39.18	1	–	–	–	–	8
v Sri Lanka	2	3	0	71	32	23.66	–	–	–	–	–	2
	41	73	6	2991	259	44.64	7	5	0	–	–	42

Test Record as Captain

				M	I	NO	Runs	HS	Avge	100s	RC	Wkts	Avge	BB	Ct
v Australia	–	L1	D1	2	4	0	78	36	19.50	–	–	–	–	–	2
v India	W1	L3	D2	6	10	0	478	117	47.80	2	–	–	–	–	8
v Pakistan	–	L2	–	2	4	0	60	49	15.00	–	–	–	–	–	3
	W1	L6	D3	10	18	0	616	117	34.22	2	–	–	–	–	13

John Morton PARKER

Northern Districts and Worcestershire

Born: Dannevirke, 21 February 1951

John Parker followed Turner to Worcestershire. A dour opening batsman, he played for the county and was an occasional wicket-keeper. He made his Test debut against Pakistan in 1973, playing in all three Tests but failing to reach double figures. He quickly asserted himself with a maiden Test century against Australia the following winter and the highest of his three Test hundreds against England in 1974–75.

He led New Zealand against Pakistan in Karachi in 1976–77 when Turner was injured. Parker's last series was against Australia in 1980–81. His brother Murray also played Test cricket.

John Parker followed Glenn Turner's path to Worcestershire and led New Zealand in his mentor's absence. His brother Murray played under him (Hulton)

Test Record

	M	I	NO	Runs	HS	Avge	100s	RC	Wkts	Avge	BB	Ct
v England	10	18	2	403	121	25.18	1	–	–	–	–	10
v Australia	11	21	0	504	108	24.00	1	–	–	–	–	14
v West Indies	3	5	0	48	42	9.60	–	–	–	–	–	1
v India	6	10	0	345	104	34.50	1	24	1	24.00	1–24	3
v Pakistan	6	9	0	198	82	22.00	–	–	–	–	–	2
	36	63	2	1498	121	24.55	3	24	1	24.00	1–24	30

Test Record as Captain

				M	I	NO	Runs	HS	Avge	100s	RC	Wkts	Avge	BB	Ct
v Pakistan	–	–	D1	1	2	0	40	48	24.00	–	–	–	–	–	–

Mark Gordon BURGESS

Auckland

Born: Auckland, 17 July 1944

No New Zealand captain has had a more sensational nor more successful first game as skipper than Mark Burgess. Replacing Turner as captain for the 1977–78 series against England, he led New Zealand to victory in the first Test. It was the 48th Test match between the two countries, and it was New Zealand's first win.

A fair-headed, purposeful batsman and a useful medium pace off-break bowler, Burgess first played for New Zealand against India in 1967–68 and hit centuries in three successive Test matches spread over 15 months from 1970 to 1972. Pakistan, England and West Indies were the opponents.

He had appeared in 38 Test matches before he became the New Zealand skipper, and in truth, his best performances were behind him. He stood down after the 1978–79 series against Pakistan but returned two years later to tour Australia under Howarth, acting as captain in Perth when Howarth was injured.

Burgess was a popular captain with a touch of the cavalier amateur about him, and he helped move New Zealand a step nearer to a highly respected place in world cricket.

Mark Burgess holds a special place in New Zealand cricket history as the first captain to lead the national side to victory over England (Hulton)

Test Record

	M	I	NO	Runs	HS	Avge	100s	RC	Wkts	Avge	BB	Ct
v England	12	21	1	610	105	30.50	2	51	0	–	–	10
v Australia	6	12	1	279	66	25.36	–	–	–	–	–	2
v West Indies	7	12	1	317	101	28.81	1	27	0	–	–	5
v India	13	24	0	725	95	30.20	–	89	5	17.80	3–23	9
v Pakistan	12	23	3	753	119*	37.65	2	45	1	45.00	1–20	8
	50	92	6	2684	119*	31.20	5	212	6	35.33	3–23	34

Test Record as Captain

				M	I	NO	Runs	HS	Avge	100s	RC	Wkts	Avge	BB	Ct
v England	W1	L4	D1	6	12	1	252	68	21.00	–	–	–	–	–	7
v Australia	–	L1	–	1	2	0	61	43	30.50	–	–	–	–	–	–
v Pakistan	–	L1	D2	3	5	0	136	71	27.20	–	–	–	–	–	1
	W1	L6	D3	10	19	1	449	68	24.94	–	–	–	–	–	8

Geoffrey Philip HOWARTH

Auckland, Northern Districts and Surrey

Born: Auckland, 29 March 1951

The younger brother of Hedley Howarth, a fine slow left-arm bowler, Geoff Howarth made his Test debut in 1974–75 against England. Three years later he became only the second batsman in New Zealand Test history – Turner was the first – to hit a century in each innings of a Test match, when his maiden Test hundred, 122 against England in his native city, was followed by 102 in the second innings. A few months later he scored 123 at Lord's, and in his next series, took a century off the Pakistan attack. For the series against West Indies in 1979–80, he was appointed captain, and so began the most successful period in New Zealand cricket history.

Howarth's career had followed a pattern similar to that of Turner's. He first played for Surrey in 1971 and became a great favourite at The Oval as a stylish batsman who frequently opened the innings. From the outset, the New Zealand selectors recognised in Howarth an intelligent and perceptive leader. He had studied the game well and had been thorough in his preparation. There was something of the amateur spirit of Burgess about him – his team considered him a 'bit of a toff' – but it was wedded to an unyielding professionalism, a total understanding of the modern game in all

England's Clive Radley takes evasive action as Geoff Howarth hits out at Lord's in 1978 (Hulton)

its aspects and a tactical acumen second to none. In the early 1980s he had no superior as a captain in world cricket.

Under Howarth, New Zealand did not lose a home series. West Indies were beaten in 1979–80, the first time that New Zealand had won a home rubber. The following season they beat India in a rubber for the first time. The greatest disappointment came when New Zealand failed to do themselves justice in England in 1983 and lost the series, but the victory at Headingley was New Zealand's first Test win in England, and the first outside New Zealand since 1969. In 1983–84 Howarth quickly gained his revenge, as New Zealand beat England in a rubber for the first time in 21 attempts.

Howarth retired after the defeat in West Indies a year later, but he had become the first New Zealand captain to win more matches than he lost, and he left New Zealand cricket in a more prosperous and respected position than it had ever previously known.

A moment of triumph for Howarth and New Zealand. Smith and Hadlee celebrate as the New Zealand captain catches Fowler off the bowling of Boock. New Zealand beat England by an innings at Christchurch and went to win a rubber against England for the first time in 1983–84 (Adrian Murrell/Allsport)

Test Record

	M	I	NO	Runs	HS	Avge	100s	RC	Wkts	Avge	BB	Ct
v England	15	27	3	910	123	37.91	3	85	1	85.00	1–47	14
v Australia	7	13	1	468	65	39.00	–	12	0	–	–	2
v West Indies	7	12	0	397	147	33.08	1	49	1	49.00	1–32	5
v India	5	9	1	216	137*	27.00	1	54	0	–	–	2
v Pakistan	8	14	0	340	114	24.28	1	71	1	71.00	1–13	3
v Sri Lanka	5	8	0	200	62	25.00	–	–	–	–	–	3
	47	83	5	2531	147	32.44	6	271	3	90.33	1–13	29

Test Record as Captain

				M	I	NO	Runs	HS	Avge	100s	RC	Wkts	Avge	BB	Ct
v England	W2	L3	D2	7	12	0	282	67	23.50	–	19	0	–	–	10
v Australia	W1	L2	D2	5	9	1	337	65	42.12	–	12	0	–	–	1
v West Indies	W1	L2	D4	7	12	0	397	147	33.08	1	49	1	49.00	1–32	5
v India	W1	–	D2	3	5	1	172	137*	43.00	1	24	0	–	–	2
v Pakistan	W2	–	D1	3	5	0	103	33	34.33	–	–	–	–	–	–
v Sri Lanka	W4	–	D1	5	8	0	200	62	25.00	–	–	–	–	–	3
	W11	L7	D12	30	51	2	1491	147	30.42	2	104	1	104.00	1–32	21

Jeremy Vernon CONEY

Wellington

Born: Wellington, 21 June 1952

Glenn Turner was injured at the start of New Zealand's tour of Australia in 1973–74, and Jeremy Coney, a young right-handed batsman and slow-medium pace bowler, was summoned as a replacement. It was a surprising choice. Coney played in two Tests in Australia and then in two against Australia in New Zealand before disappearing again into domestic cricket.

Five years later, Coney was brought back into the New Zealand side for the series against Pakistan. There was general astonishment, but it proved to be a masterstroke. Coney topped the batting averages and dealt ably with the Pakistan pace attack. Tall, lean, enthusiastic and good-humoured, Coney was a cricketer who rarely failed to make a contribution in one department of the game.

He had seemed on the verge of a Test hundred on several occasions before, in 1983–84, he hit 174 not out against England. His side trailed by 244 on the first innings and were 165 for 4 in their second when Coney went in. He batted for 490 minutes to score his first century for seven years and save the match. New Zealand went on to win the series.

He led New Zealand in Pakistan in 1984–85 when Howarth was unavailable and succeeded him as captain a year later. He enjoyed two victorious series over Australia and then led New Zealand to triumph in a rubber in England for the first time. In the home series against Australia he scored 101 not out, 98 and 93.

New Zealand's success was maintained under the likeable Jeremey Coney (Allsport/Adrian Murrell)

Following the drawn series with West Indies in 1986–87, he retired. Greatly respected, a shrewd tactician and an outstanding leader of men, Coney had built upon Howarth's success and taken New Zealand to a position of eminence in world cricket.

Edgar, Coney and Wright applaud John Bracewell's century at Trent Bridge in 1986. New Zealand won the match and a series in England for the first time, a wonderful achievement by Coney and his men (Adrian Murrell/Allsport)

Test Record

	M	I	NO	Runs	HS	Avge	100s	RC	Wkts	Avge	BB	Ct
v England	10	16	3	622	174*	47.84	1	186	5	37.20	2–21	12
v Australia	15	24	3	695	101*	33.09	1	247	10	24.70	3–47	24
v West Indies	10	17	3	458	83	32.71	–	271	6	45.16	2–38	8
v India	3	5	1	92	65	23.00	–	38	2	19.00	2–12	1
v Pakistan	9	15	2	528	111*	40.61	1	202	4	50.50	2–33	10
v Sri Lanka	5	8	2	273	92	45.50	–	22	0	–	–	9
	52	85	14	2668	174*	37.57	3	966	27	35.77	3–47	64

Test Record as Captain

				M	I	NO	Runs	HS	Avge	100s	RC	Wkts	Avge	BB	Ct
v England	W1	–	D2	3	4	1	133	51	44.33	–	48	0	–	–	2
v Australia	W3	L1	D2	6	8	1	364	101*	52.00	1	182	6	30.33	3–47	11
v West Indies	W1	L1	D1	3	6	0	77	36	12.83	–	30	0	–	–	5
v Pakistan	–	L2	D1	3	5	0	60	26	12.00	–	26	0	–	–	4
	W5	L4	D6	15	23	2	634	101*	30.19	1	286	6	47.66	3–47	22

Jeffrey John CROWE

Auckland and South Australia

Born: Auckland, 14 September 1958

Jeff Crowe played his early cricket in Australia in the Sheffield Shield. He made his Test debut against Sri Lanka in March 1983. Centuries against England 11 months later, and against West Indies in Jamaica in 1985, suggested he was of sound Test calibre, and it was apparent that he was destined to captain New Zealand.

He was popular and tactically knowledgeable as well as being an excellent fielder, and he was the obvious choice to succeed Coney. He began his captaincy with a century against Sri Lanka in difficult circumstances, but thereafter his form deserted him. After two Test matches against England in 1987–88, he was dropped, the first New Zealand captain to be replaced in the middle of a series.

There were still hopes that he could refind his form and regain the captaincy. He played against Australia under John Wright and toured England in 1990, but he did not appear in a Test match.

Jeff Crowe whose batting form deserted him when he became captain (Adrian Murrell/Allsport)

Test Record

	M	I	NO	Runs	HS	Avge	100s	RC	Wkts	Avge	BB	Ct
v England	10	16	0	343	128	21.43	1	0	0	–	–	9
v Australia	8	14	1	216	49	16.61	–	–	–	–	–	5
v West Indies	7	13	1	395	114	32.91	1	–	–	–	–	11
v Pakistan	8	13	1	355	62	29.58	–	9	0	–	–	11
v Sri Lanka	6	9	1	292	120*	36.50	1	–	–	–	–	5
	39	65	4	1601	128	26.24	3	9	0	–	–	41

Test Record as Captain

				M	I	NO	Runs	HS	Avge	100s	RC	Wkts	Avge	BB	Ct
v England	–	–	D2	2	4	0	40	28	10.00	–	–	–	–	–	2
v Australia	–	L1	D2	3	6	0	78	25	13.00	–	–	–	–	–	1
v Sri Lanka	–	–	D1	1	1	1	120	120*	–	1	–	–	–	–	–
	–	L1	D5	6	11	1	238	120*	23.80	1	–	–	–	–	3

John Geoffrey WRIGHT

Northern Districts, Canterbury and Derbyshire

Born: Darfield, 5 July 1954

One of the most charming and likeable men ever to grace the cricket field, John Wright did not seek to be captain of New Zealand. He had the job thrust upon him in the middle of the series against England in 1987–88, when Jeff Crowe lost form and confidence.

It was typical of the man that he should say that he was willing to do the job until Jeff was ready to return. A mature and intelligent person who had delighted Derbyshire supporters for many seasons with his left-handed opening batting, particularly strong on the back foot, he led New Zealand in a warm and competent manner, claiming victory in a series at home to India and in a one-Test series with Australia in 1990. He led New Zealand to England later the same year, and in wretched weather, his side lost the one Test that was decided. In truth, a fine New Zealand team was in the process of breaking up through age and retirement.

He succeeded Glenn Turner as New Zealand's opener in 1978 and played under Martin Crowe and Ian Smith in 1991. Only Martin Crowe has scored more centuries for New Zealand.

An amiable skipper and a fine opening batsman – John Wright (Allsport/Ben Radford)

Test Record

	M	I	NO	Runs	HS	Avge	100s	RC	Wkts	Avge	BB	Ct
v England	20	37	2	1260	130	36.00	3	–	–	–	–	6
v Australia	16	30	2	1040	141	37.14	2	–	–	–	–	8
v West Indies	10	18	0	535	138	29.72	1	2	0	–	–	4
v India	9	15	2	804	185	61.84	3	2	0	–	–	5
v Pakistan	11	19	0	576	107	30.31	1	1	0	–	–	5
v Sri Lanka	8	13	0	491	101	37.76	1	–	–	–	–	7
	74	132	6	4706	185	37.34	11	5	0	–	–	35

Test Record as Captain

				M	I	NO	Runs	HS	Avge	100s	RC	Wkts	Avge	BB	Ct
v England	–	L1	D3	4	6	0	213	98	35.50	–	–	–	–	–	–
v Australia	W1	–	D1	2	4	1	190	117*	63.33	1	–	–	–	–	5
v India	W2	L2	D2	6	10	1	603	185	67.00	2	–	–	–	–	3
v Pakistan	–	–	D2	2	4	0	64	36	16.00	–	–	–	–	–	–
	W3	L3	D8	14	24	2	1070	185	48.63	3	–	–	–	–	8

Martin David CROWE

Auckland, Central Districts, Wellington and Somerset

Born: Auckland, 22 September 1962

Only John Wright has scored more runs in Test cricket for New Zealand than Martin Crowe, who made his Test debut in the rain-ruined match against Australia at Wellington in February 1982. He was still seven months short of his 20th birthday. He scored his first Test hundred against England in January 1984, in his 13th match, and has now scored more Test hundreds than any other New Zealand batsman. He is certainly among the top batsmen in the world, and is the finest batsman that New Zealand has produced.

There was a reluctance to burden him with the captaincy too early in his career, but following the decline in form of his elder brother Jeff and the reluctance of Wright to continue in the last years of his career, Martin Crowe took a young and inexperienced side to Pakistan at the end of 1990. He battled bravely against heavy odds. In his first Test as captain in New Zealand, he hit 299, the highest score ever made by a New Zealander in Test cricket, as he and Andrew Jones added 467 for the third wicket against Sri Lanka, the highest partnership ever recorded in Test cricket. Crowe, who also bowls medium pace, missed the third match of the series through injury. He faces a hard task in leading a New Zealand side which is rebuilding after the loss of several leading players through retirement.

There was a hard baptism as captain of New Zealand for Martin Crowe, but he is a batsman of exceptional talent and a leader by example (Adrian Murrell/Allsport)

Test Record

	M	I	NO	Runs	HS	Avge	100s	RC	Wkts	Avge	BB	Ct
v England	16	26	2	829	143	34.54	3	202	2	101.00	2–35	15
v Australia	13	21	2	996	188	52.42	3	77	0	–	–	8
v West Indies	7	13	1	544	188	45.33	3	90	4	22.50	2–25	12
v India	3	3	0	161	113	53.66	1	–	–	–	–	1
v Pakistan	11	20	3	973	174	57.23	2	209	7	29.85	2–29	16
v Sri Lanka	6	9	1	490	299	61.25	1	73	1	73.00	1–21	3
	56	92	9	3993	299	48.10	13	651	14	46.50	2–25	55

Test Record as Captain

				M	I	NO	Runs	HS	Avge	100s	RC	Wkts	Avge	BB	Ct
v Pakistan	–	L3	–	3	6	2	244	108*	61.00	1	44	1	44.00	1–44	7
v Sri Lanka	–	–	D2	2	3	0	365	299	121.66	1	–	–	–	–	1
	–	L3	D2	5	9	2	609	299	87.00	2	44	1	44.00	1–44	8

Ian David Stockley SMITH

Central Districts and Auckland

Born: Nelson, 28 February 1957

Ian Smith succeeded Warren Lees as New Zealand's regular wicket-keeper after the tour of England in 1983, although he had made his Test debut against Australia in 1980. He now holds all the New Zealand wicket-keeping records with more than 170 victims in Test cricket. Against Sri Lanka, at Hamilton in February 1991, he equalled the world Test record with seven catches in the first innings. He led New Zealand in the final match of the series when Martin Crowe was injured.

A ferociously hard-hitting batsman, he hit his maiden Test hundred against England in February 1984, hitting the last two balls of the innings for six. More astonishing was his 173 against India at Auckland in February 1990. New Zealand were 131 for 7 when he came in, and he hit 169 off 128 balls before the end of the day. His score is the highest by a number nine batsman in Test cricket.

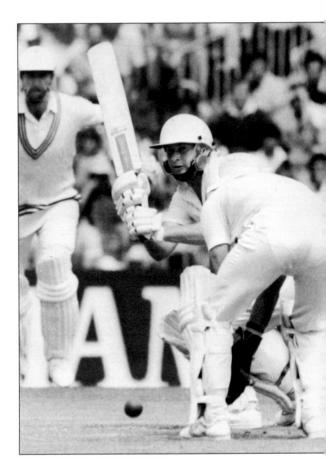

Senior assistant Ian Smith on his way to a century against England at Auckland, February 1984 (Adrian Murrell/Allsport)

Test Record

	M	I	NO	Runs	HS	Avge	100s	RC	Wkts	Avge	BB	Ct/st
v England	12	15	6	361	113*	40.11	1	–	–	–	–	37/1
v Australia	15	21	2	201	44	10.57	–	–	–	–	–	34/5
v West Indies	7	11	2	168	53	18.66	–	5	0	–	–	15/1
v India	9	12	2	439	173	43.90	1	–	–	–	–	29/–
v Pakistan	11	18	3	450	65	30.00	–	–	–	–	–	22/1
v Sri Lanka	7	8	2	154	42	22.00	–	–	–	–	–	27/–
	61	85	17	1773	173	26.07	2	5	0	–	–	164/8

Test Record as Captain

				M	I	NO	Runs	HS	Avge	100s	RC	Wkts	Avge	BB	Ct
v Sri Lanka	–	–	D1	1	1	0	3	3	3.00	–	–	–	–	–	6

WEST INDIES

Captaincy and West Indian Cricket

The British took cricket to the West Indies. The islands were colonised for commercial reasons, and in Michael Manley's words, 'As the wealth was moving from the colony to the centre of the Empire, so was cricket moving from the centre of the Empire to the colony.'

For the British, colonisation was not simply the annexation of territory for profit. It meant also that British ideals and values were implanted in the new lands. Missionaries and teachers followed close in the wake of commercial exploiters, and it was they who initiated the West Indian youngsters into the mysteries of cricket. As elsewhere, the British army, too, played a significant part in the propagation of the game. The officers augmented their practice by using the sons of former slaves to bowl at them, and these inhabitants of the islands also took care to learn how to bat.

The sons of the planters, and of the growing middle-class which served them, were educated at schools which followed traditional British patterns both in the classroom and on the playing field. The habits and practices of this elite were emulated by the other inhabitants, so West Indian cricket grew within the boundaries of clearly defined social classes.

In February 1865, what is regarded as the first first-class match in the West Indies was played at the Garrison Savannah, Bridgetown, between Barbados and Demerara. Within the next few years, Trinidad also fielded sides in first-class matches.

In 1893–94 the inter-island tournament for the Shell Shield was first held, and in 1888 there was a visit from an American side. These developments led to Lord Stamford organising a tour of the West Indies by a team of English cricketers in 1894–95. It had been hoped that Lord Hawke, who had helped to arrange the tour, would lead the side, but he was unable to make the trip and R.S. Lucas, the Middlesex amateur, was captain. The team was not a strong one, but large crowds attended the matches in which they played.

Two years later, at the invitation of Jamaica, Arthur Priestley, a future MP for Grantham who had been in Lucas's side, organised a tour of the Caribbean. His was a stronger side and included such famous names as A.E. Stoddart, Sammy Woods, R.C.N. Palariet and C.A. Beldam. Unfortunately, Lord Hawke took a side to the West Indies at the same time, and there was some altercation between him and Priestley. Hawke's side was also stronger than the one that had toured earlier; it included Pelham

Warner, born in the West Indies, and Leveson Gower.

The time was ripe for a West Indies side to tour England, or so Lord Hawke believed, and the first West Indian side arrived here in 1900. The team was led by R.S.A. Warner, Pelham's brother. It had been intended that H.B.G. Austin should captain the side, but he had to go to South Africa to fight in the Boer War. Neither Warner nor Austin was, of course, a black West Indian. They were Englishmen whose family and business had given them roots in the Caribbean.

The West Indians aroused little interest in England, but one of their number, Ollivierre, remained in England and qualified for Derbyshire. Ollivierre was a professional and he was black, and it is interesting to note that E.H.D. Sewell, who played for Essex and later became a journalist, could write that one of the West Indian's team mates at Derbyshire, Bill Storer, 'was not enamoured of importations, especially those of ebony hue.'

Sydney Gordon Smith, who toured England with Austin's side in 1906, also remained in England and played for Northamptonshire. Smith was white, and his background and social status exempted him from being considered an importation.

By the outbreak of the First World War, tours of the Caribbean had become quite frequent, but it was on their visits to England that West Indies cricketers were really measured. In 1923, Austin brought the third West Indian side to England, and the manner in which that side was chosen sheds some light on the problems that West Indian cricket faced as it moved towards international recognition. The composition of the team was determined by the four major associations – Barbados, Trinidad, British Guiana (now Guyana) and Jamaica – each being allowed a set number of players. This inter-island rivalry and appeasement was to plague West Indian cricket for some time.

In 1928, West Indies attained Test status with their first series in England. Astonishingly, it was first proposed that Austin should lead the side. Sir Harold Bruce Gardiner Austin, as he later became, was Speaker of the House of Assembly in Barbados and was 51 at the time! Wisely, he withdrew from the tour and Robert Nunes, a founder member of the Jamaican Cricket Board of Control, led the side in his place.

The outstanding cricketer of that first West Indian Test side was Learie Constantine, a dynamic all-rounder who thrilled all who saw him. Constantine joined the Lancashire League club Nelson and played for them from 1929 until 1938. Thanks to his massive contributions with bat and ball, Nelson won the title eight times in that period, a feat unapproached by any other side. Record crowds flocked to watch him wherever he played.

There was a move to enlist him by qualification for Lancashire to succeed the Australian fast bowler Ted McDonald, who had helped the Red Rose county to three Championships, but a faction within the county administration made it known that this would be unacceptable because of his colour. For a county that has since been captained by Clive Lloyd and has gloried in the deeds of Faroukh Engineer and Wasim Akram, this seems incredible today, but in the 1930s, such was the thinking. Nor was it restricted to England.

In a memorable sentence, C.L.R. James was to encapsulate Constantine's attitude to cricket and to life. 'He revolted against the revolting contrast between his first-class status as a cricketer and his third-class status as a man.'

Constantine was never to captain West Indies in a Test match, but he fought the cause of the black man with his dignity, his passion and his outstanding ability. In 1944, when he was a welfare worker with the Ministry of Labour, he won a case against a London hotel which had refused him accommodation on the grounds of his colour.

A year later came what was perhaps his greatest moment. England played the Dominions at Lord's in 'one of the finest games ever seen'. Lindsay Hassett, who was to have captained the Dominions, withdrew with injury, and the 10 white players who formed the side asked that Constantine should lead them. At one time, he and Miller put on 117 in 45 minutes, and Dominions won by 45 runs. It was to be another 15 years before a black man won his rightful place as captain of West Indies.

There were two things that militated against a black man captaining the West Indies Test team, his colour and the fact that he was invariably a professional who had earned money by playing cricket in the leagues. The attitude against a professional captaining a side had been imbibed from the English teachers. Worrell was vice-captain against England in

1953–54, but Stollmeyer and Atkinson, white West Indians, were the men for the tour of New Zealand the following season.

C.L.R. James wrote of Clyde Walcott, who left Test cricket when still at the height of his considerable powers, that he believed that Walcott put big cricket behind him when he did because 'he was tired of intrigues and manoeuvres which were not based on cricket ability . . .

'One evening in British Guiana we were talking about captaincy. Suddenly Clyde, who is always circumspect in his speech, blurted out: "You know who will be captain in England in 1963? You see that Barbados boy, Bynoe, who went to India? He has only to make fifty in one innings and he will be the captain." Bynoe is white.'

In fact, Walcott was wrong. Frank Worrell led West Indies in 1963, for the protest against the constant selection of the West Indian captain from among the European stock had reached the proportions of an international scandal. Worrell led West Indies for three series, did a splendid job, and there was to be no turning back.

Since Worrell stepped down after that 1963 tour, West Indies have had only five regular captains. One omits men like Greenidge and Murray who led on the odd occasion when the appointed skipper was injured. The chosen captains have generally been the acknowledged leading players in the side, which has the merits of at least being a clear policy even though it does not always bring forth the best man for the job. Over the past 25 years, so consistently strong have the West Indian sides been that, arguably, it has not mattered who led them.

Robert Karl NUNES

Jamaica

Born: Kingston, Jamaica, 7 June 1894
Died: Paddington, London, 22 July 1958

'R.K. Nunes was a Jamaican lawyer and of a family that came as near to aristocracy as the

West Indies in 1928, their first season in Test cricket. Back row, left to right: W.H. St Hill, E.A. Rae, E.L.G. Hoad, J.A. Small, F.R. Martin, L.N. Constantine, J.M. Neblett. Front: E.L. Bartlett, M.P. Fernandes, C.V. Wright, R.K. Nunes (captain), G. Challenor and C.R. Browne. Hoad was the second man to captain after Nunes, and Fernandes led West Indies to victory on the one occasion on which he was captain (Lemmon)

colonies can produce.' A left-handed opening batsman, Karl Nunes was educated at Dulwich College. He toured England with the West Indian side of 1923 and captained the side in the inaugural Test series of 1928. The side had no specialist wicket-keeper, and he dropped down the order and took over the gloves to the detri-

ment of his own form. He held only one catch in the three Tests.

He captained West Indies in the Jamaica Test in 1929–30 and hit 66 and 92, sharing a stand of 227 for the second wicket with George Headley.

He became a noted administrator in West Indian cricket.

Test Record as Captain

				M	I	NO	Runs	HS	Avge	100s	RC	Wkts	Avge	BB	Ct
v England	–	L3	D1	4	8	0	245	92	30.62	–	–	–	–	–	2

Edward Lisle Goldsworthy HOAD

Barbados

Born: Bridgetown, 29 January 1896
Died: Bridgetown, 5 March 1986

Teddy Hoad enjoyed a fine domestic season in the Caribbean in 1927, hitting 120 against British Guiana and 174 not out against Trinidad. In England in 1928, however, he failed to find form

early in the tour and played in only the second Test at Old Trafford. When England visited West Indies in 1929–30, a diplomatic agreement was reached whereby a local man would captain West Indies in each of the four Test centres. The first Test was played at Kensington Oval, Bridgetown, and Hoad led the side.

He was vice-captain of the side that toured England in 1933, but played in only the first two Tests.

Test Record

	M	I	NO	Runs	HS	Avge	100s	RC	Wkts	Avge	BB	Ct
v England	4	8	0	98	36	12.25	–	–	–	–	–	1

Test Record as Captain

				M	I	NO	Runs	HS	Avge	100s	RC	Wkts	Avge	BB	Ct
v England	–	–	D1	1	2	0	24	24	12.00	–	–	–	–	–	1

Nelson BETANCOURT

Trinidad

Born: Trinidad, 4 June 1887
Died: Trinidad, 12 October 1947

Making his debut for Trinidad against Jamaica in 1905, Nelson Betancourt first captained the

island in 1922. In accordance with the policy of each venue providing the captain for the Test match staged there in 1929–30, he led West Indies in the second Test at Port of Spain. Generally a wicket-keeper, he did not keep in this match, but batted at number nine and showed some courage in a vain effort to stave off defeat. He disappeared from first-class cricket after this Test match.

Test Record as Captain

				M	I	NO	Runs	HS	Avge	100s	RC	Wkts	Avge	BB	Ct
v England	–	L1	–	1	2	0	52	39	26.00	–	–	–	–	–	–

Marius Pacheco FERNANDES

British Guiana

Born: British Guiana, 12 August 1897
Died: Georgetown, Guyana, 8 May 1981

A quietly spoken man and a stubborn batsman, Fernandes toured England in 1923 and 1928, playing in the first Test at Lord's and making a 'duck' on his debut. Although he does not appear to have been captain of British Guiana at the time – W.S.M. Green leading the side in 1929 – 'Maurice' Fernandes was named as captain for the Georgetown Test in February 1930. With Roach hitting 209 and George Headley scoring a century in each innings, West Indies won by 289 runs.

Fernandes surprised many people by not enforcing the follow-on, and West Indies won with just four minutes to spare. It was only the sixth Test match that West Indies had played, and it was an historic victory. The policy on captaincy, dictated by politics and economics, was clear however, and Nunes led in the fourth and final Test in Jamaica while Fernandes did not play Test cricket again.

Test Record

	M	I	NO	Runs	HS	Avge	100s	RC	Wkts	Avge	BB	Ct
v England	2	4	0	49	22	12.25	–	–	–	–	–	–

Test Record as Captain

		M	I	NO	Runs	HS	Avge	100s	RC	Wkts	Avge	BB	Ct
v England	W1	–	–	1	2	0	41	22	20.50	–	–	–	–

George Copeland GRANT

Trinidad

Born: Port of Spain, Trinidad, 9 May 1907
Died: Cambridge, England, 26 October 1978

A student in classes taught by C.L.R. James, 'Jackie' Grant went up to Cambridge in 1928 and gained his blue in 1929 and 1930. He also represented the university at soccer.

In spite of his lack of experience in cricket in the Caribbean – he did not represent Trinidad until 1934 – he was named as captain of West Indies for the tour of Australia in 1930–31. At the age of 23 years 217 days, he is the youngest man ever to have captained West Indies.

His appointment caused something of a stir, particularly as he did not meet his team until he joined them at the Panama Canal on the voyage to Australia, but he soon made a good impression. He hit 53 not out and 71 not out on the occasion of his Test debut at Adelaide, fielded well and captained astutely. The first four Tests were lost, but West Indies won the fifth encounter at Sydney, with Grant contributing 62 and 27 not out.

The success in Australia made him an automatic choice to lead West Indies to England in 1933, but here, both he and his side were less successful.

In 1934–35, Grant captained West Indies against Wyatt's England side. In a bizarre first Test match in which batting orders were turned upside down in an attempt to counter a rain-affected wicket, he set England 73 to win and saw his side lose by four wickets. There was thought and adventure in his captaincy, and it was rewarded when West Indies won the second Test in Trinidad and the fourth in Jamaica, by an innings, to take a series for the first time.

Grant retired after this magnificent achievement and became a missionary in Africa. He worked tirelessly there, refusing every inducement to return to the Caribbean, including the offer from Prime Minister Dr Eric Williams to become Chief Officer of Education in Trinidad.

Test Record as Captain

				M	I	NO	Runs	HS	Avge	100s	RC	Wkts	Avge	BB	Ct
v England	W2	L3	D2	7	11	1	158	28	15.80	–	17	0	–	–	7
v Australia	W1	L4	–	5	10	4	255	71*	42.50	–	1	0	–	–	3
	W3	L7	D2	12	21	5	413	71*	25.81	–	18	0	–	–	10

Rolph Stewart GRANT

Trinidad

Born: Port of Spain, Trinidad, 15 December 1909
Died: Canada, 18 October 1977

The younger brother of 'Jackie' Grant, Rolph Grant followed his brother to Cambridge. He showed no outstanding ability, but he gained the last place in the University XI against Oxford in 1933 on the strength of his superb fielding. In the event, his off-spin captured three of the first four Oxford batsmen for a personal cost of 44 runs. He had already won a blue for soccer and kept goal for England in an amateur international. He was also heavyweight boxing champion of Trinidad.

He returned to the Caribbean and played in all four Tests under his brother in 1934–35, contributing significantly to West Indies' victory in the series with some brilliant fielding and an innings of 77 in the final Test which West Indies won by an innings.

He succeeded his brother as captain for the tour of England in 1939. When his side found themselves short of an opener he filled the breach and hit three sixes and four fours in his 47 in 38 minutes on a deteriorating pitch at Old Trafford. The Second World War loomed throughout the tour and brought an end to his career.

Test Record

	M	I	NO	Runs	HS	Avge	100s	RC	Wkts	Avge	BB	Ct
v England	7	11	1	220	77	22.00	–	353	11	32.09	3–68	13

Test Record as Captain

				M	I	NO	Runs	HS	Avge	100s	RC	Wkts	Avge	BB	Ct
v England	–	L1	D2	3	5	0	98	47	19.60	–	108	2	54.00	2–16	4

George Alphonso HEADLEY

Jamaica

Born: Panama, 30 May 1909
Died: Kingston, Jamaica, 30 November 1983

George Headley was one of the greatest batsmen that Test cricket has known. In the thirties, he was nicknamed the 'Black Bradman', and only four batsmen have ended their Test careers with a higher batting average in Test cricket.

Quick on his feet, a master of strokes on the off side with a natural instinct for the game, Headley had a cricket brain that was of the greatest use to the less experienced and less knowledgeable captains he served, but he was black and he was profesional. He became the first black man to lead West Indies when he captained them at Bridgetown in 1948. Grudgingly, he had been appointed captain only for the first and fourth Tests of the series, but by then he was 38 and the call had come too late. He pulled a muscle in his one Test as captain and could not play again in the series.

In 1953–54, public subscription in Jamaica raised £1000 to pay Headley's passage back from England so that he could play in the first Test match at Sabina Park. At 44 years 236 days, he was the oldest player ever to represent West Indies. He scored 16 and 1, caught Peter May and bowled five overs for 23 runs. It was the end of a legend that had begun in Bridgetown in January 1930, when he hit 176 in the second innings of his first Test match. He was the youngest player to achieve the feat. He added three more centuries before the end of the series, and was the first batsman to score three hundreds in Test cricket before his 21st birthday.

Two centuries against Australia followed, and there was 169 at Old Trafford in 1933. When England toured West Indies in 1934–35 he hit 270 in the final Test, and this remained the highest score for West Indies against England until 1973–74. In 1939, he became the first batsman to score a century in each innings of a Test match at Lord's.

Headley set a standard by which all later West Indian batsmen would be measured. He became immortalised in the history of West Indian cricket, but he was black and he played professional cricket in the Lancashire League, so he led West Indies only once.

Both his son and grandson became first-class cricketers.

George Headley, who was denied the captaincy for so long (Hulton)

Test Record

	M	I	NO	Runs	HS	Avge	100s	RC	Wkts	Avge	BB	Ct
v England	16	29	3	1852	270*	71.23	8	212	0	–	–	13
v Australia	5	10	1	336	105	37.33	2	–	–	–	–	1
v India	1	1	0	2	2	2.00	–	18	0	–	–	–
	22	40	4	2190	270*	60.83	10	230	0	–	–	14

Test Record as Captain

				M	I	NO	Runs	HS	Avge	100s	RC	Wkts	Avge	BB	Ct
v England	–	–	D1	1	2	1	36	29	36.00	–	11	0	–	–	–

Gerald Etheridge GOMEZ

Trinidad

Born: Woodbrok, Port of Spain, Trinidad, 10 October 1919

A most capable middle-order batsman and medium pace bowler, Gerry Gomez toured England in 1939 and played in two Tests. He was a prolific scorer in regional cricket just after the war, and shared a third wicket stand of 434 with Jeff Stollmeyer for Trinidad against British Guiana in March 1947. It was Stollmeyer, Gomez's school-friend, who was appointed captain of West Indies for the second Test against England in March 1948. When he was injured, Gomez replaced him. Only rain robbed West Indies of victory, but Goddard was named as leader for the rest of the series and for the tour of India, where Gomez had a particularly good series and hit his one Test century.

His last Test was against England in 1953–54. It was Sobers' first. Gomez became prominent in the administration of cricket.

Test Record

	M	I	NO	Runs	HS	Avge	100s	RC	Wkts	Avge	BB	Ct
v England	14	22	3	587	86	30.89	–	457	10	45.70	3–16	13
v Australia	5	10	1	324	55	36.00	–	256	18	14.22	7–55	3
v New Zealand	1	2	1	14	14*	14.00	–	72	3	24.00	2–25	–
v India	9	12	0	318	101	26.50	1	805	27	40.25	4–72	2
	29	46	5	1243	101	30.31	1	1590	58	27.41	7–55	18

Test Record as Captain

				M	I	NO	Runs	HS	Avge	100s	RC	Wkts	Avge	BB	Ct
v England	–	–	D1	1	1	0	62	62	62.00	–	22	1	22.00	1–22	–

John Douglas Claude GODDARD

Barbados

Born: Bridgetown, Barbados, 21 April 1919
Died: London, 26 August 1987

John Goddard played for Barbados in 1937 as a left-handed batsman and medium pace off-break bowler. He scored heavily in regional matches towards the end of the war, hitting 218 not out and sharing an unbroken fourth wicket stand of 502 with Frank Worrell against Trinidad in February 1944.

In 1946 he succeeded Pierce as captain of Barbados, and when Test cricket resumed in the Caribbean in January 1948 it was not surprising that he was in the West Indies side. As he was from a white upper-class background, it was also no surprise that his third Test match saw him as captain. He had instant success, taking 5 for 31 in England's first innings and leading his side to a seven-wicket victory. A ten-wicket victory in the fourth and final Test confirmed that he would lead West Indies in India, although his appointment came as a bitter disappointment to those who had believed that Headley would lead the side.

West Indies won a high-scoring series in India by one Test to nil, and Goddard was now sure to take the side to England in 1950. This series provided his greatest moments, although his own contributions as a player were slight. He had insisted that two little-known spinners, Ramadhin from Trinidad and Valentine from Jamaica, be included in the side, and they were the prime force as West Indies took the series by three matches to one, their first victories in England.

It was in Australia in 1951–52 that things began to turn sour for Goddard and for West Indies. His tactical vision was limited and he appeared to believe that if he bowled them long enough, his two great spinners would inevitably bring victory. They sent down more than 450 eight-ball overs between them in the five-Test series which West Indies lost four to one. There were inter-island and class tensions within the side, and Goddard, his own form poor, stood down for the last Test. He captained the team in the two Tests in New Zealand, but it seemed that his international career was at an end.

In 1955–56, however, he was surprisingly recalled to play against New Zealand in three Tests under Atkinson, and when Atkinson lost the last Test of the series he was sacked and Goddard named as captain for the 1957 tour of England. It was an attempt to recreate former glory, but that was seven years in the past.

In the first Test at Edgbaston, Ramadhin took 7 for 49; but in the second, May and Cowdrey added 411 for the fourth wicket. Ramadhin bowled 98 overs and Atkinson 72. In sending down 558 deliveries, Ramadhin bowled more balls than anyone has ever bowled in a first-class innings. Goddard showed a total lack of tactical imagination, not to say a lack of sensitivity, and West Indies were trounced in the series.

Goddard died while attending the MCC Bicentenary celebrations in 1987.

Test Record

			M	I	NO	Runs	HS	Avge	100s	RC	Wkts	Avge	BB	Ct
v England			13	21	5	340	61	21.25	–	537	19	28.26	5–31	10
v Australia			4	7	1	156	57*	26.00	–	126	4	31.50	3–36	1
v New Zealand			5	5	3	173	83*	86.50	–	36	1	36.00	1–17	7
v India			5	6	2	190	44	47.50	–	351	9	39.00	3–34	4
			27	39	11	859	83*	30.67	–	1050	33	31.81	5–31	22

Test Record as Captain

				M	I	NO	Runs	HS	Avge	100s	RC	Wkts	Avge	BB	Ct
v England	W5	L4	D2	11	18	4	285	61	20.35	–	395	15	26.33	5–31	8
v Australia	W1	L3	–	4	7	1	156	57*	26.00	–	126	4	31.50	3–36	1
v New Zealand	W1	–	D1	2	1	0	26	26	26.00	–	36	1	36.00	1–17	1
v India	W1	–	D4	5	6	2	190	44	47.50	–	351	9	39.00	3–34	4
	W8	L7	D7	22	32	7	657	61	26.28	–	908	29	31.31	5–31	14

Jeffrey Baxter STOLLMEYER

Trinidad

Born: Santa Cruz, Trinidad, 11 April 1921
Died: Miami, Florida, 10 September 1989

Jeff Stollmeyer was a gifted opening batsman who toured England in 1939 at the age of 18 and played in all three Tests. He was really the first dependable and class opening batsman that West Indies had produced and he scored heavily in inter-regional cricket during the war years. In 1947, he hit 324 for Trinidad against British Guiana, the highest score ever made in an inter-regional game.

He was an automatic choice for the series against England in 1947–48 and was appointed captain for the second Test. Injury kept him out of the match, and he did not lead West Indies until the final Test in Australia in 1951–52, when Goddard stood down. By then, he had formed a successful opening partnership with Rae which had prospered in England in 1950.

West Indies were beaten by Australia at Sydney, but Stollmeyer became the first West Indian captain to score a century in a Test match, hitting 104 in the second innings. His first Test century had come in India in 1948–49 when he hit 160 at Madras.

He replaced Goddard as captain when India visited West Indies in 1952–53, and he again led the side against England in 1953–54, but his tactics were severely criticised when England fought back to square a series in which West Indies had led two–nil. The argument which had simmered in Australia regarding the inevitability of a white West Indian captaining the Test side began to boil, yet he retained the captaincy for the visit by Australia in 1954–55, only to find that he was fit for just two of the Tests. He retired and played a major part in the administration of the game in the Caribbean.

He died tragically, shot when burglars invaded his home in 1989. He was flown to America, but died in hospital.

Test Record

	M	I	NO	Runs	HS	Avge	100s	RC	Wkts	Avge	BB	Ct
v England	14	25	2	858	78	37.30	–	119	6	19.83	3–32	8
v Australia	7	14	0	417	104	29.78	1	12	0	–	–	4
v New Zealand	2	3	0	188	152	62.66	1	12	2	6.00	2–12	3
v India	9	14	3	696	160	63.27	2	364	5	72.80	2–56	5
	32	56	5	2159	160	42.33	4	507	13	39.00	3–32	20

Test Record as Captain

				M	I	NO	Runs	HS	Avge	100s	RC	Wkts	Avge	BB	Ct
v England	W2	L2	D1	5	9	0	256	64	28.44	–	72	3	24.00	2–14	2
v Australia	–	L2	D1	3	6	0	203	110	33.83	1	12	0	–	–	2
v India	W1	–	D4	5	9	3	354	104*	59.00	1	231	3	77.00	2–56	2
	W3	L4	D6	13	24	3	813	110	38.71	2	315	6	52.50	2–14	6

Denis St Eval ATKINSON

Barbados

Born: Christ Church, Barbados, 9 August 1926

A right-handed batsman and medium pace off-break bowler, Atkinson made his Test debut in the first match in India in 1948–49. He did not hold a regular place in the West Indian side until England toured West Indies in 1953–54 and he played in the last four Tests, performing moderately well. The following season, Australia visited the Caribbean and Atkinson was appointed vice-captain to Stollmeyer for the series. Stollmeyer injured a finger in practice on the eve of the first Test and so Atkinson led West Indies for the first time.

The appointment was not well received.

Worrell had been vice-captain for the England series, but again he had been overlooked. Atkinson's experience was slight. He was not captain of Barbados, who were generally led by Goddard, and, lacking experience and the confidence of his players, he faced a difficult task.

Stollmeyer returned for the second and third Test matches against Australia, but he was again injured and Atkinson took over for the fourth Test. He hit 219 and shared a world record stand of 347 for the seventh wicket with Depeiza. The criticism died a little, but even *Wisden* was moved to comment that the West Indian cause was not advanced by having an inexperienced leader. It is astonishing that the side which contained Worrell, Weekes and Walcott should be burdened by an *inexperienced* captain.

Test Record

	M	I	NO	Runs	HS	Avge	100s	RC	Wkts	Avge	BB	Ct
v England	6	11	2	314	74	34.88	–	581	10	58.10	3–78	1
v Australia	6	11	1	334	219	33.40	1	502	13	38.61	5–56	3
v New Zealand	5	6	1	191	85	38.20	–	279	18	15.50	7–53	1
v India	4	6	2	79	45	19.75	–	224	5	44.80	2–54	5
v Pakistan	1	1	0	4	4	4.00	–	61	1	61.00	1–61	1
	22	35	6	922	219	31.79	1	1647	47	35.04	7–53	11

West Indies were well beaten by Australia, but Atkinson's double century had earned him the captaincy of the side in New Zealand. The New Zealand team was weak and West Indies won the first three Tests handsomely. The fourth was lost and Atkinson was sacked as captain, Goddard being reinstated for the tour of England.

Atkinson was in the side that toured England but he was hampered by injury. His removal from the captaincy was as harsh as his appointment had been controversial, but in scoring his 219 and taking 5 for 56 in the second innings of the match against Australia in Barbados, he had become the first West Indian captain to score a century and take five wickets in the same match.

Test Record as Captain

				M	I	NO	Runs	HS	Avge	100s	RC	Wkts	Avge	BB	Ct
v Australia	–	L2	D1	3	6	1	282	219	56.40	1	342	9	38.00	5–56	2
v New Zealand	W3	L1	–	4	5	0	183	85	36.60	–	233	16	14.56	7–53	1
	W3	L3	D1	7	11	1	465	219	46.50	1	575	25	23.00	7–53	3

Franz Copeland Murray ALEXANDER

Jamaica

Born: Kingston, Jamaica, 2 November 1928

It was the appointment of 'Gerry' Alexander as captain of West Indies which caused such an outcry as to bring to an end the policy that a white West Indian must lead the side. A fine footballer, Alexander was a wicket-keeper who won his blue at Cambridge in 1952 and 1953, but his selection for the party to tour England in 1957 was greeted with much consternation. Kanhai was also in the party and kept in the first three Tests, Alexander taking over for the last two to allow Kanhai to concentrate on his batting.

Alexander was unimpressive on the England tour and there was total astonishment when he was named as captain for the home series against Pakistan in 1957–58. It has been suggested that Worrell was offered the post but declined it. Future events would indicate that this was not the case.

West Indies were successful against Pakistan and Alexander took the side to India and Pakistan in 1958–59. He showed determination as a batsman and kept wicket well, but his captaincy was not good and he was accused of following a policy of tedium. His greatest problem concerned Roy Gilchrist, a bowler of great pace and fire. A confrontation with the 'fastest bowler in the world' over bouncers and beamers and other unspecified misdemeanours in the clos-

ing stages of the tour of India led to Gilchrist being sent home in disgrace. Although the West Indian Board did not clarify the position, Gilchrist was censured and, it transpired, banned from Test cricket for life.

Whatever the rights and wrongs of the case – and later Gilchrist would have further trouble in league cricket in England – there were a substantial number of people in the West Indies who saw the incident as a clash between the black plebeian Gilchrist and the light-skinned Cambridge graduate Alexander. C.L.R. James argues that it was the simmering discontent over issues like this and the major one on captaincy that led to disturbances during the 1959–60 series against England in which West Indies were beaten.

Throughout this series, James waged an 'Alexander Must Go' campaign in the political paper *Nation*. James wanted the best man as captain, as did the vast majority of people in the Caribbean who were irritated by the Board's conviction that the captain of West Indies should not be a black man. James agreed that Alexander kept wicket magnificently, that he was a good defensive batsman and a hard fighter, but he was not a good captain, nor was wicket-keeper the ideal place for a captain.

Alexander himself was sensitive to public feeling. He himself believed that Worrell should be captain and forwarded his cause. Worrell was appointed captain to take the side to Australia in 1960–61. A black man, the last of the three W's, was skipper of West Indies at last.

Alexander went as Worrell's vice-captain and enjoyed a splendid series, topping the batting averages and displaying his very best form as if revelling in his liberation. He retired at the end of the series, and he could be proud of the fact that he had helped West Indies cricket to mature. He had brought order and discipline and encouraged the development of some fine young players.

Test Record

				M	I	NO	Runs	HS	Avge	100s	RC	Wkts	Avge	BB	Ct/st
v England				7	12	3	119	33	13.22	–	–	–	–	–	26/1
v Australia				5	10	2	484	108	60.50	1	–	–	–	–	16/–
v India				5	5	1	156	70	39.00	–	–	–	–	–	18/–
v Pakistan				8	11	0	202	57	18.36	–	–	–	–	–	25/4
				25	38	6	961	108	30.03	–	–	–	–	–	85/5

Test Record as Captain

				M	I	NO	Runs	HS	Avge	100s	RC	Wkts	Avge	BB	Ct/st
v England	–	L1	D4	5	8	2	108	33	18.00	–	–	–	–	–	22/1
v India	W3	–	D2	5	5	1	156	70	39.00	–	–	–	–	–	18/–
v Pakistan	W4	L3	D1	8	11	0	202	57	18.36	–	–	–	–	–	25/4
	W7	L4	D7	18	24	3	466	70	22.19	–	–	–	–	–	65/5

Sir Frank Mortimer Maglinne WORRELL

Barbados and Jamaica

Born: Bank Hall, Bridgetown, Barbados, 1 August 1924
Died: Mona, Kingston, Jamaica, 13 March 1967

After the years of discussion and controversy, Worrell was the first black man to be appointed captain of West Indies for more than a single match. He had begun his cricketing career regarded primarily as a left-arm bowler, slow or medium pace, batting number 10 on his first-class debut for Barbados in 1942. He quickly climbed the order and the following season he hit 188 against Trinidad at Port of Spain.

He made his Test debut in the second match of the 1947–48 series against England and hit 97 and 28 not out. In the next Test he scored 131 not out, and a great international career, in which he was frequently linked with Walcott and Weekes, was launched.

Test Record

	M	I	NO	Runs	HS	Avge	100s	RC	Wkts	Avge	BB	Ct
v England	25	42	6	1979	261	54.97	6	1211	28	43.25	7–70	18
v Australia	14	28	0	918	108	32.78	1	997	30	33.23	6–38	8
v New Zealand	2	3	1	233	100	116.50	1	81	2	40.50	1–20	2
v India	10	14	2	730	237	60.83	1	383	9	42.55	2–12	15
	51	87	9	3860	261	49.48	9	2672	69	38.72	7–70	43

Before he became captain of West Indies, he had led the Commonwealth side in India and was admired as a man of character, all grace and dignity in the field and with a bat in his hand. When he was appointed to lead West Indies in Australia in 1960–61, the pressure upon him was immense, for the campaign for his selection had been long and strong and involved issues outside cricket.

His response to the situation was heroic, and the result romantic. His first match as captain saw the first tie in Test match history. The second was lost, the third won and the fourth drawn. The drawn game had the last Australian pair holding out for 100 minutes to save their side although West Indies were at one time leaving the field, believing they had dismissed Kline. Australia won the last Test by two wickets to take a series described as the most enterprising and exciting in living memory. West Indies left Australia to tumultuous acclaim. Worrell and cricket were winners.

He was to lead West Indies in two more series and win them both. At the end of the 1963 tour of England, he retired. His aim had been to unite West Indies into a team rather than a collection of talented individuals from regions who were vying for supremacy. He accomplished his task.

Worrell was a highly intelligent man with a natural instinct for the game and its tactics. He was a man of dignity and principle who had missed West Indies' 1948–49 tour of India after a disagreement with the Board over payment. He was also a very great all-round cricketer whose right-handed batting was a charm in its style and fluency.

He became a senator in the Jamaican parliament, was knighted and continued in cricket as an administrator. He died from leukaemia at the age of 42 and was honoured and remembered in a memorial service in Westminster Abbey, the first time that a sportsman had been so recognised.

Frank Worrell – a man of greatness with an instinctive grasp of the game and its tactics (Ken Kelly)

Test Record as Captain

				M	I	NO	Runs	HS	Avge	100s	RC	Wkts	Avge	BB	Ct
v England	W3	L1	D1	5	8	1	142	74*	20.28	–	104	3	34.66	2–12	3
v Australia	W1	L2	D1+1	5	10	0	375	82	37.50	–	357	10	35.70	3–27	2
v India	W5	–	–	5	6	2	332	98*	83.00	–	121	2	60.50	2–12	7
	W9	L3	D2+1	15	24	3	849	98*	40.42	–	582	15	38.80	3–27	12

Sir Garfield St Aubrun SOBERS

Barbados and Nottinghamshire

Born: Bridgetown, Barbados, 28 July 1936

Frank Worrell bequeathed his West Indian side to Gary Sobers, arguably the greatest all-round cricketer the game has known, for in his era he had no superior as a batsman, was the most versatile of all left-arm bowlers and a brilliant fielder in any position.

There was a languid air about all that he did on the cricket field, so supple was his movement; but he would uncoil like a spring to produce some breathtaking shots, as when he hit six sixes in an over for Nottinghamshire against Glamorgan in 1968.

He made his Test debut against England in March 1954, taking 4 for 75 in England's first innings and hitting 14 not out and 26. His first century in Test cricket came in February 1958, when he established a record for Test matches with an innings of 365 not out against Pakistan. Records continued to tumble to Sobers throughout his Test career right up until his last appearance, against England in April 1974, when he became the first West Indian to take 100 wickets against England.

About Sobers' quality as a cricketer, there is no argument; his effectiveness as a captain is less certain. There were times when his interest seemed to wander, and his grip on his side was lax. He was never forgiven for a declaration which allowed England to win the 1967–68 series in the Caribbean. In spite of injuries to key bowlers, he declared and left England 165 minutes in which to score 215 to win. England reached their target for the loss of only three wickets with three minutes to spare. At other times he became ultra-defensive and conserva-

tive, and of the last 13 Tests in which he was captain, two were lost and eleven drawn.

He relinquished the captaincy after he had won the toss in all five Tests against New Zealand in 1971–72 and drawn all five matches. He continued to delight as a player, for two more years, and it as a cricketer rather than as a captain that he is best remembered.

Gary Sobers – his captaincy did not match his all-round ability as a player (Ken Kelly)

Test Record

	M	I	NO	Runs	HS	Avge	100s	RC	Wkts	Avge	BB	Ct
v England	36	61	8	3214	174	60.64	10	3323	102	32.57	5–42	40
v Australia	19	38	3	1510	168	43.14	4	2024	51	39.68	6–73	27
v New Zealand	12	18	1	404	142	23.76	1	682	19	35.89	4–64	12
v India	18	30	7	1920	198	83.47	8	1516	59	25.69	5–63	27
v Pakistan	8	13	2	984	365*	57.78	3	454	4	113.50	2–41	4
	93	160	21	8032	365*	57.78	–	7999	235	34.03	6–73	110

Test Record as Captain

				M	I	NO	Runs	HS	Avge	100s	RC	Wkts	Avge	BB	Ct
v England	W3	L4	D6	13	23	5	1417	174	78.72	5	1371	44	31.15	5–41	16
v Australia	W3	L4	D3	10	20	1	849	113	44.68	2	1223	30	40.76	6–73	14
v New Zealand	W1	L1	D6	8	13	1	323	142	26.91	1	633	17	37.23	4–64	7
v India	W2	L1	D5	8	15	4	939	178*	85.36	3	751	26	28.88	4–56	11
	W9	L10	D20	39	71	11	3528	178*	58.80	11	3978	117	34.00	6–73	48

Rohan Babulal KANHAI

Guyana and Warwickshire

Born: Port Mourant, Berbice, British Guiana, 26 December 1935

'He was sometimes a man of moods – aren't we all? – but he let the younger generation of Warwickshire players and spectators see what real batsmanship could be, and I knew that I had really not dreamed that there were really such batsmen once.' So wrote Leslie Duckworth in *The Story of Warwickshire Cricket* about Rohan Kanhai, a batsman who believed that cricket was about the power of bat over ball. One of the most thrilling sights in cricket in the sixties was that of Kanhai on his backside as the ball thundered over the boundary at square-leg after a vicious pull.

He made his Test debut in the first match of the 1957 tour of England, and he kept wicket in the first three Tests of that series before being allowed to concentrate on his batting.

His maiden Test hundred was an innings of 256 at Calcutta in 1958–59, the highest score in a Test in India. In the next Test, he was run out for 99.

When Sobers missed the series against Australia in 1972–73 while recovering from a cartilage operation and gave up the captaincy, Kanhai, then 37 years old, succeeded him. He led West Indies in two more series, both against England, before retiring from Test cricket.

His two series against England both contained controversial incidents. At Edgbaston in 1973, umpire Fagg refused to take the field at the start of the third day because of dissent shown by Kanhai and his side when Boycott was given not out; and at Port of Spain the following winter, Tony Greig ran out Kallicharran

at the end of play and the batsman was later reinstated. In spite of these incidents, Kanhai renewed a sense of order and discipline in a West Indian side which had become very lax in the last years of Sobers' stewardship.

Rohan Kanhai brought a sense of order to the West Indian side. There has been no greater entertainer with the bat (Hulton)

Test Record

	M	I	NO	Runs	HS	Avge	100s	RC	Wkts	Avge	BB	Ct
v England	33	57	3	2267	157	41.98	5	31	0	–	–	25
v Australia	20	38	1	1694	117	45.78	5	48	0	–	–	14
v India	18	28	1	1693	256	62.70	4	6	0	–	–	10
v Pakistan	8	14	1	573	217	44.07	1	–	–	–	–	1
	79	137	6	6227	256	47.53	15	85	0	–	–	50

Test Record as Captain

				M	I	NO	Runs	HS	Avge	100s	RC	Wkts	Avge	BB	Ct
v England	W3	L1	D4	8	12	1	380	157	34.54	1	29	0	–	–	10
v Australia	–	L2	D3	5	8	1	358	105	51.14	1	34	0	–	–	7
	W3	L3	D7	13	20	2	738	157	41.00	2	63	0	–	–	17

Clive Hubert LLOYD

Guyana and Lancashire

Born: Queenstown, Georgetown, British Guiana, 31 August 1944

Clive Lloyd moved with the silkiness of a cat, whether he was dominating the crease with his left-hand batting, which could be brutal in power, or prowling in the covers, threatening to pounce. In his earlier days, he also bowled right-arm medium pace; and in his later days, he fielded at slip. He was an exceptionally fine cricketer, as 110 Test matches and over 7500 Test runs would testify.

He began his long career in Test cricket with innings of 82 and 78 not out in West Indies' victory over India at Bombay in 1966–67. In his next series, against England in 1967–68, he hit centuries in the first and third Tests.

In 1974–75, he was appointed captain of West Indies for the tour of India. He responded by hitting 163 in the first Test, his hundred coming off 85 balls, and a career-best 242 not out in the fifth, which was the first Test to be played at the Wankhede Stadium, Bombay. West Indies won the rubber and so began the most successful period of captaincy in West Indian Test his-

Power and purpose – Clive Lloyd. He led West Indies in 18 Test series and took them to the top of the world (Adrian Murrell/Allsport)

tory. Lloyd led West Indies in 18 series of which 14 were won, two lost and two drawn. There were also the World Cup triumphs of 1975 and 1979.

But the success in the inaugural World Cup was followed by the humiliating 5–1 defeat in Australia in 1975–76. This setback led Lloyd to reconsider his attitude and tactics. Holding had made his debut in the series, and within the next year were to come Croft and Garner. Fast bowling, good close catching and quick-scoring batsmen were to be the ingredients of success. There was also a corporate knowledge of the game which few teams have attained. West Indies under Lloyd were a very great side.

The results would suggest, too, that he was a very great captain, yet many would deny him this accolade. His rotation of four fast bowlers appeared to contain little that was tactically inventive, while the West Indian over-rate became moribund. His control of his side in

Clive Lloyd's side of 1984. Back row, left to right: A.L. Logie, P.J.L. Dujon, H.A. Gomes, T.R.O. Payne, E.A.E. Baptiste. Middle: J.L. Hendricks (manager), M.D. Marshall, D.L. Haynes, R.A. Harper, C.A. Walsh, M.A. Small, R.B. Richardson, W. St John (assistant manager). Front: J. Garner, I.V.A. Richards, C.H. Lloyd, C.G. Greenidge, M.A. Holding, D. Waight (physio) (Allsport)

Test Record

	M	I	NO	Runs	HS	Avge	100s	RC	Wkts	Avge	BB	Ct
v England	34	51	4	2120	132	45.10	5	146	5	29.20	2–13	32
v Australia	29	48	4	2211	178	50.25	6	223	2	111.50	2–17	24
v New Zealand	8	14	0	234	44	16.71	–	84	1	84.00	1–10	3
v India	28	44	4	2344	242*	58.60	7	169	2	84.50	2–23	20
v Pakistan	11	18	2	606	157	37.87	1	–	–	–	–	11
	110	175	14	7515	242*	46.67	19	622	10	62.20	2–13	90

terms of discipline also seemed tenuous, and the petulance of Holding and Croft in New Zealand in 1980 – the only other series lost under Lloyd's leadership – was disgraceful, yet went unpunished. In the post-Packer period, player power in West Indian cricket seemed supreme, and Lloyd was a law unto himself.

That said, Lloyd's men won 11 Tests in a row against Australia and England in 1984–85, and when Australia beat West Indies at Sydney in January 1985, it was Lloyd's first defeat in 26 matches. It was his 74th Test match as captain, a record, and his last Test.

He retired and settled in Lancashire where he had long been a great favourite, although he has continued to manage West Indies teams.

Test Record as Captain

				M	I	NO	Runs	HS	Avge	100s	RC	Wkts	Avge	BB	Ct
v England	W11	–	D7	18	24	1	1103	101	47.95	2	10	0	–	–	23
v Australia	W12	L7	D3	22	34	3	1599	149	51.58	4	56	0	–	–	21
v New Zealand	–	L1	D2	3	6	0	103	42	17.16	–	–	–	–	–	1
v India	W10	L3	D7	20	29	3	1822	242*	70.07	7	33	0	–	–	15
v Pakistan	W3	L1	D7	11	18	2	606	157	37.87	1	–	–	–	–	11
	W36	L12	D26	74	111	9	5233	242*	51.30	14	99	0	–	–	71

Alvin Isaac KALLICHARRAN

Guyana and Warwickshire

Born: Paidama, Berbice, British Guiana, 21 March 1949

A left-handed batsman of delicacy and fluency whose every movement gave delight, Kallicharran scored a century on his Test debut, against New Zealand on his home ground in Guyana in 1971–72. He followed this with another hundred in his second Test, in Trinidad.

He signed for Kerry Packer's World Series Cricket with the rest of Lloyd's highly successful West Indian side, but withdrew when he discovered he was in breach of contract with a Queensland radio station. When Lloyd and his Packer players withdrew from the series against Australia in 1977–78 after a rumpus with the West Indies Board, Kallicharran was left as the senior player to captain those who remained. It was neither a happy nor successful time for him although he continued in masterly form with the bat against both Australia and India.

Alvin Kallicharran, a left-handed batsman of great charm for West Indies and Warwickshire, led West Indies at a most difficult period (Hulton)

When Lloyd resumed the captaincy, Kallicharran's form declined and, disenchanted and possibly angered at the treatment he had received, he played Currie Cup cricket for Transvaal in 1982–83, so bringing the wrath of the West Indies politicians upon himself and ending his Test career.

He continued to excite Warwickshire supporters until injury brought about his retirement in 1990.

Test Record

	M	I	NO	Runs	HS	Avge	100s	RC	Wkts	Avge	BB	Ct
v England	16	24	1	891	158	38.73	2	59	0	–	–	13
v Australia	19	33	2	1325	127	42.74	4	53	1	53.00	1–7	16
v New Zealand	5	9	1	365	101	45.62	2	33	3	11.00	2–16	1
v India	15	25	3	1229	187	55.86	3	9	0	–	–	11
v Pakistan	11	18	3	589	115	39.26	1	4	0	–	–	10
	66	109	10	4399	187	44.43	12	158	4	39.50	2–16	51

Test Record as Captain

				M	I	NO	Runs	HS	Avge	100s	RC	Wkts	Avge	BB	Ct
v Australia	W1	L1	D1	3	6	0	273	126	45.50	1	–	–	–	–	1
v India	–	L1	D5	6	10	1	538	187	59.77	1	9	0	–	–	3
	W1	L2	D6	9	16	1	811	187	54.06	2	9	0	–	–	4

Deryck Lance MURRAY

Trinidad, Nottinghamshire and Warwickshire

Born: Port of Spain, Trinidad, 20 May 1943

Deryck Murray was the first West Indian wicket-keeper to claim 100 victims in Test cricket, and he held all records in that position until the arrival of Dujon.

He began as deputy to Allan in England in 1963, but when Allan fell ill, Murray kept in all the Tests and had a record 24 victims. He studied at both Cambridge and Nottingham Universities and played county cricket for Nottinghamshire and Warwickshire, but he did not re-establish his position in the West Indies side until 1973, after which he remained in total control.

A great spokesman on behalf of players' rights, he was a prime negotiator in the dealings over World Series Cricket and later played his part as an administrator. He led West Indies in the first Test against Australia in 1979–80 when Lloyd was recovering from a knee operation, and retired after the 1980 series in England.

Deryck Murray led West Indies only once, but he was Lloyd's right-hand man for a long time and a champion of players' rights (Ken Kelly)

Test Record

	M	I	NO	Runs	HS	Avge	100s	RC	Wkts	Avge	BB	Ct/st
v England	28	41	7	654	64	19.23	–	–	–	–	–	90/4
v Australia	15	24	0	682	90	28.41	–	–	–	–	–	40/–
v New Zealand	3	6	1	66	30	13.20	–	–	–	–	–	7/–
v India	9	14	0	343	91	24.50	–	–	–	–	–	24/3
v Pakistan	7	11	1	248	52	24.80	–	–	–	–	–	20/1
	62	96	9	1993	91	22.90	–	–	–	–	–	181/8

Test Record as Captain

				M	I	NO	Runs	HS	Avge	100s	RC	Wkts	Avge	BB	Ct/St
v Australia	–	–	D1	1	1	0	21	21	21.00	–	–	–	–	–	3/–

Isaac Vivian Alexander RICHARDS

Combined Islands, Leeward Islands, Somerset and Glamorgan

Born: St John's, Antigua, 7 March 1952

In August 1976, Viv Richards hit 291 against England at The Oval. It brought his total number of runs in Tests during the calendar year to a record 1710 at an average of 90. In a sense, it was not surprising; for by that time, Richards was recognised as the best batsman in the world, a savage and brutal destroyer of all types of bowling.

He had first played for Somerset in 1974, and the following winter, 1974–75, toured India. In the first Test he scored 4 and 3. In the second, he hit 192 not out and a mighty Test career was launched.

It was automatic that Richards would succeed Lloyd as captain of the Test side. He was the outstanding batsman in world cricket, a capable bowler, brilliant fielder, had an astute knowledge of the game and was passionately and openly committed to the West Indian cause. He had a deep sense of history which sometimes led him to believe that he was conducting a crusade to right the wrongs that had been done to the black man in the past.

He first captained West Indies against England at Headingley in 1980, when Lloyd was injured, and he led West Indies in his own right in the series with New Zealand later the same year. While his tactics and philosophy closely followed those of Lloyd, he was faced with the problems of a side that was beginning to change in character as Gomes, Holding and Garner

Viv Richards (Ben Radford/Allsport)

passed from the scene and Patterson, Ambrose, Bishop and Hooper arrived. Richards was determined that West Indies' superiority should not be lost while he was captain.

A fine natural athlete, he insisted on rigorous physical training programmes and could be a hard taskmaster with a lashing tongue to any who erred in their technique or commitment. Indeed, it is this part of his make-up which has led him to those occasions when his outstanding ability has seemed less endearing. The arro-gance which is an essential part of his batting can quickly become rudeness at the wrong moment, and he has flared at journalists and disdained spectators. None of this, however, will ever diminish his status as one of the greatest of cricketers.

By the end of 1991, West Indies had played 12 series under his leadership. Eight had been won, and four had been shared. That is an astonishing record.

Test Record

	M	I	NO	Runs	HS	Avge	100s	RC	Wkts	Avge	BB	Ct
v England	36	50	4	2869	291	62.36	8	459	6	76.50	2–24	29
v Australia	34	54	3	2266	208	44.43	5	694	7	99.14	2–65	24
v New Zealand	7	10	1	387	105	43.00	1	236	3	78.66	1–32	7
v India	28	41	3	1927	192*	50.71	8	353	5	70.60	1–14	39
v Pakistan	16	27	1	1091	123	41.96	2	222	11	20.18	2–17	23
	121	182	12	8540	291	50.23	24	1964	32	61.37	2–17	122

Test Record as Captain

				M	I	NO	Runs	HS	Avge	100s	RC	Wkts	Avge	BB	Ct
v England	W13	L3	D3	19	26	2	1102	110	45.91	1	110	0	–	–	14
v Australia	W5	L2	D4	11	18	2	696	146	43.50	1	480	6	80.00	2–65	6
v New Zealand	W3	L1	D3	7	10	1	387	105	43.00	1	236	3	78.66	1–32	7
v India	W4	L1	D3	8	11	1	430	110	43.00	2	231	4	165.25	1–28	15
v Pakistan	W2	L1	D2	5	9	0	453	123	50.33	1	53	4	13.25	2–17	7
	W27	L8	D15	50	74	6	3068	146	45.11	6	1110	17	65.29	2–17	49

Cuthbert Gordon GREENIDGE

Barbados and Hampshire

Born: Black Bess, St Peter, Barbados, 1 May 1951

One of the most exciting opening batsmen Test cricket has known, Gordon Greenidge played schoolboy cricket in England but elected to rep-resent West Indies. He formed a memorable opening partnership with Desmond Haynes, just as he had formed a thrilling one with Barry Richards for Hampshire. He led West Indies against Pakistan at Georgetown in April 1988 when Richards was recovering from surgery. He put Pakistan in to bat and saw them become the first visiting side to win in the Caribbean for 10 years.

Gordon Greenidge lost his one match as captain of West Indies and was never to succeed to Richards' throne (Adrian Murrell/Allsport)

Test Record

	M	I	NO	Runs	HS	Avge	100s	RC	Wkts	Avge	BB	Ct
v England	32	48	2	2318	223	50.39	7	4	0	–	–	29
v Australia	29	52	7	1819	226	40.42	4	0	0	–	–	22
v New Zealand	10	19	3	882	213	55.12	2	–	–	–	–	8
v India	23	39	4	1678	194	47.94	5	–	–	–	–	18
v Pakistan	14	27	0	861	100	31.88	1	–	–	–	–	19
	108	185	16	7558	226	44.72	19	4	0	–	–	96

Test Record as Captain

				M	I	NO	Runs	HS	Avge	100s	RC	Wkts	Avge	BB	Ct
v Pakistan	–	L1	–	1	2	0	60	43	30.00	–	–	–	–	–	2

Desmond Leo HAYNES

Barbados and Middlesex

Born: Holder's Hill, St James, Barbados,
15 February 1956

A cultured and consistent opening batsman and a likeable and friendly man, Haynes captained West Indies against England in 1989–90 when Richards was ill. Captaincy revealed unexpected traits in his character. He became involved in verbal exchanges with the England players and slowed the over-rate shamefully to avoid defeat.

He led West Indies to Pakistan in 1990–91, and mainly by his own efforts managed to draw the series. It seemed, however, that West Indies were looking towards Richie Richardson to succeed Richards.

Haynes made his Test debut against Australia in 1977–78. In 1990 he established a record aggregate in the Red Stripe Cup when he hit 654 runs in five matches.

Desmond Haynes led West Indies against England and Pakistan when Richards was unavailable. Here he tosses with Graham Gooch in the third Test at Port of Spain, Trinidad (Adrian Murrell/Allsport)

Test Record

	M	I	NO	Runs	HS	Avge	100s	RC	Wkts	Avge	BB	Ct
v England	32	52	8	2175	184	50.58	5	6	0	–	–	16
v Australia	28	51	6	2110	145	46.88	5	–	–	–	–	15
v New Zealand	10	20	3	843	122	49.58	3	–	–	–	–	7
v India	19	32	3	990	136	34.13	2	–	–	–	–	10
v Pakistan	13	23	1	526	117	23.90	1	2	1	2.00	1–2	11
	102	178	21	6644	184	42.31	16	8	1	8.00	1–2	59

Test Record as Captain

				M	I	NO	Runs	HS	Avge	100s	RC	Wkts	Avge	BB	Ct
v England	–	–	D1	1	2	0	45	45	22.50	–	–	–	–	–	–
v Pakistan	W1	L1	D1	3	6	0	198	117	33.00	1	–	–	–	–	1
	W1	L1	D2	4	8	0	243	117	30.37	1	–	–	–	–	1

INDIA

India and Captaincy

As Mihir Bose points out in his admirable *History of Indian Cricket*, the game began in India, 'as did all overseas cricket, with expatriate Britons – in this case British sailors playing on a beach in Western India.' The year was 1721, and by the end of 18th century, the Calcutta Cricket Club was in existence.

Cricket, like so much else in India in the days of the Raj, was the prerogative of the British. They lived in India for commercial or administrative reasons, and they followed their pursuits and hobbies in a way which, to all intents and purposes, segregated them from the Indians whose country they had conquered with ease. It was the Parsees who were to provide the link that was to turn cricket from a curious British diversion into the national game of India.

The Parsees had fled from Persia in the 6th century and settled in Western India where they maintained their own traditions and never became fully integrated into the country which had adopted them. They co-operated willingly with the European and British traders and were rewarded in return.

In the following of their masters, the Parsees took to cricket and although their early efforts were treated with some contempt, they were granted a match against the English in Bombay in 1877 and made tours of England in 1886 and 1888.

More importantly, G.F. Vernon brought a side to tour India in 1889–90. It was hardly a side of first-class strength since apart from Vernon and Lord Hawke it contained only one other, J.G. Walker, who had appeared in county cricket with any regularity. All the matches were against Englishmen in India with the exception of the match against the Parsees at Bombay in January 1890. It was a game of great significance, for the Parsees inflicted the one defeat of the tour on Vernon's side.

Two years later, in 1892–93, Lord Hawke returned with a stronger side which included F.S. Jackson. There were two matches against the Parsees on this tour; one was lost and the other won. There was also a match against All India, but the title is misleading: the side was certainly not representative of the country.

The third side from England to tour India was the Oxford Authentics, led by K.J. Key of Surrey, in 1902–03. They found the opposition stronger than anticipated and it was not until the fifth match of the tour that they could claim their first victory. The Parsees beat them convincingly by eight wickets.

What the Parsees had been able to do, the Hindus and Moslems were keen to emulate, and their interest in cricket grew. In 1892, the first Presidency Match, Europeans versus Parsees, had taken place, and it was this annual fixture that was to generate India's first cricket competition. For the 1905 and 1906 fixtures the

Hindus replaced the Parsees, but in 1907 it became a triangular tournament and with the advent of the Moslems in 1912, the Quadrangular Tournament. In 1937 it became the Pentagular Tournament, and it continued in this form until 1945 when it ceased to exist.

Tours of England by Indian sides in 1904 and 1907 had been mooted, but they had never come to fruition. The first tour was cancelled because of insufficient funding and because of disagreements among the organising committee with regard to the selection of the team. The 1907 tour was to have been led by Ranjitsinhji, but no fixture list was ever issued and the tour was abandoned.

There was talk of a tour in 1910, but this never progressed beyond the suggestion stage and it was in 1911 that the first Indian team to include the three major sections of non-European cricket made a tour of England. They won only two first-class matches but they had in Palwankar Baloo a slow left-arm bowler of the highest quality. He took more than a hundred wickets in all matches on the tour.

The problems which Baloo faced before the tour, however, give some indication of the troubles that plagued the early years of Indian cricket. He was an Untouchable who worked as a groundsman in a Bombay club, and his low caste precluded him from playing for Hindu Gymkhana, the leading Bombay Hindu club. The Parsees gave him an opportunity, and when Hindu Gymkhana realised how talented he was they made him a member and he went on to captain the Hindus.

Baloo was not, of course, captain of the Indian side that toured England in 1911. That side was led by H.H. the Maharajah of Patiala, so establishing a pattern in the captaincy of Indian sides that was to last for nearly 40 years. More than a third of India was ruled by princes who wielded great power and who were happy to collaborate with the ruling British. Cricket came to be seen as a means of increasing power and influence, and this was to have an insidious effect upon the captaincy of the Indian touring sides.

In spite of the advance made by the Hindus and the Moslems, the Europeans still dominated the organisation of cricket in India and it was at their instigation that a strong MCC side under Arthur Gilligan came to tour India in 1926–27. Lord Harris, who had been Governor of Bombay from 1890–95, gave his enthusiastic support to the lobby for the tour and Patiala helped finance it. In the event, MCC were unbeaten on the tour but there were some spirited performances by Indian cricketers and their successes were important in shaping the rapid developments which now took place.

Gilligan's enthusiasm and encouragement supported the view that Indian cricket was thriving and that the time was now ripe to establish a Board of Control to run the game in India. The inevitable political wranglings and jockeying for power delayed the setting up of the Board until December 1928, and this delay meant that a proposed tour of India by South Africa in 1929 never took place. It was to be two years after this, in 1931, that India were then scheduled to become a Test-playing nation with a tour by England, but even this plan was to be put back for a year.

This delay was partly due to bad administration and partly due to the political climate, for it was in 1930 that Gandhi began his great civil disobedience movement that was to culminate in Indian independence. Inevitably cricket suffered, with the Quadrangular tournament suspended between 1930 and 1934. Hindus who were political activists refused to have anything to do with cricket, and Vijay Merchant, destined to be one of India's greatest batsmen and just emerging as a player of the highest quality, was one of several Hindu cricketers who were persuaded not to go to the trials which were to be used to help select the side which was to tour England in 1932.

By chance, a cricketer had been appointed Viceroy of India in 1931. Strongly opposed to any hint of Indian nationalism, Lord Willingdon was, nevertheless, sympathetic to Indian cricket and cricketers. He had played for Sussex and Cambridge and had spent much of his life in India, having been Governor of both Bombay and Madras. As Governor of Bombay, he had encouraged Indian cricketers and fielded 'mixed' elevens. He now returned to India as Viceroy at a time when the country was being born as a cricketing nation and was in need of cricketing leadership.

Ranjitsinhji was the obvious man to adopt the mantle as leader of Indian cricket, but he not only refused to take on that responsibility, he also forbade his nephew Duleepsinhji to play for India. De Mello and Govan, who were the prime movers in forming the Indian Board of Control, attempted to persuade Duleepsinhji to lead India into Test cricket but he refused and elected to play for England. Ranjitsinhji's argument for his decision to prevent his nephew from playing for India was that Duleepsinhji had learned his cricket in England and that cricket in India was sub-standard.

Patiala was keen to take on the leadership of Indian cricket but Lord Willingdon would not accept him and other pretenders emerged. Foremost among them was the Maharajkumar of Vizianagram. He was not a ruling prince, but he was an enthusiast with a capacity for political cunning. He organised his own tour of India and Ceylon in 1930–31 and was acclaimed for having Hobbs and Sutcliffe in his side. His tour was a great success and he strengthened his position further by donating large sums of money to the Board, including 40 000 rupees towards the tour of England.

There was a growing belief that a European would be asked to lead the side to England in 1932. This would be politically acceptable, for it would mirror the view that the Indians were incapable of governing themselves and needed the British in order to survive.

Patiala sensed the dangers in this, and he played a master stroke by suggesting that the trials should be staged in Patiala and that he would meet all expenses for the month. Willingdon was powerless to oppose this offer. No Europeans were invited to the trials, and it was apparent, when the party was finally named, that Patiala had had the major say in selection. He himself was to captain the side, Prince Ghanshyam Singhi of Limbdi was vice-captain and Vizianagram was deputy vice-captain.

The great surprise was that the Nawab of Pataudi had opted out of the tour. He had captained one of the teams in the final trial and had already established himself with Oxford University and Worcestershire, but like Duleepsinhji, he decided to play for England rather than for his native country.

Vizianagram decided that for reasons of state he was unable to make the trip, but this was hardly credible and it seems more likely that he felt slighted at not having been named as captain. Two weeks after the party had been announced, Patiala himself stood down and the Maharaj of Porbandar, ruler of the state of Kathiawar and brother-in-law of Limbdi, was named as the new captain. It was apparent that there had been much political manoeuvring behind the scenes. It was not to be the last in the appointment of the captain of India.

Cottari Kanakyia NAYUDU

Madhya Pradesh, Andhra and United Provinces

Born: Nagpur, 31 October 1895
Died: Indore, 14 November 1967

The social system of All India in the 1930s had decreed that the leadership of the cricket team should be the monopoly of the princes, and when the side came to England in 1932 to begin their Test career they were managed by Major E.W.C. Ricketts, who had served in the Indian army, and led by a prince who, unfortunately, could not play cricket. The Maharaj of Porbandar appeared in the first four matches of the tour and scored 0, 2, 0, 2 and 2. He did not play again. As Mihir Bose so eloquently pointed out, 'He was said to be the only first-class cricketer in England to have more Rolls-Royces than runs.' Limbdi fared somewhat better and was a better cricketer, but both men wisely decided to stand down from the Test side and the captaincy passed to C.K. Nayudu.

This move was not unanimously accepted by the Indian side but a cable from Patiala confirmed the appointment. Nayudu led the side admirably. He badly damaged his hand while attempting a catch in England's first innings but he dismissed Paynter and Jardine at a personal cost of 40 runs and was top scorer in India's first innings with 40.

He won praise from the English press, but there were still factions within the Indian side itself who were jealous and critical of him. An open rift appeared between Nayudu and India's leading bowler Amar Singh, and on his return to India, Nayudu, hailed as a hero by the majority, was still the victim of political machinations and petty jealousies.

Two of the three selectors for the side to meet England in 1933–34 were Englishmen, but Nayadu survived all the political intrigue and religious rivalry to be retained as captain. His younger brother, C.S., joined him in the side.

A tall, elegant, agile and powerful batsman and an accurate slow-medium pace bowler, Nayudu made his debut in representative cricket in 1916 when he played for the Hindus against the Europeans in the Bombay Quadrangular tournament. In December 1926 he caused a sensation when he hit 11 sixes and 13 fours in an innings of 153 (out of 187) in 100 minutes for the Hindus against the MCC touring side who numbered Tate, Geary, Mercer and Astill in their attack. To the Bombay crowd of 45 000 he became a national hero, and in spite of the underhand criticisms of lesser men, he held that position for the rest of his life and beyond.

Honoured as one of *Wisden*'s Five Cricketers of the Year in 1933, Nayudu was already 37 years old when India entered the Test arena, but he played in his country's first seven Tests.

Inevitably, the intrigue and the loss of the series against Jardine's side in India in 1933–34 by two to nil was to cost Nayudu the captaincy, but he came to England with the Maharaj of Vizianagram's team in 1936 and played in all three Tests. In the second innings of the final Test at The Oval, he was struck a fearful blow by a ball from Allen, but he refused to retire and batted for two and a half hours for 81, an innings which saved his side from the indignity of an innings defeat.

Nayudu played in the Ranji Trophy from the year of its inception, 1934–35, until 1956–57 when he was 62 years old. He played innings of 84 against Rajasthan and 52 against Bombay in his final season.

Above: The statue to the memory of India's first Test captain, C.K. Nayudu (Adrian Murrell/ Allsport)

Left: Nayudu pictured with his opposite number Douglas Jardine before India's first home Test match, against England at Bombay (Hulton)

A lieutenant-colonel in the army, Nayudu was a dedicated cricketer who prepared himself meticulously. He was an astute captain and a strong disciplinarian, and his name is revered in Indian cricket. In Indore, a statue has been erected to honour his achievements.

Test Record

	M	I	NO	Runs	HS	Avge	100s	RC	Wkts	Avge	BB	Ct
v England	7	14	0	350	81	25.00	–	386	9	42.88	3–40	4

Test Record as Captain

				M	I	NO	Runs	HS	Avge	100s	RC	Wkts	Avge	BB	Ct
v England	–	L3	D1	4	8	0	210	67	26.25	–	181	5	36.20	3–40	2

Maharajah Kumar Sir Vijaya Anand VIZIANAGRAM

United Provinces

Born: Benares, 28 December 1905
Died: Benares, 2 December 1965

Vizianagram was a wealthy and influential figure in Indian cricket for much of his life, and in the early part of the 1930s he was engaged for most of the time in a struggle for power with Patiala. Vizianagram was helped in his struggle by Lord Willingdon, the Viceroy, who was a consistent ally, and by his own clever political manipulating. He had lost the battle to captain the 1932 side to England, but he was determined to lead the 1936 side. In spite of Nayudu's stature as a player and success as a captain, it was apparent that he was no longer a contender to lead the side to England. He was, after all, a commoner, and as *Wisden* phrased it, 'For reasons apart from cricket, the necessity existed of having a person of distinction and importance at the head of affairs.'

Vizianagram was obviously a strong contender to take the side to England, but the Nawab of Pataudi, who had prospered for Oxford University and Worcestershire and scored a century on his Test debut for England, returned to India and it was he who, in October 1935, was appointed captain of the side to tour England in 1936. Pataudi later withdrew on grounds of ill-health, but as he confessed later, the real reason was that he saw no joy in trying to unite the warring factions. Having undermined the candidature of the other contenders, Vizianagram was appointed captain, with Major R.J. Brittain-Jones, the Comptroller of Willingdon's Household, as manager.

No vice-captain was appointed and there was no selection committee on the tour. This was unfortunate as Vizianagram himself was below first-class standard, and it has been argued that the reason he scored 600 runs on the tour owed as much to the generous gifts he would give to opposing captains before each match as it did to his ability.

The tour was marred by the fact that there were two main factions, one of which was friendly to Nayudu who was not favoured by the captain. Worst of all, however, was that on the eve of the first Test, Vizianagram and Brittain-Jones sent home Lala Amarnath, the party's outstanding cricketer, for disciplinary reasons. There were pleas on the player's behalf, and the Indian Board of Control wished him to be reinstated, but Lord Willingdon attacked the all-rounder in a speech at The Oval as he was on his way back to India, and the captain and manager refused to accept his return. Amarnath was later to be exonerated, and he went on to become a captain of India and a chairman of selectors.

Senior members of the party and Merchant, a young batsman of outstanding talent, tried to persuade Vizianagram to stand down and allow Nayudu to lead the side in the Test series, but captain and manager maintained a despotic regime. It was no coincidence that when Vizianagram was absent from the side receiving the knighthood which was conferred on him between the first and second Tests, India, led by Nayudu, gained their first victory over a county.

Vizianagram was at one time a member of the Indian Parliament, and from 1954 to 1956 he was President of the Board of Control. He donated much money to Indian cricket and was an undoubted enthusiast with a passion for the game. He was also a very clever politician.

Test Record as Captain

				M	I	NO	Runs	HS	Avge	100s	RC	Wkts	Avge	BB	Ct
v England	-	L2	D1	3	6	2	33	19*	8.25	–	–	–	–	–	1

Nawab Iftikar Ali PATAUDI

Worcestershire and Southern Punjab

Born: Pataudi, 16 March 1910
Died: New Delhi, 5 January 1952

The only cricketer to have played for both England and India, the Nawab of Pataudi was a stylish middle-order batsman who won his blue at Oxford in 1929 and established a record by scoring 238 not out in the Varsity match of 1931. He was a contender for the captaincy of India in 1932 and 1936, but chose to play for Worcestershire and England. His Test debut came in the first match of the body-line series in 1932–33, and he hit 102, so emulating the feat of Ranjitsinhji and Duleepsinhji, both of whom had hit centuries on their Test debuts. He was dropped after the second Test, and his third and last appearance came in the 1934 series.

Vijay Merchant seemed sure to captain the Indian side to England in 1946, but early that year Pataudi reappeared on the scene. He had played little first-class cricket for ten years, but his knowledge of English cricket and the inevitable power struggle within the Indian Board led to Pataudi winning the captaincy by ten votes to eight. Merchant, one of India's truly great cricketers, was never to captain his country.

Although there was talk that Pataudi would return to Worcestershire for the 1952 season, he virtually retired from cricket after the 1946 tour of England. He died of a heart attack while playing polo in January 1952, on his son's eleventh birthday; and that son was destined to follow his father to Oxford and to captain India.

The Nawab of Pataudi was a fine all-round sportsman who represented India at hockey in the Olympic Games in Amsterdam in 1928.

The Nawab of Pataudi who scored a century for England against Australia and who led India against England in 1946 (Hulton)

Test Record

	M	I	NO	Runs	HS	Avge	100s	RC	Wkts	Avge	BB	Ct
for England v Australia	3	5	0	144	102	28.80	1	–	–	–	–	–
v England	3	5	0	55	22	11.00	–	–	–	–	–	–
	6	10	0	199	102	19.90	1	–	–	–	–	–

Test Record as Captain

	M	I	NO	Runs	HS	Avge	100s	RC	Wkts	Avge	BB	Ct
v England	–	L1	D2	*Details as above*								

Lala AMARNATH

Southern Punjab, Gujarat, Patiala, United Provinces and Railways

Born: Lahore, 11 September 1911

Known always as Lala Armanath, this great all-rounder's real given names were Nanik Bhardwaj. By the time MCC toured India in 1933–34 he had become an accomplished attacking batsman and was selected for the first Test match that season. He hit a century in the second innings, the first to be hit for India in a Test match. He arrived in England in 1936 with the reputation of being an all-rounder of the highest quality. Three centuries and 32 wickets at moderate cost in the first part of the tour confirmed that view, but his disenchantment with the way in which the tour was being led and managed caused this impetuous and instinctive cricketer to erupt, and he was sent home for disciplinary reasons. An enquiry by the Indian Board of Control later found him 'not guilty'.

He played in the Lancashire League and toured England in 1946, taking eight wickets in the second Test at Old Trafford. Merchant withdrew from the 1947–48 tour of Australia because of injury and Amarnath replaced him as captain. Although confronted by Bradman's great side, he was the leading wicket-taker in the series; but he could not find his batting form.

He retained the captaincy for the visit of West Indies in 1948–49, and kept wicket in the fifth Test after Sen was injured. He held five catches behind the stumps.

At the end of that series, Amarnath demanded more money and better travelling conditions and accommodation for the players. The result was that he infuriated De Mello, the powerful member of the Board who had been his supporter, and was suspended from domestic cricket. His apology was later accepted, but he played no cricket in India for two years, and Hazare was named as captain for the series against England in 1951–52. Amarnath played in three Tests in that series but, incomprehensibly, he was omitted from the party to tour England in 1952.

That tour was a disaster and Amarnath, now supported by Vizianagram who had once been his enemy, was reinstated as captain for the inaugural series against Pakistan in 1952–53. He enjoyed a good series and led India to their first victory in a Test rubber, but he ended the series a bitter man, having learned that he had

Test Record

	M	I	NO	Runs	HS	Avge	100s	RC	Wkts	Avge	BB	Ct
v England	9	15	1	339	118	24.21	1	650	20	32.50	5–96	5
v Australia	5	10	0	140	46	14.00	–	366	13	28.15	4–78	–
v West Indies	5	10	2	294	62	36.75	–	263	3	87.66	2–75	6
v Pakistan	5	5	1	101	61*	26.25	–	202	9	22.44	4–40	2
	24	40	4	878	118	24.38	1	1481	45	32.91	5–96	13

already been replaced as captain for the trip to West Indies. His Test career was at an end.

Never far from controversy, Lala Amarnath was a batsman of explosive power. He was a bowler whose short run disguised a brisk pace and prodigious movement. He was a respected and capable captain who was confronted by the strongest of opposition.

Test Record as Captain

				M	I	NO	Runs	HS	Avge	100s	RC	Wkts	Avge	BB	Ct
v Australia	–	L4	D1	5	10	0	140	46	14.00	–	366	13	28.15	4–78	–
v West Indies	–	L1	D4	5	10	2	294	62	36.75	–	263	3	87.66	2–75	6
v Pakistan	W2	L1	D2	5	5	1	101	61*	26.25	–	202	9	22.44	4–40	2
	W2	L6	D7	15	25	3	539	62	24.50	–	831	25	33.24	4–40	8

Vijay Samuel HAZARE

Maharashtra, Central India and Baroda

Born: Sangli, Maharashtra, 11 March 1915

Vijay Hazare played his early cricket in Maharashtra and represented them in their first Ranji Trophy match in 1935. He was then employed by Vikram Singh, the ruler of Dewas, who was a cricket fanatic. He and his brother-in-law engaged Clarrie Grimmett, the great Australian leg-spinner, to teach Hazare wrist-spin and to improve his batting. The wily Grimmett, who was actually born in New Zealand, concentrated on allowing Hazare to develop his medium-pace bowling and taught him patience in his batting. The result was to be a fine all-round cricketer, a batsman who scored Test centuries against every country whom he played.

He was to suffer the frustration of having his Test debut delayed by the war, but by 1946, he was an automatic choice for the tour of England. His reputation had been established in 1939–40 when Maharashtra won the Ranji Trophy for the first time and Hazare hit 316 not out against Baroda. This was the first triple century hit by an Indian cricketer although Duleepsinhji, who played all his cricket in England, had made three hundred for Sussex.

Records were to be part of Hazare's career. He became the first Indian to hit two triple centuries, and he and Gul Mohamed shared the highest partnership in first-class cricket, 577 for Baroda against Holkar in 1946–47. By then Hazare had made his Test debut and had scored more than a thousand runs on the tour of England.

In the fourth Test match against Australia at Adelaide in 1948, Hazare became the first batsman to score a century in each innings for India. His success continued with two centuries in the series against West Indies in 1948–49, and while playing league cricket in Lancashire he learned that he was to replace Amarnath and lead India against England in 1951–52.

As a batsman and as a personality he was unable to impose himself upon the series, but under his leadership India won a Test match for the first time, beating England by an innings and eight runs in the final Test at Madras.

The selectors had not helped Hazare in the series against England, opting for three different wicket-keepers and four different sets of openers as they made constant changes, and they served him as ill when they appointed him to take the side to England in 1952. The party did not include Amarnath, Mushtaq Ali and, most importantly, the great Vinoo Mankad who could get no guarantee from the Board that he would be selected and signed to play in the Lancashire League. In fact, Mankad was released to play in four Tests in the series, but in spite of Hazare's brave and durable batting, India were trounced, and the tour was a disaster.

Failure is not easily tolerated by Indian selectors and Hazare was deposed as captain for the inaugural series against Pakistan. He still managed a century in the Test in Bombay which India won, and he was then reinstated as captain when it was decided to dispense with Amarnath at the end of the series.

Hazare took the side to the West Indies in 1952–53, and although India were beaten they gave a reasonably good account of themselves and fielded brilliantly. They had in Gupte an outstanding leg-spin bowler.

Hazare did not enjoy a successful series and he decided to relinquish the captaincy. In fact, his Test career was at an end.

The number of runs he accumulated in Test cricket is testimony to Hazare's quality as a player. He was by nature cautious, and the dire straits in which he often found his side added to that caution and led to him being a captain not noted for adventure; but he led India to their first victory in Test cricket, and he was a very fine batsman.

Test Record

		M	I	NO	Runs	HS	Avge	100s	RC	Wkts	Avge	BB	Ct
v England		12	19	2	803	164*	50.18	2	382	7	54.57	2–53	1
v Australia		5	10	1	429	145	47.66	2	382	7	54.57	4–29	1
v West Indies		10	20	2	737	134*	40.94	2	391	5	78.20	2–13	7
v Pakistan		3	3	1	223	146	111.50	1	65	1	65.00	1–21	1
		30	52	6	2192	164*	47.65	7	1220	20	61.00	4–29	11

Test Record as Captain

				M	I	NO	Runs	HS	Avge	100s	RC	Wkts	Avge	BB	Ct
v England	W1	L4	D4	9	14	2	680	164*	56.66	2	203	5	40.60	2–53	–
v West Indies	–	L1	D4	5	10	0	194	63	19.40	–	132	3	44.00	2–13	4
	W1	L5	D8	14	24	2	874	164*	39.72	2	335	8	41.87	2–13	4

Mulwantrai Himatlal MANKAD

Western India, Nawanagar, Gujarat, Bengal, Bombay and Rajasthan

Born: Jamnagar, 12 April 1917
Died: Bombay, 21 August 1978

India had produced no finer all-round cricketer than 'Vinoo' Mankad, a tenacious right-handed batsman who frequently opened the innings, and a slow left-arm bowler who was the first of the great Indian spinners and, many would argue, the best.

He began with aspirations to be a fast bowler, but under the tutelage of A.F. Wensley, the Sussex all-rounder, he became a spinner. He was outstanding with bat and ball against Lord Tennyson's side in 1937–38, but the war delayed his Test debut until 1946. He performed admirably in the three Tests, took 5 for 101 at Old Trafford, impressed all with his bowling and completed the 'double' in first-class matches. He was one of *Wisden's* Five Cricketers of the Year.

He hit two centuries in the Test series against Australia in 1947–48 and remained an automatic choice for the Indian side for the next decade. His first great moment against England came at Madras in February 1952 when he took 8 for 55 and 4 for 53 to bowl India to an innings victory, their first win in Test cricket. He claimed 34 wickets in the series, which was a record until 1972–73 when Chandrasekhar took 35 wickets in a series against England.

Mankad had received an offer from Haslingden in the Lancashire League, but he said that he would not accept it if the Indian Board would assure him that he would be picked for the tour of England. With an arrogance and stupidity that bedevilled Indian cricket at that time, the Board refused to give him that assurance, and Hazare's side left for England without him.

In the event, Haslingden released him to play in three of the four Tests when it was seen what a sorry plight the Indian side was in. He responded by playing a memorable innings at Lord's. He hit 72, and then bowled 73 overs to take 5 for 196 as England made 537. Mankad then scored 184 out of India's 378 before bowling another 24 overs for 35 runs, but he was unable to stop England winning by eight wickets.

He bowled India to their first series victory by taking 25 wickets in four Tests against Pakistan in 1952–53, his most memorable achievement being his 13 for 131 in the first Test at Delhi. He was appointed vice-captain for the tour to West Indies which immediately followed the series against Pakistan, but there was a reluctance to give him the captaincy and it proved to be justified.

When he finally led India on the tour of Pakistan in 1955, he proved to be an unimaginative captain who seemed unable to make decisions or seize the initiative. As a player, he had always shown a sharp brain, an unrivalled understanding of the game and a mastery of tactics, but these qualities deserted him when he was asked to lead India.

He played in two Tests in 1958–59 against West Indies and captained India at Madras when Umrigar resigned shortly before the start of the match. Illness prevented Mankad from playing after the first innings, and the next Test, at Delhi, was his last.

He was one of India's greatest cricketers, but not one of their better captains.

India's first great all-round cricketer, 'Vinoo' Mankad, also the first of the great Indian spinners (Lemmon)

Test Record

	M	I	NO	Runs	HS	Avge	100s	RC	Wkts	Avge	BB	Ct
v England	11	18	1	618	184	36.35	1	1249	54	23.12	8–55	9
v Australia	8	16	0	388	116	24.25	2	943	23	41.00	4–49	2
v West Indies	12	22	2	397	96	19.85	–	1802	36	50.05	5–228	8
v Pakistan	9	11	2	180	41	20.00	–	913	37	24.70	8–52	10
v New Zealand	4	5	0	526	231	105.20	2	328	12	27.33	4–65	4
	44	72	5	2109	231	31.47	5	5235	162	32.31	8–52	33

Test Record as Captain

				M	I	NO	Runs	HS	Avge	100s	RC	Wkts	Avge	BB	Ct
v Pakistan	–	–	D5	5	6	1	51	33	10.20	–	399	12	33.25	5–64	6
v West Indies	–	L1	–	1	1	0	4	4	4.00	–	95	4	23.75	4–95	–
	–	L1	D5	6	7	1	55	33	9.16	–	494	16	30.87	5–64	6

Ghulam AHMED

Hyderabad

Born: Hyderabad, 4 July 1922

A tall off-spinner who learned his bowling on matting wickets, Ghulam Ahmed lacked consistency and became a victim of the web of Indian cricket politics. He developed phobias about playing in certain centres, and he should have played in more than 22 Tests. He was a stop-gap captain for India against New Zealand at Hyderabad – he did not appear again in the series – and against West Indies in two Tests in 1958–59. He has served Indian cricket well as an administrator.

Test Record

	M	I	NO	Runs	HS	Avge	100s	RC	Wkts	Avge	BB	Ct
v West Indies	5	9	3	35	11	5.83	–	523	9	58.11	4–94	3
v England	6	10	5	27	14	5.40	–	581	25	23.24	5–70	2
v Pakistan	8	8	1	96	50	13.71	–	659	21	31.38	5–109	3
v New Zealand	1	–	–	–	–	–	–	92	1	92.00	1–56	2
v Australia	2	4	0	34	13	8.50	–	197	12	16.41	7–49	1
	22	31	9	192	50	8.72	–	2052	68	30.17	7–49	11

Test Record as Captain

				M	I	NO	Runs	HS	Avge	100s	RC	Wkts	Avge	BB	Ct
v New Zealand	–	–	D1	1	–	–	–	–	–	–	92	1	92.00	1–56	2
v West Indies	–	L2	–	2	4	1	4	4	1.33	–	162	1	162.00	1–52	–
	–	L2	D1	3	4	1	4	4	1.33	–	254	2	127.00	1–52	2

Pahelam Ratanji UMRIGAR

Bombay and Gujarat

Born: Solapur, Maharashtra, 28 March 1926

A dashing cricketer, 'Polly' Umrigar was a shrewd captain who led Bombay to five successive Ranji Trophy victories, the beginning of their 15 years of domination of the tournament which started in 1959. A tall, forceful batsman, a medium-pace bowler and a splendid fielder, he was the leading Indian batsman of his generation.

He made his first-class debut in the Pentagular tournament in 1945 and made his Test debut against West Indies in Bombay in December 1948. He had to wait another three years for his second Test appearance. In the last match of that series, against England in 1951–52, he hit 130 not out, India won by an innings, and Umrigar's Test career was saved.

Like other Indian batsmen, he had a wretched time in the Test series against

Hutton's side in 1952, but he re-established his reputation in the inaugural series with Pakistan the following winter. In the Caribbean in 1952–53 he topped the batting averages in the Test series.

In the first Test against New Zealand at Hyderabad in 1955–56, Umrigar became the first Indian batsman to reach 200 in a Test innings. When Ghulam Ahmed stepped down from the second Test through illness, Umrigar was appointed captain, and India won a high-scoring series. He led his country in all three Tests against Australia in 1956–57, but after one Test against West Indies in 1958–59 the cap-

taincy was returned to Ghulam Ahmed. India were to have four captains in that series.

Four days before the fourth Test of the series in Madras, Ghulam Ahmed announced that he was retiring from Test cricket. Umrigar was once more named as captain, but an altercation with Board officials over the composition of the side led him to resign on the eve of the match, and Mankad hastily took over. Umrigar was never to captain India again, although he played Test cricket until April 1962. He was a shrewd captain, but those were difficult times in which to pull an Indian side together.

Test Record

	M	I	NO	Runs	HS	Avge	100s	RC	Wkts	Avge	BB	Ct
v England	17	28	2	770	147*	29.61	3	277	2	138.50	2–46	4
v Australia	6	11	0	227	78	20.63	–	203	8	25.37	4–27	2
v West Indies	16	30	3	1372	172*	50.81	3	547	11	49.72	5–107	9
v New Zealand	5	6	1	351	223	70.20	1	21	0	–	–	8
v Pakistan	15	19	2	911	117	53.58	5	425	14	30.35	6–74	10
	59	94	8	3631	223	42.22	12	1473	35	42.08	6–74	33

Test Record as Captain

				M	I	NO	Runs	HS	Avge	100s	RC	Wkts	Avge	BB	Ct
v Australia	–	L2	D1	3	6	0	175	78	29.16	–	68	0	–	–	2
v West Indies	–	–	D1	1	2	0	91	55	45.50	–	34	0	–	–	–
v New Zealand	W2	–	D2	4	5	1	128	79*	32.25	–	21	0	–	–	7
	W2	L2	D4	8	13	1	394	79*	32.83	–	123	0	–	–	9

Hemchandra Ramachandra ADHIKARI

Gujarat, Baroda and Services

Born: Pune, Baroda, 31 July 1919

Adhikari was India's fourth captain in the 1958–59 series against West Indies in what was, in fact, his last Test match. He first played for India

against Australia in 1947–48. Originally a free-scoring batsman, he became more circumspect as his Test career lengthened. He was a brilliant cover point. Adhikari managed the Indian side in England in 1971.

Test Record

	M	I	NO	Runs	HS	Avge	100s	RC	Wkts	Avge	BB	Ct
v England	6	10	1	187	60	20.77	–	–	–	–	–	2
v Australia	7	14	2	216	51	18.00	–	4	0	–	–	3
v West Indies	6	10	3	357	114*	51.00	1	10	0	–	–	1
v Pakistan	2	2	2	112	81*	–	–	68	3	22.66	3–68	2
	21	36	8	872	114*	31.14	1	82	3	27.33	3–68	8

Test Record as Captain

				M	I	NO	Runs	HS	Avge	100s	RC	Wkts	Avge	BB	Ct
v West Indies	–	–	D1	1	2	0	103	63	51.50	–	68	3	22.66	3–68	1

Dattajirao Krishnarao GAEKWAD

Baroda

Born: Baroda, 27 October 1928

A right-handed opening batsman with a sound defence and a fine and fearless fielder, Dattajirao Gaekwad, as a member of the ruling family of Baroda, seemed an appropriate captain of India. He led Baroda to the Ranji Trophy in 1957–58, interrupting Bombay's long sequence, but his appointment as captain of India for the 1959 tour of England was a surprise to everyone, including Gaekwad himself.

He had toured England in 1952 but played in only the first Test against Hutton's team. Since that time, he had not held a regular place in the Indian side and had played in only the final Test in the series against West Indies in which India had had four captains.

He contracted typhoid in between the time of his selection and the beginning of the tour of England, and he was never fully fit on the tour, missing the Lord's Test. He played only once more for India after that tour, against Pakistan in 1961.

In spite of his princely background, Gaekwad lacked the authority to unite a group of disparate characters, and he was too retiring to be a good captain. His son, Anshuman, also played for India.

Test Record

	M	I	NO	Runs	HS	Avge	100s	RC	Wkts	Avge	BB	Ct
v England	5	10	0	137	33	13.70	–	–	–	–	–	3
v West Indies	3	5	0	125	52	25.00	–	8	0	–	–	1
v Pakistan	3	5	1	88	32	22.00	–	4	0	–	–	1
	11	20	1	350	52	18.42	–	12	0	–	–	5

Test Record as Captain

				M	I	NO	Runs	HS	Avge	100s	RC	Wkts	Avge	BB	Ct
v England	–	L4	–	4	8	0	128	33	16.00	–	–	–	–	–	3

Pankaj Khirodroy ROY

Bengal

Born: Calcutta, 31 May 1928

Pankaj Roy was a schoolboy protegé who hit a century on his first-class debut. An opening batsman, he made his Test debut against England in 1951–52 and hit 140 in his second match. He toured England in 1952 but had a disastrous series, failing to score in five of his seven Test innings.

He was a contender for the captaincy of the side to tour England in 1959, but he was named as second in command to Gaekwad. He led India in the second Test at Lord's when Gaekwad was unwell. He played his last Test against Pakistan in December 1960.

Pankaj Roy has continued as an administrator in Indian cricket, and his son, Pronob, has also played for India.

Test Record

	M	I	NO	Runs	HS	Avge	100s	RC	Wkts	Avge	BB	Ct
v England	14	25	1	620	140	25.83	2	5	0	–	–	5
v Australia	8	16	0	432	99	27.00	–	6	1	6.00	1–6	3
v West Indies	9	18	0	717	150	39.83	1	47	0	–	–	4
v New Zealand	3	4	0	301	173	72.75	2	–	–	–	–	1
v Pakistan	9	16	3	372	77	28.61	–	8	0	–	–	3
	43	79	4	2442	173	32.56	5	66	1	66.00	1–6	16

Test Record as Captain

				M	I	NO	Runs	HS	Avge	100s	RC	Wkts	Avge	BB	Ct
v England	–	L1	–	1	2	0	15	15	7.50	–	4	0	–	–	–

Gulabari Sipahimalani RAMCHAND

Sind, Bombay and Rajasthan

Born: Karachi (now Pakistan), 26 July 1927

An all-round cricketer of great enthusiasm, Ramchand was a product of Bombay University who hit four centuries in successive years in the Ranji Trophy Final from 1960–63. Like Gaekwad, he made his Test debut against England at Headingley in 1952; and like Gooch, he collected two ducks on his debut. He gained valuable experience as a professional in the Lancashire and North Staffordshire Leagues.

He hit his first Test century against New Zealand at Calcutta in the 1955–56 series and helped save a game which looked lost. He captained India briefly in the fourth Test against West Indies in 1958–59, when Mankad was off

Test Record

	M	I	NO	Runs	HS	Avge	100s	RC	Wkts	Avge	BB	Ct
v England	4	7	0	68	42	9.71	–	304	4	76.00	2–61	4
v Australia	8	15	0	269	109	17.93	1	297	3	99.00	1–6	5
v West Indies	8	16	1	399	67*	26.60	–	649	13	49.92	2–31	3
v New Zealand	5	6	2	234	106*	58.50	1	276	5	55.20	2–48	1
v Pakistan	8	9	2	210	56	30.00	–	373	16	23.31	6–49	7
	33	53	5	1180	109	24.58	2	1899	41	46.31	6–49	20

the field, and so impressed the selectors that they decided to make him captain for the final Test. He had already left for Bombay, however, and the selectors decided to let Adhikari captain the side rather than chase after Ramchand. Astonishingly, Ramchand was not even selected for the side to tour England in 1959, such were the politics which plagued Indian cricket at that time.

Following the debacle in England where all five Tests were lost, Ramchand was named as captain for the series against Australia in 1959–60. India lost the series by two Tests to one, but in leading his side to victory by 119 runs in the second Test at Kanpur, Ramchand made history, for this was India's first victory over Australia. He retired from Test cricket at the end of the series, having brought some stability and honour to the Indian team.

Test Record as Captain

				M	I	NO	Runs	HS	Avge	100s	RC	Wkts	Avge	BB	Ct
v Australia	W1	L2	D2	5	9	0	111	24	12.33	–	200	1	200.00	1–27	2

Nariman Jamshedji CONTRACTOR

Gujarat and Railways

Born: Godra, Gujarat, 7 March 1934

At the age of 18, Nari Contractor hit a century in each innings for Gujarat against Baroda on the occasion of his first-class debut. A left-handed opening batsman with a sound defence, he made his Test debut against New Zealand in 1955–56, but in spite of playing in four Tests in the series, he did not establish a regular place in the side until West Indies visited India in 1958–59. He toured England the following summer and met with more success than the majority of Indian batsman on that tour.

He scored his solitary Test hundred in the Bombay Test with Australia in 1959–60, and following the retirement of Ramchand, Contractor became captain of India. A drawn series with Pakistan was followed by an historic 2–0 series victory over England in 1961–62. This was the first time that India had ever won a rubber against England, and Contractor, in spite of his defensive approach and his failure to save the great leg-spinner Gupte from exile from Test cricket, was a national hero.

He took India to the Caribbean a few weeks later and seemed lifted, emboldened by the success, but West Indies won the first two Tests. Indeed, they were to win all five. In between the second and third Tests, the Indians met Barbados. Contractor was struck on the head by a ball from Charlie Griffith, his skull was fractured and for a few days his life was in the balance. He had a metal plate inserted in his skull and even played cricket again, but his Test career was at an end.

Test Record

	M	I	NO	Runs	HS	Avge	100s	RC	Wkts	Avge	BB	Ct
v England	9	16	1	413	86	27.53	–	9	0	–	–	8
v Australia	6	12	0	480	108	40.00	1	14	1	14.00	1–9	3
v West Indies	7	14	0	254	92	18.14	–	17	0	–	–	3
v New Zealand	4	4	0	145	62	36.25	–	17	0	–	–	–
v Pakistan	5	6	0	319	92	53.16	–	23	0	–	–	4
	31	52	1	1611	108	31.58	1	80	1	80.00	1–9	18

Test Record as Captain

				M	I	NO	Runs	HS	Avge	100s	RC	Wkts	Avge	BB	Ct
v England	W2	–	D3	5	8	0	180	86	22.50	–	9	0	–	–	5
v West Indies	–	L2	–	2	4	0	26	10	6.50	–	6	0	–	–	2
v Pakistan	–	–	D5	5	6	0	319	92	53.16	–	23	0	–	–	4
	W2	L2	D8	12	18	0	525	92	29.16	–	38	0	–	–	11

Mansur Ali Khan, Nawab of PATAUDI jnr.

Sussex, Delhi and Hyderabad

Born: Bhopal, 5 January 1941

Educated in England, the son of the only man to have played cricket for both England and India, the Nawab of Pataudi junior made his first-class debut for Sussex in 1957. He was a dazzling batsman, an exciting, if often unorthodox player, who earned the nickname 'Tiger'.

He won his first blue at Oxford in 1960 and was due to captain the university against Cambridge in 1961, but he was involved in a road accident on the eve of the Varsity match and lost the sight of one eye; most believed that he would not be able to play first-class cricket again. He proved people wrong, and a few months after his accident he made his Test debut against England. In the final Test of the series, his third appearance for India, he hit his first Test century.

He went to West Indies a few weeks later as vice-captain to Contractor, who suffered the dreadful head injury which ended his Test career. Thus in his sixth Test match, 'Tiger' Pataudi found himself captain of India. He was 21 years 77 days old, the youngest captain in Test history. He was to lead his country in 40 Test matches, and his influence on India's approach to Test cricket would be profound. As Mihir Bose has written, 'In India it does not matter how many Tests he won or lost, what stands out is the way he changed the game. To a nation that for 20 years regarded a draw as a victory and whose cricket had a certain predictability, he brought the prospect of victory, often unexpected victories, and his captaincy had an element of daring, at times maddeningly unpredictable; so that even when

India failed, the impression was of having attempted the impossible.'

He had been sent to West Indies to learn the job of captaincy under Contractor and had suddenly found himself with the responsibility thrust upon him in tragic circumstances. When England visited India in 1963–64, he was appointed captain only on the casting vote of the chairman. The series was drawn. Pataudi put England in in the final Test, and India were forced to follow-on. They saved the game. Had they lost it, Pataudi's reign as captain might well have come to an end in spite of the fact that in the fourth Test he had become the first Indian to hit a double century against England.

It was the drawn series with Australia a year later that really established Pataudi as India's captain and enabled him to capture the imagination of the cricket-loving public. He became a romantic hero, and in spite of one or two stumbles he has remained so until this day. In the first Test, he hit the highest score by an Indian captain against Australia, 128 not out, but India lost. In the second, he played innings of 84 and 53, and India won a dramatic and exciting victory by two wickets.

Defeats by West Indies, England – in conditions alien to the Indian spinners – and Australia did not detract from the belief that India were a more eager and better side. From Australia, India went to New Zealand in the spring of 1968 and won the series by three matches to one. It was the first time that India had won a Test match abroad.

This success was not sustained. In India in 1969–70 the series with New Zealand was drawn, with the visitors being robbed of victory only by the weather. Then Australia took a five-match series by three to one, and Pataudi came in for severe criticism as the crowds showed their displeasure in a vocal and physical manner. It was said that Pataudi's tactics were often questionable and that India lacked the ultimate will to win. Pataudi had raised expectations which were not being fulfilled.

Tours to West Indies and to England were scheduled for 1971. The selectors met to choose the sides under a new chairman, the great Vijay Merchant. It was he who used his casting vote to decide that Wadekar, not Pataudi, should lead India in 1971. The public were astonished and Pataudi decided not to go on tour. He fought a political campaign which he lost. Princely privileges and titles were abolished and the Nawab of Pataudi became Mansur Ali Khan.

He abandoned his political ambitions and began to score freely in domestic cricket. He was recalled for the third Test against England in 1972–73 and his willingness to play under a man junior to himself was seen as a magnanimous gesture. He batted in a royal manner and India won. He did not tour England in 1974, and the series was a disaster of disharmony for India.

Pataudi was unanimously elected as captain when West Indies visited India in 1974–75, but injury caused him to miss the second Test. Remarkably, under his leadership India came from 2–0 down to level the series, only to be beaten in the last Test. The revival reflected much credit on Pataudi whose batting was now past its best. He had restored India's pride and self-respect, and the whole of India knew it. The 'Tiger' had had his final triumph, and he moved into retirement as a national hero, a position that he has never lost.

Nawab of Pataudi junior, Mansur Ali Khan, the youngest cricketer ever to captain India. He remains a national hero (Hulton)

Test Record

	M	I	NO	Runs	HS	Avge	100s	RC	Wkts	Avge	BB	Ct
v England	14	25	2	946	203*	41.33	3	75	1	75.00	1–10	10
v Australia	11	20	1	829	128	43.63	1	4	0	–	–	4
v West Indies	10	19	0	352	53	18.52	–	–	–	–	–	5
v New Zealand	11	19	0	666	153	35.05	2	9	0	–	–	8
	46	83	3	2793	203*	34.91	6	88	1	88.00	1–10	27

Test Record as Captain

				M	I	NO	Runs	HS	Avge	100s	RC	Wkts	Avge	BB	Ct
v England	–	L3	D5	8	15	1	577	203*	41.21	2	71	1	71.00	1–10	9
v Australia	W2	L7	D2	11	20	1	829	128	43.63	1	4	0	–	–	4
v West Indies	W2	L7	D1	10	19	0	352	53	18.52	–	–	–	–	–	5
v New Zealand	W5	L2	D4	11	19	0	666	153	35.05	2	9	0	–	–	8
	W9	L19	D12	40	73	2	2424	203*	34.14	5	84	1	84.00	1–10	26

Chandrakant Gulabrao BORDE

Maharashtra and Baroda

Born: Pune, 21 July 1934

The first Indian cricketer to score 3000 runs and take 50 wickets in Test cricket, Borde could well have expected to succeed Contractor as captain of India, but Pataudi took over. Borde was again in contention when Pataudi was sacked in 1971, but at the age of 36 he was considered too old. As it was, he led India only once, when Pataudi had a hamstring injury, in the first Test against Australia in 1967–68.

Test Record

	M	I	NO	Runs	HS	Avge	100s	RC	Wkts	Avge	BB	Ct
v England	17	30	5	746	84	29.84	–	1083	29	37.34	5–88	15
v Australia	13	25	2	502	69	21.82	–	371	8	46.37	3–23	9
v West Indies	12	23	0	870	125	37.82	3	684	9	76.00	2–65	5
v New Zealand	8	13	2	613	109	55.72	1	18	1	18.00	1–18	6
v Pakistan	5	6	2	330	177*	82.50	1	261	5	52.20	4–21	2
	55	97	11	3061	177*	35.59	5	2147	52	46.48	5–88	37

Test Record as Captain

			M	I	NO	Runs	HS	Avge	100s	RC	Wkts	Avge	BB	Ct
v Australia	–	L1	–	1	2	0	81	69	40.50	–	–	–	–	–	3

Ajit Laxman WADEKAR

Bombay

Born: Bombay, 1 April 1941

A stylish, left-handed middle-order batsman, Wadekar made his Test debut against West Indies at Bombay in 1966–67. He went to England, Australia and New Zealand under Pataudi's captaincy, and having got into the nineties on several occasions, he hit his one Test hundred against New Zealand at Wellington in 1967–68.

To the surprise of cricket followers in India, he was named as captain in place of Pataudi for the tours of West Indies and England in 1971, winning the position on the casting vote of Vijay Merchant, the chairman of selectors. No less surprising to cricket followers everywhere was the fact that, under his leadership, India won their first Tests and first series in both countries.

When England, under Tony Lewis, came to

India in 1972–73, India were beaten in the first Test, but Wadekar led his team to a 2–1 victory in the series. Three successive series victories was a feat previously unknown in Indian cricket. Wadekar was the most successful captain in Indian history and, not surprisingly, he was acclaimed everywhere, garlanded and lavishly praised.

He led India to England in 1974 with hopes high, but everything was against the Indians. An experimental law concerning leg-side fielders militated against their spinners, and the tour was at the beginning of the English season when the weather was at its less friendly. England won all three Tests. Wadekar appeared to lose confidence and control. There were unfortunate incidents with Indian diplomats in England and team morale was low. The triumphs of 1971 and 1973 were quickly forgotten. Wadekar's house in Bombay was stoned. He was dropped from the West Zone team for the Duleep Trophy. He announced his retirement and, belatedly, the Indian Board granted him a benefit match. Pataudi returned as captain.

Wadekar's decline was even quicker than his rise. No man has been more shabbily treated.

Ajit Wadekar, pictured during the disastrous series in England in 1974 (Hulton)

Test Record

	M	I	NO	Runs	HS	Avge	100s	RC	Wkts	Avge	BB	Ct
v England	14	28	1	840	91	31.11	–	17	0	–	–	15
v Australia	9	18	1	548	99	32.23	–	17	0	–	–	8
v West Indies	7	11	0	230	67	20.90	–	21	0	–	–	7
v New Zealand	7	14	1	495	143	38.07	1	–	–	–	–	16
	37	71	3	2113	143	31.07	1	55	0	–	–	46

Test Record as Captain

				M	I	NO	Runs	HS	Avge	100s	RC	Wkts	Avge	BB	Ct
v England	W3	L4	D4	11	22	1	598	90	28.47	–	–	–	–	–	9
v West Indies	W1	–	D4	5	7	0	151	54	21.57	–	12	0	–	–	5
	W4	L4	D8	16	29	1	749	90	26.75	–	12	0	–	–	14

Srinivasaraghavan VENKATARAGHAVAN

Tamil Nadu and Derbyshire

Born: Madras, 21 April 1945

Venkataraghavan made four tours of England, and he was with Derbyshire from 1973 to 1975. His Test debut was against New Zealand in Madras in 1964–65, and it was in the fourth and final Test of that series that he produced his best performance in international cricket, taking 8 for 72 and 4 for 80, and bowling India to victory.

An intelligent off-break bowler and a fine close to the wicket fielder, he led India in the World Cup in 1975 without much distinction. He had been vice-captain to Pataudi in the Test series against West Indies a few months earlier, had led the side in the second Test and been dropped for the third. The problem was that he vied for his place with Prasanna who was a more attacking off-spinner.

Gavaskar was named as captain for the World Cup of 1979 and for the tour of England that followed, but the rumours that he was associated with Packer's World Series Cricket organisation caused him to be stripped of the leadership. Venkataraghavan was chosen in his place. India had a dreadful World Cup and, in spite of the brilliance of Gavaskar, an unsuccessful series against Brearley's side. Venkataraghavan, perhaps uncertain of his position and his place, tended to berate his players angrily. He lacked control and was defensively minded. With their customary tact, the Indian Board sacked him before the team had arrived home in India.

He played ten more Test matches under the captaincy of Gavaskar and Kapil Dev, the last being against Pakistan in 1983–84.

Test Record

	M	I	NO	Runs	HS	Avge	100s	RC	Wkts	Avge	BB	Ct
v England	13	20	3	179	28	10.52	–	1073	23	46.52	4–59	9
v Australia	9	14	2	147	37	12.25	–	769	20	38.45	4–71	7
v West Indies	23	28	4	267	51	11.12	–	2684	68	39.47	5–95	15
v New Zealand	10	12	3	144	64	16.00	–	1004	44	22.81	8–72	13
v Pakistan	2	2	0	11	6	5.50	–	104	1	104.00	1–49	–
	57	76	12	748	64	11.68	–	5634	156	36.11	8–72	44

Test Record as Captain

				M	I	NO	Runs	HS	Avge	100s	RC	Wkts	Avge	BB	Ct
v England	–	L1	D3	4	5	0	36	28	7.20	–	345	6	57.50	3–59	1
v West Indies	–	L1	–	1	2	0	18	13	9.00	–	107	1	107.00	1–107	–
	–	L2	D3	5	7	0	54	28	7.71	–	452	7	64.57	3–59	1

Sunil Manohar GAVASKAR

Bombay and Somerset

Born: Bombay, 10 July 1949

Sunil Gavaskar is the greatest batsman that Indian cricket has produced and his record in Test cricket places him supreme among open-

ing batsmen. He has played in more Test matches, scored more runs and hit more centuries than any other Test cricketer.

He made his first-class debut in the Moin-ud-Dowla Gold Cup tournament in 1966–67, played for Somerset in 1980 and made his Test debut on the tour of West Indies in 1970–71. His debut coincided with India's first victory over West Indies, Gavaskar making 65 and 67 not

The most successful batsman in Test history, Sunil Gavaskar (Adrian Murrell/Allsport)

out. In the last three Tests of the series, he scored 116 and 64 not out, 1 and 117 not out, and 124 and 220. His aggregate of 774 runs (average 154.80) remains a record for a batsman in his first rubber – and he had missed the first Test through injury.

He never lost his appetite for runs, and his concentration and dedication to the game marked him as a batsman of exceptional talent. It is likely that he would have become captain of India earlier than he did, for he was a model of consistency, had he not batted through the entire 60 overs for 36 not out against England in a World Cup match at Lord's in 1975 and been unable to offer any explanation for his performance. Bedi was named as captain for the tour of New Zealand in 1975–76 but was injured before the first Test; Gavaskar captained, hit a century and won.

Bedi survived defeats in West Indies and at home to England, but defeat in Pakistan inevitably meant the end of his reign as captain. Gavaskar led India against a weakened West Indies side in 1978–79 and hit three centuries in the series, which India won. There were rumours, however, that Gavaskar was flirting with the idea of joining Packer's World Series Cricket and he was deprived of the captaincy for the tour of England. Wicket-keeper Kirmani, whose name had also been linked with Packer, was dropped altogether.

Gavaskar played wonderfully well at The Oval on the 1979 tour of England but India lost the series; Venkataraghavan was sacked and Gavaskar reinstated as captain. His reappointment coincided with the busiest period Indian cricket has known, 26 Test matches in 13 months. There were victories over Australia and Pakistan, but Gavaskar declared himself unavailable for the tour of West Indies, a tour which, in fact, never took place. Gavaskar was not accorded the praise that was his due for the 1979–80 triumph over Pakistan, in particular. He remained something of a cold, controversial figure. Indians were not used to seeing such consistency from a batsman, and his approach to Test cricket as a captain was solid, the accumulation of runs and the avoidance of defeat before all else. He now had a strong rival for the affections of the Indian cricket-loving public, for a star had arisen in the North: Kapil Dev.

Inevitably, political factions began to develop as Gavaskar was perceived as being biased in favour of Bombay and ignoring the talent in the North. As India began to lose, in New Zealand and in England, criticism of Gavaskar increased. When Pakistan beat India by three matches to nil in 1982–83, their third win coming by an innings as they lost only three wickets, Gavaskar's reign was at an end. Kapil Dev took the side to the Caribbean and then led India to an unexpected triumph in the World Cup of 1983.

Kapil's success was not to last, however, and the struggle for the captaincy of India began again. At times, it was bitter and unpleasant. For the 1984–85 series in Pakistan, Gavaskar was reinstated as captain. The first match, at Lahore, was his 100th Test.

The tour was cut short by the assassination of Mrs Gandhi, but the series with England went ahead. India won by eight wickets in Bombay, their first victory for 31 Tests, but lost the series. Gavaskar personally suffered the worst series of his entire Test career, averaging only 17.50. He took India to victory in the Benson and Hedges World Championship in Australia, but

Test Record

	M	I	NO	Runs	HS	Avge	100s	RC	Wkts	Avge	BB	Ct
v England	38	67	2	2483	221	38.20	4	84	0	–	–	35
v Australia	20	31	1	1550	172	51.66	8	17	0	–	–	19
v West Indies	27	48	6	2749	236*	65.45	13	10	0	–	–	17
v New Zealand	9	16	1	651	119	43.40	2	11	0	–	–	11
v Pakistan	24	41	4	2089	166	56.45	5	84	1	84.00	1–34	19
v Sri Lanka	7	11	2	600	176	66.66	2	–	–	–	–	7
	125	214	16	10122	236*	51.12	34	206	1	206.00	1–34	108

he deemed that that would be the last time he would captain India.

He played Test cricket until March 1987. In his final Test innings, against Pakistan, he batted for 323 minutes to score 96 in an effort to save his side. Nobody else reached 30 and India lost by 16 runs.

Test Record as Captain

				M	I	NO	Runs	HS	Avge	100s	RC	Wkts	Avge	BB	Ct
v England	W2	L3	D9	14	20	1	714	172	37.57	1	24	0	–	–	14
v Australia	W3	L1	D5	9	14	0	543	123	38.78	2	10	0	–	–	6
v West Indies	W1	–	D5	6	9	1	732	205	91.50	4	–	–	–	–	4
v New Zealand	W1	L1	D2	4	7	1	277	116	46.16	1	11	0	–	–	6
v Pakistan	W2	L3	D8	13	22	2	1024	166	51.20	2	18	0	–	–	13
v Sri Lanka	–	–	D1	1	2	1	159	155	159.00	1	–	–	–	–	2
	W9	L8	D30	47	74	6	3449	205	50.72	11	63	0	–	–	45

Bishansingh Giansingh BEDI

Northern Punjab, Southern Punjab, Delhi and Northamptonshire

Born: Amritsar, 25 September 1946

One of the great slow left-arm bowlers, surprisingly unsuccessful in his four Test series in England, Bedi bowled in the classical style and his variations of flight were masterly. His bowling was a beauty to behold.

Making his first-class debut before his 16th birthday, he played his first Test match in 1966–67 against West Indies. He became one of a quartet of spin bowlers who were the dominant factor in India's victories in three Test series.

Mihir Bose describes him as 'always a fretful character', and he led a faction on the 1974 tour of England which pressed for better payment. On his return to India, he was banned for one Test match for giving a live television interview, so ending a sequence of 30 consecutive Tests.

He made no secret of his desire to lead India, and he had a strong following and could command respect from most of the side. Following India's disasters in the 1975 World Cup he was

Bishen Bedi, supreme left-arm spinner, controversial captain who declared India's innings closed in Jamaica in April 1976 as a protest against West Indies' intimidatory bowling. He later managed Indian sides effectively (Adrian Murrell/ Allsport)

appointed captain for the tour of New Zealand, but he missed the first Test in which he should have been captain because of injury.

Outspoken and never far from controversy, Bedi was also much involved in the political intrigues of Indian cricket. He led India in 22 consecutive Tests between 1975–76 and 1978–

79. Two crushing defeats in Pakistan brought an end to his reign.

Like other notable Indian cricketers, he was honoured with the title of Padma Shri by the Government of India, and he has been both a Test selector and manager of touring sides.

Test Record

	M	I	NO	Runs	HS	Avge	100s	RC	Wkts	Avge	BB	Ct
v England	22	35	9	179	20*	6.88	–	2539	85	29.87	6–71	6
v Australia	12	21	11	131	26*	13.10	–	1395	56	24.91	7–98	6
v West Indies	18	24	4	140	20*	7.00	–	2163	62	34.88	6–104	7
v New Zealand	12	16	3	196	50*	15.07	–	1091	57	19.14	6–42	6
v Pakistan	3	5	1	10	4	2.50	–	449	6	74.83	3–124	1
	67	101	28	656	26*	8.98	–	7637	266	28.71	7–98	26

Test Record as Captain

				M	I	NO	Runs	HS	Avge	100s	RC	Wkts	Avge	BB	Ct
v England	W1	L3	D1	5	10	3	81	20*	11.57	–	574	25	22.96	6–71	2
v Australia	W2	L3	–	5	9	6	68	26*	22.66	–	740	31	23.87	5–55	2
v West Indies	W1	L2	D1	4	3	0	10	10	3.33	–	456	18	25.33	5–82	–
v New Zealand	W2	L1	D2	5	6	1	125	50*	25.00	–	412	26	15.84	5–27	1
v Pakistan	–	L2	D1	3	5	1	10	4	2.50	–	449	6	74.83	3–124	1
	W6	L11	D5	22	33	11	294	50*	13.36	–	2631	106	24.82	6–71	6

Gundappa Rangnath VISWANATH

Karnataka

Born: Bhadravati, Mysore, 12 February 1949

Brother-in-law to Gavaskar, Viswanath hit 230 in 340 minutes on the occasion of his first-class debut for Karnataka (then Mysore) against Andhra in 1967. He also hit a century on his Test debut, against Australia in November

Test Record

	M	I	NO	Runs	HS	Avge	100s	RC	Wkts	Avge	BB	Ct
v England	30	54	4	1880	222	37.60	4	14	0	–	–	19
v Australia	18	31	2	1538	161*	53.03	4	19	1	19.00	1–11	15
v West Indies	18	28	1	1455	179	53.88	4	–	–	–	–	15
v New Zealand	9	17	2	585	103*	39.00	1	–	–	–	–	5
v Pakistan	15	23	1	611	145	27.77	1	13	0	–	–	8
v Sri Lanka	1	2	0	11	9	5.50	–	–	–	–	–	1
	91	155	10	6080	222	41.93	14	46	1	46.00	1–11	63

1969. He was to play 91 times for India, with 87 of his appearances consecutive.

A delightful batsman, as befits a kind and gentle man, he led India twice: against Pakistan in 1979–80 when Gavaskar had declared himself unavailable for the coming tour of West Indies, a tour which was subsequently cancelled, and against England in the Golden Jubilee Test a fortnight later. In this Test, he recalled Bob Taylor who had been given out caught behind, and his action tended to confirm the view that he was too soft a person to captain a Test side in the cauldron of the 1980s.

Test Record as Captain

				M	I	NO	Runs	HS	Avge	100s	RC	Wkts	Avge	BB	Ct
v England	–	L1	–	1	2	0	16	11	8.00	–	–	–	–	–	–
v Pakistan	–	–	D1	1	2	0	26	13	13.00	–	–	–	–	–	–
	–	L1	D1	2	4	0	42	13	10.50	–	–	–	–	–	–

Ramlal Nikhanj KAPIL DEV

Haryana, Northamptonshire and Worcestershire

Born: Chandigarh, 6 January 1959

At the time of writing, only Ian Botham and Richard Hadlee have taken more wickets in Test cricket than Kapil Dev, who also has more than 4500 runs to his credit. A fast-medium pace bowler and a violent batsman, he is the greatest all-round cricketer India has produced.

He made his Test debut against Pakistan in October 1978, and in his 25th Test, with Pakistan again the opponents, he completed 1000 runs and 100 wickets. At 21 years 27 days, he was the youngest cricketer to perform the 'double' in Test cricket.

The arrival of Kapil Dev coincided with the resurgence of cricket in Northern India which had been brought about by the dynamism of Bishen Bedi. Kapil Dev was the new hero of the north and a serious challenge to the leadership of Gavaskar and the dominance of Bombay. There was much political intrigue and conflict, and when Gavaskar's side was heavily beaten in Pakistan – an unforgivable crime – Bedi, one of the selectors, was the prime mover in seeing that Kapil Dev led the party to the West Indies in 1982–83. He celebrated his first Test as captain by reaching 2000 runs in Test cricket. In the

Kapil Dev, all-rounder supreme, signals Roger Harper's dismissal in the 1983–84 home series against West Indies (Adrian Murrell/Allsport)

next Test, he hit a century and became the youngest player to reach 200 wickets and 2000 runs in Test cricket.

Victory in the 1983 World Cup elevated Kapil Dev to a position that no other Indian cricketer had ever enjoyed, but in three Test series he had not gained a single victory. In the third Test against West Indies, Kapil Dev took a remarkable 9 for 83 in the second innings, but his side lost, and when West Indies took the fifth Test and the series there were angry scenes from members of the 80 000 crowd, and the Indian players had to have police protection. Gavaskar returned as captain for the next series.

Gavaskar's return to the captaincy was brief. He took the side to Pakistan and then lost to Gower's side in 1984–85. His own form suffered. He resigned the captaincy and, with no other contenders, Kapil Dev was reinstated.

His return to the leadership could not have had a worse start. India were beaten by Sri Lanka, who won a Test and a series for the first time. In Australia, all three Tests were drawn. Kapil Dev took 8 for 106 in the first, and India had the better of every Test, but the fact remained that Kapil Dev had now led India in 20 Tests and had not recorded a victory.

The Indian press had maintained a running saga on the feud that was said to exist between Kapil Dev and Gavaskar and which was undermining team morale. Certainly the men had their differences. They were very different personalities. In England in 1986, manager Raj Singh called a press conference. Gavaskar and Kapil Dev were present. The imagined feud was brought to an official end. India beat England comprehensively in the three-match series, and Kapil Dev was once again the hero he had been in 1983. Like Wadekar, he was to find that the period of idolisation could be brief.

There was a century in the tied Test with Australia, and the fastest century by an Indian in Test cricket as revenge was taken against Sri Lanka. The series in Pakistan was lost narrowly, but, more importantly, India failed to win the World Cup in 1987. They were beaten by England in the semi-final in a match which they had looked to be winning. The disappointment was intense. Memories were short. In future, Kapil Dev would play for India only as the great all-rounder, no longer as captain. A player of flair, not a tactical genius, like Botham he is better remembered for the glorious entertainment he provided.

Test Record

	M	I	NO	Runs	HS	Avge	100s	RC	Wkts	Avge	BB	Ct
v England	24	36	5	1254	116	40.45	2	3041	78	38.98	6–91	8
v Australia	15	18	1	522	119	30.70	1	1358	54	25.14	8–106	12
v West Indies	25	39	4	1079	126*	30.82	3	2217	89	24.91	9–83	17
v New Zealand	9	13	0	189	40	14.53	–	792	23	34.43	4–34	5
v Pakistan	29	41	2	1054	84	27.02	–	2982	99	30.12	8–85	9
v Sri Lanka	8	12	1	427	163	38.81	1	860	33	26.06	5–110	3
	110	159	13	4252	163	30.99	7	11250	376	29.92	9–83	54

Test Record as Captain

			M	I	NO	Runs	HS	Avge	100s	RC	Wkts	Avge	BB	Ct
v England	W2 –	D1	3	5	1	81	31	20.25	–	306	10	30.60	4–52	2
v Australia	– –	D5+1	6	5	0	255	119	51.00	1	400	12	33.33	8–106	7
v West Indies	– L5	D6	11	19	2	438	100*	25.76	1	961	46	20.89	9–83	8
v Pakistan	– L1	D7	8	10	1	228	66	25.33	–	655	23	28.47	5–68	6
v Sri Lanka	W2 L1	D3	6	9	1	362	163	45.25	1	603	20	30.15	4–69	3
	W4 L7	D22+1	34	48	5	1364	163	31.72	3	2925	111	26.35	9–83	26

Dilip Balwant VENGSARKAR

Bombay

Born: Bombay, 6 April 1946

The appointment of Vengsarkar as captain in succession to Kapil Dev was something of a surprise. A batsman of high quality, a true artist with three centuries in Lord's Tests to his credit, Vengsarkar was too much of an introvert to be a successful captain. He did well enough in home series against West Indies and New Zealand, but in the Caribbean, his lack of communication with his side proved to be disastrous. His flirtation with journalism while still captain, and a trip to North America with members of his side which reputedly brought them a larger income than they had received for playing the Test series against West Indies marked the end of a reign in which he showed glimpses of a positive approach to the game and no loss of his own form.

Dilip Vengsarkar enjoyed outstanding success for India as a batsman, but had a less happy time as captain (Adrian Murrell/Allsport)

Test Record

	M	I	NO	Runs	HS	Avge	100s	RC	Wkts	Avge	BB	Ct
v England	26	43	6	1589	157	42.94	5	–	–	–	–	15
v Australia	19	29	4	1146	164*	45.84	2	–	–	–	–	14
v West Indies	25	40	4	1596	159	44.33	6	14	0	–	–	13
v New Zealand	11	17	1	440	75	27.50	–	3	0	–	–	13
v Pakistan	22	35	6	1284	146*	44.27	2	19	0	–	–	13
v Sri Lanka	8	12	1	655	166	59.54	2	–	–	–	–	6
	111	176	22	6710	166	43.57	17	36	0	–	–	74

Test Record as Captain

				M	I	NO	Runs	HS	Avge	100s	RC	Wkts	Avge	BB	Ct
v West Indies	–	L4	D3	7	11	2	415	102*	46.11	2	–	–	–	–	–
v New Zealand	W2	L1	–	3	4	0	132	75	33.00	–	–	–	–	–	6
	W2	L5	D3	10	15	2	547	102*	42.07	2	–	–	–	–	6

Ravishankar Jayadritha SHASTRI

Bombay and Glamorgan

Born: Bombay, 27 May 1962

In many ways Ravi Shastri remains an unfulfilled talent. A right-handed batsman who equalled Sobers' record by hitting six sixes in one over and a slow left-arm bowler, Shastri was seen as an all-rounder of the highest quality, but his bowling has fallen just short of the standard that had been anticipated. He was also seen as a future captain of India, leading the under-22 side and, more recently, Bombay. The Indian Board have seemed to nurture some suspicions as to his conduct over the years, and as one captain has succeeded another, Shastri has always been passed over. He appears to be the permanent vice-captain, and it was as Vengsarkar's deputy that he led India for the only time, squaring the series against West Indies in 1987–88.

His Test debut came in 1980–81 when he was summoned to New Zealand as a late replacement for the injured Doshi. On his Test debut he had match figures of 6 for 63.

So long seen as a future Indian captain, Ravi Shastri has led his country only once (Allsport/ Adrian Murrell)

Test Record

	M	I	NO	Runs	HS	Avge	100s	RC	Wkts	Avge	BB	Ct
v England	20	31	4	1026	187	38.00	4	1629	30	54.30	4–83	12
v Australia	6	5	2	322	121*	107.33	1	769	21	36.61	4–87	2
v West Indies	19	33	5	847	107	30.25	2	1606	37	43.40	4–43	6
v New Zealand	6	9	2	182	54	26.00	–	414	20	20.70	5–125	5
v Pakistan	15	22	1	801	139	38.14	3	1112	24	46.33	5–75	6
v Sri Lanka	7	10	0	282	88	28.20	–	384	11	34.90	4–11	5
	73	110	14	3460	187	36.04	10	5914	143	41.35	5–75	36

Test Record as Captain

		M	I	NO	Runs	HS	Avge	100s	RC	Wkts	Avge	BB	Ct
v West Indies	W1	–	–	1	2	1	43	23	43.00	–	54	1	54.00	1–29	–

Krishnamachari SRIKKANTH

Tamil Nadu

Born: Madras, 21 December 1959

A right-handed opening batsman aggressive even to the point of irresponsibility, Srikkanth made his Test debut against the England side led by Keith Fletcher in 1981–82. He did not hold a regular place in the Indian side, and it was not until 1985–86 that he hit his first Test hundred. It was against Australia, and he reached three figures off 97 balls.

He was a rather surprising choice as captain for the 1989–90 tour of Pakistan, but he was popular and commanded the respect of his players and the loyalty of Kapil Dev. India drew all four Tests, but Srikkanth had a poor series with the bat. He was also in contention with the Indian Board over the payment his players were being offered. He was dropped as captain and from the team, and his form has declined over the past two seasons.

Excitingly unpredictable batsman and a captain who clashed with authority – Kris Srikkanth (Allsport/Adrian Murrell)

Test Record

	M	I	NO	Runs	HS	Avge	100s	RC	Wkts	Avge	BB	Ct
v England	9	16	1	365	84	24.33	–	21	0	–	–	5
v Australia	6	8	0	433	116	54.12	1	19	0	–	–	5
v West Indies	4	7	0	204	71	29.14	–	7	0	–	–	2
v New Zealand	3	6	2	240	94	60.00	–	7	0	–	–	6
v Pakistan	11	18	0	436	123	24.22	1	50	0	–	–	8
v Sri Lanka	6	9	0	249	64	27.66	–	4	0	–	–	7
	39	64	3	1927	123	31.59	2	108	0	–	–	33

Test Record as Captain

				M	I	NO	Runs	HS	Avge	100s	RC	Wkts	Avge	BB	Ct
v Pakistan	–	–	D4	4	7	0	97	36	13.85	–	33	0	–	–	1

Mohammad AZHARUDDIN

Hyderabad and Derbyshire

Born: Hyderabad, 8 February 1963

One of the most exciting batsmen in world cricket, Azharuddin created a record when he began his Test career with three centuries in successive matches against England in 1984–85. His form in international cricket lapsed somewhat after that brilliant start, but by the end of the 1980s he had re-established himself as one of the foremost batsmen in the world.

He was named as captain for the tour of New Zealand in 1989–90, and for the tour to England that followed. A Moslem, he was something of a controversial choice, but he has proved to be a sympathetic leader who is gradually becoming more tactically aware.

He was chosen to lead a new-look Indian team into the nineties, but the history of captains of India would suggest that only time and results will tell how long his stewardship lasts.

Appointed to lead India into the nineties –
Mohammad Azharuddin (Allsport/Ben Radford)

Test Record

	M	I	NO	Runs	HS	Avge	100s	RC	Wkts	Avge	BB	Ct
v England	9	16	2	1022	179	73.00	5	8	0	–	–	5
v Australia	6	7	1	239	59*	39.83	–	–	–	–	–	3
v West Indies	6	9	0	298	61	33.11	–	–	–	–	–	4
v New Zealand	6	8	0	456	192	57.00	1	–	–	–	–	2
v Pakistan	9	13	0	627	141	48.23	3	–	–	–	–	12
v Sri Lanka	5	8	0	334	199	41.75	1	–	–	–	–	6
	41	61	3	2976	199	51.31	10	8	0	–	–	32

Test Record as Captain

				M	I	NO	Runs	HS	Avge	100s	RC	Wkts	Avge	BB	Ct
v England	–	L1	D2	3	5	0	426	179	85.20	2	–	–	–	–	1
v New Zealand	–	L1	D2	3	4	0	303	192	75.75	1	–	–	–	–	–
v Sri Lanka	W1	–	–	1	1	0	23	23	23.00	–	–	–	–	–	1
	W1	L2	D4	7	10	0	752	192	75.20	3	–	–	–	–	2

PAKISTAN

Pakistan in Test Cricket

Until 15 August 1947, India and Pakistan were one country. When India toured England in 1932, 1936 and 1946 they were always referred to as 'All India', for that term embraced not only the India we know today but also the present-day countries of Pakistan and Bangladesh.

The majority of those who first represented Pakistan at Test level had played their earliest first-class cricket before partition and were immersed in the mood and manners of the Ranji Trophy. Pakistan's first captain, A.H. Kardar, had played Test cricket for India, been educated at Oxford and played in the county championship for Warwickshire. Alimuddin had played for Rajputana and Gujarat in the Ranji Trophy and had made his debut before his 13th birthday. However carefully the boundaries were drawn in 1947, the spirit of Indian cricket was to shape Pakistan cricket for some years.

There was, and is, a certain lack of urgency in domestic cricket in India. The major competition, the Ranji Trophy, can be won by a side who, in the course of a season, may not claim an outright victory in any match. The points system in the zonal rounds is such that high scores and a few wickets in the first 25 overs of the second innings will take a side through to the quarter-finals. In the knockout stage of the tournament, a lead on the first innings is sufficient to gain a place in the next round.

In 1989–90, for example, Bengal qualified for the quarter-finals of the Ranji Trophy by winning one of their four matches in the East Zone. In the quarter-final match against Bombay in Calcutta, neither side completed an innings in four days' cricket, but Bengal moved into the semi-final under the quotient rule: number of runs scored divided by number of wickets lost. In the semi-final, which again lasted four days, Bengal hit 539 for 8 and Hyderabad made 417. Bengal moved into the final by virtue of their first innings lead; and they beat Baroda in the final by means of the quotient rule.

Indian cricket accepts such passivity and initially a similar attitude was acceptable in Pakistan cricket, but 44 years after partition, the character has changed. As Dr Khadim Hussain, an authority on Pakistan cricket, has pointed out, the instincts of the Muslim warrior are now apparent in Pakistan cricket. To play Pakistan today is to play a side very different in character from the side that first represented Pakistan in 1952.

Pakistan's introduction to Test cricket was in Delhi, in October of that year. Two of the Pakistan side, Kardar and Amir Elahi, had played for India; the rest of the side were new to international cricket. India won the inaugural Test match by an innings, but in the second Test, the only one ever to be played at Lucknow, on the jute matting at the University Ground, Pakistan reversed the result.

No side new to Test cricket had previously gained a victory as early as the second Test match in which they appeared. The hero was Nazar Mohammad, whose son Mudassar Nazar later gave distinguished service to Pakistan. Nazar Mohammad hit 124 not out, carrying his bat through the innings and becoming the first man to be on the field for an entire Test match.

India won the third Test to take the series, the last two being drawn. It was an encouraging beginning for Pakistan, but greater glory was to follow quickly. In 1954 they played a four-match series in England. The games at Lord's and Old Trafford were ruined by rain, and at Trent Bridge, the inexperienced Pakistan bowlers were hammered by Denis Compton whose 278 was his highest score in Test cricket. At The Oval, with Tyson and Loader making their debuts for England, Pakistan won by 24 runs to square the rubber. Never before had a country won a Test match in their first rubber in England.

Buoyant from their success in England, Pakistan engaged in a five-match home series with India in 1954–55, but this rubber was to give an ominous foretaste of the character of the cricket that was to dominate encounters between these two sides over the next few years. The political and religious differences which separate them mean that national prestige and national honour are at stake every time that India and Pakistan meet, and the fear of defeat was so great in 1954–55 that the scoring rate was under two runs an over for the series. In the fourth Test, it declined as low as 1.61, 638 runs being scored in four days from 395.3 overs. Inevitably, such tedium produced a stalemate of five drawn matches in the rubber, the first time such a thing had happened in Test cricket.

Memories of this dreadful series were obliterated a year later when Pakistan beat New Zealand by two matches to nil, so giving them their first victory in a rubber at their fourth attempt. When Australia were trounced in 1956–57, Pakistan completed a most impressive entry into Test cricket, having not lost a rubber since their inaugural series in India. They found West Indies in the Caribbean formidable opposition and were beaten in three Tests, but even here they won the final Test, and in the first, Hanif Mohammad played the longest innings in Test cricket and scored 337.

From the outset, there was a confidence in Pakistan cricket and Kardar's experience gave them a stability which proved to be a great asset to a side new to Test cricket. He stepped down at the end of the tour to West Indies, and for some years, the captaincy of Pakistan was to pose problems.

The selection of Pakistan Test sides and touring parties has always aroused heated debate. Many close observers of Pakistan cricket will argue that the best possible side has rarely been selected. Social and political pressures have led to the exclusion of one player to accommodate a lesser man, and the captaincy has had its share of arguments in this context.

Not until the 1980s, the regimes of Javed Miandad and Imran Khan, has a sense of equanimity been achieved, and then only by Javed's willingness to step down whenever Imran made himself available. In their different ways, they have taken Pakistan to a position of eminence in world cricket.

Abdul Hafeez KARDAR

Northern India, Services and Warwickshire

Born: Lahore, 17 January 1925

Touring England in 1946 under the name of Abdul Hafeez, A.H. Kardar went up to Oxford the following year and won his blue in all three years at university. A stylish left-handed batsman and a bowler of left-arm spin or medium pace, he assisted Warwickshire between 1948 and 1950. He took Pakistani citizenship following partition, and he was an obvious choice to lead Pakistan into Test cricket. A man of position and authority, he captained Pakistan in their first 23 Tests and quickly established his country as a credible force in world cricket.

Criticised for his part in the attritional series with India in 1954–55, he was, nevertheless, without a rival for the captaincy during his period of office. Orthodox rather than inventive in his leadership, he gave Pakistan a very necessary initial stability and self-confidence. He varied his place in the batting order, and his highest Test score came at Karachi in 1954–55 when, in the fifth Test, he hit 93 and shared a stand of 155 for the fifth wicket with Alimuddin in even time, abnormal in that series. A year later he had his best bowling return, against New Zealand on the same ground.

He retired after the tour of West Indies in 1957–58, and he has since remained a very powerful figure in the administration of cricket in Pakistan.

Test Record for India

	M	I	NO	Runs	HS	Avge	100s	RC	Wkts	Avge	BB	Ct
v England	3	5	0	80	43	16.00	–	–	–	–	–	1

Test Record as Captain of Pakistan

				M	I	NO	Runs	HS	Avge	100s	RC	Wkts	Avge	BB	Ct
v England	W1	L1	D2	4	7	1	96	36	16.00	–	110	1	110.00	1–110	3
v Australia	W1	–	–	1	1	0	69	69	69.00	–	12	0	–	–	1
v West Indies	W1	L3	D1	5	9	1	253	57	31.62	–	385	2	192.50	1–71	5
v New Zealand	W2	–	D1	3	4	0	49	22	12.25	–	151	10	15.10	3–35	1
v India	W1	L2	D7	10	16	1	380	93	25.33	–	296	8	37.00	2–20	5
	W6	L6	D11	23	37	3	847	93	24.91	–	954	21	45.42	3–35	15

Test Record

M	I	NO	Runs	HS	Avge	100s	RC	Wkts	Avge	BB	Ct
26	42	3	927	93	23.76	–	954	21	45.42	3–35	16

FAZAL MAHMOOD

Northern India, Punjab and Lahore

Born: Lahore, 18 February 1927

Fazal Mahmood was selected for India's tour of Australia in 1947–48, but he waited for Pakistan's entry into Test cricket before he claimed international recognition. A right-arm fast-medium pace bowler, he took 5 for 52 and 7 for 42 in his second match to bring Pakistan their first victory in Test cricket. Particularly effective on matting, he proved to be equally devastating in England in 1954. He captured four wickets in the first rain-ruined Test, took another four at Old Trafford and won the match at The Oval with figures of 6 for 53 and 6 for 46.

A happy, popular and successful cricketer, he was chosen to lead Pakistan when Kardar stepped down. Without the social status or authority of Kardar, and with the responsibility of being his side's main strike bowler, Fazal struggled. His stewardship began in spectacular

fashion. He won the toss against West Indies at Karachi, put them in on the matting wicket, took seven wickets in the match, became the first bowler to capture 100 Test wickets for Pakistan, and led his side to a 10-wicket victory. Twelve wickets for Fazal in the second Test brought another victory, and in spite of losing at home for the first time, in Lahore, Pakistan took the series.

The following season, 1959–60, saw defeat at home to Australia, and then in 1960–61 there were five draws with India in another tedious series. Fazal's captaincy was severely criticised. He was accused of favouritism, and factions formed which were to have an adverse effect on Pakistan cricket for several years. His own bowling was a shadow of its former glory, and he was replaced as captain and dropped from the side.

Not chosen for the tour of England in 1962, he was flown to England as a replacement when the new-ball bowlers broke down. He was dreadfully overworked and took five expensive wickets in the last two Tests. He had been sent for in a desperate attempt to revive the glories of eight years previously, but by now he was a spent force. He left Test cricket with a record 139 wickets to his credit.

Test Record

	M	I	NO	Runs	HS	Avge	100s	RC	Wkts	Avge	BB	Ct
v England	7	11	0	89	36	8.09	–	838	25	33.52	6–46	2
v Australia	3	5	1	33	11	8.25	–	327	24	13.62	7–80	1
v West Indies	8	14	1	192	60	14.76	–	1097	41	26.75	6–34	3
v New Zealand	2	1	1	34	34*	–	–	92	5	18.40	3–34	–
v India	14	19	3	272	33	17.00	–	1080	44	24.54	7–42	5
	34	50	6	620	60	14.09	–	3434	139	24.70	7–42	11

Test Record as Captain

				M	I	NO	Runs	HS	Avge	100s	RC	Wkts	Avge	BB	Ct
v Australia	–	L1	D1	2	4	0	23	11	5.75	–	213	11	19.36	5–71	–
v West Indies	W2	L1	–	3	5	1	33	14	8.25	–	333	21	15.85	6.34	1
v India	–	–	D5	5	6	0	60	18	10.00	–	239	9	26.55	3–86	3
	W2	L2	D6	10	15	1	116	18	8.28	–	785	41	19.14	6–34	4

IMTIAZ AHMED

Northern India, Punjab, Services and P.A.F.

Born: Lahore, 5 January 1928

Imtiaz Ahmed played in the first 39 Test matches in Pakistan's history. He missed the 40th, the third Test in England in 1962, but appeared in the last two matches of the series, which marked the end of his international career.

Originally chosen for his batting, he took over the wicket-keeping duties from Hanif Mohammad in his fourth match for Pakistan and thereafter performed capably, keeping to both the leg-cutters of Fazal and a variety of spinners without show or fuss.

He had made no significant mark with the bat until the second Test match against New Zealand at Lahore in October 1955 when he hit 209, the highest score ever made by a No. 8 in Test cricket. It was, at the time, also the highest score ever made by a wicket-keeper in Test cricket. He later moved up the order and was particularly successful as an opener in the Caribbean.

A shy and courteous man, he led Pakistan against Australia at Lahore in November 1959

Test Record

	M	I	NO	Runs	HS	Avge	100s	RC	Wkts	Avge	BB	Ct/st
v England	11	20	0	488	86	24.40	–	–	–	–	–	21/ 3
v Australia	4	7	0	131	54	18.71	–	–	–	–	–	13/ 1
v West Indies	8	14	0	423	122	30.21	1	–	–	–	–	13/ 8
v New Zealand	3	4	0	284	209	71.00	1	–	–	–	–	7/ 2
v India	15	27	1	753	135	35.85	1	0	0	–	–	23/ 2
	41	72	1	2079	209	29.28	3	0	0	–	–	77/16

when Fazal was injured, and succeeded him as captain when the medium pace bowler was dropped. His quiet approach was hardly likely to be appropriate in the stressful times which had begun to prevail, and following defeat at the hands of England in Pakistan, he was replaced for the tour of England in 1962, which was his last series as a Test player.

He later served as a selector.

Test Record as Captain

				M	I	NO	Runs	HS	Avge	100s	RC	Wkts	Avge	BB	Ct/st
v England	–	L1	D2	3	6	0	102	86	17.00	–	–	–	–	–	4/ 2
v Australia	–	L1	–	1	2	0	72	64	36.00	–	–	–	–	–	4/ 1
	–	L2	D2	4	8	0	174	86	21.75	–	–	–	–	–	8/ 3

JAVED BURKI

Punjab, Lahore, Karachi, Rawalpindi and N.W.F.P.

Born: Meerut, 8 May 1938

Educated at Oxford University where he won his blue in all three years (1958–60) and had a good record, Javed Burki made his Test debut against India at Bombay in December 1960. A right-handed middle-order batsman who sometimes opened the innings, Javed Burki is a cousin to both Imran Khan and Majid Khan and a member of a wealthy and influential family. Two centuries in the series against England in 1961–62 convinced the Pakistani selectors that he had the ability to ally to his social standing, and he replaced Imtiaz as captain for the tour of England in 1962.

In Burki, the Pakistan Board saw the opportunity to reinstate the type of regime that Kardar had had, a captain able to lead through the authority of his social status. Unfortunately, Burki turned out to be a poor leader. He hit a century at Lord's, but his side was overwhelmed and he was replaced as captain after the one series.

Although he was to appear in another 10 Tests after being relieved of the captaincy, he was never again to capture the form that he displayed in his first seven matches for Pakistan.

Test Record

	M	I	NO	Runs	HS	Avge	100s	RC	Wkts	Avge	BB	Ct
v England	11	22	0	674	140	30.63	3	17	0	–	–	2
v Australia	2	4	0	146	62	36.50	–	3	0	–	–	–
v New Zealand	7	13	2	196	63	14.27	–	–	–	–	–	2
v India	5	9	2	325	79	46.42	–	3	0	–	–	3
	25	48	4	1341	140	30.47	3	23	0	–	–	7

Test Record as Captain

			M	I	NO	Runs	HS	Avge	100s	RC	Wkts	Avge	BB	Ct
v England	–	L4 D1	5	10	0	252	140	25.20	1	14	0	–	–	2

HANIF MOHAMMAD

Karachi, Bahawalpur and Pakistan
International Airlines

Born: Junagadh, 21 December 1934

The most famous member of one of the most distinguished cricketing families in the world, Hanif Mohammad still holds the world record with his innings of 499 for Karachi against Bahawalpur in 1958–59. A right-handed opening batsman of infinite patience, he made his first-class debut in 1951–52 and his quality was instantly recognised, for he was in the Pakistan side for the inaugural Test match against India a year later.

He kept wicket in the first three Test matches and was top scorer for Pakistan in the first game with an innings of 51. He gave up wicket-keeping to concentrate on his batting, and centuries against India and New Zealand were followed by an innings of 337 against West Indies at Bridgetown in January 1958. Hanif batted for 16 hours 10 minutes, and this remains the longest ever first-class innings.

Four years later he became the first Pakistan batsman to score a hundred in each innings of a Test match. This was against England at Dacca and Hanif batted for 893 minutes in the course of the match. Small, with a look of innocence on a boyish face, Hanif was by now more of a legend than a national hero of Pakistan, and his appointment as captain was something of an inevitability.

His first Tests as captain were against Australia in 1964–65. In the second of these, at Melbourne, he hit 104 and 93, took over the wicket-keeping duties when Abdul Kadir was injured, and held five catches. Captaincy did not affect his form with the bat, although he had now dropped down the order. He scored 203 not out against New Zealand at Lahore in April 1965 and 187 not out in the Lord's Test of 1967 in what proved to be his last series as captain.

Hanif's defensive approach to his batting was mirrored in his approach to the captaincy. He was criticised for his negative attitude and there was an undercurrent of discontent from those in authority. He relinquished the captaincy, although he played in four more Test matches after the tour of England.

His last appearance was against New Zealand at Karachi in October 1969 when he opened the innings with his brother Sadiq, and another brother, Mushtaq, was also in the side. As well as Sadiq, another batsman was making his debut for Pakistan in that match: Zaheer Abbas, destined to take on Hanif's mantle as Pakistan's leading batsman.

Hanif played in all but two of Pakistan's first 57 Test matches.

Test Record

	M	I	NO	Runs	HS	Avge	100s	RC	Wkts	Avge	BB	Ct
v England	18	33	2	1039	187*	33.51	3	13	0	–	–	13
v Australia	6	12	1	548	104	49.81	2	–	–	–	–	5
v West Indies	6	11	1	736	337	73.60	2	21	0	–	–	5
v New Zealand	10	15	2	622	203*	47.84	3	2	0	–	–	12
v India	15	26	2	970	160	40.41	2	59	1	59.00	1–1	5
	55	97	8	3915	337	43.98	12	95	1	95.00	1–1	40

Test Record as Captain

				M	I	NO	Runs	HS	Avge	100s	RC	Wkts	Avge	BB	Ct
v England	–	L2	D1	3	5	1	228	187*	57.00	1	4	0	–	–	3
v Australia	–	–	D2	2	4	0	239	104	59.75	1	–	–	–	–	5
v New Zealand	W2	–	D4	6	9	2	414	203*	59.14	2	–	–	–	–	8
	W2	L2	D7	11	18	3	881	203*	58.73	4	4	0	–	–	16

SAEED AHMED

Punjab, Railways, Lahore, Pakistan
International Airlines, Karachi and P.W.D.

Born: Jullundur, 1 October 1937

Saeed Ahmed first played for Pakistan on the tour of West Indies in 1957–58 and proved himself to be a most entertaining right-handed middle-order batsman with 150 in the fourth Test. He prospered against Australia, India and New Zealand, and his off-break bowling became ever more useful. It was something of a surprise when he succeeded Hanif as captain for the series against England in 1968–69, for he was seen as an eccentric, ever in dispute with the Board. His form was also in decline by that time and it was no shock that his captaincy was limited to that series.

He completely failed to find his form in England in 1971 and played only in the last Test. In Australia in 1972–73, he was hit on the hand by a ball from Lillee in the second Test and forced to retire, but he returned to complete his innings and hit an unorthodox 50. He and Lillee exchanged heated words, and Lillee made it known that he would try to exploit to the full the green and well-grassed wicket in the third Test at Sydney and that Saeed would be his prime target.

On the eve of the Test, Saeed declared that he had a back injury and would be unable to play. The team management were not satisfied with Saeed's explanation, and he was flown back to Pakistan after the third Test and excluded from the tour of New Zealand. He did not play Test cricket again.

Test Record

	M	I	NO	Runs	HS	Avge	100s	RC	Wkts	Avge	BB	Ct
v England	15	28	1	791	74	29.29	–	493	13	37.92	4–64	7
v Australia	7	14	0	611	166	43.64	1	138	4	34.50	3–41	2
v West Indies	8	15	1	707	150	50.50	1	44	1	44.00	1–19	1
v New Zealand	6	11	1	422	172	42.20	1	125	4	31.25	2–15	3
v India	5	10	1	460	121	51.11	2	2	0	–	–	–
	41	78	4	2991	172	40.41	5	802	22	36.45	4–64	13

Test Record as Captain

				M	I	NO	Runs	HS	Avge	100s	RC	Wkts	Avge	BB	Ct
v England	–	–	D3	3	4	0	109	39	27.25	–	224	9	24.88	4–64	1

INTIKHAB ALAM Khan

Pakistan International Airlines, P.W.D.,
Sind, Punjab and Surrey

Born: Hoshiarpur, 28 December 1941

By the 1970s, the post of captain of Pakistan was no sinecure. Appointed in deference to his background, Javed Burki had been summarily dismissed after one series against England. Appointed in respect to his position as a player, Hanif Mohammad had seen his reign end in rancour, accusation and pressure to stand down. Saeed Ahmed had led for one three-match series which had been played against a backdrop of political unrest and had come to an abrupt conclusion when the Karachi Test was abandoned because of an angry demonstration by a mob who broke down the gates and swarmed onto the outfield. Relationships with India were such that the countries did not meet in a Test match between 1961 and 1978. It was in the context of these events and attitudes that Intikhab Alam was named as captain of Pakistan.

A burly, powerful, cheerful all-rounder,

Intikhab was the first Pakistan cricketer to complete the 'double' in Test matches. He was a gloriously aggressive batsman, and a leg-spin bowler of the highest quality in an age when that style of bowling was becoming a rarity. He was an immense favourite at The Oval during his 12 years with Surrey, and a most popular cricketer wherever he went.

He first played for Pakistan in the last Test of the 1959–60 series against Australia, and he toured England in 1962 with limited success in the Test matches. He first captained Pakistan against New Zealand at Karachi in October 1969, in what was Hanif's last Test and the one occasion when that great batsman and his two brothers, Sadiq and Mushtaq, appeared in the Pakistan side together. That match was drawn but New Zealand won the second match at Lahore and drew at Dacca to gain their first victory in a Test rubber. Intikhab took 10 for 182 in the last match, but defeat at the hands of New Zealand was a major setback.

He led the side to England in 1971 and, arguably, was only denied victory in the first Test because of rain. Rain also ruined the second Test, but England won the third by a narrow margin to take the series. Intikhab was retained as captain for the tours of Australia and New Zealand in 1972–73.

In New Zealand, Intikhab was outstanding, taking 18 wickets for 323 runs in the three Tests and leading Pakistan to their first victory in a Test rubber outside Pakistan, but this success had been preceded by defeat in Australia and a series attended by disagreements with Saeed Ahmed and Mohammad Ilyas, and some dreadful out cricket; and although neither of these players made the trip to New Zealand, it was decided to replace Intikhab as captain with Majid Khan.

Majid Khan lasted only one series, while, relieved of the captaincy, Intikhab hit his one Test century in that series. He was reinstated as captain for the tour of England and led his side through the tour unbeaten, all three Tests being drawn. He proved an able captain, and when Pakistan met West Indies in February 1975, the first meeting between the two sides for 16 years, he was again captain. Both Tests were drawn. Intikhab was dropped from the side altogether for the home series against New Zealand in 1976–77. At the last moment, he was recalled to the side and was Pakistan's leading wicket-taker in a successful series.

When six of Pakistan's leading players were involved in a pay dispute with the BCCP, Intikhab was then named as captain of the party to tour Australia and West Indies. When the dispute was settled he was relegated to the position of an ordinary member of the party. He appeared in one Test in West Indies and none in Australia. Not surprisingly, he decided that it was time to retire.

He later managed Pakistan touring sides and formed an excellent partnership with Imran Khan, with whom he deserves considerable credit for forging Pakistan into the formidable unit that they are today.

Intikhab Alam – astute captain, happy cricketer, later successful manager (Hulton)

Test Record

	M	I	NO	Runs	HS	Avge	100s	RC	Wkts	Avge	BB	Ct
v England	20	30	3	569	138	21.07	1	2145	49	43.77	5–116	6
v Australia	6	12	1	381	68	34.63	–	552	9	61.33	2–49	3
v West Indies	3	6	0	100	34	16.66	–	296	8	37.00	3–122	–
v New Zealand	15	24	5	353	53*	18.57	–	1317	54	24.38	7–52	7
v India	3	5	1	90	56	22.50	–	184	5	36.80	2–33	4
	47	77	10	1493	138	22.28	1	4494	125	35.95	7–52	20

Test Record as Captain

				M	I	NO	Runs	HS	Avge	100s	RC	Wkts	Avge	BB	Ct
v England	–	L1	D5	6	9	1	98	32*	12.25	–	601	16	37.56	5–116	1
v Australia	–	L3	–	3	6	0	227	68	37.83	–	308	4	77.00	2–101	1
v West Indies	–	–	D2	2	4	0	88	34	22.00	–	200	6	33.33	3–122	–
v New Zealand	W1	L1	D4	6	11	2	195	53*	21.66	–	605	28	21.60	7–52	4
	W1	L5	D11	17	30	3	608	68	22.51	–	1714	54	31.74	7–52	6

MAJID Janahgir KHAN

Lahore, Punjab, Pakistan International Airlines and Glamorgan

Born: Ludhiana, 28 September 1946

Son of Jahangir Khan who played for India in the 1930s and cousin of Javed Burki and Imran Khan, Majid Khan had all the necessary qualifications to be captain of Pakistan. He was an outstanding success at Cambridge (1970–72) where he captained the side in his last two years and so impressed Glamorgan that they signed him.

Originally a medium pace bowler who opened the bowling in his first Test match, against Australia in 1964–65, Majid later turned to off-breaks and bowled less and less. His greatest value was as a batsman of exceptional talent. He had the widest range of strokes, and he was ever eager to use them. Surprisingly, it took him until the 1972–73 series against Australia to register his first Test century. So impressed were the Australians by his batting that he was later invited to spend a year with Queensland.

The Pakistan Board of Control did Majid no favours in the manner in which they appointed him captain. He was in New Zealand under the successful captaincy of Intikhab when the BCCP announced that he and not Intikhab would be captain in the next home series against England in 1973. Intikhab was deeply upset and the Pakistan players were both upset and mystified. To the Board, Majid was the aristocrat in whom they were ever eager to place their trust.

Majid had just succeeded Tony Lewis as captain of Glamorgan and it was Lewis who was leading the England side in the 1973 series. It is suggested that Wilf Wooller, still very much in control at Glamorgan at the time, spent the series sending telegrams to both captains offering them advice.

For Majid, his short period of captaincy was an unhappy time. Tony Lewis recalled in his book, *Playing Days*, 'When I got to talk to the Pakistan players I could feel dissent. It was the first time I had ever heard Majid's name buffeted by criticism; it was the first moment when I realised how a delightful cricketer of pleasing, rather old-fashioned virtues, could be mauled by the machinations of professional cricketers who treat the game, understandably, as their next plate of curry.'

Betrayed by those who had made him captain of Pakistan, Majid suffered a similar fate at

Glamorgan whom he left in 1976 with both sadness and bitterness. He fought for better payment for Pakistan's players who were paid a pittance by the Board in spite of the fact that huge crowds flocked to see them, and eventually he joined the Packer revolution as much out of disenchantment as anything else.

His was an amateur spirit which became submerged by the wave of commercialism which swept the game. Few men have been more shabbily treated by those in authority in both Pakistan and Wales.

Test Record

	M	I	NO	Runs	HS	Avge	100s	RC	Wkts	Avge	BB	Ct
v England	15	25	1	751	99	31.29	–	329	8	41.12	2–32	14
v Australia	15	24	2	915	158	41.59	3	589	8	73.62	2–55	14
v West Indies	11	21	1	821	167	41.05	2	82	4	20.50	4–45	13
v New Zealand	11	17	1	936	119*	58.50	3	266	4	66.50	1–9	19
v India	10	18	0	445	56	24.72	–	190	3	63.33	3–55	9
v Sri Lanka	1	1	0	63	63	63.00	–	0	0	–	–	1
	63	**106**	**5**	**3931**	**167**	**38.92**	**8**	**1456**	**27**	**53.92**	**4–45**	**70**

Test Record as Captain

	M	I	NO	Runs	HS	Avge	100s	RC	Wkts	Avge	BB	Ct
v England	–	–	D3	3	5	0	214	99	42.80	–	67	2	33.50	2–51	4

MUSHTAQ MOHAMMAD

Karachi, Pakistan International Airlines and Northamptonshire

Born: Junagadh, 22 November 1943

When Mushtaq Mohammad first played for Pakistan against West Indies at Lahore in March 1959, he was 15 years 124 days old, the youngest player ever to appear in a Test match. He next played against India some 15 months later, and from that point onwards he was a regular member of the Pakistan side.

An exciting right-handed middle-order batsman and an excellent leg-spin bowler, he hit his first Test century against India at Delhi in February 1961. He was then 17 years 82 days old and the youngest batsman to register a Test hundred. Twelve years later, he became only the second cricketer to score a double century and take five wickets in an innings in the same Test match when he hit 201 and took 5 for 49 against New Zealand at Dunedin.

A highly successful captain of Northamptonshire for three seasons, he replaced Intikhab as captain of Pakistan for the series against New Zealand in 1976–77; Mushtaq hit two centuries in the series, one in the same match as his brother Sadiq, and led his side to a resounding victory in the rubber.

He now seemed assured of leading Pakistan in Australia and West Indies, but he and other leading players entered into a contractual dispute with the BCCP, from whom they demanded higher salaries and allowances. The argument was long and ugly, but with a reconstruction of the Board it was eventually resolved to the satisfaction of the players, and Mushtaq did indeed lead the party in two fine series, drawing in Australia, where Pakistan won a Test for the first time, and losing narrowly in a highly competitive rubber in the Caribbean.

Mushtaq had proved a most able skipper, shrewd and tactically aware, uniting disparate personalities and bringing the best out of men like former captain Majid Khan. The arrival of Javed Miandad and the maturation of Imran Khan had given Pakistan an exciting and outstanding side in the making. Then in May 1977, Mushtaq, Majid, Zaheer Abbas, Imran and Asif

Iqbal declared their association with the World Series Cricket organisation and were banned from Test cricket by the BCCP.

In their absence, a much-weakened Pakistan side fared badly, and when Test cricket with India was renewed in 1978–79, Mushtaq was reinstated as captain and the ban on the other Packer cricketers lifted. Mushtaq led his side to a mighty win over India, their first victory in a rubber against their closest rivals. It was a cause for much rejoicing and Mushtaq was hailed as a hero.

Victory in New Zealand followed, and then one Test in Australia was won and the other lost. Australia were still bereft of their leading players and the second Test, in particular, was acrimonious. Sikhander was run out backing up, and Hilditch was given out 'handled ball' when he picked up a wayward delivery and returned it to the bowler. It was Mushtaq's final

The Northamptonshire side of the late 1970s contained three Test players from Asia and two Test captains. In the back row, third from right, is Bishen Bedi, captain of India, standing next to the Pakistan fast bowler Sarfraz Nawaz. Second from left in the front row is the Northamptonshire and Pakistan captain Mushtaq Mohammad (Lemmon)

Test Record

	M	I	NO	Runs	HS	Avge	100s	RC	Wkts	Avge	BB	Ct
v England	23	41	4	1554	157	42.00	3	793	27	29.37	4–80	13
v Australia	8	16	1	409	121	27.26	1	318	8	39.75	4–58	6
v West Indies	8	16	0	488	123	30.50	2	438	14	31.28	5–28	2
v New Zealand	10	17	1	779	201	48.48	3	513	24	21.37	5–49	17
v India	8	10	1	413	101	45.88	1	247	6	41.16	4–55	4
	57	100	7	3643	201	39.17	10	2309	79	29.22	5–28	42

Test match, and when he went to the wicket in the second innings he became the first Pakistan cricketer to play 100 innings in Test matches.

He bequeathed to Imran and Javed a fine side, united and competitive, overtly so, and on the threshold of great achievements.

Test Record as Captain

				M	I	NO	Runs	HS	Avge	100s	RC	Wkts	Avge	BB	Ct
v Australia	W2	L2	D1	5	10	1	165	37	18.33	–	205	4	51.25	4–58	4
v West Indies	W1	L2	D2	5	10	0	314	121	31.40	1	328	13	25.23	5–28	2
v New Zealand	W3	–	D3	6	10	1	406	107	45.11	2	357	15	23.80	5–59	10
v India	W2	–	D1	3	3	0	150	78	50.00	–	235	6	39.16	4–55	4
	W8	L4	D7	19	33	2	1035	121	33.38	3	1125	38	29.60	5–28	20

WASIM BARI

Karachi, Pakistan International Airlines and Sind

Born: Karachi, 23 March 1948

Unquestionably the finest wicket-keeper to have played for Pakistan, Wasim Bari was the first Asian to claim 200 dismissals behind the wicket and shares the world Test record with his seven catches against New Zealand at Auckland in 1979. This was shortly after he had relinquished the captaincy to Mushtaq Mohammad on Mushtaq's return from World Series Cricket.

Wasim led Pakistan in two series against England following the defection of leading players to the Packer organisation. He was a reluctant skipper who did an admirable job in a very difficult period. He retired after the World Cup in 1983 and the tour of Australia that followed.

Wasim Bari – an outstanding wicket-keeper and a reluctant skipper (Adrian Murrell/Allsport)

Test Record

	M	I	NO	Runs	HS	Avge	100s	RC	Wkts	Avge	BB	Ct/st
v England	24	32	6	384	63	14.76	–	2	0	–	–	50/ 4
v Australia	19	28	4	198	72	8.25	–	–	–	–	–	56/10
v West Indies	9	17	6	227	60*	20.63	–	–	–	–	–	18/ 3
v New Zealand	11	15	8	216	37*	30.85	–	–	–	–	–	27/ 5
v India	18	20	2	341	85	18.94	–	–	–	–	–	50/ 5
	81	112	26	1366	85	15.88	–	2	0	–	–	201/27

Test Record as Captain

			M	I	NO	Runs	HS	Avge	100s	RC	Wkts	Avge	BB	Ct/st
v England	–	L2	D4	6	8	1	45	17	6.42	–	2	0	–	–	8/ –

ASIF IQBAL Razvi

Hyderabad, Karachi, Pakistan International
Airlines, National Bank and Kent

Born: Hyderabad, 6 June 1943

Asif Iqbal began his Test cricket by batting at
No. 10 and opening the bowling with his right-
arm medium pace, but as he bowled less so his
batting prospered and he is best remembered as
an exhilarating batsman who could adapt himself to any occasion. His maiden Test century
came at The Oval in 1967 when, at No. 9, he hit
146 in 200 minutes and shared a record ninth-
wicket stand of 190 in 170 minutes with
Intikhab.

He was highly successful with Kent, whom
he captained in 1968, and held a regular place in
the Pakistan side. Between his debut against
Australia in October 1964 and the match against
West Indies in April 1977, he played a record 45
consecutive Tests for Pakistan. He then
announced his retirement from Test cricket and
a month later joined Packer's World Series
Cricket, for whom he had been a major
recruiter. He had long pressed for better financial rewards for Pakistan players.

When the differences between Packer and
the cricketing authorities were resolved he
made himself available again for Test cricket
and led Pakistan against India in 1979–80. This
was the first time that Pakistan had played in
India for almost 19 years, and Asif had played

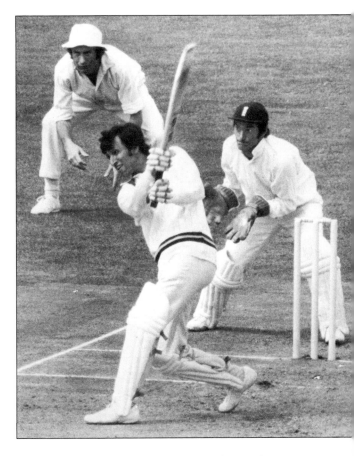

*Asif Iqbal hits out against England at The Oval in
1974. Asif appeared in a record 45 consecutive
Tests for Pakistan, but his period as captain was
not successful (Hulton)*

Test Record

	M	I	NO	Runs	HS	Avge	100s	RC	Wkts	Avge	BB	Ct
v England	15	22	1	813	146	38.71	3	467	17	27.47	3–37	6
v Australia	10	19	2	758	152*	44.58	3	413	8	51.62	3–52	8
v West Indies	7	14	0	416	135	29.71	1	45	0	–	–	3
v New Zealand	17	28	2	1122	175	43.15	3	505	26	19.42	5–48	14
v India	9	16	2	466	104	33.28	1	72	2	36.00	1–3	5
	58	99	7	3575	175	38.85	11	1502	53	28.33	5–48	36

his initial first-class cricket in India, representing Hyderabad in the Ranji Trophy before emigrating to Pakistan. Asif failed to sparkle in the series, nor could he inspire a very strong side who were well beaten. He retired from all cricket at the end of the series, but he has remained involved in the game, mainly in his role as an entrepreneur.

Test Record as Captain

				M	I	NO	Runs	HS	Avge	100s	RC	Wkts	Avge	BB	Ct
v India	–	L2	D4	6	10	1	267	64	29.66	–	72	2	36.00	1–3	4

JAVED MIANDAD Khan

Karachi, Sind, Habib Bank, Sussex and Glamorgan

Born: Karachi, 12 June 1957

On the occasion of his Test debut, against New Zealand at Lahore in October 1976, Javed Miandad hit 163 to become only the second Pakistan batsman to score a century on his Test debut. In the third Test of the same series he made 206, and at 19 years 141 days, he was the youngest batsman ever to score a double century in a Test match. He has continued to plunder records ever since with his brilliant right-handed batting, and within a decade he had become the most prolific run-scorer in Pakistan Test history.

In 1979–80 he captained Pakistan for the first time, leading them in the home series against Australia. At 22 years 260 days, he was Pakistan's youngest Test captain and third only to the Nawab of Pataudi and to Ian Craig as the youngest in Test history. He retained the captaincy for the visit of West Indies and for the 1981–82 tour of Australia where he and Lillee came close to blows in the first Test.

When Sri Lanka came to Pakistan later the same year, those who had been in the Pakistan side in Australia refused to play under Javed unless a new captain was appointed for the forthcoming tour of England. After the second Test, which the weakened Pakistan side came close to losing, Javed announced that he would

Javed Miandad, a most capable captain who has never been far from controversy. Here he leaves the field after his innings of 260 against England at The Oval in 1987 (Adrian Murrell/Allsport)

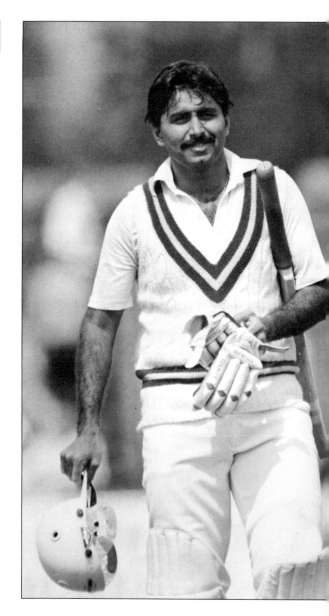

relinquish the captaincy at the end of the series. Imran, Zaheer, Majid and the rest returned for the third Test which Pakistan won easily, and Imran led the side in England.

When Imran was unable to captain the side against Australia in 1983–84, Zaheer took over the leadership, but Javed was reinstated for the visit to New Zealand in 1984–85 and for Sri Lanka's tour of Pakistan in 1985–86. Imran and Zaheer played under Javed who, after the second Test, again announced that he would relinquish the captaincy at the end of the series in order to concentrate on his batting – which, as he had scored 203 not out in the first Test, hardly seemed necessary.

Imran became captain once more and the position since has been that Javed has captained the side whenever Imran has felt disinclined to play as, for example, in the 1990–91 series against New Zealand, when he considered the opposition too weak.

As in his captaincy, so in his cricket, Javed has never been far from controversy. He was sacked by Glamorgan when he lengthened his celebrations for winning a one-day international in Sharjah by hitting the last ball for six, and he upset both Gatting's England side and Border's Australian side with his gamesmanship. The Javed Miandad on the field is a very different man from the Javed off it.

In spite of the controversy and the lack of popularity, Javed is considered by the majority of Pakistan's former Test players to be the best captain the country has had. He has a deep tactical awareness and a remarkable perception in his field placings. He has what one Pakistan writer refers to as a 'street wisdom' which Imran does not possess, and Imran relies heavily upon him. Javed's part in taking Pakistan to their present position of eminence should not be underestimated.

Test Record

	M	I	NO	Runs	HS	Avge	100s	RC	Wkts	Avge	BB	Ct/st
v England	17	24	4	965	260	48.25	1	60	1	60.00	1–4	14/–
v Australia	25	40	2	1797	211	47.28	6	312	6	52.00	3–85	12/1
v West Indies	13	23	0	714	114	31.04	2	53	1	53.00	1–22	12/–
v New Zealand	17	27	5	1815	271	82.50	7	214	8	26.75	3–74	20/–
v India	28	39	6	2228	280*	67.51	5	42	1	42.00	1–7	19/–
v Sri Lanka	9	12	1	545	203*	49.54	1	1	0	–	–	10/–
	109	165	18	8064	280*	54.85	22	682	17	40.11	3–74	87/1

Test Record as Captain

				M	I	NO	Runs	HS	Avge	100s	RC	Wkts	Avge	BB	Ct/st
v England	W1	–	D2	3	3	0	88	65	29.33	–	–	–	–	–	4/–
v Australia	W3	L2	D4	9	14	1	798	211	61.38	3	64	0	–	–	3/1
v West Indies	–	L1	D3	4	7	0	230	60	32.85	–	–	–	–	–	7/–
v New Zealand	W3	L2	D1	6	9	0	288	79	32.00	–	7	0	–	–	5/–
v Sri Lanka	W4	–	D2	6	8	1	482	203*	68.85	1	1	0	–	–	7/–
	W11	L5	D11	28	41	2	1886	211	48.35	4	72	0	–	–	26/1

IMRAN KHAN Niazi

Lahore, Pakistan International Airlines,
Worcestershire and Sussex

Born: Lahore, 25 November 1952

Imran Khan is one of the greatest all-rounders that Test cricket has seen. A genuinely fast bowler and an attacking middle-order batsman, he is one of only four players to have taken 300 wickets and scored 3000 runs in Test cricket.

Educated at Worcester Royal Grammar School and Oxford University, he played for Worcestershire from 1971 to 1976 when he joined Sussex in controversial circumstances. He made his Test debut on the 1971 tour of England, and as he matured, he combined with Sarfraz Nawaz to form a lethal new-ball attack. He was always a contester with the BCCP: he was one of those who agitated over financial terms, and he also joined World Series Cricket.

His elevation to the captaincy for the 1982 tour of England was really brought about by 'player power' after the senior members of the side that toured Australia had refused to play under Javed Miandad. Imran led Pakistan to their first victory at Lord's, but narrowly lost the three-match series. From the outset, it was apparent that his captaincy was based on strength of personality rather than on tactical genius, but few men have commanded a side so thoroughly.

Imran captained Pakistan to a spectacular triumph over India in 1982–83 but a stress fracture of the left shin meant that he was unable to bowl a ball in Test cricket for three years. The doubts regarding his fitness led the selectors to ignore him for the 1983–84 tour of Australia. The politics so often attendant on Pakistani cricket raged. The selectors were dismissed, and the team reselected with Imran as captain. Even then he was unable to play until the fourth Test and could not bowl.

Rumours of his retirement were squashed by President Zia, who asked him to return. Imran assisted New South Wales for a season and returned to Test cricket against Sri Lanka after two years' absence in October 1985. By the end of the series, Javed had resigned, and Imran was reinstated as captain for the tour of Sri Lanka in 1985–86. In the past five years, he has been captain of Pakistan when he has chosen to make himself available.

Imran's career has not been without criticism. He was accused of favouring Abdul Qadir and Mansoor Akhtar, and whenever either of them failed he was held responsible. On the reverse side, he has blighted the careers of Qasim Omar and Asif Mujtaba, a young all-rounder of talent which Imran fails to recognise. Imran has not played domestic cricket in Pakistan for more than a decade, yet he is a law unto himself in matters concerning the composition and running of the national side.

Imran is a patrician. He is a man who is aware of his own worth. The power of his personality has united a group of highly talented individuals and welded them into a side which has no superior in the world. His achievements have made him a legendary figure in Pakistan Test history.

*Opposite: The Lion of Pakistan – Imran Khan
(Ben Radford/Allsport)*

Test Record

	M	I	NO	Runs	HS	Avge	100s	RC	Wkts	Avge	BB	Ct
v England	12	17	3	500	118	35.71	1	1158	47	24.63	7–52	6
v Australia	18	28	5	862	136	37.47	1	1598	64	24.96	6–63	5
v West Indies	18	33	5	775	123	27.67	1	1695	80	21.18	7–40	4
v New Zealand	7	9	3	308	71	51.33	–	874	31	31.41	5–106	1
v India	23	29	8	1091	135*	51.95	3	2260	94	24.04	8–60	7
v Sri Lanka	7	7	0	156	63	22.28	–	657	46	14.28	8–58	5
	85	123	24	3692	136	37.29	6	8242	362	22.76	8–58	28

Test Record as Captain

				M	I	NO	Runs	HS	Avge	100s	RC	Wkts	Avge	BB	Ct
v England	W2	L2	D4	8	10	2	403	118	50.37	1	845	42	20.11	7–40	3
v Australia	W3	L2	D3	8	12	4	513	136	64.12	1	338	17	19.88	4–35	1
v West Indies	W3	L3	D3	9	16	5	356	73*	32.36	–	669	45	14.86	7–80	2
v New Zealand	–	–	D2	2	2	1	140	71	140.00	–	198	7	28.28	3–34	–
v India	W4	–	D11	15	17	5	833	135*	69.41	3	1454	61	23.83	8–60	7
v Sri Lanka	W1	L1	D1	3	4	0	48	33	12.00	–	270	15	18.00	4–69	4
	W13	L8	D24	45	61	17	2293	136	52.11	5	3774	187	20.18	8–60	17

Syed ZAHEER ABBAS

P.W.D., Karachi, Pakistan International Airlines, Sind and Gloucestershire

Born: Sialkot, 24 July 1947

A happy batsman with an infinite capacity to entertain a crowd with his repertoire of beautiful strokes, Zaheer Abbas, who initially batted in spectacles, made a spectacular entrance into Test cricket when, in his second Test match, his first in England, he hit 274 at Edgbaston in 1971. When he was next in England, in 1974, he hit 240 at The Oval.

In 1982–83 at Lahore, he hit 215 against India and so emulated Boycott in scoring his 100th hundred in a Test match. In that series, he became the first Pakistan batsman to score centuries in three successive innings. He was also the first Pakistan batsman to reach 5000 runs in Test cricket.

As a captain, he took over from Imran in 1983–84, acting as a buffer between Javed and his critics, relinquishing the job to Javed in 1984–85. He was not the man to lead a side, popular though he was, for he was neither a great tactician nor a driving force, and he tended to become defensively minded. His final Test was against Sri Lanka in February 1985.

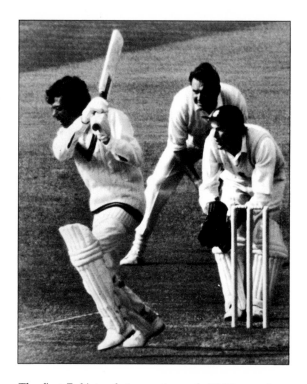

The first Pakistan batsman to reach 5000 runs in Test cricket and 100 hundreds in first-class cricket, Zaheer Abbas was less happy as a captain than as a batsman. He is pictured here during his innings of 274 at Edgbaston in 1971 (Ken Kelly)

Test Record

	M	I	NO	Runs	HS	Avge	100s	RC	Wkts	Avge	BB	Ct
v England	14	24	3	1086	274	51.71	2	2	0	–	–	5
v Australia	20	34	2	1411	126	44.09	2	50	0	–	–	14
v West Indies	8	15	1	259	80	18.50	–	0	0	–	–	5
v New Zealand	14	24	0	428	135	17.83	1	39	2	19.50	2–21	4
v India	19	25	5	1740	235*	87.00	6	41	1	41.00	1–14	6
v Sri Lanka	3	2	0	138	134	69.00	1	–	–	–	–	–
	78	124	11	5062	274	44.79	12	132	3	44.00	2–21	34

Test Record as Captain

				M	I	NO	Runs	HS	Avge	100s	RC	Wkts	Avge	BB	Ct
v England	W1	–	D2	3	6	2	195	82*	48.75	–	–	–	–	–	–
v Australia	–	L1	D2	3	5	1	135	56	33.75	–	–	–	–	–	1
v New Zealand	W2	–	D1	3	5	0	93	43	18.60	–	39	2	19.50	2–21	–
v India	–	–	D5	5	5	1	350	168*	87.50	1	17	1	17.00	1–14	2
	W3	L1	D10	14	21	4	773	168*	45.47	1	56	3	18.66	2–21	3

SRI LANKA

Sri Lanka and Test Cricket

The voyage from England to Australia for a Test series was once a gentle and luxurious cruise lasting some six weeks. In 1911, when Pelham Warner led the MCC party in quest of the 'Ashes' there were stops at Gibraltar, Marseilles, Taranto, Port Said and Colombo.

Fearing that his men were becoming stiff with inactivity, Warner cabled the Colombo Club and suggested that, during the ship's call at the city, the MCC and the Club should play a one-day match. As no English side had played in Sri Lanka, then called Ceylon, for 17 years, the Colombo Club readily agreed.

Warner and his side were overwhelmed by the enthusiasm and hospitality with which they were welcomed, and Warner advocated that the island should be a regular venue for England sides on their way to Australia. 'Cricket has become more than a game,' he wrote. 'It is an institution, a passion, one might almost say a religion. It has gone into the blood of the nation.'

Several Sri Lankan cricketers appeared in first-class cricket in England in the years after Warner's visit. Dr C.H.Gunasekera was a member of Warner's Middlesex side that won the Championship in 1920, while F.C. de Saram won his blue at Oxford in 1934 and was considered to be one of the finest batsmen to come out of either of the older universities in the thirties. On his first-class debut, he hit 176 in three hours against Gloucestershire, and he followed it with a century against the Australians.

After the Second World War, Goonesena made his mark with Cambridge University and Nottinghamshire, and Leicestershire had Inman and Jayasinghe in their side at the same period. These men were able to return home and help fertilise the cricket in their own country, bringing experience and expertise.

By the end of the sixties, Sri Lanka was nursing hopes of being granted Test status. Extended tours of India and Pakistan were taken, and Sri Lanka proved they could match the best.

They were led by Anura Tennekoon, an extremely talented batsman and astute captain, and it was his dignity and tenacity that helped the Sri Lankan cause as they argued their case for Test status. He captained the side in the inaugural World Cup in England in 1975, where, in spite of losing all three matches, Sri Lanka created a very good impression.

At The Oval, Australia made 328 for 5. Wettimuny and Mendis, future Test players, were struck by bouncers from Thomson and forced to retire hurt, but Sri Lanka reached a gallant 276 for 4 and were acclaimed. They had met the fire of Thomson and Lillee with an array of glorious strokes.

That Sri Lanka were the strongest of the ICC Associate members was well known before they won the ICC Trophy. What was not known was quite how strong they were, but this was revealed at the World Cup of 1979. Tennekoon had now retired, and opening batsman Warnapura was captain when Sri Lanka beat India at Old Trafford by 47 runs. Wettimuny hit 67, Mendis took the individual award with an exciting 64, and leg-spinner Somachandra de Silva claimed three front-line wickets.

This victory did much to enhance Sri Lanka's case that they should be granted Test status. They won the argument, and in February 1982 they played England in the inaugural Test match in Colombo. At the end of the third day, with Sri Lanka on 152 for 3, the home side had every chance of victory, but they collapsed on the fourth morning and were beaten by seven wickets. It was a portent of what was to come as Sri Lanka have so often been in contention for three of the five days of a Test match, only to fade in the closing stages of the game.

The main reasons for this have been the lack of an established first-class cricket programme in the island and the unwillingness of the major nations to accord Sri Lanka more than one Test match at irregular intervals. Only recently has a domestic first-class competition been introduced, while Pakistan, India and New Zealand are the only countries to have played Sri Lanka in a three-match series. Moreover, Sri Lanka

have yet to meet West Indies in a Test match.

A rebel tour to South Africa in 1982–83 deprived Sri Lanka of some experienced players while the continuing civil strife caused by the Tamil separatists has kept away visitors and led to one series being abandoned.

In spite of these obstacles and disappointments, Sri Lankan cricketers remain the most cheerful and, one would suggest, the most dignified in the world. The game is in their blood. Their batsmen are rich in strokes if not strong in patience. The standard at school level is astonishingly high.

To captain the Sri Lankan side is not an easy task when several of those whom you are leading may be playing in a first-class match for the first time. The Sri Lankan Board has tried to provide as much experience of leadership as possible to those playing in 'A' sides and has frequently changed the captain for this reason. The captaincy of the national side has generally been in the hands of the most experienced cricketer, but all too often the responsibility has taken toll of his form.

The Sri Lankans are an exciting and happy band of cricketers as befits the youngest Test nation. What is now needed is the encouragement of the other Test playing countries, not least England and Australia.

Bandula WARNAPURA

Bloomfield

Born: Rambukkana, Colombo, 1 March 1953

A consistent right-handed opening batsman and a popular and respected cricketer with a good knowledge of the game, Warnapura succeeded Tennekoon as captain and was captaining the side when India were beaten in the World Cup of 1979. He captained Sri Lanka in the inaugural Test match in Colombo in 1982, opening both the batting and the bowling. He led the side to Pakistan a few weeks later but missed the second Test through injury. He was

Sri Lanka's first Test captain, Bandula Warnapura, whose career ended when he went to South Africa (Adrian Murrell/Allsport)

also captain in the first official Test against India, in September 1982, but an ill-judged venture in South Africa a few months later caused him to be banned from Test cricket for life.

Test Record as Captain

				M	I	NO	Runs	HS	Avge	100s	RC	Wkts	Avge	BB	Ct
v England	–	L1	–	1	2	0	40	38	20.00	–	10	0	–	–	1
v India	–	–	D1	1	2	0	10	6	5.00	–	27	0	–	–	1
v Pakistan	–	L2	–	2	4	0	46	26	11.50	–	9	0	–	–	–
	–	L3	D1	4	8	0	96	38	12.00	–	46	0	–	–	2

Louis Rohan Duleep MENDIS

Sinhalese

Born: Moratuwa, 25 August 1952

Mendis had played league cricket in England with considerable success by the time Sri Lanka achieved Test status, and he was vice-captain to Warnapura in the earlier matches. He led the side in the second Test in Pakistan in 1981–82.

In the first generation of Sri Lankan batsmen after Test status had been granted, he was supreme. An abundant stroke-player, he hit a century in each innings against India in Madras in September 1982, reaching his hundred in the first innings with a six. He nearly repeated the feat when, having succeeded Warnapura as captain, he hit 111 and 94 in the Lord's Test of 1984. His side drew the match, but led England by 121 runs on the first innings.

His greatest moment came when he captained Sri Lanka to victory against India in Colombo in 1985. Sri Lanka won the series, and Mendis' contribution was 124 and three fifties in six innings. He was also captain when Sri Lanka drew the series with Pakistan in 1985–86, so that he remains the only Sri Lankan captain to have tasted victory.

He last led Sri Lanka in 1987 when the series against New Zealand was abandoned because of civil disturbances, but he was recalled for the tour of England in 1988 and, under Madugalle's captaincy, hit 21 and 56 in the Test match at Lord's.

Duleep Mendis, an exciting batsman and a talented captain, the most successful leader in Sri Lanka's brief Test history (Adrian Murrell/Allsport)

Test Record

	M	I	NO	Runs	HS	Avge	100s	RC	Wkts	Avge	BB	Ct
v England	3	6	0	326	111	54.33	1	–	–	–	–	2
v Australia	1	2	0	80	74	40.00	–	–	–	–	–	–
v New Zealand	4	7	0	83	36	11.85	–	–	–	–	–	1
v India	7	13	1	596	124	49.66	3	–	–	–	–	1
v Pakistan	9	15	0	244	58	16.26	–	–	–	–	–	4
	24	43	1	1329	124	31.64	4	–	–	–	–	8

Test Record as Captain

				M	I	NO	Runs	HS	Avge	100s	RC	Wkts	Avge	BB	Ct
v England	–	–	D1	1	2	0	205	111	102.50	1	–	–	–	–	–
v Australia	–	L1	–	1	2	0	80	74	40.00	–	–	–	–	–	–
v New Zealand	–	L2	D2	4	7	0	83	36	11.85	–	–	–	–	–	1
v India	W1	L2	D3	6	11	1	386	124	38.60	1	–	–	–	–	1
v Pakistan	W1	L3	D3	7	11	0	144	58	13.09	–	–	–	–	–	2
	W2	L8	D9	19	33	1	898	124	28.06	2	–	–	–	–	4

Dandeniyage Somachandra DE SILVA

Moratuwa

Born: Galle, 11 June 1942

A most able bowler of leg-breaks at quite a brisk pace, and a useful late order batsman, Somachandra de Silva was something of a veteran by the time Sri Lanka attained Test status. He was well known in league cricket in England and played in the Minor Counties Championship for Lincolnshire and Shropshire.

With Mendis a clever skipper who used his limited bowling resources with great intelligence, and the stylish Dias as his right-hand man, there was little chance of de Silva leading Sri Lanka, but when both were injured in New Zealand in 1982–83, he led the side.

His final Test was Sri Lanka's first in England, in 1984, and he claimed the wickets of Tavare and Ellison for 85 runs in 45 overs.

Somachandra de Silva, the veteran leg-spinner, who led Sri Lanka in New Zealand in 1982–83 (Allsport/Adrian Murrell)

Test Record

	M	I	NO	Runs	HS	Avge	100s	RC	Wkts	Avge	BB	Ct
v England	2	2	0	4	3	2.00	–	177	5	35.40	3–54	–
v Australia	1	2	0	31	26	15.50	–	122	1	122.00	1–122	–
v New Zealand	5	10	1	162	61	18.00	–	365	11	33.18	3–59	4
v India	1	2	1	95	49	47.50	–	191	3	63.66	2–162	1
v Pakistan	3	6	1	114	26	22.80	–	492	17	28.94	5–59	–
	12	22	3	406	61	21.36	–	1347	37	36.40	5–59	5

Test Record as Captain

				M	I	NO	Runs	HS	Avge	100s	RC	Wkts	Avge	BB	Ct
v New Zealand	–	L2	–	2	4	0	120	61	30.00	–	72	3	24.00	1–13	2

Ranjan Senerath MADUGALLE

Nondescripts

Born: Kandy, 22 April 1959

In the inaugural Test match against England in 1982, Ranjan Madugalle hit the top score of 65. He played in the first 18 Test matches in which Sri Lanka were engaged, and as a stylish right-handed batsman, he prospered in the middle-order, hitting his one Test century against India at Colombo in 1985. His promotion to number three did not seem to suit him, however, and he lost his place after the series against Pakistan two months later.

He returned to play against New Zealand in 1987, but the series was abandoned after one Test in which he scored 60. As the most senior and perceptive of Sri Lanka's cricketers, he was appointed captain against Australia and England in 1988, but his side was twice beaten heavily.

A knowledgeable captain of great dignity and charm, he had the misfortune to lead Sri Lanka at the most difficult time when their appearances in international cricket were very limited.

A cultured batsman whose form was lost when he became captain – Ranjan Madugalle (Adrian Murrell/Allsport)

Test Record

	M	I	NO	Runs	HS	Avge	100s	RC	Wkts	Avge	BB	Ct
v England	3	6	0	99	65	16.50	–	4	0	–	–	1
v Australia	2	4	0	22	9	5.50	–	–	–	–	–	–
v New Zealand	6	11	2	451	89*	50.11	–	6	0	–	–	2
v India	4	7	1	227	103	37.83	–	10	0	–	–	1
v Pakistan	6	11	1	230	91*	23.00	–	18	0	–	–	5
	21	39	4	1029	103	29.40	–	38	0	–	–	9

Test Record as Captain

				M	I	NO	Runs	HS	Avge	100s	RC	Wkts	Avge	BB	Ct
v England	–	L1	–	1	2	0	23	20	11.50	–	–	–	–	–	–
v Australia	–	L1	–	1	2	0	13	7	6.50	–	–	–	–	–	–
	–	L2	–	2	4	0	36	20	9.00	–	–	–	–	–	–

Arjuna RANATUNGA

Sinhalese

Born: Colombo, 1 December 1963

A left-handed batsman and right-arm medium pace bowler, he played in the inaugural Test match against England at the age of 18 years 78 days while still attending Ananda College, and he hit 54, Sri Lanka's first fifty in Test cricket. In 1983 he made 90 against Australia, and the following year came his maiden Test century, against India.

In England in 1984, he had revealed himself as a joyous cricketer; plump and enthusiastic, he delighted in hitting the ball and made a splendidly entertaining 84 at Lord's. His second and higher Test hundred came against Pakistan in Colombo in 1986, when he and Gurusinha batted throughout the last day and shared a record fourth wicket stand of 240.

Ranatunga continued to score consistently in a happy manner, and as the senior player, he replaced Madugalle as captain for the tour of Australia in 1989–90. The itinerary was of no help to his side, but he displayed sympathy and understanding in a lost cause. It was not an easy time at which to be captain, although Sri Lanka

A cheerful cricketer who led Sri Lanka at a most difficult time, Arjuna Ranatunga (Allsport/Ben Radford)

were now playing more Test matches. There was a heavy defeat in India and a drawn series in New Zealand in 1991. Ranatunga's own form was moderate, but it came as something of a surprise that he was deprived of the captaincy and dropped for the tour of England. He is a keen cricketer and is young enough to return to Test cricket.

Test Record

	M	I	NO	Runs	HS	Avge	100s	RC	Wkts	Avge	BB	Ct
v England	3	6	0	223	84	37.16	–	20	2	10.00	1–6	2
v Australia	4	7	0	306	90	43.71	–	164	1	164.00	1–72	3
v New Zealand	7	12	1	346	55	31.45	–	249	7	35.57	2–17	4
v India	8	14	0	416	111	29.71	1	215	2	107.50	1–8	2
v Pakistan	8	14	2	533	135*	44.41	1	161	2	80.50	1–26	4
	30	53	3	1824	135*	36.48	2	809	14	57.78	2–17	15

Test Record as Captain

				M	I	NO	Runs	HS	Avge	100s	RC	Wkts	Avge	BB	Ct
v Australia	–	L1	D1	2	3	0	84	38	28.00	–	74	0	–	–	3
v New Zealand	–	–	D3	3	5	1	160	55	40.00	–	117	3	39.00	2–60	1
v India	–	L1	–	1	2	0	43	42	21.50	–	4	0	–	–	–
	–	L2	D4	6	10	1	287	55	31.88	–	195	3	65.00	2–60	4

Pinnaduwage Aravinda DE SILVA

Nondescripts

Born: Colombo, 17 October 1965

Aravinda de Silva is the most exciting batsman that Sri Lanka has yet produced, and before his 26th birthday, he had made the highest score for Sri Lanka in a Test match, scored the most centuries, and been appointed captain of his country. He was the first Sri Lankan captain not to have played in the inaugural Test match against England.

His Test debut was against England at Lord's in 1984, by which time he was known in England for his prolific scoring in club cricket. He reached his maiden Test century against Pakistan in 1986, the day after his 20th birthday, reaching three figures with a six off Imran. He hit a second century in the third Test of the same series.

The hope for the future as batsman and captain, record holder Aravinda de Silva (Allsport/Chris Cole)

In Australia in 1989–90, he played innings of 167, 75 and 72, and the following year he hit two centuries in the series in New Zealand. In the first game in Wellington he scored 267, the highest by a Sri Lankan in Test cricket.

Appointed captain for the tour of England in 1991, he displayed some glorious strokes in a breathtaking innings of 42 on the Friday evening of the Test, only to be out in the first over the next morning. His captaincy was somewhat fretful, but he has many years ahead of him.

Test Record

	M	I	NO	Runs	HS	Avge	100s	RC	Wkts	Avge	BB	Ct
v England	3	6	0	100	42	16.66	–	–	–	–	–	5
v Australia	3	5	0	327	167	65.40	1	112	3	37.33	2–65	1
v New Zealand	3	5	0	493	267	98.60	2	73	0	–	–	2
v India	7	13	1	274	75	22.83	–	–	–	–	–	3
v Pakistan	6	11	1	345	122	34.50	2	22	0	–	–	4
	22	40	2	1539	267	40.50	5	207	3	69.00	2–65	15

Test Record as Captain

	M	I	NO	Runs	HS	Avge	100s	RC	Wkts	Avge	BB	Ct
v England – L1 –	1	2	0	60	42	30.00	–	–	–	–	–	2

Bibliography

Wisden Book of Test Cricket, two vols, Bill Frindall
England Test Cricketers Bill Frindall
England v Australia, 1877–1985 David Frith
Who's Who of Cricketers Philip Bailey, Philip Thorne and Peter Wynne-Thomas
Cricketer International Quarterly ed. Richard Lockwood
Wisden, various years
Benson and Hedges Cricket Year, I–IX
Australian Cricket Jack Pollard
A History of West Indian Cricket Michael Manley
Statistics of West Indies Cricket, 1865–1989 Jimmy Richards and Mervyn Wong
The Complete Record of West Indian Test Cricketers Bridgette Lawrence and Ray Goble
Beyond a Boundary C.L.R. James
The Playfair Book of Test Cricket, two vols, Roy Webber
Compendium of Indian Test Cricketers L.N. Mathur
A History of Indian Cricket Mihir Bose
Men in White D.O. Neely, R.P. King and F.K. Payne
The Shell Cricket Almanack of New Zealand ed. Francis Payne and Ian Smith
First-Class Cricket in New Zealand Brian Croudy
Pakistan Book of Cricket, various years, ed. Qamar Ahmed
Playing Days Tony Lewis

Appendix

Captains' success rate in Tests

As a point of interest, one offers the following tables which attempt to indicate the amount of success enjoyed by those who have led Test sides. Allowing two points for a win and one for a draw, the percentage of success is the number of points gained from the number possible.

England

	M	W	L	D	Pts	%
WW Read	2	2	–	–	4	100.00
CA Smith	1	1	–	–	2	100.00
MP Bowden	1	1	–	–	2	100.00
TC O'Brien	1	1	–	–	2	100.00
Lord Hawke	4	4	–	–	8	100.00
DB Close	7	6	–	1	13	92.85
CB Fry	6	4	–	2	10	83.33
DR Jardine	15	9	1	5	23	76.66
AG Steel	4	3	1	–	6	75.00
DS Sheppard	2	1	–	1	3	75.00
JM Brearley	31	18	4	9	45	72.58
A Shrewsbury	7	5	2	–	10	71.42
APF Chapman	17	9	2	6	24	70.58
FS Jackson	5	2	–	3	7	70.00
WG Grace	13	8	3	2	18	69.23
RE Foster	3	1	–	2	4	66.66
RWV Robins	3	1	–	2	4	66.66
L Hutton	23	11	4	8	30	65.21
FG Mann	7	2	–	5	9	64.28
Lord Harris	4	2	1	1	5	62.50
RT Stanyforth	4	2	1	1	5	62.50
AHH Gilligan	4	1	–	3	5	62.50
ND Howard	4	1	–	3	5	62.50
PBH May	41	20	10	11	51	62.19
R Illingworth	31	12	5	14	38	61.29
FT Mann	5	2	1	2	6	60.00
AW Carr	6	1	–	5	7	58.33
MC Cowdrey	27	8	4	15	31	57.40
RGD Willis	18	7	5	6	20	55.55
GA Gooch	20	7	5	8	22	55.00
MJK Smith	25	5	3	17	27	54.00
ER Dexter	30	9	7	14	32	53.33
MH Denness	19	6	5	8	20	52.63
WR Hammond	20	4	3	13	21	52.50
J Lillywhite	2	1	1	–	2	50.00
Hon. Ivo Bligh	4	2	2	–	4	50.00
JWHT Douglas	18	8	8	2	18	50.00
AER Gilligan	9	4	4	1	9	50.00
JC White	4	1	1	2	4	50.00
FSG Calthorpe	4	1	1	2	4	50.00
K Cranston	1	–	–	1	1	50.00
TW Graveney	1	–	–	1	1	50.00
G Boycott	4	1	1	2	4	50.00

	M	W	L	D	Pts	%
KWR Fletcher	7	1	1	5	7	50.00
FR Brown	15	5	6	4	14	46.66
GOB Allen	11	4	5	2	10	45.45
AE Stoddart	8	3	4	1	7	43.75
RES Wyatt	16	3	5	8	14	43.75
AR Lewis	8	1	2	5	7	43.75
MW Gatting	23	2	5	16	20	43.47
AW Greig	14	3	5	6	12	42.85
PF Warner	10	4	6	–	8	40.00
FL Fane	5	2	3	–	4	40.00
NWD Yardley	14	4	7	3	11	39.28
AC MacLaren	22	4	11	7	15	34.09
HDG Leveson Gower	3	1	2	–	2	33.33
Lord Tennyson	3	–	1	2	2	33.33
IT Botham	12	–	4	8	8	33.33
DI Gower	32	5	18	9	19	29.68
A Shaw	4	–	2	2	4	25.00
AN Hornby	2	–	1	1	1	25.00
AO Jones	2	–	2	–	0	0.00
GTS Stevens	1	–	1	–	0	0.00
CF Walters	1	–	1	–	0	0.00
DB Carr	1	–	1	–	0	0.00
JH Edrich	1	–	1	–	0	0.00
JE Emburey	2	–	2	–	0	0.00
CS Cowdrey	1	–	1	–	0	0.00
AJ Lamb	3	–	3	–	0	0.00

Australia

	M	W	L	D	Pts	%
HH Massie	1	1	–	–	2	100.00
RN Harvey	1	1	–	–	2	100.00
WA Brown	1	1	–	–	2	100.00
H Trumble	2	2	–	–	4	100.00
WW Armstrong	10	8	–	2	18	90.00
VJ Richardson	5	4	–	1	9	90.00
ID Craig	5	3	–	2	8	80.00
DG Bradman	24	15	3	6	36	75.00
AL Hassett	24	14	4	6	34	70.83
DW Gregory	3	2	1	–	4	66.66
IM Chappell	30	15	5	10	40	66.66
R Benaud	28	12	4	12*	36	64.28
WM Woodfull	25	14	7	4	32	64.00

	M	W	L	D	Pts	%
HL Collins	11	5	2	4	14	63.63
GHS Trott	8	5	3	–	10	62.50
MA Noble	15	8	5	2	18	60.00
SE Gregory	6	2	1	3	7	58.33
GS Chappell	48	21	13	14	56	58.33
J Darling	21	7	4	10	24	57.14
IW Johnson	17	7	5	5	19	55.88
WM Lawry	25	9	8	8	26	52.00
AR Border	62	17	16	29*	63	50.80
G Giffen	4	2	2	–	4	50.00
C Hill	10	5	5	–	10	50.00
W Bardsley	2	–	–	2	2	50.00
RR Lindwall	1	–	–	1	1	50.00
RB Simpson	39	12	12	15	39	50.00
JM Blackham	8	3	3	2	8	50.00
BN Jarman	1	–	–	1	1	50.00
WL Murdoch	16	5	7	4	14	43.75
KJ Hughes	28	4	13	11	19	33.92
BC Booth	2	–	1	1	1	25.00
J Ryder	5	1	4	–	2	20.00
PS McDonnell	6	1	5	–	2	16.66
GN Yallop	7	1	6	–	2	14.28
TP Horan	2	–	2	–	0	0.00
HJH Scott	3	–	3	–	0	0.00
AR Morris	2	–	2	–	0	0.00

* includes one match tied

	M	W	L	D	Pts	%
JH Anderson	1	–	1	–	0	0.00
F Mitchell	3	–	3	–	0	0.00

New Zealand

	M	W	L	D	Pts	%
GP Howarth	30	11	7	12	34	56.66
JV Coney	15	5	4	6	16	53.33
JG Wright	14	3	3	8	14	50.00
ME Chapple	1	–	–	1	1	50.00
JM Parker	1	–	–	1	1	50.00
IDS Smith	1	–	–	1	1	50.00
GT Dowling	19	4	7	8	16	42.10
JJ Crowe	6	–	1	5	5	41.16
WA Hadlee	8	–	2	6	6	37.50
TC Lowry	7	–	2	5	5	35.71
BW Sinclair	3	–	1	2	2	33.33
BE Congdon	17	1	7	9	11	32.35
ML Page	7	–	3	4	4	28.57
JR Reid	34	3	18	13	19	27.94
GM Turner	10	1	6	3	5	25.00
MG Burgess	10	1	6	3	5	25.00
WM Wallace	2	–	1	1	1	25.00
HB Cave	9	–	5	4	4	22.22
MD Crowe	5	–	3	2	2	20.00
B Sutcliffe	4	–	3	1	1	12.50
GO Rabone	5	–	4	1	1	10.00

South Africa

	M	W	L	D	Pts	%
A Bacher	4	4	–	–	8	100.00
EP Nupen	1	1	–	–	2	100.00
PL van der Merwe	8	4	1	3	11	68.75
SJ Snooke	5	3	2	–	6	60.00
JE Cheetham	15	7	5	3	17	56.66
HM Taberer	1	–	–	1	1	50.00
TL Goddard	13	1	2	10	12	46.15
PW Sherwell	13	5	6	2	12	46.15
DJ McGlew	14	4	6	4	12	42.85
HG Deane	12	2	4	6	10	41.66
CB van Ryneveld	8	2	4	2	6	37.50
HF Wade	10	1	4	5	7	35.00
HB Cameron	9	2	5	2	6	33.33
A Melville	10	–	4	6	6	30.00
HW Taylor	18	1	10	7	9	25.00
AD Nourse	15	1	9	5	7	23.33
LJ Tancred	3	–	2	1	1	16.66
OR Dunnell	1	–	1	–	0	0.00
WH Milton	2	–	2	–	0	0.00
EA Halliwell	3	–	3	–	0	0.00
AR Richards	1	–	1	–	0	0.00
M Bisset	2	–	2	–	0	0.00

West Indies

	M	W	L	D	Pts	%
MP Fernandes	1	1	–	–	2	100.00
FM Worrell	15	9	3	3*	21	70.00
IVA Richards	50	27	8	15	69	69.00
CH Lloyd	74	36	12	26	98	66.21
FCM Alexander	18	7	4	7	21	58.33
JDC Goddard	22	8	7	7	23	52.27
ELG Hoad	1	–	–	1	1	50.00
GA Headley	1	–	–	1	1	50.00
GE Gomez	1	–	–	1	1	50.00
D St E Atkinson	7	3	3	1	7	50.00
RB Kanhai	13	3	3	7	13	50.00
DL Murray	1	–	–	1	1	50.00
DL Haynes	4	1	1	2	4	50.00
G St A Sobers	39	9	10	20	38	48.71
JB Stollmeyer	13	3	4	6	12	46.15
AI Kallicharran	9	1	2	6	8	44.44
GC Grant	12	3	7	2	8	33.33
RS Grant	3	–	1	2	2	33.33
RK Nunes	4	–	3	1	1	12.50
N Betancourt	1	–	1	–	0	0.00
CG Greenidge	1	–	1	–	0	0.00

* includes one match tied

India

	M	W	L	D	Pts	%
RJ Shastri	1	1	–	–	2	100.00
SM Gavaskar	47	9	8	30	48	51.06
K Srikkanth	4	–	–	4	4	50.00
AL Wadekar	16	4	4	8	16	50.00
NJ Contractor	12	2	2	8	12	50.00
HR Adhikari	1	–	–	1	1	50.00
PR Umrigar	8	2	2	4	8	50.00
Kapil Dev	34	4	7	23*	31	45.58
M Azharuddin	7	1	2	4	6	42.85
MH Mankad	6	–	1	5	5	41.66
GS Ramchand	5	1	2	2	4	40.00
BS Bedi	22	6	11	5	17	38.63
Nawab of Pataudi jnr	40	9	19	12	30	37.50
L Amarnath	15	2	6	7	11	36.66
VS Hazare	14	1	5	8	10	35.71
DB Vengsarkar	10	2	5	3	7	35.00
Nawab of Pataudi snr	3	–	1	2	2	33.33
S Venkataraghavan	5	–	2	3	3	30.00
GR Viswanath	2	–	1	1	1	25.00
Maharaj of Vizianagram	3	–	2	1	1	16.66
Ghulam Ahmed	3	–	2	1	1	16.66
CK Nayudu	4	–	3	1	1	12.50
DK Gaekwad	4	–	4	–	0	0.00
PK Roy	1	–	1	–	0	0.00
CG Borde	1	–	1	–	0	0.00

includes one match tied

Pakistan

	M	W	L	D	Pts	%
Javed Miandad	28	11	5	12	34	60.71
Mushtaq Mohammad	19	8	4	7	23	60.52
Zaheer Abbas	14	3	1	10	16	57.14
Imran Khan	45	13	8	24	40	55.55
Hanif Mohammad	11	2	2	7	11	50.00
Saeed Ahmed	3	–	–	3	3	50.00
Majid J Khan	3	–	–	3	3	50.00
AH Kardar	23	6	6	11	23	50.00
Fazal Mahmood	10	2	6	6	10	50.00
Intikhab Alam	17	1	5	11	13	38.23
Wasim Bari	6	–	2	4	4	33.33
Asif Iqbal	6	–	2	4	4	33.33
Imtiaz Ahmed	4	–	2	2	2	25.00
Javed Burki	5	–	4	1	1	10.00

Sri Lanka

	M	W	L	D	Pts	%
LRD Mendis	19	2	8	9	13	34.21
A Ranatunga	6	–	2	4	4	33.33
B Warnapura	4	–	3	1	1	12.50
DS de Silva	2	–	2	–	0	0.00
RS Madugalle	2	–	2	–	0	0.00
PA de Silva	1	–	1	–	0	0.00

Top 20 Test Captains

(qualification – captain in a minimum of five Tests)

		M	W	L	D	Pts	%
1	DB Close	7	6	–	1	13	92.85
2	WW Armstrong	10	8	–	2	18	90.00
	VJ Richardson	5	4	–	1	9	90.00
4	CB Fry	6	4	–	2	10	83.33
5	ID Craig	5	3	–	2	8	80.00
6	DR Jardine	15	9	1	5	23	76.66
7	DG Bradman	24	15	3	6	36	75.00
8	JM Brearley	31	18	4	9	45	72.58
9	A Shrewsbury	7	5	2	–	10	71.42
10	AL Hassett	24	14	4	6	34	70.83
11	APF Chapman	17	9	2	6	24	70.58
12	FS Jackson	5	2	–	3	7	70.00
	FM Worrell	15	9	3	3*	21	70.00
14	WG Grace	13	8	3	2	18	69.23
15	IVA Richards	50	27	8	15	69	69.00
16	PL van der Merwe	8	4	1	3	11	68.75
17	IM Chappell	30	15	5	10	40	66.66
18	CH Lloyd	74	36	12	26	98	66.21
19	L Hutton	23	11	4	8	30	65.21
20	FG Mann	7	2	–	5	9	64.28
	R Benaud	28	12	4	12*	36	64.28

Index of Captains

(With First-class Career Records)

Page references in brackets after captain's name.

England

	M	I	NO	Runs	HS	Avge	100s	RC	Wkts	Avge	Ct	St
Lillywhite, James jnr *(15)*	256	445	59	5523	126*	14.30	2	18436	1210	15.23	109	–
Harris, Lord *(15)*	224	395	23	9990	176	26.85	11	1758	70	25.11	190	–
Shaw, A *(16)*	404	630	101	6585	88	12.83	–	24579	2027	12.12	368	–
Hornby, AN *(17)*	437	710	41	16109	188	24.07	16	258	11	23.45	313	3
Bligh, Hon IFW *(18)*	84	143	11	2734	113*	20.71	2	–	–	–	81	–
Shrewsbury, A *(19)*	498	813	90	26505	267	36.65	59	2	0	–	376	–
Steel, AG *(19)*	162	261	23	7000	171	29.41	8	11667	788	14.80	137	–
Read, WW *(20)*	467	749	52	22349	338	32.06	38	3483	108	32.25	381	20
Grace, WG *(21)*	869	1478	104	54211	344	39.45	124	50982	2808	18.15	874	5
Smith, CA *(23)*	143	247	28	2986	85	13.63	–	7728	345	22.40	97	–
Bowden, MP *(23)*	86	123	17	2316	189*	20.13	3	33	2	16.50	73	14
Stoddart, AE *(24)*	309	537	16	16738	221	32.12	26	6571	278	23.63	257	–
O'Brien, TC *(25)*	266	452	30	11397	202	27.00	15	340	4	85.00	173	2
Hawke, Lord *(25)*	633	936	105	16749	166	20.15	13	16	0	–	209	–
MacLaren, AC *(26)*	424	703	52	22237	424	34.15	47	267	1	267.00	452	–
Warner, PF *(27)*	519	875	75	29028	244	36.28	60	636	15	42.40	183	–
Jackson, FS *(28)*	309	505	35	15901	160	33.83	31	15767	774	20.37	197	–
Foster, RE *(29)*	139	234	17	9076	287	41.82	22	1153	25	46.12	179	–
Fane, FL *(30)*	417	721	44	18548	217	27.39	25	49	2	24.50	194	–
Jones, AO *(31)*	472	774	47	22935	296	31.54	34	10929	333	32.81	577	2
Leveson Gower, HDG *(31)*	277	400	78	7638	155	23.72	4	1378	46	29.95	103	–
Douglas, JWHT *(32)*	651	1035	156	24531	210*	27.90	26	44159	1893	23.32	364	–
Fry, CB *(34)*	394	658	43	30886	258*	50.22	94	4872	166	29.34	240	–
Tennyson, Lord *(36)*	477	759	38	16828	217	23.33	19	2976	55	54.10	172	–
Mann, FT *(36)*	398	612	47	13235	194	23.42	9	249	3	83.00	174	–
Gilligan, AER *(37)*	337	510	55	9140	144	20.08	12	20141	868	23.20	180	–
Carr, AW *(38)*	468	709	42	21051	206	31.56	45	1150	31	37.09	393	1
Chapman, APF *(39)*	394	554	44	16309	260	31.97	27	921	22	41.86	356	–
Stanyforth, RT *(42)*	61	79	16	1092	91	17.33	–	–	–	–	72	21
Stevens, GTS *(42)*	243	387	36	10376	182	29.56	12	18364	684	26.84	213	–
White, JC *(43)*	472	765	101	12202	192	18.40	6	43759	2356	18.57	426	–
Gilligan, AHH *(44)*	321	525	31	8873	143	17.96	1	3872	115	33.66	123	–
Calthorpe, FSG *(44)*	369	576	52	12596	209	24.03	13	23390	782	29.91	216	–
Wyatt, RES *(45)*	739	1141	157	39405	232	40.04	85	29597	901	32.84	413	1
Jardine, DR *(46)*	262	378	61	14848	214	46.83	35	1493	48	31.10	188	–
Walters, CF *(49)*	244	427	32	12145	226	30.94	21	380	5	76.00	101	–
Allen, GOB *(49)*	265	376	54	9232	180	28.67	11	17518	788	22.23	131	–
Robins, RWV *(51)*	379	565	39	13884	140	26.39	11	22580	969	23.30	221	–
Hammond, WR *(52)*	634	1005	104	50551	336*	56.10	167	22389	732	30.58	819	3

	M	I	NO	Runs	HS	Avge	100s	RC	Wkts	Avge	Ct	St
Yardley, NWD (54)	446	658	75	18173	183*	31.17	27	8506	279	30.48	328	1
Cranston, K (55)	78	104	15	3099	156*	34.82	3	4985	178	28.00	46	–
Mann, FG (55)	166	262	17	6350	136*	25.91	7	389	3	129.66	72	–
Brown, FR (56)	355	536	49	13325	212	27.36	22	32007	1221	26.21	212	–
Howard, ND (57)	198	279	30	6152	145	24.70	3	52	1	52.00	153	–
Carr, DB (57)	446	745	72	19257	170	38.61	24	11396	328	34.74	499	–
Hutton, L (57)	513	814	91	40140	364	55.51	129	5106	173	29.51	400	–
Sheppard, DS (60)	230	395	31	15838	239*	43.51	45	88	2	44.00	195	–
May, PBH (60)	388	618	77	27592	285*	51.00	85	49	0	–	282	–
Cowdrey, MC (62)	692	1130	134	42719	307	42.89	107	3329	65	51.21	638	–
Dexter, ER (63)	327	567	48	21150	205	40.75	51	12539	419	29.92	233	–
Smith, MJK (64)	637	1091	139	39832	204	41.84	69	205	5	61.00	593	–
Close, DB (65)	786	1225	173	34994	198	33.26	52	30947	1171	26.42	813	1
Graveney, TW (66)	732	1223	159	47793	258	44.91	122	3037	80	37.96	550	1
Illingworth, R (67)	787	1073	213	24134	162	28.06	22	42023	2072	20.28	446	–
Lewis, AR (68)	409	708	76	20495	223	32.42	30	432	6	72.00	193	–
Denness, MH (69)	501	838	65	25886	195	33.48	33	62	2	31.00	411	–
Edrich, JH (70)	564	979	104	39790	310*	45.47	103	53	0	–	311	–
Greig, AW (71)	350	579	45	16660	226	31.19	26	24702	856	28.85	345	–
Brearley, JM (73)	455	768	102	25185	312*	37.81	45	192	3	64.00	418	12
Boycott, G (75)	609	1014	162	48426	261*	56.83	151	1459	45	32.42	264	–
Botham, IT (76)	372	572	42	18221	228	34.37	36	30088	1126	26.72	336	–
Fletcher, KWR (77)	730	1167	170	37665	228*	37.77	63	2296	51	45.01	644	–
Willis, RGD (79)	308	333	145	2690	72	14.30	–	22468	899	24.99	134	–
Gower, DI (80)	412	666	62	23978	228	39.69	48	227	4	56.75	255	1
Gatting, MW (81)	408	640	101	26512	258	49.18	66	4428	154	28.75	360	–
Emburey, JE (83)	423	535	106	9762	133	22.75	4	33530	1285	26.09	382	–
Cowdrey, CS (84)	297	451	68	12202	159	31.85	21	7962	200	39.81	290	–
Gooch, GA (85)	459	777	62	33897	333	47.40	89	7644	219	34.90	456	–
Lamb, AJ (87)	389	648	95	26472	294	47.86	72	193	8	24.12	305	–

Australia

	M	I	NO	Runs	HS	Avge	100s	RC	Wkts	Avge	Ct	St
Gregory, DW (89)	41	68	7	889	85	14.57	–	553	29	19.06	35	–
Murdoch, WL (89)	391	679	48	16953	321	26.86	19	430	10	43.00	218	25
Horan, TP (90)	106	187	14	4027	141*	23.27	8	829	35	23.68	39	–
Massie, HH (91)	64	113	5	2485	206	23.00	1	60	2	30.00	35	–
Blackham, JM (91)	275	442	61	6395	109	16.78	1	138	2	69.00	273	180
Scott, HJH (92)	85	141	15	2863	123	22.72	4	494	18	27.44	56	–
McDonnell, PS (93)	166	285	10	6470	239	23.52	7	247	2	123.50	98	–
Giffen, G (93)	251	421	23	11758	271	29.54	18	21782	1023	21.29	195	–
Trott, GHS (94)	222	393	19	8804	186	23.54	9	9700	386	25.12	183	–
Darling, J (95)	202	333	25	10635	210	34.52	19	55	1	55.00	148	–

	M	I	NO	Runs	HS	Avge	100s	RC	Wkts	Avge	Ct	St
Trumble, H (96)	213	344	67	5395	107	19.47	3	17134	929	18.44	328	–
Noble, MA (97)	248	377	34	13975	284	40.74	37	14445	625	23.11	191	–
Hill, C (97)	252	416	21	17213	365*	43.57	45	323	10	32.30	168	1
Gregory, SE (98)	368	587	55	15192	201	28.55	25	394	2	197.00	174	–
Armstrong, WW (99)	269	406	61	16158	303*	46.83	45	16406	832	19.71	274	–
Collins, HL (101)	168	258	10	9224	282	40.01	32	3871	181	21.38	115	–
Bardsley, W (101)	250	376	35	17025	264	49.92	53	41	0	–	112	–
Ryder, J (102)	177	274	37	10499	295	44.29	24	7064	238	29.68	132	–
Woodfull, WM (102)	174	245	39	13388	284	64.99	49	24	1	24.00	78	–
Richardson, VJ (103)	184	297	12	10727	231	37.63	27	545	8	68.12	213	4
Bradman, DG (104)	234	338	43	28067	452*	95.14	117	1367	36	37.97	131	1
Brown, WA (106)	189	284	15	13838	265*	51.44	39	110	6	18.33	110	1
Hassett, AL (108)	216	322	32	16890	232	58.24	59	703	18	39.05	170	–
Morris, AR (108)	162	250	15	12614	290	53.67	46	592	12	49.33	73	–
Johnson, IW (109)	189	243	29	4905	132*	22.92	2	14423	619	23.30	137	–
Lindwall, RR (110)	228	270	39	5042	134*	21.82	5	16956	794	21.35	123	–
Craig, ID (111)	144	208	15	7328	213*	37.96	15	127	1	127.00	70	–
Benaud, R (112)	259	365	44	11719	187	36.50	23	23370	945	24.73	254	–
Harvey, RN (113)	306	461	35	21699	231*	50.93	67	1106	30	36.86	228	–
Simpson, RB (114)	257	436	62	21029	359	56.22	60	13287	349	38.07	383	–
Booth, BC (116)	183	283	35	11265	214*	45.42	26	956	16	59.75	119	–
Lawry, WM (116)	249	417	49	18734	266	50.90	50	188	5	37.60	121	–
Jarman, BN (117)	191	284	37	5615	196	22.73	5	98	3	32.66	431	129
Chappell, IM (118)	262	448	41	19680	209	48.35	59	6614	176	37.57	312	1
Chappell, GS (119)	321	542	72	24535	247*	52.20	74	8717	291	29.96	376	–
Yallop, GN (121)	156	272	28	11063	268	45.34	29	772	11	70.18	115	1
Hughes, KJ (122)	216	368	20	12711	213	36.52	26	97	3	32.33	155	–
Border, AR (124)	305	500	79	22071	205	52.42	61	3229	89	36.28	296	–

South Africa

	M	I	NO	Runs	HS	Avge	100s	RC	Wkts	Avge	Ct	St
Dunell, OR (129)	3	6	1	79	26*	15.80	–	–	–	–	3	–
Milton, WH (129)	6	11	0	151	47	13.72	–	63	2	31.50	4	–
Halliwell, EA (130)	60	96	8	1702	92	19.34	–	175	3	58.33	75	37
Richards, AR (130)	9	15	0	346	108	23.06	1	–	–	–	13	2
Bisset, M (131)	40	70	9	1436	184	23.54	2	122	5	24.40	51	13
Taberer, HM (131)	11	20	3	222	47*	13.05	–	446	22	20.27	5	–
Anderson, JH (131)	14	24	2	511	109	23.22	1	26	1	26.00	14	–
Sherwell, PW (132)	58	91	16	1808	144	24.10	3	–	–	–	67	52
Snooke, SJ (132)	124	202	16	4821	187	25.91	7	3017	120	25.14	83	–
Mitchell, F (133)	198	304	19	9117	194	31.98	17	828	35	23.65	147	2
Tancred, LJ (134)	130	219	12	5695	160	27.51	11	190	8	23.75	73	–
Taylor, HW (134)	206	340	27	13105	250*	41.86	30	560	22	25.45	75	–

	M	I	NO	Runs	HS	Avge	100s	RC	Wkts	Avge	Ct	St
Deane, HG *(135)*	100	138	12	3795	165	30.11	6	99	3	33.00	63	–
Nupen, EP *(136)*	74	105	14	1635	89	17.96	–	6077	334	18.19	34	–
Cameron, HB *(136)*	107	161	17	5396	182	37.47	11	13	0	–	155	69
Wade, HF *(137)*	74	118	9	3858	190	35.39	9	–	–	–	50	–
Melville, A *(137)*	190	295	15	10598	189	37.85	25	3959	132	29.99	156	–
Nourse, AD *(138)*	175	269	27	12472	260*	51.53	41	124	0	–	135	–
Cheetham, JE *(139)*	108	170	35	5697	271*	42.20	8	376	8	47.00	67	–
McGlew, DJ *(140)*	190	299	34	12170	255*	45.92	27	932	35	26.62	103	–
van Ryneveld, CB *(141)*	101	171	12	4803	150	30.20	4	6230	206	30.24	71	–
Goddard, TL *(142)*	179	297	19	11279	222	40.57	26	11563	534	21.65	174	–
van der Merwe, PL *(143)*	94	152	12	4086	128	29.18	4	2108	82	25.70	73	–
Bacher, A *(143)*	120	212	10	7894	235	39.07	18	87	2	43.50	110	1

New Zealand

	M	I	NO	Runs	HS	Avge	100s	RC	Wkts	Avge	Ct	St
Lowry, TC *(147)*	198	322	20	9421	181	31.19	18	1323	49	27.00	189	48
Page, ML *(147)*	132	213	17	5857	206	29.88	9	2365	73	32.39	117	–
Hadlee, WA *(148)*	116	202	17	7421	198	40.11	17	293	6	48.83	67	–
Sutcliffe, B *(148)*	232	405	39	17283	385	47.22	44	3264	86	37.95	158	1
Wallace, WM *(149)*	120	190	17	7609	211	43.98	16	18	0	–	68	–
Rabone, GO *(150)*	82	135	14	3425	125	28.30	3	4835	173	27.94	76	–
Cave, HB *(150)*	117	175	39	2187	118	16.08	2	8664	362	23.93	69	–
Reid, JR *(151)*	264	418	28	16128	296	41.35	39	10535	466	22.60	240	7
Chapple, ME *(152)*	119	201	16	5344	165	28.88	4	3559	142	25.06	67	–
Sinclair, BW *(153)*	118	204	18	6114	148	32.87	6	86	2	43.00	45	–
Dowling, GT *(153)*	158	282	13	9399	239	34.94	16	378	9	42.00	111	–
Congdon, BE *(154)*	241	416	40	13101	202*	34.84	23	6125	204	30.02	201	–
Turner, GM *(156)*	455	792	101	34346	311*	49.70	103	189	5	37.80	410	–
Parker, JM *(157)*	207	362	39	11254	195	34.84	21	681	14	48.64	177	–
Burgess, MG *(158)*	192	322	35	10281	146	25.82	20	1148	30	38.26	151	–
Howarth, GP *(159)*	338	584	42	17294	183	31.90	32	3593	112	32.08	229	–
Coney, JV *(161)*	165	272	48	7872	174*	35.14	8	3460	111	31.17	192	–
Crowe, JJ *(163)*	170	285	32	9170	159	36.24	18	55	1	55.00	186	–
Wright, JG *(164)*	350	605	43	23842	192	42.42	56	339	2	169.50	186	–
Crowe, MD *(165)*	205	336	53	16359	299	57.80	58	3807	117	32.53	195	–
Smith, IDS *(166)*	173	243	40	5465	173	26.92	6	38	0	–	402	36

West Indies

	M	I	NO	Runs	HS	Avge	100s	RC	Wkts	Avge	Ct	St
Nunes, RK *(169)*	61	94	8	2695	200*	31.33	6	83	3	27.66	31	8
Hoad, ELG *(170)*	63	104	13	3502	174*	38.48	8	1923	53	36.28	26	–
Betancourt, N *(170)*	16	28	4	442	71*	18.41	–	98	1	98.00	6	–

	M	I	NO	Runs	HS	Avge	100s	RC	Wkts	Avge	Ct	St
Fernandes, MP *(171)*	46	79	5	2087	141	28.20	4	183	5	36.60	30	–
Grant, GC *(171)*	81	136	17	3831	115	32.19	4	969	19	51.00	71	–
Grant, RS *(172)*	48	74	8	1883	152	28.53	1	1989	79	25.17	66	–
Headley, GA *(172)*	103	164	22	9921	344*	69.86	33	1842	51	36.11	76	–
Gomez, GA *(173)*	126	182	27	6764	216*	43.63	14	5052	200	25.26	92	–
Goddard, JD *(174)*	111	145	32	3769	218*	33.35	5	3845	146	26.33	94	–
Stollmeyer, JB *(175)*	117	194	16	7942	324	44.61	14	2482	55	45.12	93	–
Atkinson, D St E *(176)*	78	115	16	2812	219	28.40	5	5291	200	26.45	39	–
Alexander, FCM *(177)*	92	141	30	3238	108	29.17	1	7	0	–	217	39
Worrell, FMM *(178)*	208	326	49	15025	308*	54.24	39	10115	349	28.98	139	–
Sobers, G St A *(180)*	383	609	93	28315	365*	54.87	86	28941	1043	27.74	407	–
Kanhai, RB *(181)*	416	669	82	28774	256	49.01	83	1009	18	56.05	318	7
Lloyd, CH *(182)*	490	730	96	31232	242*	49.26	79	4104	114	36.00	377	–
Kallicharran, AI *(184)*	505	834	86	32650	243*	43.64	87	4030	84	47.97	323	–
Murray, DL *(185)*	367	554	85	13291	166*	28.33	10	367	5	73.40	741	108
Richards, IVA *(186)*	476	741	56	34255	322	50.07	111	9801	219	44.75	430	1
Greenidge, CG *(187)*	522	888	75	37330	273*	45.91	92	479	18	26.61	516	–
Haynes, DL *(189)*	274	468	56	19147	255*	46.47	45	196	6	32.66	152	–

India

	M	I	NO	Runs	HS	Avge	100s	RC	Wkts	Avge	Ct	St
Nayudu, CK *(193)*	207	344	15	11825	200	35.94	26	12029	411	29.26	170	1
Vizianagram, Maharaj of *(195)*	47	73	7	1228	77	18.60	–	139	4	34.75	18	–
Pataudi, Nawab of, snr *(196)*	127	204	24	8750	238*	48.61	29	529	15	35.26	58	–
Amarnath, L *(197)*	184	282	33	10323	262	41.45	31	10488	457	22.94	90	2
Hazare, VS *(198)*	239	369	46	18754	316*	58.06	60	14648	595	24.61	166	–
Mankad, MH *(199)*	232	359	27	11566	231	34.83	26	19159	781	24.53	188	–
Ghulam Ahmed *(201)*	98	126	30	1341	90	13.96	–	9190	407	22.57	57	–
Umrigar, PR *(201)*	243	350	41	16155	252*	52.28	49	8350	325	25.69	216	–
Adhikari, HR *(202)*	152	236	28	8683	230*	41.74	17	1859	49	37.93	97	–
Gaekwad, DK *(203)*	110	172	13	5788	249*	36.40	17	1016	25	40.64	50	–
Roy, PK *(204)*	185	298	18	11868	202*	42.38	33	648	21	30.85	75	–
Ramchand, GS *(204)*	145	202	36	6027	230*	36.30	16	7518	255	29.48	105	–
Contractor, NJ *(205)*	138	234	18	8611	176	39.86	22	1040	26	40.00	72	–
Pataudi, Nawab of, jnr *(206)*	310	499	41	15425	203*	33.67	33	776	10	77.60	208	–
Borde, CG *(208)*	251	370	57	12805	207*	40.91	30	9044	331	27.32	159	–
Wadekar, AL *(208)*	237	360	33	15380	323	47.03	36	908	21	43.23	271	–
Venkataraghavan, S *(210)*	341	457	84	6617	137	17.73	1	33568	1390	24.14	318	–
Gavaskar, SM *(210)*	348	563	61	25834	340	51.46	81	1240	22	56.36	294	–
Bedi, BS *(213)*	370	426	111	3584	61	11.37	–	33843	1560	21.69	172	–
Viswanath, GR *(214)*	308	486	47	17970	247	40.93	44	736	15	49.06	225	–
Kapil Dev *(215)*	248	353	37	10332	193	32.69	16	20754	765	27.12	178	–

	M	I	NO	Runs	HS	Avge	100s	RC	Wkts	Avge	Ct	St
Vengsarkar, DB *(217)*	251	375	51	17288	258*	53.35	54	126	1	126.00	172	–
Shastri, RJ *(218)*	221	318	54	11650	217	44.12	29	15684	466	33.65	127	–
Srikkanth, K *(219)*	118	186	3	6695	172	36.58	10	1317	26	50.65	72	–
Azharuddin, M *(220)*	121	184	23	9038	226	56.13	30	533	7	76.14	104	–

Pakistan

	M	I	NO	Runs	HS	Avge	100s	RC	Wkts	Avge	Ct	St
Kardar, AH *(222)*	174	262	33	6832	173	29.83	8	8448	344	24.55	110	–
Fazal Mahmood *(223)*	111	146	33	2602	100*	23.02	1	8792	460	19.11	38	–
Imtiaz Ahmed *(224)*	179	309	32	10323	300*	37.26	22	166	4	41.50	314	77
Javed Burki *(225)*	177	290	31	9421	227	36.37	22	1554	35	44.40	100	–
Hanif Mohammad *(226)*	238	370	44	17059	499	52.32	55	1509	53	28.50	178	12
Saeed Ahmed *(227)*	213	346	25	12847	203*	40.02	34	8217	332	24.75	122	–
Intikhab Alam *(227)*	489	725	78	14331	182	22.14	9	43472	1571	27.67	228	–
Majid Khan *(229)*	410	700	62	27444	241	43.01	73	7197	224	32.12	410	–
Mushtaq Mohammad *(230)*	500	840	104	31044	303*	42.17	72	22758	936	24.31	346	–
Wasim Bari *(232)*	286	357	92	5749	177	21.69	2	30	1	30.00	674	145
Asif Iqbal *(233)*	441	703	76	23375	196	37.28	45	8776	291	30.15	304	–
Javed Miandad *(234)*	379	598	90	27468	311	54.07	78	6395	191	33.48	328	3
Imran Khan *(236)*	377	576	98	17614	170	36.84	30	28658	1287	22.26	117	–
Zaheer Abbas *(238)*	459	768	92	34843	274	51.54	108	1146	30	38.20	278	–

Sri Lanka

	M	I	NO	Runs	HS	Avge	100s	RC	Wkts	Avge	Ct	St
Warnapura, B *(241)*	57	99	8	2280	154	25.05	2	628	13	48.30	23	–
Mendis, LRD *(242)*	121	190	16	6233	194	35.82	12	52	1	52.00	49	1
de Silva, DS *(243)*	64	95	16	1735	97	21.96	–	6714	238	28.21	34	–
Madugalle, RS *(244)*	81	118	15	3301	142*	32.04	2	159	2	79.50	42	–
Ranatunga, A *(245)*	82	119	11	3981	135*	36.86	5	2373	68	34.89	50	–
de Silva, PA *(246)*	75	114	13	4575	267	45.29	12	750	11	68.18	53	–